PHILIP'S

MODERN SCHOOL ·ATLAS·

In association with Heinemann Educational

George Philip Limited
Michelin House, 81 Fulham Road
London SW3 6RB

Heinemann Educational
Halley Court, Jordan Hill
Oxford OX2 8EJ

CONTENTS

Published in Great Britain in 1994
by George Philip Limited,
an imprint of Reed Consumer Books Limited,
Michelin House, 81 Fulham Road,
London SW3 6RB

Cartography by Philip's

Ninetieth edition
© 1994 Reed International Books Limited

ISBN 0-540-05815-7 Paperback edition
ISBN 0-540-05795-9 Hardback edition

BRITISH ISLES MAPS

A separate map key is provided on the first page of the World Maps section.

SETTLEMENTS

■ **LONDON**　　■ **GLASGOW**　　▣ **BRADFORD**　　▣ Brighton　　● Gateshead

◉ Aylesbury　　◉ Sligo　　⊙ Selkirk　　○ Burford　　○ Lampeter

Settlement symbols and type styles vary according to the population and importance of towns

▨ Built up areas　　　　　　□ London Boroughs

ADMINISTRATION

——— International boundaries

——— National boundaries

- - - - Administrative boundaries

W A L E S　Country names

K E N T　Administrative area names

EXMOOR　National park names

COMMUNICATIONS

═══ Motorways
=== *under construction*

——— Major roads
- - - *under construction*
╪- - - ╪ *in tunnels*

——— Other important roads
- - - *under construction*
╪- - - ╪ *in tunnels*

⊕　Major airports

——— Main passenger railways
- - - *under construction*
╪- - - ╪ *in tunnels*

——— Other passenger railways
- - - *under construction*
╪- - - ╪ *in tunnels*

——— Canals
- - - *in tunnels*

⊕　Other airports

PHYSICAL FEATURES

〰 Perennial rivers

▨ Tidal flats

⬭ Lakes or reservoirs

⌇⌇ Reservoirs under construction

▲ 444　Elevations in metres

△ 1342　Elevations-highest in county
(or region in Scotland)
in metres

▾ 38　Depths below sea level
in metres

ELEVATION AND DEPTH TINTS

Height of Land above Sea Level	Land below Sea Level	Depth of Sea

in metres	1000	750	500	400	200	100	0							in feet
								150	300	600	1500	3000	6000	
in feet	3000	2250	1500	1200	600	300								in metres
							0	20	50	100	200	500	1000	2000

SHETLAND ISLANDS on same scale

Projection : Conical with two standard parallels

West from Greenwich

ORKNEY ISLANDS on same scale

1:1 000 000

CARTOGRAPHY BY PHILIP'S. COPYRIGHT REED INTERNATIONAL BOOKS LTD

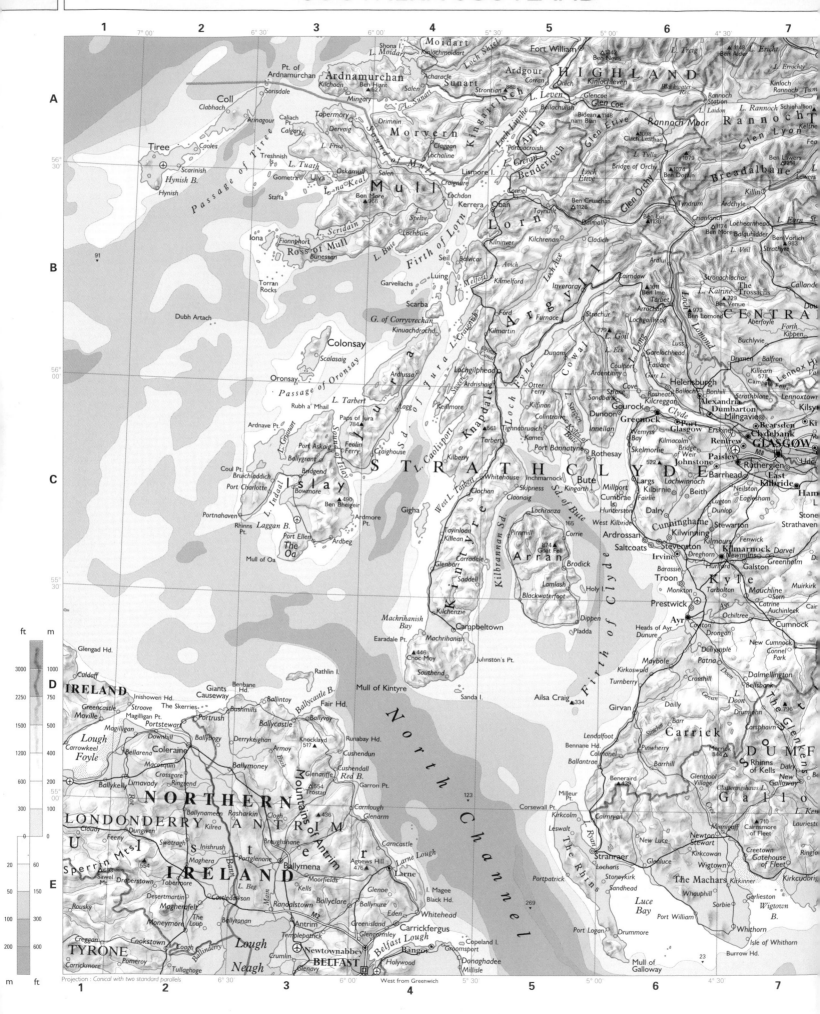

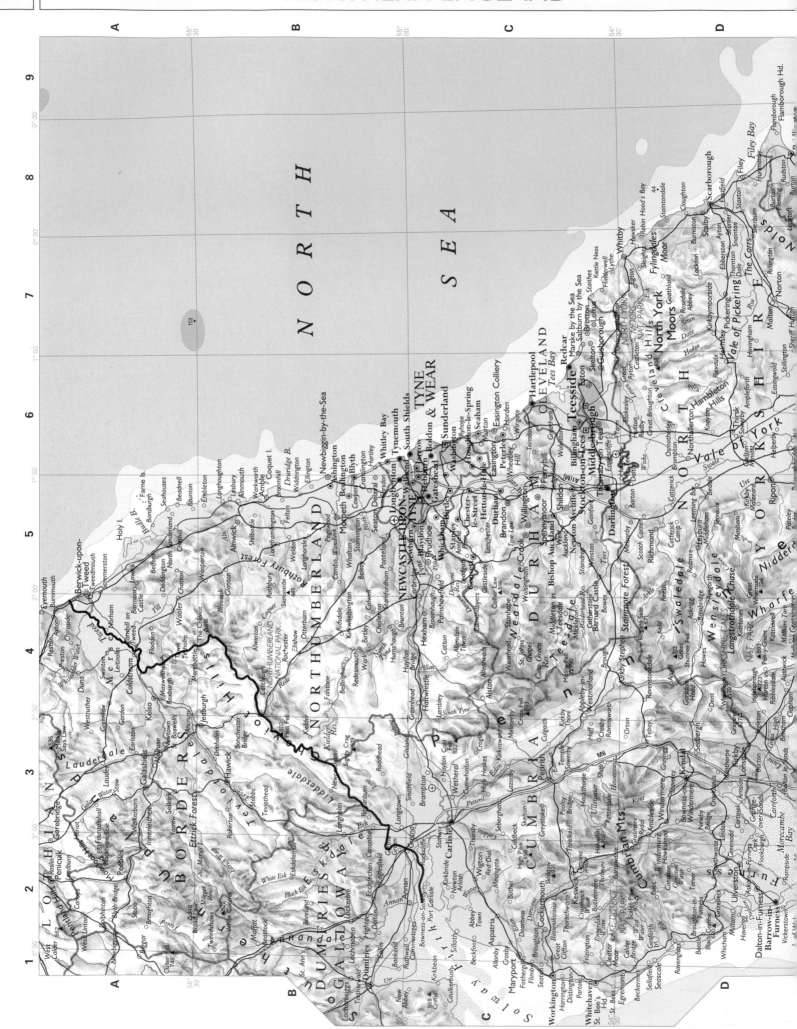

East from Greenwich

1:1 000 000

CARTOGRAPHY BY PHILIP'S. COPYRIGHT REED INTERNATIONAL BOOKS LTD

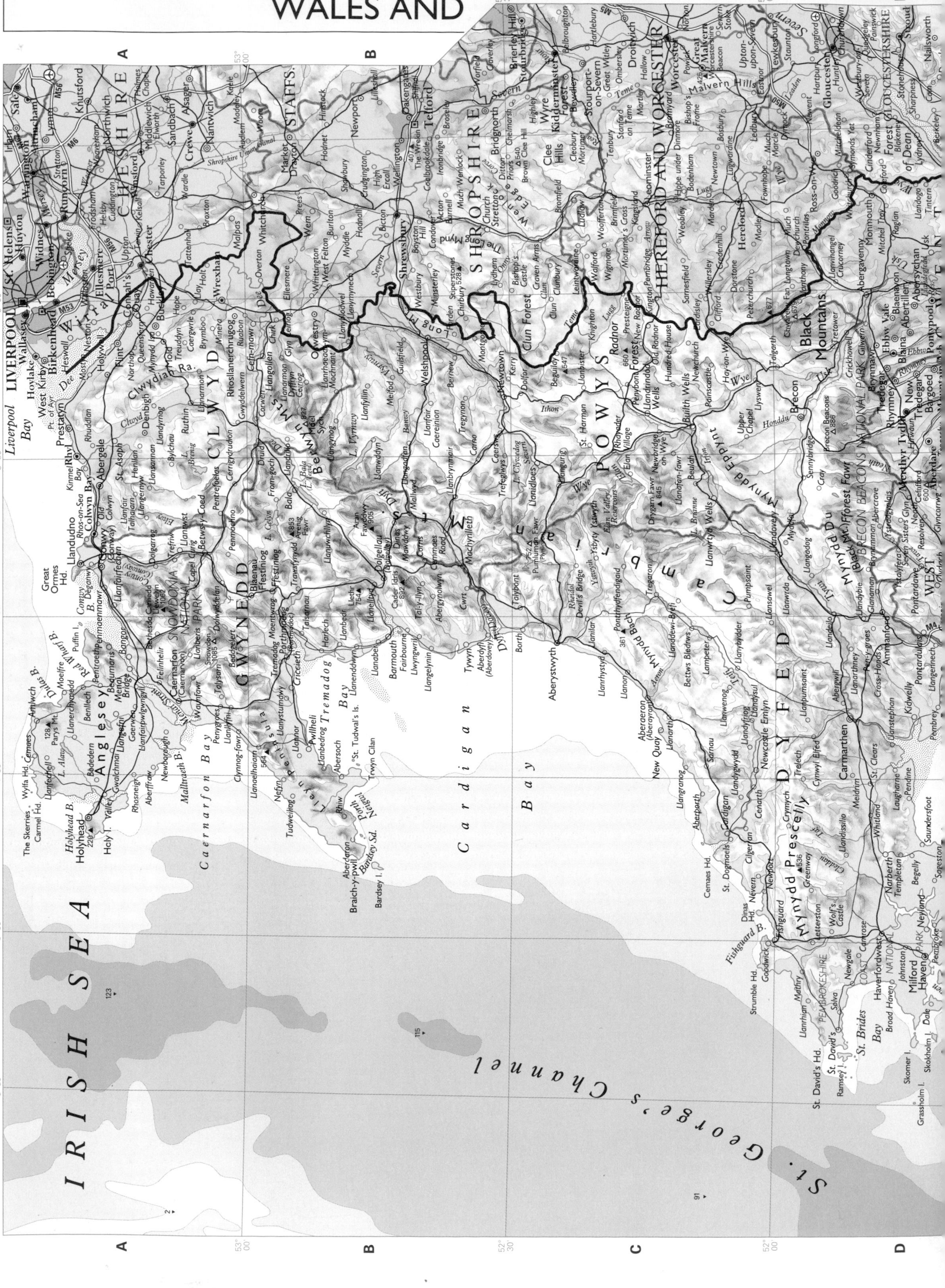

IRISH SEA

CHESHIRE
STAFFS.
SHROPSHIRE
HEREFORD AND WORCESTER
CLWYD
GWYNEDD
POWYS
DYFED
GWENT

Liverpool Bay
Caernarfon Bay
Cardigan Bay
St. George's Channel
Tremadog Bay

SNOWDONIA NATIONAL PARK
BRECON BEACONS NATIONAL PARK
PEMBROKESHIRE COAST NATIONAL PARK

Liverpool
Birkenhead
Chester
Wrexham
Shrewsbury
Telford
Bridgnorth
Worcester
Kidderminster
Hereford
Leominster
Ludlow
Oswestry
Welshpool
Newtown
Llandrindod Wells
Builth Wells
Brecon
Aberystwyth
Cardigan
Haverfordwest
Milford Haven
Fishguard
Carmarthen
Merthyr Tydfil
Ebbw Vale
Pontypool
Abergavenny
Monmouth

Anglesey
Holyhead
Caernarfon
Bangor
Llandudno
Colwyn Bay
Rhyl
Prestatyn
Llangollen
Bala
Dolgellau
Machynlleth
Barmouth
Harlech
Pwllheli
Lleyn Peninsula
Bardsey I.

CARTOGRAPHY BY PHILIP'S. COPYRIGHT REED INTERNATIONAL BOOKS LTD

FRANCE

CHANNEL ISLANDS on same scale

CHANNEL ISLANDS

Alderney
Guernsey
St. Peter Port
Jersey
St. Helier

Passage de la Déroute

SCILLY ISLES on same scale

Isles of Scilly

1:1 000 000

Projection: Conical with two standard parallels

West from Greenwich

m
ft
3000
2250
1500
1200
600
300
0

ft
1000
750
500
400
200
100
0
60
150
300
m

miles
km

ATLANTIC

OCEAN

Projection : Conical with two standard parallels   West from Greenwich

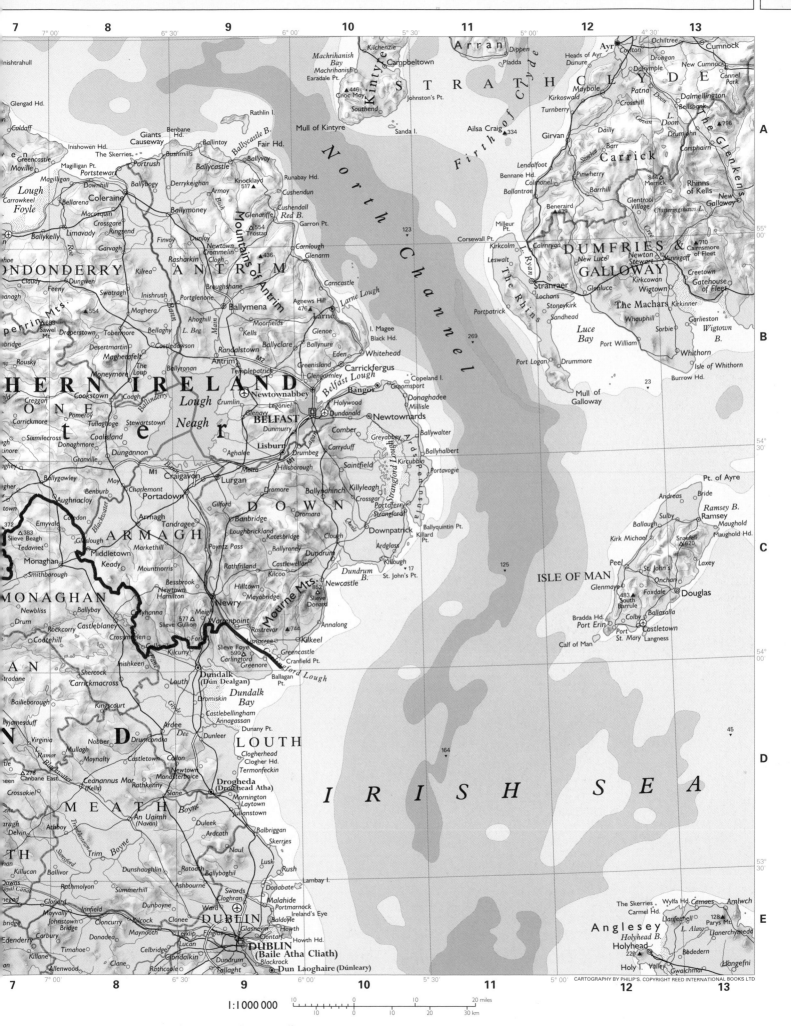

7 7° 00' **8** 6° 30' **9** 6° 00' **10** 5° 30' **11** 5° 00' **12** 4° 30' **13**

A

B

55° 00'

54° 30'

C

54° 00'

D

53° 30'

E

7 7° 00' **8** 6° 30' **9** 6° 00' **10** 5° 30' **11** 5° 00' **12** 4° 30' **13**

CARTOGRAPHY BY PHILIP'S. COPYRIGHT REED INTERNATIONAL BOOKS LTD

1:1 000 000

10   0   20 miles
10   0   10   20   30 km

Inishtrahull

Machrihanish
Bay
Machrihanish
Earadale Pt.

Kilchenzie
Campbeltown

Arran

Dippen
Pladda

Heads of Ayr
Dunure

Ayr
Coylton

Ochiltree

Cumnock

New Cumnock

Connel
Park

Glengad Hd.
Culdaff
Moville
Greencastle
Inishowen Hd.

Magilligan Pt.
Magilligan

Giants
Causeway

Benbane
Hd.

Bushmills
Ballintoy

Ballycastle B.

Mull of Kintyre

Sanda I.

Kintyre

Johnston's Pt.

Gnoc Moy

Southend

STRATHCLYDE

Firth of Clyde

Maybole
Kirkoswald
Crosshill

Drongan
Dalrymple

Patna
L.
Doon

Bellsbank

Dalmellington

New
Galloway

796

Lough
Foyle
Carrowkeel

Ballykelly
hoe

Rathlin I.

Fair Hd.

Ballycastle

Turnberry

Girvan

Dailly

Drumjohn

The Glenkens

Carsphairn

Portstewart
Downhill
Coleraine
Macosquin
Crossgare
Ringsend

Portrush

Ballyvoy

Runabay Hd.

Ailsa Craig
334

Lendalfoot

Barr

Carrick

Merrick
844

Rhinns
of Kells

Limavady
Bellarena
Garvagh

Ballybogy
Derrykeighan

Knocklayd
517

Cushendun

North

Bennane Hd.
Ballantrae

Pinwherry
Barrhill

Glentrool
Village

Beneraird
439

Clatteringshaws L.

710

Moville

DONDONDERRY

Kilrea
Claudy
Feeny
Dungiven

Ballymoney

Finvoy
Dunloy

Armoy

Trostan
554

Glenariffe
Red B.

Cushendall

Channel

123

Corsewall Pt.

DUMFRIES &
GALLOWAY

Minnigaff

Creetown

Gatehouse
of Fleet

Cairnsmore
of Fleet

Swatragh
Maghera

Rasharkin
Clogh

Newtown
Crommelin

Garron Pt.

Kirkcolm
Leswalt

Cairnryan

New Luce

Newton
Stewart

Kirkcowan

Wigtown

anagh
bridge

Draperstown
Tobermore

ANTRIM

436

Carnlough
Glenarm

L. Ryan
Stranraer

Lochans

Stoneykirk

Glenluce

The Machars

Kirkinner

eperim Mts.
Sawel
Mt.
693

Desertmartin
Magherafelt
Moneymore

Ballymena

Mountains of Antrim

Carncastle

Larne Lough
Agnews Hill
476

Portpatrick

The Rhins

Sandhead

Whauphill

Garlieston

Sorbie

Wigtown
B.

Rousky
554

Belaghy
Castledawson

Ahoghill
Broughshane

Moorfields

Larne

269

Port Logan

Luce
Bay

Port William

Whithorn

Isle of Whithorn

Tobermore
Coagh

Moneymore
Cookstown

The
Loup

Randalstown
Antrim

Ballymena

Kells

Glenoe

I. Magee
Black Hd.

Drummore

Mull of
Galloway

Burrow Hd.

HERN IRELAND
ONE ter

Lough
Neagh

Ballyronan
Toomebridge

Templepatrick

Ballyclare

Ballynure
Whitehead

Sixmilecross
Donaghmore
Pomeroy
Stewartstown
Coalisland

Crumlin

Newtownabbey

Eden

Greenisland
Carrickfergus

Copeland I.

23

Dungannon
Granville

Aghalee
Moira

Glengormley

Bangor
Holywood

Groomsport
Donaghadee
Millisle

Ballygawley
Benburn
Moy
Charlemont

Craigavon
Lurgan

Lisburn

BELFAST

Dundonald

Newtownards

Comber

Greyabbey

Ballywalter

Aughnacloy
Caledon
Emyvale
383
372

Armagh

Portadown

ARMAGH
Tandragee

Gilford
Banbridge

Dromore

Hillsborough
Drumbeg

Carryduff

Saintfield

Killyleagh
Crossgar

Portaferry

Strangford L.

Ardkeen

Portavogie

Slieve Beagh
Tedavnet
Monaghan
Smithborough

Glaslough
Middletown

Keady

Mountnorris

Loughbrickland
Katesbridge

Ballynahinch

Dromara

Crossgar
Strangford

DOWN

Ballyquintin
Pt.

MONAGHAN

Newbliss
Drum

Rockcorry
Cootehill

Castleblaney
Ballybay

Clontibret

Newtown
Hamilton

Bessbrook

Poyntz Pass

Ballyroney

Rathfriland

Kilcoo

Castlewellan

Dundrum

Clough

Downpatrick
Ardglass

Killard
Pt.

St. John's Pt.

ISLE OF MAN

Pt. of Ayre

Bride
Andreas

Ramsey B.

Sulby
Ballaugh

Ramsey
Maughold

Maughold Hd.

Shercock
Carrickmacross

Crossmaglen
Cullyhanna

Newry
Meigh
Warrenpoint

Hilltown
Mayobridge

Newcastle

Mourne Mts.

Slieve
Donard
852

Dundrum
B.

17

Killough

Kirk Michael

Snaefell
620

Laxey

Bailieborough
stradone

Inishkeen
Louth

Kilcurry
Carlingford

Slieve Gullion
577

Forkill

Slieve Foye
590

Greenore

125

South
Barrule
483

Foxdale

Onchan

St. John's

Douglas

Virginia
L. Ramor

Nobber
Drumconrath

Dromiskin

Rostrevor

Annalong
744

Kilkeel

Greencastle
Cranfield Pt.

Calf of Man

Bradda Hd.
Port Erin

Port
St. Mary

Ballasalla

Colby

Castletown
Langness

Kingscourt
Mullagh
Moynalty

Castletown
Collon

Ardee
Dunleer

Dundalk
(Dún Dealgan)

Carlingford Lough

Ballagan
Pt.

Dundalk
Bay

Carling ford Lough

45

Canbane East
278

Virginia
Crossakiel

Ceanannus Mor
(Kells)
Rathkenny
Slane

MEATH

Castlebellingham
Annagassan
Dunany Pt.

Clogherhead
Clogher Hd.
Termonfeckin

164

IRISH   SEA

Delvin
aragh
th

Killucan
Ballivor
Rathmolyon

An Uaimh
(Navan)

Trim
Stamford

Duleek

Drogheda
(Drochead Atha)

Mornington
Laytown
Julianstown

Boyne

Ardcath

Balbriggan
Skerries

Downs
Royal Canal
Edenderry

Clonard
Johnstown
Bridge

Innfield

Dunshaughlin

Ratoath
Ballyboghil

Naul

Lambay I.

Lusk
Rush

Donabate

The Skerries
Carmel Hd.

Wylfa Hd. Cemaes

Llanfechell

Amlwch

128
Parys Mt.

bridge
Timahoe
Allenwood

Kilcock
Maynooth

Summerhill
Dunboyne
Cloncurry
Donadea

Leixlip
Lucan
Clane

Ward

Swords
Cloghran

Malahide
Portmarnock

Ireland's Eye

Anglesey

Holyhead B.

Llanerchymedd

Llangefni

Carbury
Donadea

Celbridge

Clondalkin
Rathcoole

DUBLIN
(Baile Atha Cliath)

Glasnevin
Finglas
Clontarf

Howth Hd.

Holyhead
220

L. Alaw

Bodedern

Carlingford
Killane

Allenwood

Clane

Tallaght
Dundrum

DUBLIN
Blackrock

Dun Laoghaire (Dúnleary)

Holy I.
Valley

Gwalchmai

Llangefni

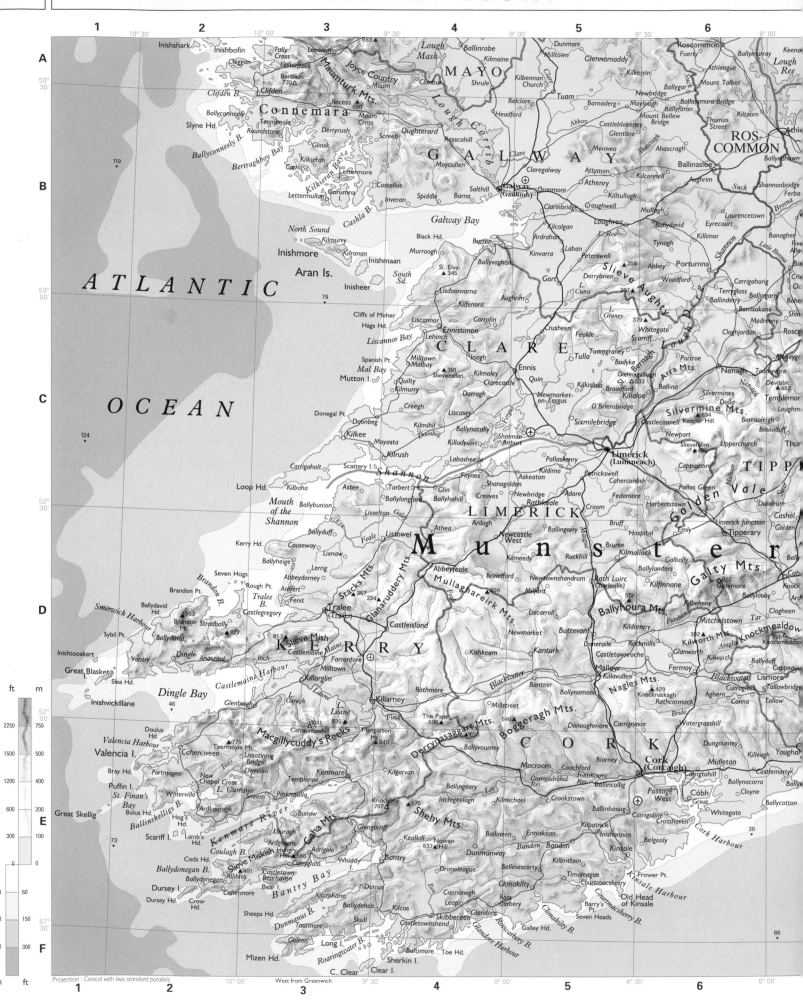

Projection : Conical with two standard parallels

West from Greenwich

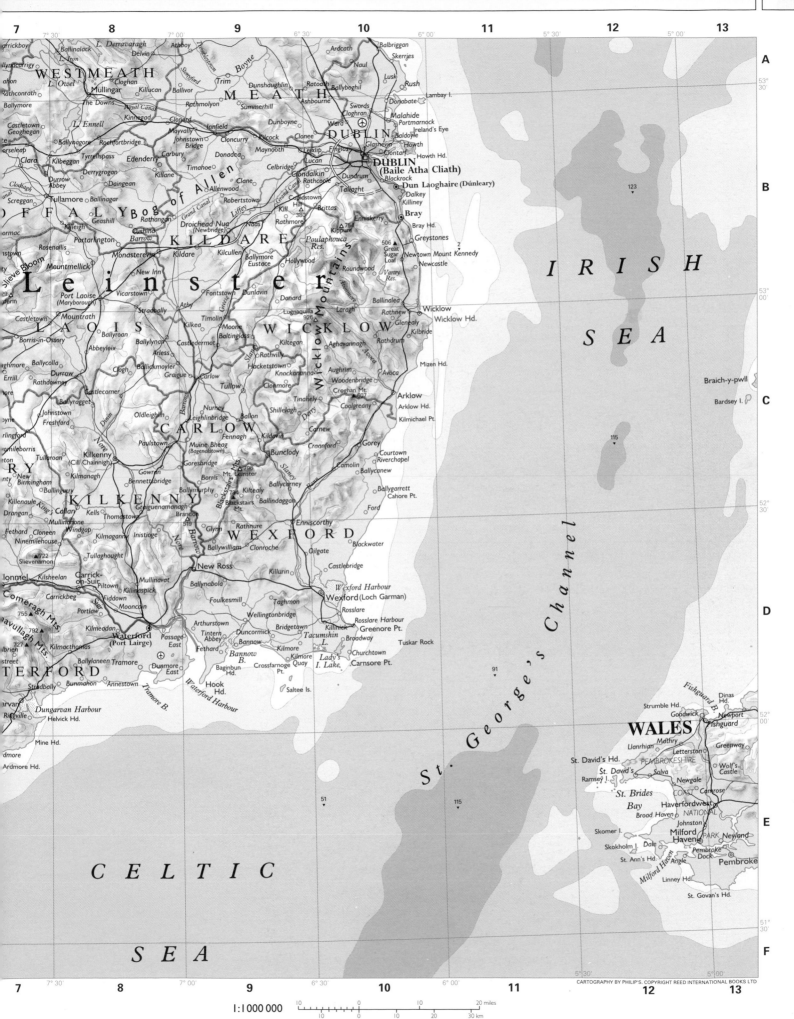

7   8   9   10   11   12   13

A

B

IRISH

SEA

C

D

WALES

E

CELTIC

SEA

F

7   8   9   10   11   12   13

CARTOGRAPHY BY PHILIP'S. COPYRIGHT REED INTERNATIONAL BOOKS LTD

1:1 000 000

10   0   10   20 miles
10   0   10   20   30 km

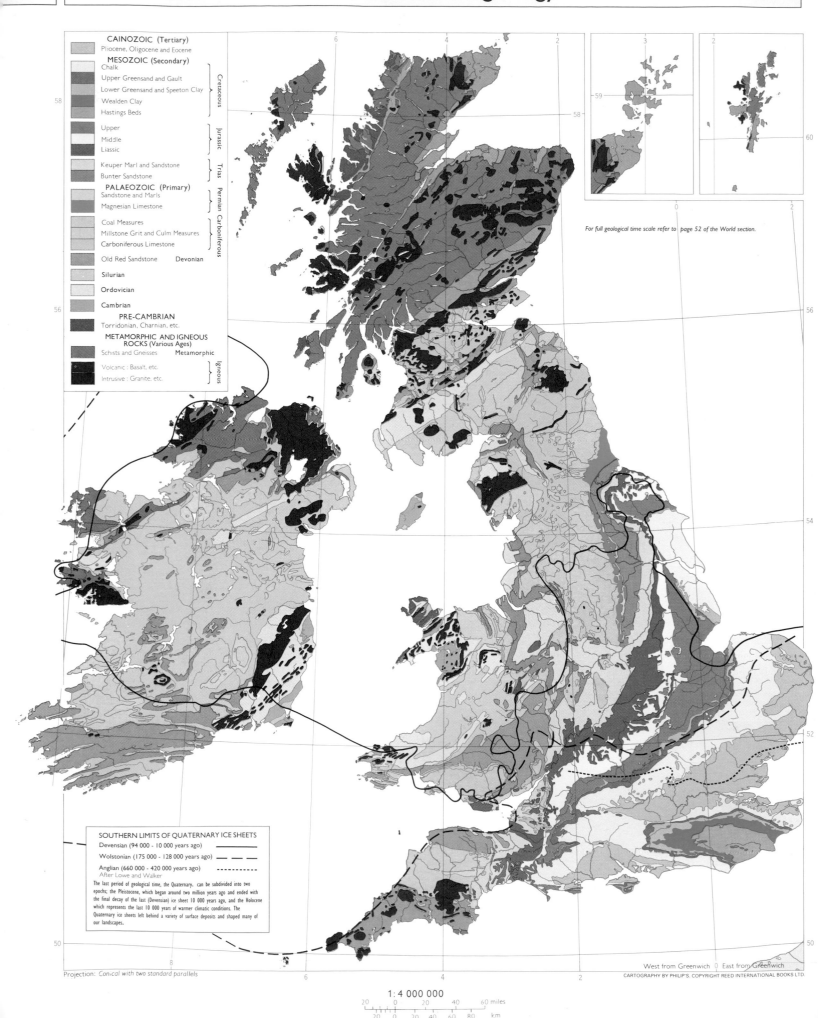

CAINOZOIC (Tertiary)
  Pliocene, Oligocene and Eocene
MESOZOIC (Secondary)
  Chalk
  Upper Greensand and Gault
  Lower Greensand and Speeton Clay
  Wealden Clay
  Hastings Beds
    Cretaceous
  Upper
  Middle
  Liassic
    Jurassic
  Keuper Marl and Sandstone
  Bunter Sandstone
    Trias
PALAEOZOIC (Primary)
  Sandstone and Marls
  Magnesian Limestone
    Permian
  Coal Measures
  Millstone Grit and Culm Measures
  Carboniferous Limestone
    Carboniferous
  Old Red Sandstone   Devonian
  Silurian
  Ordovician
  Cambrian
PRE-CAMBRIAN
  Torridonian, Charnian, etc.
METAMORPHIC AND IGNEOUS
  ROCKS (Various Ages)
  Schists and Gneisses   Metamorphic
  Volcanic : Basalt, etc.
  Intrusive : Granite, etc.
    Igneous

For full geological time scale refer to page 52 of the World section.

SOUTHERN LIMITS OF QUATERNARY ICE SHEETS
  Devensian (94 000 - 10 000 years ago) ————
  Wolstonian (175 000 - 128 000 years ago) — — —
  Anglian (660 000 - 420 000 years ago) ··········
  After Lowe and Walker

The last period of geological time, the Quaternary, can be subdivided into two epochs; the Pleistocene, which began around two million years ago and ended with the final decay of the last (Devensian) ice sheet 10 000 years ago, and the Holocene which represents the last 10 000 years of warmer climatic conditions. The Quaternary ice sheets left behind a variety of surface deposits and shaped many of our landscapes.

Projection: Conical with two standard parallels

West from Greenwich 0 East from Greenwich

CARTOGRAPHY BY PHILIP'S. COPYRIGHT REED INTERNATIONAL BOOKS LTD.

1 : 4 000 000
20   0   20   40   60 miles
20 0   20 40 60 80   km

Projection: Conical with two standard parallels

1 : 4 000 000

CARTOGRAPHY BY PHILIP'S. COPYRIGHT REED INTERNATIONAL BOOKS LTD.

JANUARY TEMPERATURE
Actual surface temperature

°C
7
6
5
4
3
2
1
0

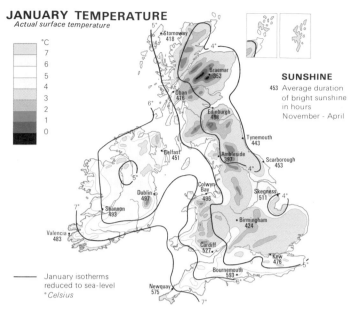

SUNSHINE

453 Average duration
of bright sunshine
in hours
November - April

January isotherms
reduced to sea-level
°Celsius

JULY TEMPERATURE
Actual surface temperature

°C
17
16
15
14
13
12
11
10

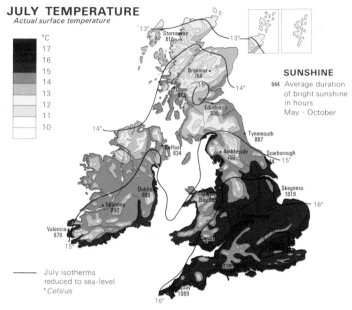

SUNSHINE

944 Average duration
of bright sunshine
in hours
May - October

July isotherms
reduced to sea-level
°Celsius

ANNUAL RAINFALL

mm
2500
2000
1500
1000
750
625

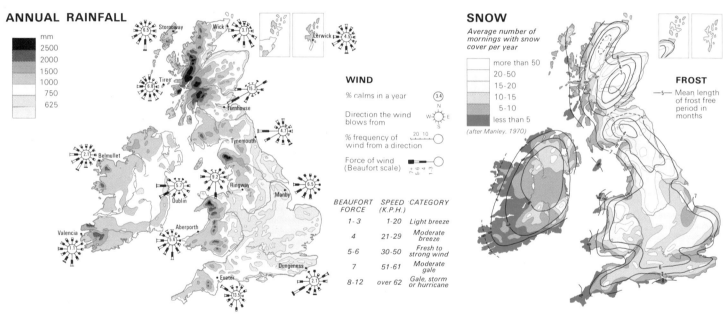

WIND

% calms in a year

Direction the wind
blows from

% frequency of
wind from a direction

Force of wind
(Beaufort scale)

BEAUFORT FORCE	SPEED (K.P.H.)	CATEGORY
1-3	1-20	Light breeze
4	21-29	Moderate breeze
5-6	30-50	Fresh to strong wind
7	51-61	Moderate gale
8-12	over 62	Gale, storm or hurricane

SNOW
*Average number of
mornings with snow
cover per year*

more than 50
20-50
15-20
10-15
5-10
less than 5

(after Manley, 1970)

FROST

—5— Mean length
of frost free
period in
months

VARIABILITY OF RAIN

*The percentage frequency with
which rainfall varies from the
normal rainfall regime in an area:
the higher the percentage figure,
the more variable the rainfall.*

over 20%
18-20%
16-18%
14-16%
12-14%
10-12%
under 10%

(after Gregory, 1955)

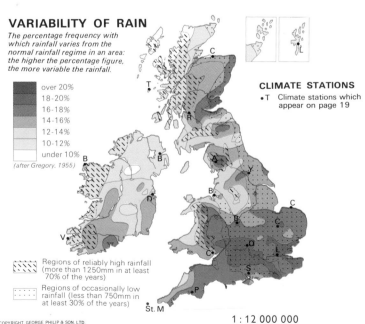

CLIMATE STATIONS

•T Climate stations which
appear on page 19

Regions of reliably high rainfall
(more than 1250mm in at least
70% of the years)

Regions of occasionally low
rainfall (less than 750mm in
at least 30% of the years)

1 : 12 000 000

SYNOPTIC CHART FOR A TYPICAL WINTER DEPRESSION
21st January 1971

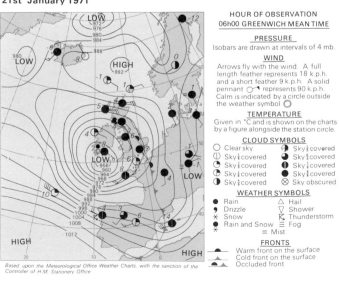

HOUR OF OBSERVATION
06h00 GREENWICH MEAN TIME

PRESSURE
Isobars are drawn at intervals of 4 mb.

WIND
Arrows fly with the wind. A full
length feather represents 18 k.p.h.
and a short feather 9 k.p.h. A solid
pennant represents 90 k.p.h.
Calm is indicated by a circle outside
the weather symbol O

TEMPERATURE
Given in °C and is shown on the charts
by a figure alongside the station circle.

CLOUD SYMBOLS
○ Clear sky
◐ Sky ½ covered
◑ Sky ⅛ covered
◓ Sky ⅝ covered
◔ Sky ¼ covered
◕ Sky ¾ covered
◑ Sky ⅜ covered
● Sky ⅞ covered
◒ Sky ½ covered
⊗ Sky obscured

WEATHER SYMBOLS
● Rain   △ Hail
, Drizzle   ▽ Shower
✳ Snow   Ҡ Thunderstorm
✲ Rain and Snow ≡ Fog
                = Mist

FRONTS
Warm front on the surface
Cold front on the surface
Occluded front

*Based upon the Meteorological Office Weather Charts, with the sanction of the
Controller of H.M. Stationery Office*

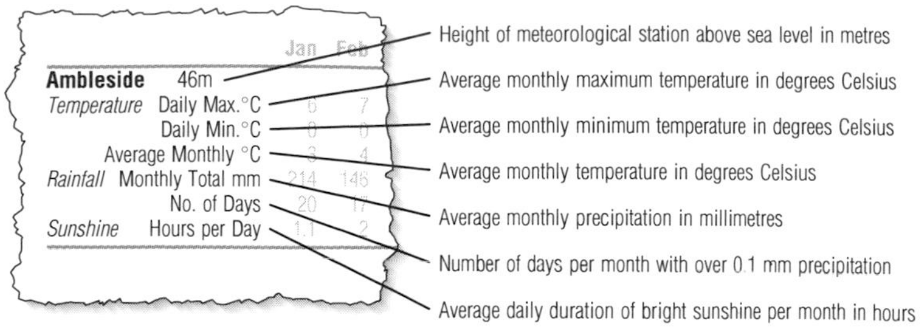
Ambleside 46m
Temperature Daily Max.°C
Daily Min.°C
Average Monthly °C
Rainfall Monthly Total mm
No. of Days
Sunshine Hours per Day
Height of meteorological station above sea level in metres
Average monthly maximum temperature in degrees Celsius
Average monthly minimum temperature in degrees Celsius
Average monthly temperature in degrees Celsius
Average monthly precipitation in millimetres
Number of days per month with over 0.1 mm precipitation
Average daily duration of bright sunshine per month in hours

	Jan	Feb	Mar	Apr	May	June	July	Aug	Sep	Oct	Nov	Dec	Year
Ambleside 46m													
Temperature Daily Max.°C	6	7	9	12	16	19	20	19	17	13	9	7	13
Daily Min.°C	0	0	2	4	6	9	11	11	9	6	3	1	5
Average Monthly °C	3	4	6	8	11	14	15	15	13	10	6	4	9
Rainfall Monthly Total mm	214	146	112	101	90	111	134	139	184	196	209	215	1851
No. of Days	20	17	15	15	14	15	18	17	18	19	19	21	208
Sunshine Hours per Day	1.1	2	3.2	4.5	6	5.7	4.5	4.2	3.3	2.2	1.4	1	3.3
Belfast 4m													
Temperature Daily Max.°C	6	7	9	12	15	18	18	18	16	13	9	7	12
Daily Min.°C	2	2	3	4	6	9	11	11	9	7	4	3	6
Average Monthly °C	4	4	6	8	11	13	15	15	13	10	7	5	9
Rainfall Monthly Total mm	80	52	50	48	52	68	94	77	80	83	72	90	845
No. of Days	20	17	16	16	15	16	19	17	18	19	19	21	213
Sunshine Hours per Day	1.5	2.3	3.4	5	6.3	6	4.4	4.4	3.6	2.6	1.8	1.1	3.5
Belmullet 9m													
Temperature Daily Max.°C	8	9	10	12	14	16	17	17	16	14	10	9	12
Daily Min.°C	3	4	4	6	8	10	11	11	10	8	5	4	7
Average Monthly °C	5	6	7	9	11	13	14	14	13	11	8	6	10
Rainfall Monthly Total mm	108	64	82	70	75	80	76	95	108	116	127	131	1132
No. of Days	18	13	16	15	14	12	14	17	16	18	20	22	195
Sunshine Hours per Day	1.9	2.5	3.4	5.2	7	6	4.6	5.1	3.9	2.9	1.9	1.3	3.8
Birkenhead 60m													
Temperature Daily Max.°C	6	6	9	11	15	17	19	19	16	13	9	7	12
Daily Min.°C	2	2	3	5	8	11	13	13	11	8	5	3	7
Average Monthly °C	4	4	6	8	11	14	16	16	14	10	7	5	10
Rainfall Monthly Total mm	64	46	40	41	55	55	67	80	66	71	76	65	726
No. of Days	18	13	13	13	13	13	15	15	15	17	17	19	181
Sunshine Hours per Day	1.6	2.4	3.5	5.3	6.3	6.7	5.7	5.4	4.2	2.9	1.8	1.3	3.9
Birmingham 163m													
Temperature Daily Max.°C	5	6	9	12	16	19	20	20	17	13	9	6	13
Daily Min.°C	2	2	3	5	7	10	12	12	10	7	5	3	7
Average Monthly °C	3	4	6	8	11	15	16	16	14	10	7	5	10
Rainfall Monthly Total mm	74	54	50	53	64	50	69	69	61	69	84	67	764
No. of Days	17	15	13	13	14	13	15	14	14	15	17	18	178
Sunshine Hours per Day	1.4	2.1	3.2	4.6	5.4	6	5.4	5.1	3.9	2.8	1.6	1.2	3.6
Cambridge 12m													
Temperature Daily Max.°C	6	7	11	14	17	21	22	22	19	15	10	7	14
Daily Min.°C	1	1	2	4	7	10	12	12	10	6	4	2	6
Average Monthly °C	3	4	6	9	12	15	17	17	14	10	7	5	10
Rainfall Monthly Total mm	49	35	36	37	45	45	58	55	51	51	54	41	558
No. of Days	15	13	10	11	11	11	12	12	11	13	14	14	147
Sunshine Hours per Day	1.7	2.5	3.8	5.1	6.2	6.7	6	5.7	4.6	3.4	1.9	1.4	4.1
Cardiff 62m													
Temperature Daily Max.°C	7	7	10	13	16	19	20	21	18	14	10	8	14
Daily Min.°C	2	2	3	5	8	11	12	13	11	8	5	3	7
Average Monthly °C	4	5	7	9	12	15	16	17	14	11	8	6	10
Rainfall Monthly Total mm	108	72	63	65	76	63	89	97	99	109	116	108	1065
No. of Days	18	14	13	13	13	13	14	15	16	16	17	18	180
Sunshine Hours per Day	1.7	2.7	4	5.6	6.4	6.9	6.2	6	4.7	3.4	1.9	1.5	4.3
Craibstone 91m													
Temperature Daily Max.°C	5	6	8	10	13	16	18	17	15	12	8	6	11
Daily Min.°C	0	0	2	3	5	8	10	10	8	6	3	1	5
Average Monthly °C	3	3	5	7	9	12	14	13	12	9	6	4	8
Rainfall Monthly Total mm	78	55	53	51	63	54	95	75	67	92	93	80	856
No. of Days	19	16	15	15	14	14	18	15	16	18	19	18	197
Sunshine Hours per Day	1.8	2.9	3.5	4.9	5.9	6.1	5.1	4.8	4.3	3.1	2	1.5	3.8
Cromer 54m													
Temperature Daily Max.°C	6	7	9	12	15	18	21	20	18	14	10	8	13
Daily Min.°C	1	1	3	5	7	10	12	13	11	8	5	3	7
Average Monthly °C	4	4	6	8	11	14	16	16	15	11	7	5	10
Rainfall Monthly Total mm	58	46	37	39	48	39	63	56	54	61	64	53	618
No. of Days	18	16	13	13	11	11	13	12	14	16	18	18	173
Sunshine Hours per Day	1.8	2.6	4	5.4	6.4	6.8	6.3	5.8	5	3.6	2	1.9	4.3
Dublin 47m													
Temperature Daily Max.°C	8	8	10	13	15	18	20	19	17	14	10	8	14
Daily Min.°C	1	2	3	4	6	9	11	11	9	6	4	3	6
Average Monthly °C	4	5	7	8	11	14	15	15	13	10	7	6	10
Rainfall Monthly Total mm	67	55	51	45	60	57	70	74	72	70	67	74	762
No. of Days	13	10	10	11	10	11	13	12	12	11	12	14	139
Sunshine Hours per Day	1.9	2.5	3.4	5	6.2	6	4.8	4.9	3.9	3.2	2.1	1.6	3.8
Durham 102m													
Temperature Daily Max.°C	6	6	9	12	15	18	20	19	17	13	9	7	13
Daily Min.°C	0	0	1	3	6	9	11	10	9	6	3	2	5
Average Monthly °C	3	3	5	7	10	13	15	15	13	9	6	4	9
Rainfall Monthly Total mm	59	51	38	38	51	49	61	67	60	63	66	55	658
No. of Days	17	15	14	13	13	14	15	14	14	16	17	17	179
Sunshine Hours per Day	1.7	2.5	3.3	4.6	5.4	6	5.1	4.8	4.1	3	1.9	1.4	3.6
Lerwick 82m													
Temperature Daily Max.°C	5	5	6	8	11	13	14	14	13	10	8	6	9
Daily Min.°C	1	1	2	3	5	7	10	10	8	6	4	3	5
Average Monthly °C	3	3	4	5	8	10	12	12	11	8	6	4	7
Rainfall Monthly Total mm	109	87	69	68	52	55	72	71	87	104	111	118	1003
No. of Days	25	22	20	21	15	15	17	17	19	23	24	25	243
Sunshine Hours per Day	0.8	1.8	2.9	4.4	5.3	5.3	4	3.8	3.5	2.2	2.2	0.5	3
London (Kew) 5m													
Temperature Daily Max.°C	6	7	10	13	17	20	22	21	19	14	10	7	14
Daily Min.°C	2	2	3	6	8	12	14	13	11	8	5	4	7
Average Monthly °C	4	5	7	9	12	16	18	17	15	11	8	5	11
Rainfall Monthly Total mm	54	40	37	37	46	45	57	59	49	57	64	48	593
No. of Days	15	13	11	12	12	11	12	11	13	13	15	15	153
Sunshine Hours per Day	1.5	2.3	3.6	5.3	6.4	7.1	6.4	6.1	4.7	3.2	1.8	1.3	4.1
Oxford 63m													
Temperature Daily Max.°C	7	7	11	14	17	20	22	22	19	14	10	8	14
Daily Min.°C	1	1	2	5	7	10	12	12	10	7	4	2	6
Average Monthly °C	4	4	6	9	12	15	17	17	14	11	7	5	10
Rainfall Monthly Total mm	61	44	43	41	55	52	55	60	59	64	69	57	660
No. of Days	13	10	9	9	10	9	10	10	10	11	12	13	126
Sunshine Hours per Day	1.7	2.6	3.9	5.3	6.1	6.6	5.9	5.7	4.4	3.2	2.1	1.6	4.1
Plymouth 27m													
Temperature Daily Max.°C	8	8	10	12	15	18	19	19	18	15	11	9	14
Daily Min.°C	4	4	5	6	8	11	13	13	12	9	7	5	8
Average Monthly °C	6	6	7	9	12	15	16	16	15	12	9	7	11
Rainfall Monthly Total mm	99	74	69	53	63	53	70	77	78	91	113	110	950
No. of Days	19	15	14	12	12	12	14	14	15	16	17	18	178
Sunshine Hours per Day	1.9	2.9	4.3	6.1	7.1	7.4	6.4	6.4	5.1	3.7	2.2	1.7	4.6
Renfrew 6m													
Temperature Daily Max.°C	5	7	9	12	15	18	19	19	16	13	9	7	12
Daily Min.°C	1	1	2	4	6	9	11	11	9	6	4	2	6
Average Monthly °C	3	4	6	8	11	14	15	15	13	9	7	4	9
Rainfall Monthly Total mm	111	85	69	67	63	70	97	93	102	119	106	127	1109
No. of Days	19	16	15	15	14	15	17	17	17	18	18	20	201
Sunshine Hours per Day	1.1	2.1	2.9	4.7	6	6.1	5.1	4.4	3.7	2.3	1.4	0.8	3.4
St Helier 9m													
Temperature Daily Max.°C	9	8	11	13	16	19	21	21	19	16	12	10	15
Daily Min.°C	5	4	6	7	10	13	15	15	14	11	8	6	9
Average Monthly °C	7	6	8	10	13	16	18	18	17	13	10	8	12
Rainfall Monthly Total mm	89	68	57	43	44	39	48	67	69	77	101	99	801
No. of Days	19	15	13	12	11	10	11	12	15	15	17	19	169
Sunshine Hours per Day	2.3	3.1	5	6.7	7.8	8.5	7.8	7.6	5.6	4.1	2.5	1.8	5.3
St Mary's 50m													
Temperature Daily Max.°C	9	9	11	12	14	17	19	19	18	15	12	10	14
Daily Min.°C	6	6	7	7	9	12	13	14	13	11	9	7	9
Average Monthly °C	8	7	9	10	12	14	16	16	15	13	10	9	12
Rainfall Monthly Total mm	91	71	69	46	56	49	61	64	67	80	96	94	844
No. of Days	22	17	16	13	14	14	16	15	16	17	19	21	200
Sunshine Hours per Day	2	2.9	4.2	6.4	7.6	7.6	6.7	6.7	5.2	3.9	2.5	1.8	4.8
Southampton 20m													
Temperature Daily Max.°C	7	8	11	14	17	20	22	22	19	15	11	8	15
Daily Min.°C	2	2	3	5	8	11	13	13	11	7	5	3	7
Average Monthly °C	5	5	7	10	13	16	17	17	15	11	8	6	11
Rainfall Monthly Total mm	83	56	52	45	56	49	60	69	70	86	94	84	804
No. of Days	17	13	13	12	12	12	13	13	14	14	16	17	166
Sunshine Hours per Day	1.8	2.6	4	5.7	6.7	7.2	6.5	6.4	4.9	3.6	2.2	1.6	4.5
Tiree 9m													
Temperature Daily Max.°C	7	7	9	10	13	15	16	16	15	12	10	8	12
Daily Min.°C	4	3	4	5	7	10	11	11	10	8	6	5	7
Average Monthly °C	5	5	6	8	10	12	14	14	13	10	8	6	9
Rainfall Monthly Total mm	117	77	67	64	55	70	91	90	118	129	122	128	1128
No. of Days	23	19	17	17	15	16	20	18	20	23	22	24	234
Sunshine Hours per Day	1.3	2.6	3.7	5.7	7.5	6.8	5.2	5.3	4.2	2.6	1.6	0.9	4
Valencia 9m													
Temperature Daily Max.°C	9	9	11	13	15	17	18	18	17	14	12	10	14
Daily Min.°C	5	4	5	6	8	11	12	13	11	9	7	6	8
Average Monthly °C	7	7	8	9	11	0	15	15	14	12	9	8	11
Rainfall Monthly Total mm	165	107	103	75	86	81	107	95	122	140	151	168	1400
No. of Days	20	15	14	13	13	13	15	15	16	17	18	21	190
Sunshine Hours per Day	1.6	2.5	3.5	5.2	6.5	5.9	4.7	4.9	3.8	2.8	2	1.3	3.7
York 17m													
Temperature Daily Max.°C	6	7	10	13	16	19	21	21	18	14	10	7	13
Daily Min.°C	1	1	2	4	7	10	12	12	10	7	4	2	6
Average Monthly °C	3	4	6	9	12	15	17	16	14	10	7	5	10
Rainfall Monthly Total mm	59	46	37	41	50	50	62	68	55	56	65	50	639
No. of Days	17	15	13	13	13	14	15	14	14	15	17	17	177
Sunshine Hours per Day	1.3	2.1	3.2	4.7	6.1	6.4	5.6	5.1	4.1	2.8	1.6	1.1	3.7

WATER SUPPLY

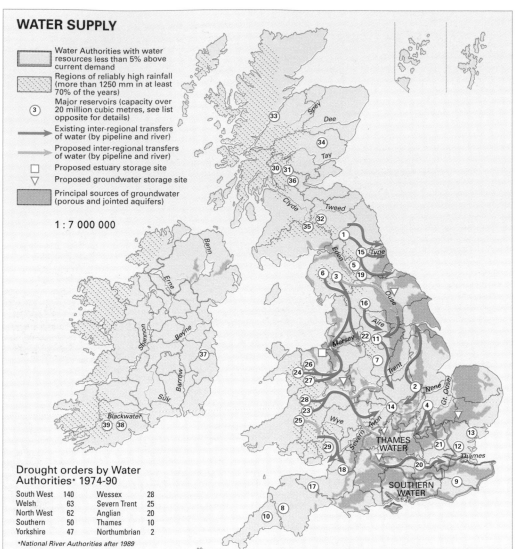

Water Authorities with water resources less than 5% above current demand

Regions of reliably high rainfall (more than 1250 mm in at least 70% of the years)

③ Major reservoirs (capacity over 20 million cubic metres, see list opposite for details)

→ Existing inter-regional transfers of water (by pipeline and river)

→ Proposed inter-regional transfers of water (by pipeline and river)

□ Proposed estuary storage site

▽ Proposed groundwater storage site

Principal sources of groundwater (porous and jointed aquifers)

1 : 7 000 000

Drought orders by Water Authorities* 1974-90

South West	140	Wessex	28
Welsh	63	Severn Trent	25
North West	62	Anglian	20
Southern	50	Thames	10
Yorkshire	47	Northumbrian	2

*National River Authorities after 1989

Major reservoirs (with capacity in million m³)

England			Wales	
1	Kielder Res.	198	23 Elan Valley	99
2	Rutland Water	123	24 Llyn Celyn	74
3	Haweswater	85	25 Llyn Brianne	62
4	Grafham Water	59	26 Llyn Brenig	60
5	Cow Green Res.	41	27 Llyn Vyrnwy	60
6	Thirlmere	41	28 Llyn Clywedog	48
7	Carsington Res.	36	29 Llandegfedd Res.	22
8	Roadford Res.	35		
9	Bewl Water Res.	31	**Scotland**	
10	Colliford Lake	29	30 Loch Lomond	86
11	Ladybower Res.	28	31 Loch Katrine	64
12	Hanningfield Res.	27	32 Megget Res.	64
13	Abberton Res.	25	33 Loch Ness	26
14	Draycote Water	23	34 Backwater Res.	25
15	Derwent Res.	22	35 Daer Res.	23
16	Grimwith Res.	22	36 Carron Valley Res.	21
17	Wimbleball Lake	21		
18	Chew Valley Lake	20	**Ireland**	
19	Balderhead Res.	20	37 Poulaphouca Res.	168
20	Thames Valley (linked reservoirs)		38 Inishcarra Res.	57
21	Lea Valley (linked reservoirs)		39 Carrigadrohid Res.	33
22	Longdendale (linked reservoirs)			

Average daily domestic water use in England and Wales (1990)

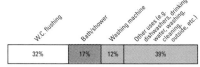

W.C. flushing	Bath/shower	Washing machine	Other uses (e.g. dishwashers, drinking water, washing, cleaning, outside, etc.)
32%	17%	12%	39%

Water abstractions in England and Wales (1990) 35 249 megalitres per day* of which:

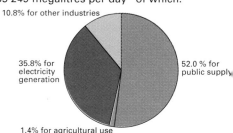

10.8% for other industries

35.8% for electricity generation

52.0 % for public supply

1.4% for agricultural use

*average daily domestic consumption per head 136 litres.

WATER ABSTRACTIONS   1 : 12 000 000

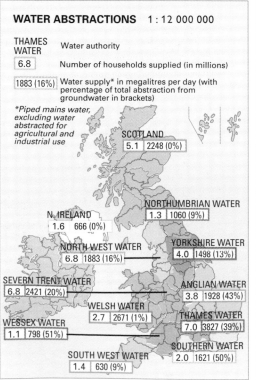

THAMES WATER   Water authority

6.8   Number of households supplied (in millions)

1883 (16%)   Water supply* in megalitres per day (with percentage of total abstraction from groundwater in brackets)

*Piped mains water, excluding water abstracted for agricultural and industrial use

SCOTLAND   5.1   2248 (0%)

N. IRELAND   1.6   666 (0%)

NORTHUMBRIAN WATER   1.3   1060 (9%)

YORKSHIRE WATER   4.0   1498 (13%)

NORTH WEST WATER   6.8   1883 (16%)

SEVERN TRENT WATER   6.8   2421 (20%)

ANGLIAN WATER   3.8   1928 (43%)

WELSH WATER   2.7   2671 (1%)

THAMES WATER   7.0   3827 (39%)

WESSEX WATER   1.1   798 (51%)

SOUTH WEST WATER   1.4   630 (9%)

SOUTHERN WATER   2.0   1621 (50%)

WATER QUALITY   1 : 12 000 000

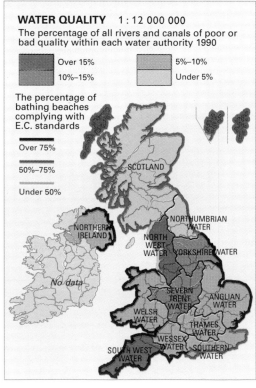

The percentage of all rivers and canals of poor or bad quality within each water authority 1990

Over 15%

10%–15%

5%–10%

Under 5%

The percentage of bathing beaches complying with E.C. standards

Over 75%

50%–75%

Under 50%

No data

SOILS   1 : 12 000 000

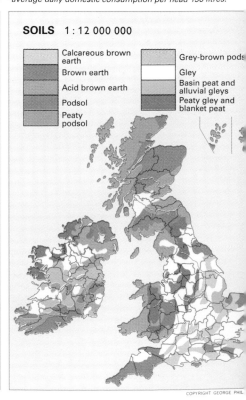

Calcareous brown earth

Brown earth

Acid brown earth

Podsol

Peaty podsol

Grey-brown pods...

Gley

Basin peat and alluvial gleys

Peaty gley and blanket peat

AIR QUALITY : Emissions in thousand tonnes

	Sulphur dioxide			Nitrogen oxides		
	1975	1981	1987	1975	1981	1987
Belgium	–	856	610	–	317	271
Denmark	418	363	248	182	212	266
France	3 329	2 735	1 517	1 608	1 779	1 652
Germany	3 325	3 034	2 223	2 532	2 851	2 969
Greece	–	546	–	–	217	–
Irish Republic	186	189	138	60	68	68
Italy	3 250	3 211	2 075	1 499	1 585	1 570
Luxembourg	–	24	13	–	23	22
Netherlands	386	445	274	447	547	560
Portugal	178	266	286	104	166	303
Spain	–	2 543	–	–	937	–
United Kingdom	5 310	4 387	3 863	2 365	2 328	2 429

FORESTRY 1 : 12 000 000

The percentage of the total area covered by woodland and forest

- Over 20%
- 15%-20%
- 10%-15%
- 5%-10%
- Under 5%
- △ 50%-80% coniferous
- △ Over 80% coniferous

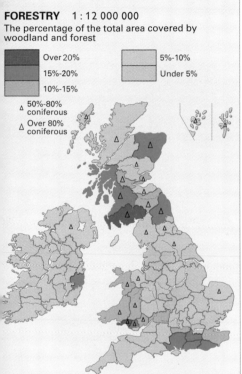

NATURAL VEGETATION 1 : 12 000 000

The plant cover associated with a particular environment if it is unaffected by human activity

- Oak
- Beech and Oak
- Ash and Oak
- Birch and Oakwood
- Scots Pine
- Heath, moorland, water meadows, fen, bog and marsh

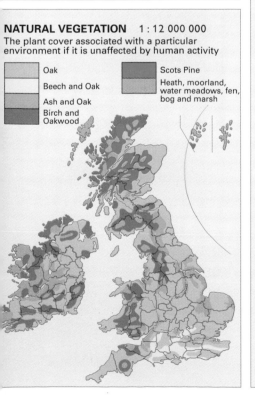

ACID RAIN 1 : 12 000 000

Average acidity of precipitation in the U.K. (pH scale)

- 4.29 and under (most acidic)
- 4.30-4.39
- 4.40-4.49
- 4.50-4.59
- 4.60-4.69
- 4.70-4.79
- 4.80 and over (least acidic)

No data

E.S.As.
Environmentally Sensitive Areas in the U.K.

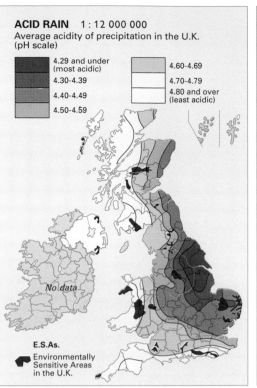

AIR QUALITY 1 : 12 000 000

Hourly average of tropospheric ozone (O_3) exceeding 100 parts per billion (summer 1990)*

- Over 45
- 30-45
- 15-30
- Under 15

Ground-level concentrations of smoke in the U.K., by region
U.K. average:
12 micrograms per m³

- Less than the U.K. average
- More than the U.K. average
- Over 3x the U.K. average

SCOTLAND
NORTH
NORTHERN IRELAND
YORKSHIRE AND HUMBERSIDE
NORTH WEST
EAST MIDLANDS
WALES
WEST MIDLANDS
EAST ANGLIA
SOUTH WEST
SOUTH EAST

* W.H.O. recommends 75-100 ppb maximum

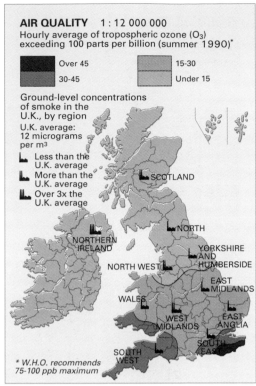

CONSERVATION

- National Parks
- Areas of Outstanding Natural Beauty
- National Scenic Areas
- Forest Parks and Special Protected Areas
- Green Belts (and the urban areas they surround)
- Heritage Coast (England and Wales)/Coastal Conservation Zones (Scotland)
- * World Heritage Sites in the U.K.

(also designated but not shown, St. Kilda, Outer Hebrides and Henderson Island, South Pacific Ocean)

1 : 7 000 000

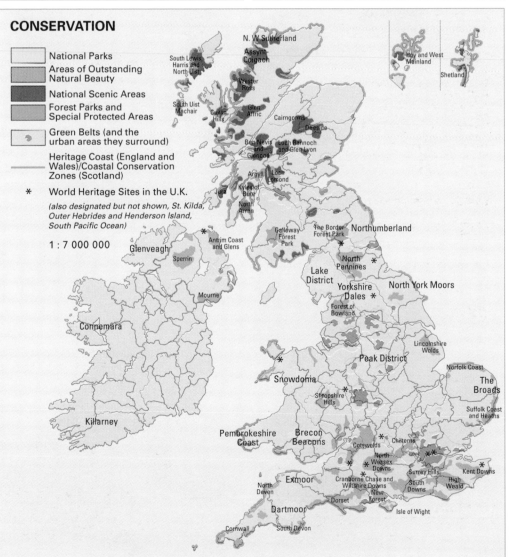

N. W. Sutherland
South Lewis, Harris and North Uist
Assynt-Coigach
Hoy and West Mainland
Wester Ross
Shetland
South Uist Machair
Cuillin Hills
Glen Affric
Cairngorms
Deeside
Ben Nevis and Glencoe
Loch Rannoch and Glen Lyon
Argyll
Loch Lomond
Jura
Kyles of Bute
North Arran
Glenveagh
Antrim Coast and Glens
Galloway Forest Park
The Border Forest Park
Northumberland
Sperrin
Mourne
Lake District
North Pennines
Yorkshire Dales
North York Moors
Connemara
Forest of Bowland
Lincolnshire Wolds
Peak District
Norfolk Coast
Snowdonia
Shropshire Hills
The Broads
Killarney
Suffolk Coast and Heaths
Pembrokeshire Coast
Brecon Beacons
Cotswolds
Chilterns
North Wessex Downs
Surrey Hills
Kent Downs
Exmoor
Cranborne Chase and Wiltshire Downs
South Downs
High Weald
North Devon
New Forest
Dorset
Dartmoor
Isle of Wight
Cornwall
South Devon

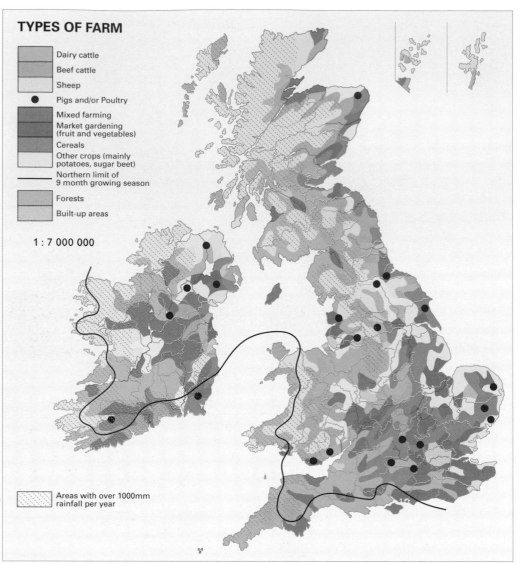

TYPES OF FARM

- Dairy cattle
- Beef cattle
- Sheep
- ● Pigs and/or Poultry
- Mixed farming
- Market gardening (fruit and vegetables)
- Cereals
- Other crops (mainly potatoes, sugar beet)
- —— Northern limit of 9 month growing season
- Forests
- Built-up areas

1 : 7 000 000

Areas with over 1000mm rainfall per year

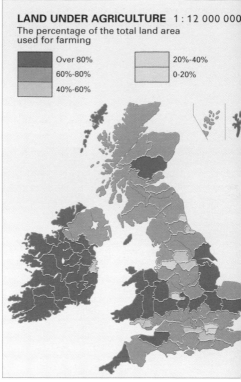

LAND UNDER AGRICULTURE   1 : 12 000 000
The percentage of the total land area used for farming

- Over 80%
- 60%-80%
- 40%-60%
- 20%-40%
- 0-20%

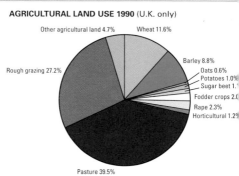

AGRICULTURAL LAND USE 1990 (U.K. only)

- Other agricultural land 4.7%
- Wheat 11.6%
- Rough grazing 27.2%
- Barley 8.8%
- Oats 0.6%
- Potatoes 1.0%
- Sugar beet 1.
- Fodder crops 2.0
- Rape 2.3%
- Horticultural 1.2%
- Pasture 39.5%

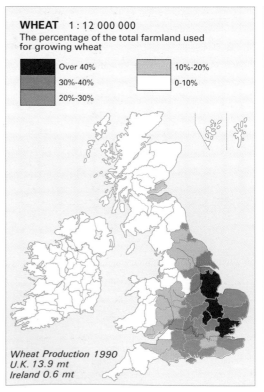

WHEAT   1 : 12 000 000
The percentage of the total farmland used for growing wheat

- Over 40%
- 30%-40%
- 20%-30%
- 10%-20%
- 0-10%

Wheat Production 1990
U.K. 13.9 mt
Ireland 0.6 mt

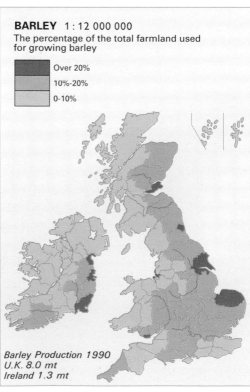

BARLEY   1 : 12 000 000
The percentage of the total farmland used for growing barley

- Over 20%
- 10%-20%
- 0-10%

Barley Production 1990
U.K. 8.0 mt
Ireland 1.3 mt

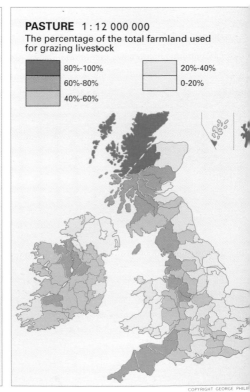

PASTURE   1 : 12 000 000
The percentage of the total farmland used for grazing livestock

- 80%-100%
- 60%-80%
- 40%-60%
- 20%-40%
- 0-20%

NUMBER AND SIZE OF AGRICULTURAL HOLDINGS IN THE U.K.

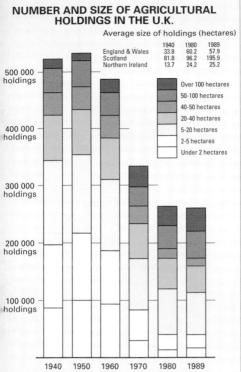

Average size of holdings (hectares)

	1940	1980	1989
England & Wales	33.8	60.2	57.9
Scotland	81.8	96.2	195.9
Northern Ireland	13.7	24.2	25.2

Over 100 hectares
50-100 hectares
40-50 hectares
20-40 hectares
5-20 hectares
2-5 hectares
Under 2 hectares

POTATOES 1 : 12 000 000

The percentage of the total farmland used for growing potatoes

- Over 3%
- 2%-3%
- 1%-2%
- Under 1%

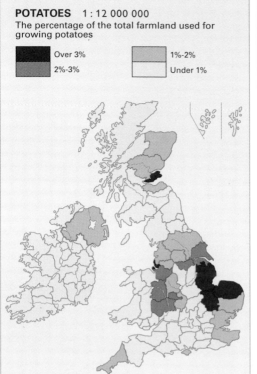

MARKET GARDENING 1 : 12 000 000

The percentage of the total farmland used for market gardening

- Over 5%
- 2.5%-5%
- 1.0%-2.5%
- Under 1%

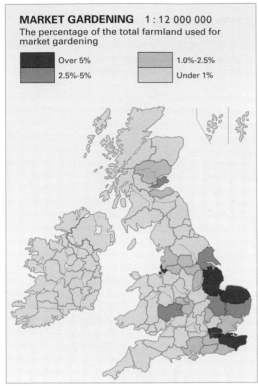

FISHING

('000 tonnes)

Quantities of fish landed at major ports (port districts in Scotland) in 1989

100
50
10
5

Type of fish landed

- Demersal (Deep Sea Fish)
- Pelagic (Shallow Water Fish)
- Shellfish

Fishing Regions
IV North Sea
VIa West Scotland
VIIa Irish Sea
VIIb South & West Ireland
VIId English Channel
VIIf Bristol Channel

Fish landed according to region of capture (1989)
Demersal
Pelagic
1 fish represents 10 000 caught
Region boundary

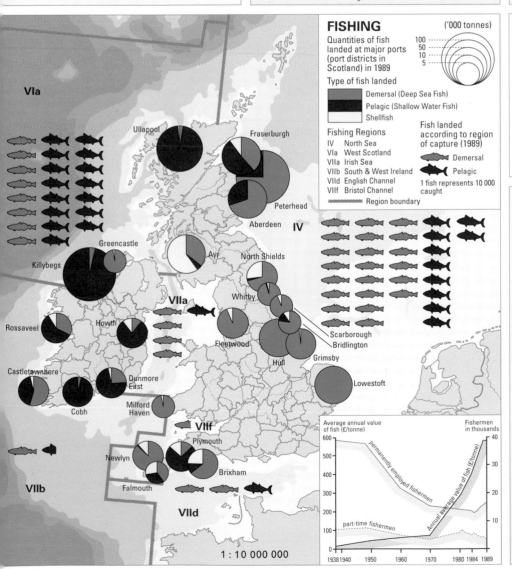

1 : 10 000 000

1000 500 200 100 50 m

VALUE OF AGRICULTURAL OUTPUT (U.K. only)

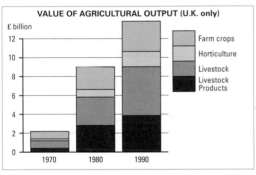

£ billion

- Farm crops
- Horticulture
- Livestock
- Livestock Products

1970 1980 1990

AGRICULTURAL LAND & LIVESTOCK, 1970-90 (U.K. only)

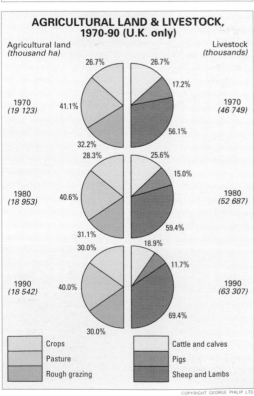

Agricultural land (thousand ha)

1970 (19 123)
1980 (18 953)
1990 (18 542)

Livestock (thousands)

1970 (46 749)
1980 (52 687)
1990 (63 307)

- Crops
- Pasture
- Rough grazing
- Cattle and calves
- Pigs
- Sheep and Lambs

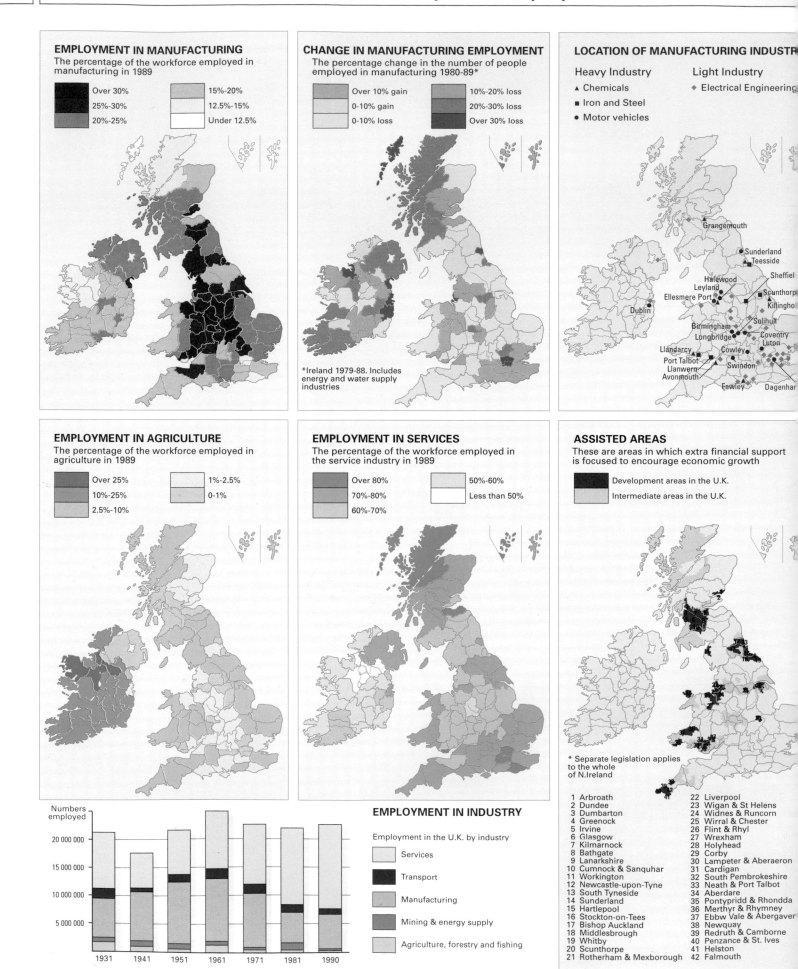

EMPLOYMENT IN MANUFACTURING

The percentage of the workforce employed in manufacturing in 1989

- Over 30%
- 25%-30%
- 20%-25%
- 15%-20%
- 12.5%-15%
- Under 12.5%

CHANGE IN MANUFACTURING EMPLOYMENT

The percentage change in the number of people employed in manufacturing 1980-89*

- Over 10% gain
- 0-10% gain
- 0-10% loss
- 10%-20% loss
- 20%-30% loss
- Over 30% loss

*Ireland 1979-88. Includes energy and water supply industries

LOCATION OF MANUFACTURING INDUSTR

Heavy Industry
- ▲ Chemicals
- ■ Iron and Steel
- ● Motor vehicles

Light Industry
- ◆ Electrical Engineering

Grangemouth
Sunderland
Teesside
Sheffiel
Halewood
Leyland
Scunthorp
Ellesmere Port
Killingho
Dublin
Solihull
Birmingham
Coventry
Longbridge
Luton
Llandarcy
Cowley
Port Talbot
Llanwern
Swindon
Avonmouth
Dagenhar
Fawley

EMPLOYMENT IN AGRICULTURE

The percentage of the workforce employed in agriculture in 1989

- Over 25%
- 10%-25%
- 2.5%-10%
- 1%-2.5%
- 0-1%

EMPLOYMENT IN SERVICES

The percentage of the workforce employed in the service industry in 1989

- Over 80%
- 70%-80%
- 60%-70%
- 50%-60%
- Less than 50%

ASSISTED AREAS

These are areas in which extra financial support is focused to encourage economic growth

- Development areas in the U.K.
- Intermediate areas in the U.K.

* Separate legislation applies to the whole of N.Ireland

1 Arbroath	22 Liverpool
2 Dundee	23 Wigan & St Helens
3 Dumbarton	24 Widnes & Runcorn
4 Greenock	25 Wirral & Chester
5 Irvine	26 Flint & Rhyl
6 Glasgow	27 Wrexham
7 Kilmarnock	28 Holyhead
8 Bathgate	29 Corby
9 Lanarkshire	30 Lampeter & Aberaeron
10 Cumnock & Sanquhar	31 Cardigan
11 Workington	32 South Pembrokeshire
12 Newcastle-upon-Tyne	33 Neath & Port Talbot
13 South Tyneside	34 Aberdare
14 Sunderland	35 Pontypridd & Rhondda
15 Hartlepool	36 Merthyr & Rhymney
16 Stockton-on-Tees	37 Ebbw Vale & Abergaver
17 Bishop Auckland	38 Newquay
18 Middlesbrough	39 Redruth & Camborne
19 Whitby	40 Penzance & St. Ives
20 Scunthorpe	41 Helston
21 Rotherham & Mexborough	42 Falmouth

Numbers employed

20 000 000
15 000 000
10 000 000
5 000 000

1931 1941 1951 1961 1971 1981 1990

EMPLOYMENT IN INDUSTRY

Employment in the U.K. by industry

- Services
- Transport
- Manufacturing
- Mining & energy supply
- Agriculture, forestry and fishing

1 : 12 000 000

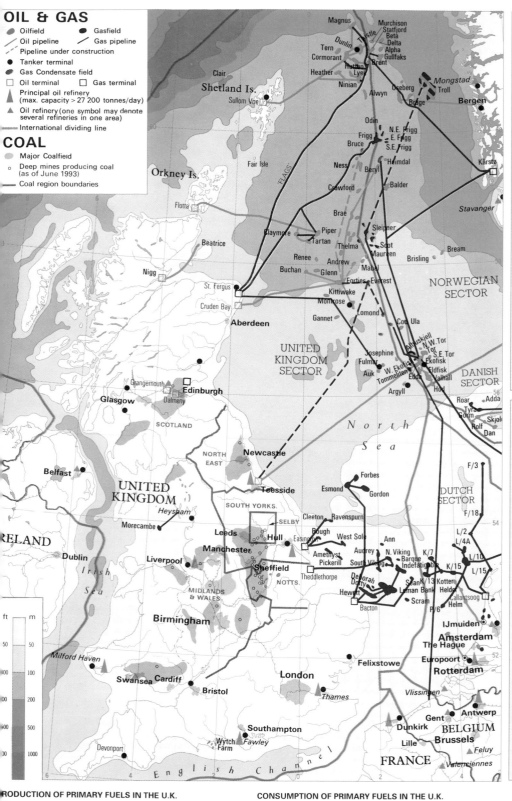

OIL & GAS

- ◆ Oilfield
- ● Gasfield
- ⟋ Oil pipeline
- ⟍ Gas pipeline
- ⟋ Pipeline under construction
- ● Tanker terminal
- ▲ Gas Condensate field
- □ Oil terminal
- □ Gas terminal
- ▲ Principal oil refinery (max. capacity > 27 200 tonnes/day)
- ▲ Oil refinery (one symbol may denote several refineries in one area)
- — International dividing line

COAL

- Major Coalfield
- ○ Deep mines producing coal (as of June 1993)
- — Coal region boundaries

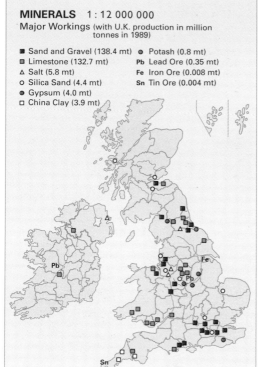

MINERALS 1 : 12 000 000
Major Workings (with U.K. production in million tonnes in 1989)

- ■ Sand and Gravel (138.4 mt)
- ■ Limestone (132.7 mt)
- △ Salt (5.8 mt)
- ○ Silica Sand (4.4 mt)
- ● Gypsum (4.0 mt)
- □ China Clay (3.9 mt)
- ● Potash (0.8 mt)
- Pb Lead Ore (0.35 mt)
- Fe Iron Ore (0.008 mt)
- Sn Tin Ore (0.004 mt)

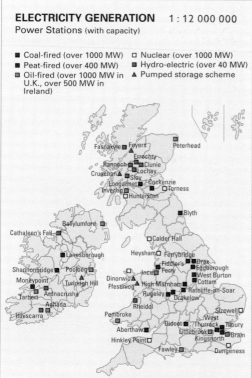

ELECTRICITY GENERATION 1 : 12 000 000
Power Stations (with capacity)

- ■ Coal-fired (over 1000 MW)
- ■ Peat-fired (over 400 MW)
- ■ Oil-fired (over 1000 MW in U.K., over 500 MW in Ireland)
- □ Nuclear (over 1000 MW)
- ▲ Hydro-electric (over 40 MW)
- ▲ Pumped storage scheme

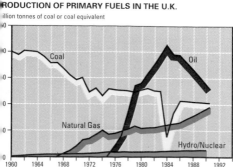

PRODUCTION OF PRIMARY FUELS IN THE U.K.
million tonnes of coal or coal equivalent

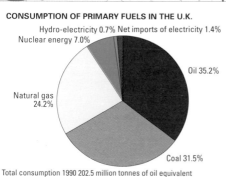

CONSUMPTION OF PRIMARY FUELS IN THE U.K.

Hydro-electricity 0.7% Net imports of electricity 1.4%
Nuclear energy 7.0%
Oil 35.2%
Natural gas 24.2%
Coal 31.5%

Total consumption 1990 202.5 million tonnes of oil equivalent

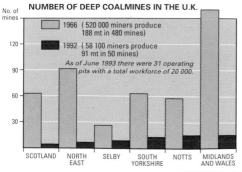

NUMBER OF DEEP COALMINES IN THE U.K.

No. of mines

- 1966 (520 000 miners produce 188 mt in 480 mines)
- 1992 (58 100 miners produce 91 mt in 50 mines)

As of June 1993 there were 31 operating pits with a total workforce of 20 000.

SCOTLAND · NORTH EAST · SELBY · SOUTH YORKSHIRE · NOTTS · MIDLANDS AND WALES

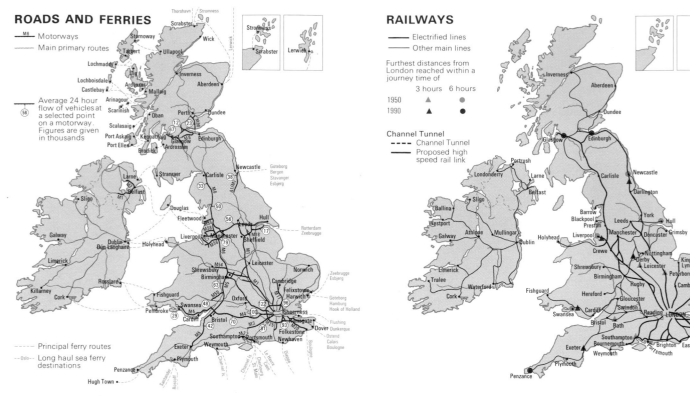

ROADS AND FERRIES

— M6 — Motorways
— Main primary routes

(56) Average 24 hour flow of vehicles at a selected point on a motorway. Figures are given in thousands

----- Principal ferry routes
--Oslo- Long haul sea ferry destinations

RAILWAYS

— Electrified lines
— Other main lines

Furthest distances from London reached within a journey time of

	3 hours	6 hours
1950	▲	●
1990	▲	●

Channel Tunnel

--- Channel Tunnel
--- Proposed high speed rail link

CHANNEL TUNNEL

Estimated journey times between London-Brussels and London-Paris

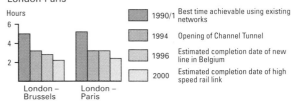

Hours

- 1990/1 Best time achievable using existing networks
- 1994 Opening of Channel Tunnel
- 1996 Estimated completion date of new line in Belgium
- 2000 Estimated completion date of high speed rail link

London – Brussels
London – Paris

MEANS OF TRANSPORTATION WITHIN THE U.K.

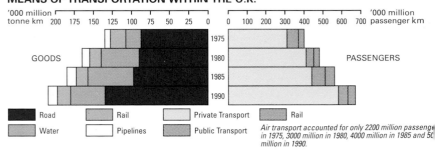

'000 million tonne km   GOODS   '000 million passenger km

PASSENGERS

1975, 1980, 1985, 1990

Road · Rail · Water · Pipelines
Private Transport · Public Transport · Rail

Air transport accounted for only 2200 million passengers in 1975, 3000 million in 1980, 4000 million in 1985 and 5000 million in 1990.

PORTS

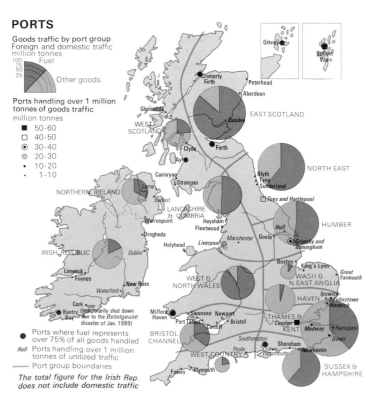

Goods traffic by port group
Foreign and domestic traffic
million tonnes

Fuel
Other goods

Ports handling over 1 million tonnes of goods traffic
million tonnes

- 50-60
- 40-50
- 30-40
- 20-30
- 10-20
- 1-10

● Ports where fuel represents over 75% of all goods handled

Hull Ports handling over 1 million tonnes of unitized traffic

— Port group boundaries

The total figure for the Irish Rep. does not include domestic traffic

AIRPORTS

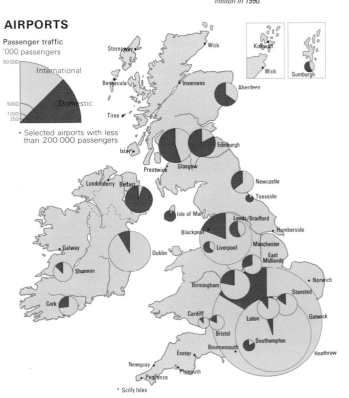

Passenger traffic
'000 passengers

International
Domestic

· Selected airports with less than 200 000 passengers

1 : 10 000 000

The DISTRICTS of Northern Ireland have been numbered and can be identified by reference to this table.

1	Londonderry	14	Craigavon
2	Limavady	15	Armagh
3	Coleraine	16	Newry & Mourne
4	Ballymoney	17	Banbridge
5	Moyle	18	Down
6	Larne	19	Lisburn
7	Ballymena	20	Antrim
8	Magherafelt	21	Newtownabbey
9	Cookstown	22	Carrickfergus
10	Strabane	23	North Down
11	Omagh	24	Ards
12	Fermanagh	25	Castlereagh
13	Dungannon	26	Belfast

ORKNEY

SHETLAND

HIGHLAND

Kirkwall

Lerwick

WESTERN ISLES

Stornoway

HIGHLAND

GRAMPIAN

Inverness

Aberdeen

SCOTLAND

TAYSIDE

Dundee

FIFE

Glenrothes

CENTRAL

Stirling

Edinburgh

Glasgow

LOTHIAN

STRATHCLYDE

BORDERS

Newtown St. Boswells

NORTHUMBERLAND

Morpeth

DUMFRIES AND GALLOWAY

Dumfries

Newcastle

TYNE AND WEAR

Carlisle

Durham

DURHAM

CLEVELAND

Middlesbrough

CUMBRIA

Northallerton

NORTH YORKSHIRE

ISLE OF MAN

Douglas

HUMBERSIDE

Beverley

LANCASHIRE

Preston

WEST YORKSHIRE

Wakefield

Barnsley

GREATER MANCHESTER

SOUTH YORKSHIRE

MERSEYSIDE

Manchester

Liverpool

ENGLAND

Lincoln

Chester

CHESHIRE

DERBYSHIRE

NOTTINGHAMSHIRE

LINCOLNSHIRE

Matlock

Nottingham

Caernarfon

Mold

CLWYD

GWYNEDD

Stafford

STAFFORDSHIRE

Leicester

NORFOLK

Norwich

Shrewsbury

SHROPSHIRE

WEST MIDLANDS

Birmingham

LEICESTERSHIRE

WARWICKSHIRE

Warwick

NORTHAMPTONSHIRE

Northampton

CAMBRIDGESHIRE

Cambridge

SUFFOLK

Ipswich

WALES

POWYS

HEREFORD AND WORCESTER

Worcester

Bedford

BEDFORDSHIRE

Hertford

HERTFORDSHIRE

ESSEX

Chelmsford

Llandrindod Wells

Gloucester

GLOUCESTERSHIRE

Oxford

OXFORDSHIRE

Aylesbury

BUCKINGHAMSHIRE

GREATER LONDON

Kingston

Maidstone

DYFED

Carmarthen

GWENT

Cwmbran

Reading

BERKSHIRE

SURREY

KENT

WEST GLAMORGAN

Swansea

MID GLAMORGAN

Cardiff

SOUTH GLAMORGAN

Bristol

AVON

WILTSHIRE

Trowbridge

HAMPSHIRE

Winchester

WEST SUSSEX

EAST SUSSEX

Lewes

Chichester

SOMERSET

Taunton

DORSET

Dorchester

Newport

ISLE OF WIGHT

DEVON

Exeter

CORNWALL

Truro

NORTH SEA

NORTH CHANNEL

IRISH SEA

ATLANTIC OCEAN

CELTIC SEA

ENGLISH CHANNEL

St. George's Channel

FRANCE

DONEGAL

Lifford

NORTHERN IRELAND

Londonderry

Antrim

Tyrone

Fermanagh

Belfast

Down

Armagh

SLIGO

Sligo

LEITRIM

Carrick-on-Shannon

MONAGHAN

Monaghan

MAYO

Castlebar

ROSCOMMON

Roscommon

Longford

LONGFORD

CAVAN

Cavan

Dundalk

LOUTH

An Uaimh (Navan)

Mullingar

WESTMEATH

MEATH

GALWAY

Galway

IRELAND

OFFALY

Tullamore

DUBLIN

Dublin

KILDARE

Naas

CLARE

Ennis

LAOIS

Port Laoise

WICKLOW

Wicklow

LIMERICK

Limerick

TIPPERARY

Kilkenny

KILKENNY

CARLOW

Carlow

Tralee

Clonmel

WEXFORD

Wexford

KERRY

WATERFORD

Waterford

CORK

Cork

○ Norwich — Administrative headquarters

MERSEYSIDE — Metropolitan counties

Antrim — Former Northern Ireland counties

Projection: Conical with two standard parallels

1 : 4 000 000

20 0 20 40 60 miles

20 0 20 40 60 80 km

West from Greenwich 0 East from Greenwich

COPYRIGHT. GEORGE PHILIP & SON. LTD.

POPULATION DENSITY 1891 1 : 12 000 000

See map at right for reference to colours

Density in 1891 by country :
U.K. 142 people per km²
Ireland 49 people per km²

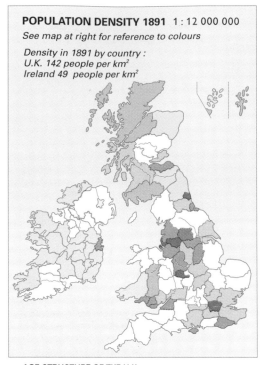

AGE STRUCTURE OF THE U.K.

The bars represent the percentage of males and the percentage of females in the age group shown

□ 1901   □ 1990   — Projected 2150

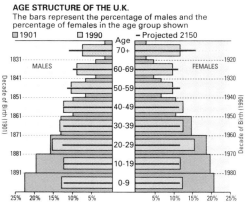

POPULATION DENSITY 1991

Persons per km²

	Over 1000
	500-1000
	200-500
	100-200
	50-100
	25-50
	Under 25

The density for the whole of the U.K. is 223 people per km², the density for Ireland is 51.

1 : 7 000 000

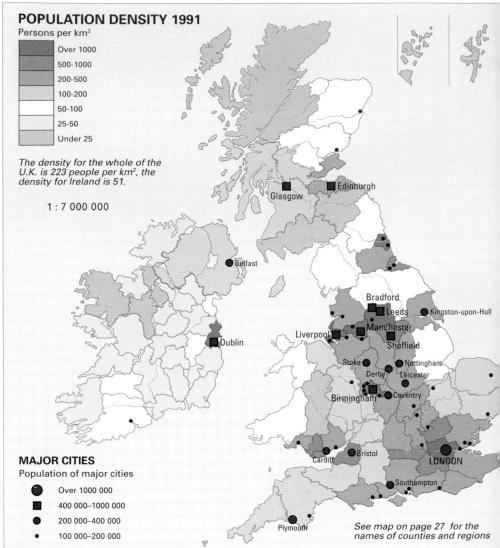

Glasgow   Edinburgh

Belfast

Bradford
Leeds   Kingston-upon-Hull
Liverpool   Manchester
Sheffield
Dublin
Stoke   Nottingham
Derby   Leicester
Birmingham   Coventry

Cardiff   Bristol   LONDON

Southampton

Plymouth

MAJOR CITIES

Population of major cities

● Over 1000 000
■ 400 000–1000 000
● 200 000–400 000
• 100 000–200 000

See map on page 27 for the names of counties and regions

YOUNG PEOPLE 1 : 12 000 000

The percentage of the population under 15 years old in 1990 (Ireland 1986)

	Over 30%		19%-20%
	25%-30%		18%-19%
	20%-25%		Under 18%

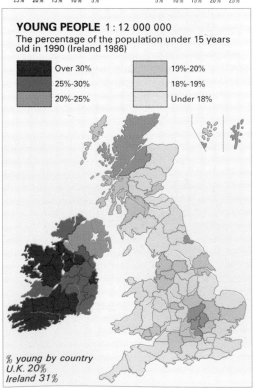

% young by country
U.K. 20%
Ireland 31%

OLD PEOPLE 1 : 12 000 000

The percentage of the population over pensionable age* in 1989

	Over 20%		12.5%-15%
	17.5%-20%		10%-12.5%
	15%-17.5%		Under 10%

* Pensionable age is 65 for males, 60 for females

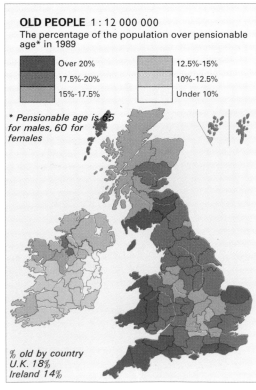

% old by country
U.K. 18%
Ireland 14%

URBANIZATION 1 : 12 000 000

The percentage of the population living in towns and cities (latest available year)

	Over 90%		60%-70%
	80%-90%		50%-60%
	70%-80%		Under 50%

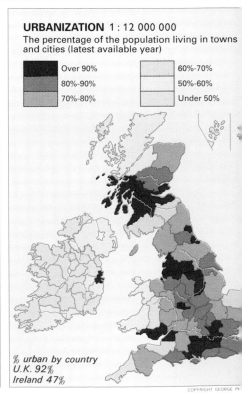

% urban by country
U.K. 92%
Ireland 47%

NATURAL POPULATION CHANGE

The difference between the number of births and the number of deaths per thousand inhabitants in 1990

- Over 10 more births
- 5-10 more births
- 2.5-5 more births
- 0-2.5 more births
- 0-2.5 more deaths
- Over 2.5 more deaths

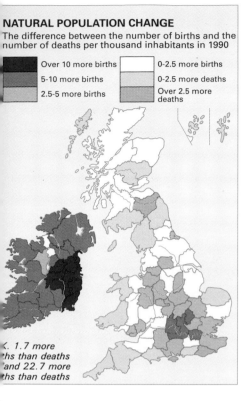

K. 1.7 more
ths than deaths
and 22.7 more
ths than deaths

ETHNIC GROUP

Ethnic minority groups

Thousands
- 500
- 100
- 50

Other — Indian/ Pakistani/ Bangladeshi
W. Indian/ African

No available data for Ireland or Northern Ireland

Ethnic minorities as a % of total population in each region named

- Over 6%
- 4%-6%
- 2%-4%
- 0-2%

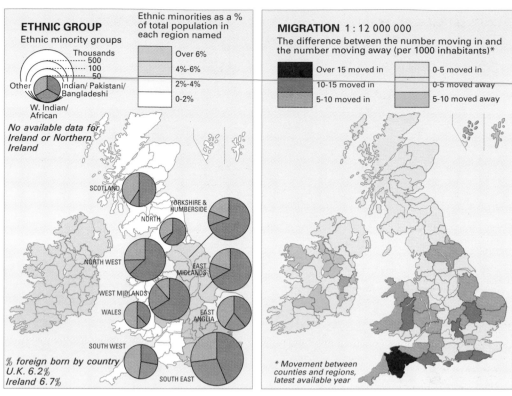

SCOTLAND
YORKSHIRE & HUMBERSIDE
NORTH
NORTH WEST
EAST MIDLANDS
WEST MIDLANDS
WALES
EAST ANGLIA
SOUTH WEST
SOUTH EAST

% foreign born by country
U.K. 6.2%
Ireland 6.7%

MIGRATION 1 : 12 000 000

The difference between the number moving in and the number moving away (per 1000 inhabitants)*

- Over 15 moved in
- 10-15 moved in
- 5-10 moved in
- 0-5 moved in
- 0-5 moved away
- 5-10 moved away

* Movement between counties and regions, latest available year

U.K. VITAL STATISTICS 1900-2000

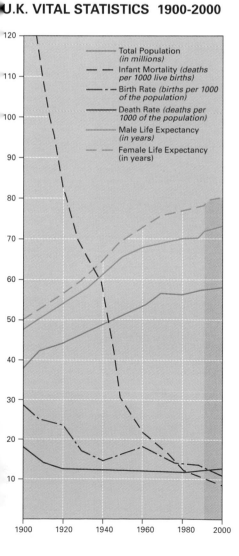

- Total Population (in millions)
- Infant Mortality (deaths per 1000 live births)
- Birth Rate (births per 1000 of the population)
- Death Rate (deaths per 1000 of the population)
- Male Life Expectancy (in years)
- Female Life Expectancy (in years)

POPULATION CHANGE 1961-1991

The percentage change in the number of people between 1961 and 1991

- Over 30% gain
- 25%-30% gain
- 20%-25% gain
- 15%-20% gain
- 10%-15% gain
- 5%-10% gain
- 0-5% gain
- 0-5% loss
- 5%-10% loss
- Over 10% loss

1 : 7 000 000

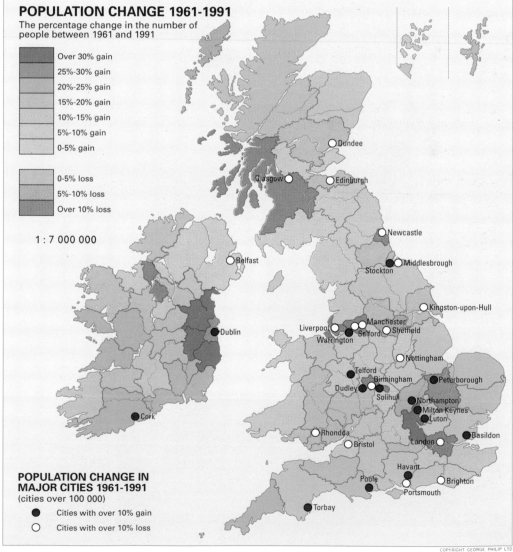

POPULATION CHANGE IN MAJOR CITIES 1961-1991
(cities over 100 000)

- ● Cities with over 10% gain
- ○ Cities with over 10% loss

COPYRIGHT GEORGE PHILIP LTD

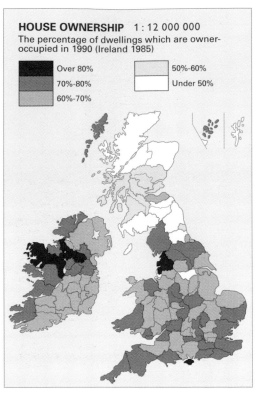

HOUSE OWNERSHIP 1 : 12 000 000
The percentage of dwellings which are owner-occupied in 1990 (Ireland 1985)

- Over 80%
- 70%-80%
- 60%-70%
- 50%-60%
- Under 50%

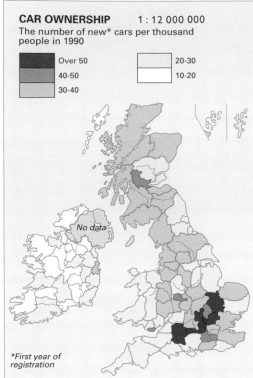

CAR OWNERSHIP 1 : 12 000 000
The number of new* cars per thousand people in 1990

- Over 50
- 40-50
- 30-40
- 20-30
- 10-20

No data

*First year of registration

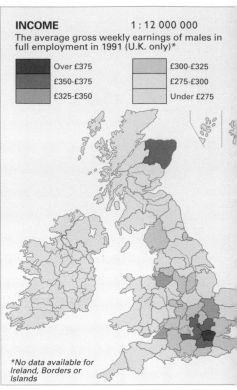

INCOME 1 : 12 000 000
The average gross weekly earnings of males in full employment in 1991 (U.K. only)*

- Over £375
- £350-£375
- £325-£350
- £300-£325
- £275-£300
- Under £275

*No data available for Ireland, Borders or Islands

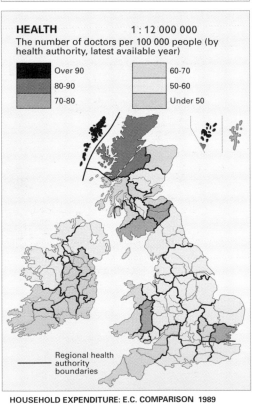

HEALTH 1 : 12 000 000
The number of doctors per 100 000 people (by health authority, latest available year)

- Over 90
- 80-90
- 70-80
- 60-70
- 50-60
- Under 50

— Regional health authority boundaries

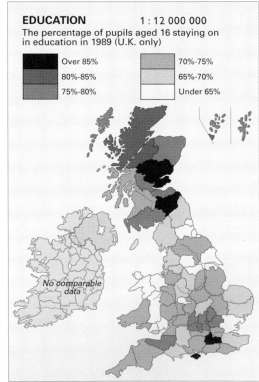

EDUCATION 1 : 12 000 000
The percentage of pupils aged 16 staying on in education in 1989 (U.K. only)

- Over 85%
- 80%-85%
- 75%-80%
- 70%-75%
- 65%-70%
- Under 65%

No comparable data

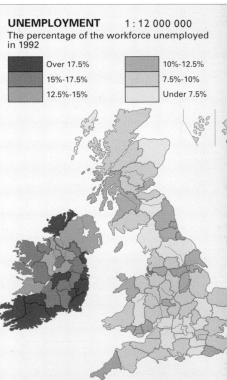

UNEMPLOYMENT 1 : 12 000 000
The percentage of the workforce unemployed in 1992

- Over 17.5%
- 15%-17.5%
- 12.5%-15%
- 10%-12.5%
- 7.5%-10%
- Under 7.5%

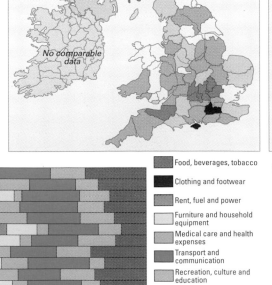

HOUSEHOLD EXPENDITURE: E.C. COMPARISON 1989

U.K.
Belgium
Denmark
France
Germany
Greece
Irish Rep.
Italy
Luxembourg
Netherlands
Portugal
Spain

0   10% 20% 30% 40% 50% 60% 70% 80% 90% 100%
Medical expenses are provided free in the U.K. and Denmark

- Food, beverages, tobacco
- Clothing and footwear
- Rent, fuel and power
- Furniture and household equipment
- Medical care and health expenses
- Transport and communication
- Recreation, culture and education
- Miscellaneous goods and services

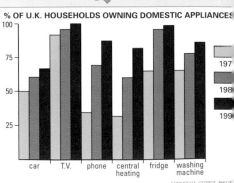

% OF U.K. HOUSEHOLDS OWNING DOMESTIC APPLIANCES

100
75
50
25

car   T.V.   phone   central heating   fridge   washing machine

197
198
199

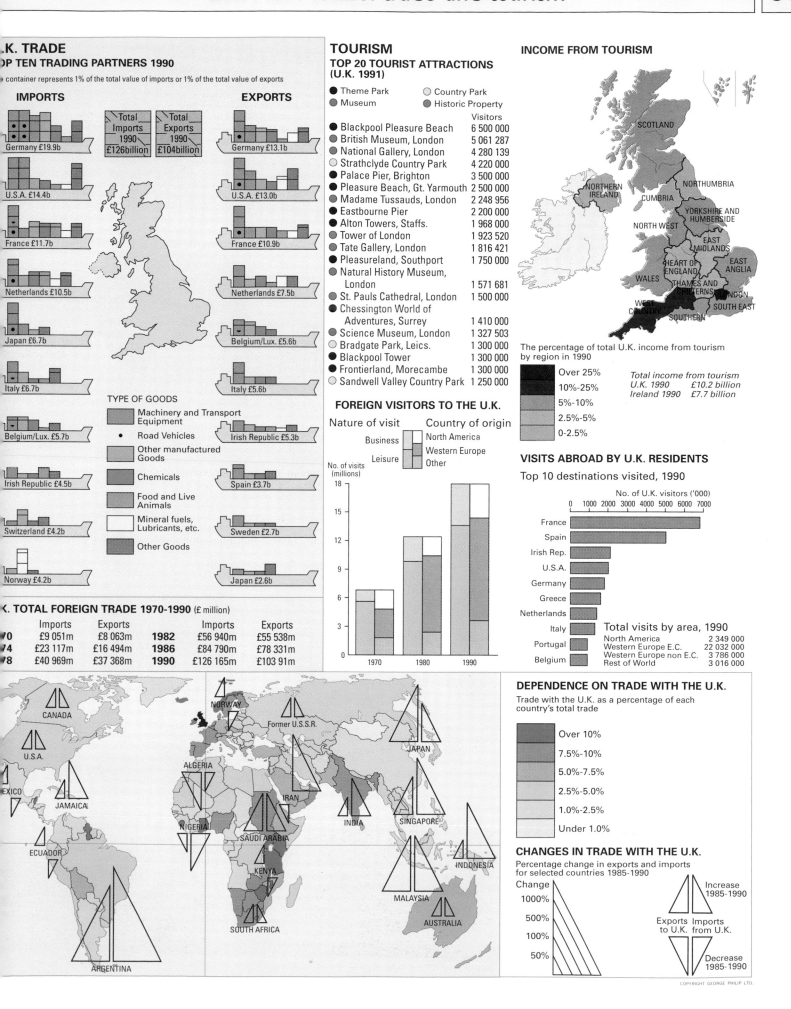

U.K. TRADE
TOP TEN TRADING PARTNERS 1990

• container represents 1% of the total value of imports or 1% of the total value of exports

IMPORTS

- Germany £19.9b
- U.S.A. £14.4b
- France £11.7b
- Netherlands £10.5b
- Japan £6.7b
- Italy £6.7b
- Belgium/Lux. £5.7b
- Irish Republic £4.5b
- Switzerland £4.2b
- Norway £4.2b

Total Imports 1990 £126billion
Total Exports 1990 £104billion

EXPORTS

- Germany £13.1b
- U.S.A. £13.0b
- France £10.9b
- Netherlands £7.5b
- Belgium/Lux. £5.6b
- Italy £5.6b
- Irish Republic £5.3b
- Spain £3.7b
- Sweden £2.7b
- Japan £2.6b

TYPE OF GOODS

- Machinery and Transport Equipment
- • Road Vehicles
- Other manufactured Goods
- Chemicals
- Food and Live Animals
- Mineral fuels, Lubricants, etc.
- Other Goods

U.K. TOTAL FOREIGN TRADE 1970-1990 (£ million)

	Imports	Exports		Imports	Exports
70	£9 051m	£8 063m	**1982**	£56 940m	£55 538m
74	£23 117m	£16 494m	**1986**	£84 790m	£78 331m
78	£40 969m	£37 368m	**1990**	£126 165m	£103 91m

TOURISM
TOP 20 TOURIST ATTRACTIONS (U.K. 1991)

- ● Theme Park
- ● Museum
- ○ Country Park
- ● Historic Property

	Visitors
● Blackpool Pleasure Beach	6 500 000
● British Museum, London	5 061 287
● National Gallery, London	4 280 139
○ Strathclyde Country Park	4 220 000
● Palace Pier, Brighton	3 500 000
● Pleasure Beach, Gt. Yarmouth	2 500 000
● Madame Tussauds, London	2 248 956
● Eastbourne Pier	2 200 000
● Alton Towers, Staffs.	1 968 000
● Tower of London	1 923 520
● Tate Gallery, London	1 816 421
● Pleasureland, Southport	1 750 000
● Natural History Museum, London	1 571 681
● St. Pauls Cathedral, London	1 500 000
● Chessington World of Adventures, Surrey	1 410 000
● Science Museum, London	1 327 503
○ Bradgate Park, Leics.	1 300 000
● Blackpool Tower	1 300 000
● Frontierland, Morecambe	1 300 000
○ Sandwell Valley Country Park	1 250 000

FOREIGN VISITORS TO THE U.K.

Nature of visit
- Business
- Leisure

Country of origin
- North America
- Western Europe
- Other

No. of visits (millions)

1970 1980 1990

INCOME FROM TOURISM

The percentage of total U.K. income from tourism by region in 1990

- Over 25%
- 10%-25%
- 5%-10%
- 2.5%-5%
- 0-2.5%

Total income from tourism
U.K. 1990   £10.2 billion
Ireland 1990   £7.7 billion

VISITS ABROAD BY U.K. RESIDENTS

Top 10 destinations visited, 1990

No. of U.K. visitors ('000)
0 1000 2000 3000 4000 5000 6000 7000

- France
- Spain
- Irish Rep.
- U.S.A.
- Germany
- Greece
- Netherlands
- Italy
- Portugal
- Belgium

Total visits by area, 1990
North America	2 349 000
Western Europe E.C.	22 032 000
Western Europe non E.C.	3 786 000
Rest of World	3 016 000

DEPENDENCE ON TRADE WITH THE U.K.

Trade with the U.K. as a percentage of each country's total trade

- Over 10%
- 7.5%-10%
- 5.0%-7.5%
- 2.5%-5.0%
- 1.0%-2.5%
- Under 1.0%

CHANGES IN TRADE WITH THE U.K.

Percentage change in exports and imports for selected countries 1985-1990

Change
- 1000%
- 500%
- 100%
- 50%

Increase 1985-1990

Exports to U.K.   Imports from U.K.

Decrease 1985-1990

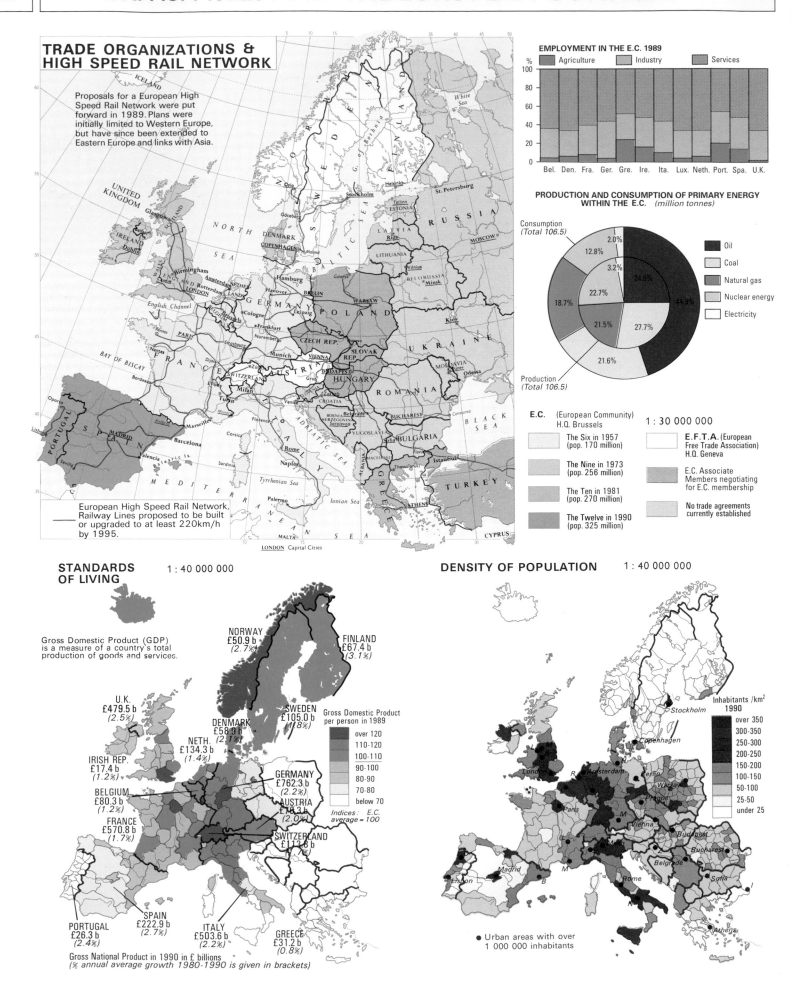

TRADE ORGANIZATIONS & HIGH SPEED RAIL NETWORK

Proposals for a European High Speed Rail Network were put forward in 1989. Plans were initially limited to Western Europe, but have since been extended to Eastern Europe and links with Asia.

European High Speed Rail Network, Railway Lines proposed to be built or upgraded to at least 220km/h by 1995.

LONDON Capital Cities

EMPLOYMENT IN THE E.C. 1989

Agriculture   Industry   Services

Bel. Den. Fra. Ger. Gre. Ire. Ita. Lux. Neth. Port. Spa. U.K.

PRODUCTION AND CONSUMPTION OF PRIMARY ENERGY WITHIN THE E.C. *(million tonnes)*

Consumption (Total 106.5)

2.0%
12.8%
3.2%
22.7%
24.9%
18.7%
21.5%
44.9%
21.6%
27.7%

Production (Total 106.5)

Oil
Coal
Natural gas
Nuclear energy
Electricity

E.C. (European Community) H.Q. Brussels   1 : 30 000 000

The Six in 1957 (pop. 170 million)

The Nine in 1973 (pop. 256 million)

The Ten in 1981 (pop. 270 million)

The Twelve in 1990 (pop. 325 million)

E.F.T.A. (European Free Trade Association) H.Q. Geneva

E.C. Associate Members negotiating for E.C. membership

No trade agreements currently established

STANDARDS OF LIVING   1 : 40 000 000

Gross Domestic Product (GDP) is a measure of a country's total production of goods and services.

NORWAY £50.9 b (2.7%)

FINLAND £67.4 b (3.1%)

U.K. £479.5 b (2.5%)

SWEDEN £105.0 b (1.8%)

DENMARK £58.9 b (2.1%)

NETH. £134.3 b (1.4%)

IRISH REP. £17.4 b (1.2%)

GERMANY £762.3 b (2.2%)

BELGIUM £80.3 b (1.2%)

AUSTRIA £83 b (2.0%)

FRANCE £570.8 b (1.7%)

SWITZERLAND £113.8 b

PORTUGAL £26.3 b (2.4%)

SPAIN £222.9 b (2.7%)

ITALY £503.6 b (2.2%)

GREECE £31.2 b (0.8%)

Gross Domestic Product per person in 1989

over 120
110-120
100-110
90-100
80-90
70-80
below 70

Indices : E.C. average = 100

Gross National Product in 1990 in £ billions (% annual average growth 1980-1990 is given in brackets)

DENSITY OF POPULATION   1 : 40 000 000

Inhabitants /km² 1990

over 350
300-350
250-300
200-250
150-200
100-150
50-100
25-50
under 25

● Urban areas with over 1 000 000 inhabitants

INDEX TO BRITISH ISLES MAPS

This index lists the major placenames which appear on the large-scale maps of the British Isles (pages *2–15* with the yellow band). Placenames for the rest of the world can be found in the World Index, with the turquoise band.

The first number beside each name in the index gives the map page on which that feature or place will be found. The letter and figure immediately after the page number give the grid square within which the feature is situated. The letter represents the latitude and the figure the longitude. In some cases the feature may fall within the specified square, while the name is outside. This is usually the case only with very large features. Rivers are indexed to their mouths or confluence.

The 'geographical co-ordinates' which follow the letter-figure references give the latitude and longitude of each place. The first co-ordinate indicates latitude – the distance north of the Equator. The second co-ordinate indicates longitude – the distance east or west of the Greenwich Meridian. Both latitude and longitude are measured in degrees and minutes (there are 60 minutes in a degree).

Thus the entry in the index for Runcorn reads:

Runcorn............. **7 F3** 53 20N 2 44W

This indicates that Runcorn appears on map page 7 in grid square F3 at latitude 53 degrees, 20 minutes north and at longitude 2 degrees, 44 minutes west. To find Runcorn by using the geographical co-ordinates, look at the edges of the map. The degrees of latitude are indicated by blue figures on the left-hand edge of the map and the degrees of longitude are marked on the bottom edge of the map. Runcorn will be found where lines extended from the two points on the map edge would cross on the map.

An open square □ indicates that the name refers to an administrative unit such as a county or region; rivers are indicated by an arrow →. Names composed of a proper name (Wight) and a description (Isle of) are positioned alphabetically by the proper name. All names beginning St. are alphabetized under Saint. A list of abbreviations used can be found in the World Index at the end of the atlas.

A

Abberton Res. **9 C10** 51 50N 0 52 E
Abbeyfeale **14 D4** 52 23N 9 20W
Aberaeron **10 C5** 52 15N 4 16W
Aberayron = Aberaeron **10 C5** 52 15N 4 16W
Abercarn **10 D7** 51 39N 3 9W
Aberchirder **3 G12** 57 34N 2 40W
Aberdare **10 D7** 51 43N 3 27W
Aberdeen **3 H13** 57 9N 2 6W
Aberdovey = Aberdyfi **10 B5** 52 33N 4 3W
Aberdyfi **10 B5** 52 33N 4 3W
Aberfeldy **5 A8** 56 37N 3 50W
Abergavenny **10 D7** 51 49N 3 1W
Abergele **10 A6** 53 17N 3 35W
Abersychan **10 D7** 51 44N 3 3W
Abertillery **10 D7** 51 44N 3 9W
Aberystwyth **10 C5** 52 25N 4 6W
Abingdon **8 C6** 51 40N 1 17W
Aboyne **3 H12** 57 4N 2 48W
Accrington **7 E4** 53 46N 2 22W
Achill Hd. **12 D1** 53 59N 10 15W
Achill I. **12 D1** 53 58N 10 5W
A'Chralaig **2 H7** 57 11N 5 10W
Adlington **7 E3** 53 36N 2 36W
Adwick le Street **7 E6** 53 35N 1 12W
Agnews Hill **13 B10** 54 51N 5 55W
Ailsa Craig **4 D5** 55 15N 5 7W
Ainsdale **7 E2** 53 37N 3 2W
Aird Brenish **2 F3** 58 8N 7 8W
Airdrie **5 C8** 55 53N 3 57W
Aire → **7 E7** 53 42N 0 55W
Alcester **8 B5** 52 13N 1 52W
Aldbrough **7 E8** 53 50N 0 7W
Aldeburgh **9 B12** 52 9N 1 35 E
Alderley Edge **7 F4** 53 18N 2 15W
Alderney **11 H9** 49 42N 2 12W
Aldershot **9 D7** 51 15N 0 43W
Aldridge **7 G5** 52 36N 1 55W
Alexandria **4 C6** 55 59N 4 40W
Alford, *Gramp.* **3 H12** 57 13N 2 42W
Alford, *Lincs.* **7 F9** 53 16N 0 10 E
Alfreton **7 F6** 53 6N 1 22W
Allen, Bog of **15 B9** 53 15N 7 0W
Allen, L. **12 C5** 54 12N 8 5W
Alloa **5 B8** 56 7N 3 49W
Alness **3 G9** 57 41N 4 15W
Alnmouth **6 B5** 55 24N 1 37W
Alnwick **6 B5** 55 25N 1 42W
Alsager **7 F4** 53 7N 2 20W
Alsh, L. **2 H6** 57 15N 5 39W
Alston **6 C4** 54 48N 2 26W
Alton **9 D7** 51 8N 0 59W
Altrincham **7 F4** 53 25N 2 21W
Alva **5 B8** 56 9N 3 49W
Alyth **5 A9** 56 38N 3 15W
Amble **6 B5** 55 20N 1 36W
Ambleside **6 D3** 54 26N 2 58W
Amersham **9 C7** 51 40N 0 38W
Amesbury **8 D5** 51 10N 1 46W
Amlwch **10 A5** 53 24N 4 21W
Ammanford **10 D5** 51 48N 4 0W
Ampthill **9 B8** 52 3N 0 30W
An Teallach **2 G7** 57 49N 5 18W
An Uaimh **13 D8** 53 39N 6 40W
Andover **8 D6** 51 13N 1 29W
Anglesey **10 A5** 53 17N 4 20W
Angus, Braes of **3 J11** 56 51N 3 10W
Annagh Hd. **12 C1** 54 15N 10 5W
Annalee → **13 C7** 54 3N 7 15W
Annan **5 E9** 54 57N 3 17W
Annan → **5 E9** 54 58N 3 18W
Annandale **5 D9** 55 10N 3 25W
Anstey **7 G6** 52 41N 1 14W
Anstruther **5 B10** 56 14N 2 40W
Antrim **13 B9** 54 43N 6 13W
Antrim □ **13 B9** 54 55N 6 20W
Antrim, Mts. of **13 B9** 54 57N 6 8W
Appin **4 A5** 56 37N 5 20W
Appleby-in-Westmorland **6 C4** 54 35N 2 29W
Appledore **11 E5** 51 3N 4 12W
Aran Fawddwy **10 B6** 52 48N 3 40W
Aran I. **12 B4** 55 0N 8 30W
Aran Is. **14 B3** 53 5N 9 42W
Arbroath **5 A10** 56 34N 2 35W
Arbury Hill **8 B6** 52 13N 1 12W
Ardee **13 D8** 53 51N 6 32W
Arderin **15 B7** 53 3N 7 40W
Ardgour **4 A5** 56 45N 5 25W
Ardivachar Pt. **2 H3** 57 23N 7 25W
Ardmore Hd. **15 E7** 51 58N 7 43W
Ardmore Pt. **4 C3** 55 40N 6 2W
Ardnamurchan **4 A4** 56 43N 6 0W
Ardnamurchan, Pt. of **4 A3** 56 44N 6 14W
Ardnave Pt. **4 C3** 55 54N 6 20W
Ardrossan **4 C6** 55 39N 4 50W
Ards Pen. **13 B10** 54 30N 5 30W
Arenig Fawr **10 B6** 52 56N 3 45W
Argyll **4 B5** 56 14N 5 10W
Arisaig **2 J6** 56 55N 5 50W
Arisaig, Sd. of **2 J6** 56 50N 5 50W
Arkaig, L. **2 J7** 56 58N 5 10W
Arklow **15 C10** 52 48N 6 10W
Arklow Hd. **15 C10** 52 46N 6 10W
Armadale **5 C8** 55 54N 3 42W
Armagh **13 C8** 54 22N 6 40W
Armagh □ **13 C8** 54 18N 6 37W
Armthorpe **7 E6** 53 32N 1 3W
Arnold **7 F6** 53 2N 1 8W
Arran **4 C5** 55 34N 5 12W
Arrow, L. **12 C5** 54 3N 8 20W
Arun → **9 E7** 50 48N 0 33W
Arundel **9 E7** 50 52N 0 32W
Ascot **9 D7** 51 24N 0 41W
Ash **9 D7** 51 14N 0 43W
Ashbourne **7 F5** 53 2N 1 44W
Ashburton **11 F6** 50 31N 3 45W
Ashby de la Zouch **7 G6** 52 45N 1 29W
Ashdown Forest **9 D9** 51 4N 0 2 E
Ashford **9 D10** 51 8N 0 53 E
Ashington **6 B5** 55 12N 1 35W
Ashton-in-Makerfield **7 F3** 53 29N 2 39W
Ashton under Lyne **7 F4** 53 30N 2 8W
Aspatria **6 C2** 54 45N 3 20W
Assynt **2 F7** 58 20N 5 10W
Athboy **13 D8** 53 37N 6 55W
Athenry **14 B5** 53 18N 8 45W
Atherstone **7 G5** 52 35N 1 32W
Atherton **7 E3** 53 32N 2 30W
Athlone **14 B7** 53 26N 7 57W
Atholl, Forest of **3 J10** 56 51N 3 50W
Athy **15 C9** 53 0N 7 0W
Attleborough **9 A11** 52 32N 1 1 E
Auchterarder **5 B8** 56 18N 3 43W
Auchtermuchty **5 B9** 56 18N 3 15W
Aughnacloy **13 C8** 54 25N 6 58W
Aviemore **3 H10** 57 11N 3 50W
Avoca **15 C10** 52 52N 6 13W
Avoca → **15 C10** 52 48N 6 9W
Avon □ **8 D3** 51 30N 2 40W
Avon →, *Avon* **8 D3** 51 30N 2 43W
Avon →, *Hants.* **8 E5** 50 44N 1 45W
Avon →, *Warks.* **8 C4** 51 57N 2 9W
Avonmouth **8 C3** 51 30N 2 42W
Awe, L. **4 B5** 56 15N 5 15W
Axe Edge **7 F5** 53 14N 1 59W
Axminster **11 F7** 50 47N 3 1W
Aylesbury **9 C7** 51 48N 0 49W
Aylsham **9 A11** 52 48N 1 16 E
Ayr **4 D6** 55 28N 4 37W
Ayr → **4 D6** 55 29N 4 40W
Ayr, Heads of **4 D6** 55 25N 4 43W
Ayr, Pt. of **10 A7** 53 21N 3 19W
Ayre, Pt. of **3 E12** 58 55N 2 43W

B

Bacton **9 A11** 52 50N 1 29 E
Bacup **7 E4** 53 42N 2 12W
Badenoch **3 J9** 56 59N 4 15W
Bagenalstown = Muine Bheag **15 C9** 52 42N 6 57W
Baggy Pt. **11 E5** 51 11N 4 12W
Bagh nam Faoileann **2 H3** 57 22N 7 13W
Baginbun Hd. **15 D9** 52 10N 6 50W
Bagshot **9 D7** 51 22N 0 41W
Baildon **7 E5** 53 52N 1 46W
Baile Atha Cliath = Dublin **15 B10** 53 20N 6 18W
Bakewell **7 F5** 53 13N 1 40W
Bala **10 B6** 52 54N 3 36W
Bala, L. **10 B6** 52 53N 3 38W
Balbriggan **13 D9** 53 35N 6 10W
Baldock **9 C8** 51 59N 0 11W
Ballachulish **4 A5** 56 40N 5 10W
Ballagan Pt. **13 D9** 54 0N 6 6W
Ballaghaderreen **12 D4** 53 55N 8 35W
Ballater **3 H11** 57 2N 3 2W
Ballina, *Mayo* **12 C3** 54 7N 9 10W
Ballina, *Tipp.* **14 C6** 52 49N 8 27W
Ballinasloe **14 B6** 53 20N 8 12W
Ballinderry → **13 B8** 54 40N 6 32W
Ballinrobe **12 D3** 53 36N 9 13W
Ballinskelligs B. **14 E2** 51 46N 10 11W
Ballybunion **14 C3** 52 30N 9 40W
Ballycastle **13 A9** 55 12N 6 15W
Ballyclare **13 B10** 54 46N 6 0W
Ballyconneely B. **14 B2** 53 23N 10 8W
Ballydavid Hd. **14 D2** 52 15N 10 20W
Ballydonegan B. **14 E2** 51 38N 10 6W
Ballyhaunis **12 D4** 53 47N 8 47W
Ballyhoura Mts. **14 D5** 52 18N 8 33W
Ballymena **13 B9** 54 53N 6 18W
Ballymoney **13 A8** 55 5N 6 30W
Ballymote **12 C4** 54 5N 8 31W
Ballynahinch **13 C10** 54 24N 5 55W
Ballyquintin Pt. **13 C11** 54 20N 5 30W
Ballyshannon **12 B5** 54 30N 8 10W
Balmoral Forest **3 J11** 57 0N 3 15W
Baltimore **14 F4** 51 29N 9 22W
Bamber Bridge **7 E3** 53 44N 2 39W
Bamburgh **6 A5** 55 36N 1 42W
Banbridge **13 C9** 54 21N 6 17W
Banbury **8 B6** 52 4N 1 21W
Banchory **3 H13** 57 3N 2 30W
Bandon **14 E5** 51 44N 8 45W
Bandon → **14 E5** 51 40N 8 41W
Banff **3 G12** 57 40N 2 32W
Bangor, *Down* **13 B10** 54 40N 5 40W
Bangor, *Gwynedd* **10 A5** 53 13N 4 9W
Bann →, *Down* **13 C8** 54 30N 6 31W
Bann →, *L'derry.* **13 A8** 55 10N 6 40W
Bannockburn **5 B8** 56 5N 3 55W
Bannow B. **15 D9** 52 13N 6 48W
Banstead **9 D8** 51 19N 0 10W
Bantry **14 E4** 51 40N 9 28W
Bantry B. **14 E3** 51 35N 9 50W
Bard Hd. **2 B15** 60 6N 1 5W
Bardsey Sd. **10 B4** 52 47N 4 46W
Bargoed **10 D7** 51 42N 3 22W
Barking and Dagenham **9 C9** 51 31N 0 10 E
Barmouth **10 B5** 52 44N 4 3W
Barnard Castle **6 C5** 54 33N 1 55W
Barnet **9 C8** 51 37N 0 15W
Barnoldswick **7 E4** 53 55N 2 11W
Barns Ness **5 C11** 55 59N 2 27W
Barnsley **7 E6** 53 33N 1 29W
Barnstaple **11 E5** 51 5N 4 3W
Barnstaple B. **11 E5** 51 5N 4 20W
Barra **2 J3** 57 0N 7 30W
Barra Hd. **2 J2** 56 47N 7 40W
Barrhead **4 C7** 55 48N 4 23W
Barrow → **15 D9** 52 14N 6 58W
Barrow-in-Furness **6 D2** 54 8N 3 15W
Barrow upon Humber **7 E8** 53 41N 0 22W
Barrowford **7 E4** 53 51N 2 14W
Barry **8 E7** 51 23N 3 19W
Barry I. **8 E7** 51 23N 3 17W
Barry's Pt. **14 E5** 51 36N 8 40W
Barton upon Humber **7 E8** 53 41N 0 27W
Basildon **9 C9** 51 34N 0 29 E
Basingstoke **8 D6** 51 15N 1 5W
Bass Rock **5 B10** 56 5N 2 40W
Bath **8 D4** 51 22N 2 22W
Bathgate **5 C8** 55 54N 3 38W
Batley **7 E5** 53 43N 1 38W
Battle **9 E9** 50 55N 0 30 E
Beachy Hd. **9 E9** 50 44N 0 16 E
Beaconsfield **9 C7** 51 36N 0 39W
Beaminster **8 E3** 50 48N 2 44W
Bearsden **4 C7** 55 55N 4 21W
Beauly **3 H9** 57 29N 4 27W
Beauly → **3 H9** 57 26N 4 28W
Beauly Firth **3 H9** 57 30N 4 20W
Beaumaris **10 A5** 53 16N 4 7W
Bebington **7 F2** 53 23N 3 1W
Beccles **9 B12** 52 27N 1 33 E
Bedford **9 B8** 52 8N 0 29W
Bedford Level **9 A8** 52 35N 0 15W
Bedfordshire □ **9 B8** 52 4N 0 28W
Bedlington **6 B5** 55 8N 1 35W
Bedwas **11 D7** 51 36N 3 10W
Bedworth **8 B6** 52 28N 1 29W
Bee, L. **2 H3** 57 22N 7 21W
Beeston **7 G6** 52 55N 1 11W
Beighton **7 F6** 53 21N 1 21W
Beinn a' Ghlo **3 J10** 56 51N 3 42W
Beinn Mhor **2 G4** 57 59N 6 39W
Beith **4 C6** 55 45N 4 38W
Belfast **13 B10** 54 35N 5 56W
Belfast L. **13 B10** 54 40N 5 50W
Belmullet **12 C2** 54 13N 9 58W
Belper **7 F6** 53 2N 1 29W
Belturbet **12 C7** 54 6N 7 28W
Bembridge **8 E6** 50 41N 1 4W
Ben Alder **3 J9** 56 50N 4 30W
Ben Avon **3 H11** 57 6N 3 28W
Ben Bheigeir **4 C3** 55 43N 6 6W
Ben Chonzie **5 B8** 56 27N 4 0W
Ben Cruachan **4 B5** 56 26N 5 8W
Ben Dearg, *Highl.* **3 G8** 57 47N 4 58W
Ben Dearg, *Tayside* **3 J10** 56 52N 3 52W
Ben Dhorain **3 F10** 58 7N 3 50W
Ben Dorain **4 A6** 56 32N 4 42W
Ben Eighie **2 G7** 57 37N 5 30W
Ben Hee **3 F8** 58 16N 4 43W
Ben Hiant **4 A3** 56 42N 6 1W

Ben Hope 3 F8 58 24N 4 36W
Ben Ime 4 B6 56 14N 4 49W
Ben Klibreck 3 F9 58 14N 4 25W
Ben Lawers 4 A7 56 33N 4 13W
Ben Lomond 4 B6 56 12N 4 39W
Ben Loyal 3 F9 58 25N 4 25W
Ben Lui 4 B6 56 24N 4 50W
Ben Macdhui . . . 3 H10 57 4N 3 40W
Ben Mholach . . . 2 F4 58 14N 6 33W
Ben Mhor 2 H3 57 16N 7 21W
Ben More, *Central* 4 B6 56 23N 4 31W
Ben More, *Strath.* 4 B3 56 26N 6 2W
Ben More Assynt . 3 F8 58 7N 4 51W
Ben Nevis 3 J7 56 48N 5 2W
Ben Rinnes 3 H11 57 25N 3 15W
Ben Stack 3 F8 58 20N 4 58W
Ben Tharsuinn . . . 3 G9 57 47N 4 20W
Ben Venue 4 B7 56 13N 4 28W
Ben Vorlich 4 B7 56 22N 4 15W
Ben Wyvis 3 G8 57 40N 4 35W
Benbane Hd. 13 A9 55 15N 6 30W
Benbaun 12 D2 53 30N 9 50W
Benbecula 2 H3 57 26N 7 21W
Benderloch 4 A5 56 30N 5 22W
Beneraird 4 D6 55 4N 4 57W
Bennane Hd. 4 D6 55 8N 4 59W
Bentley 7 E6 53 33N 1 9W
Benwee Hd. 12 C2 54 20N 9 50W
Berkeley 8 C4 51 41N 2 28W
Berkhamsted . . . 9 C7 51 45N 0 33W
Berkshire □ 8 D6 51 30N 1 20W
Berkshire Downs . 8 C5 51 30N 1 30W
Berry Hd. 11 G7 50 24N 3 29W
Berst Ness 3 D12 59 16N 3 0W
Bertraghboy B. . . 14 B3 53 22N 9 54W
Berwick-upon-
Tweed 6 A5 55 47N 2 0W
Berwyn Mts. 10 B7 52 54N 3 26W
Betws-y-Coed . . . 10 A6 53 4N 3 49W
Beverley 7 E8 53 52N 0 26W
Bewdley 8 B4 52 23N 2 19W
Bexhill . . . . 9 E9 50 51N 0 29 E
Bexley . . . . 9 D9 51 26N 0 10 E
Bicester 8 C6 51 53N 1 9W
Biddulph 7 F4 53 8N 2 11W
Bidean nam Bian . 4 A5 56 39N 5 6W
Bideford 11 E5 51 1N 4 13W
Bideford B. =
Barnstaple B. . . 11 E5 51 5N 4 20W
Bigbury B. 11 G6 50 18N 3 58W
Biggar 5 C8 55 38N 3 31W
Biggleswade 9 B8 52 6N 0 16W
Billericay . . . . . . 9 C9 51 38N 0 25 E
Billinge Hill 7 E3 53 32N 2 42W
Billingham 6 C6 54 36N 1 18W
Billingshurst 9 D8 51 2N 0 28W
Bilston 7 G4 52 34N 2 5W
Bingley 7 E5 53 51N 1 50W
Birdlip 8 C4 51 50N 2 7W
Birkenhead 7 F2 53 24N 3 1W
Birmingham 8 B5 52 30N 1 55W
Birr 14 B7 53 7N 7 55W
Birtley 6 C5 54 53N 1 34W
Bishop Auckland . 6 C5 54 40N 1 40W
Bishop's Stortford 9 C9 51 52N 0 11 E
Bishop's Waltham 8 E6 50 57N 1 13W
Bla Bheinn 2 H5 57 14N 6 7W
Black Combe 6 D2 54 16N 3 20W
Black Hd., *Ireland* 14 B4 53 9N 9 18W
Black Hd., *Ant.* . . 13 B10 54 56N 5 42W
Black Hd., *Corn.* . 11 H3 50 0N 5 6W
Black Isle 3 G9 57 35N 4 15W
Black Mts. 10 D7 51 52N 3 5W
Black Mt. =
Mynydd Du 10 D6 51 45N 3 45W
Blackburn 7 E4 53 44N 2 30W
Blackdown Hill . . . 8 D7 51 4N 41 7W
Blackdown Hills . . 8 E2 50 57N 3 15W
Blackhill 7 E5 53 32N 1 53W
Blackhope Scar . . 5 C9 55 44N 3 5W
Blackmoor Vale . . 8 E4 50 54N 2 28W
Blackpool 7 E2 53 48N 3 3W
Blacksod B. 12 C2 54 6N 10 0W
Blacksod Pt. 12 C1 54 7N 10 5W
Blackstairs Mt. . . 15 C9 52 33N 6 50W
Blackwater →,
Munst. 14 E7 51 55N 7 50W
Blackwater →,
Essex . . . . . . 9 C10 51 44N 0 53 E
Blackwater →,
Tyrone 13 B8 54 31N 6 35W
Blackwood 10 D7 51 40N 3 13W
Blaenau Ffestiniog 10 B6 52 59N 3 57W
Blaenavon 10 D7 51 46N 3 5W
Blaina 10 D7 51 46N 3 10W
Blair Atholl 3 J10 56 46N 3 50W
Blairgowrie 5 A9 56 36N 3 20W
Blakeney . . . . 9 A11 52 57N 1 0 E
Blandford Forum . . 8 E4 50 52N 2 10W
Blarney 14 E5 51 57N 8 35W
Blaydon 6 C5 54 56N 1 47W
Bletchley 9 C7 51 59N 0 44W
Bloody Foreland . 12 A5 55 10N 8 18W
Bluemull Sd. 2 A16 60 45N 1 0W
Blyth 6 B5 55 8N 1 32W
Blyth Bridge 7 G4 52 58N 2 4W
Boderg, L. 12 D6 53 55N 8 0W
Bodmin 11 G4 50 28N 4 44W
Bodmin Moor 11 F4 50 33N 4 36W
Boggeragh Mts. . . 14 D5 52 2N 8 55W
Bognor Regis . . . 9 E7 50 47N 0 40W
Bogrie Hill 5 D8 55 8N 3 54W
Boisdale, L. 2 H3 57 9N 7 19W
Boldon 6 C6 54 57N 1 26W
Bolsover 7 F6 53 14N 1 18W
Bolt Hd. 11 G6 50 13N 3 48W
Bolt Tail 11 G6 50 13N 3 55W
Bolton 7 E4 53 35N 2 26W
Bolus Hd. 14 E2 51 48N 10 20W
Bo'ness 5 B8 56 1N 3 38W
Bonnyrigg 5 C9 55 52N 3 8W
Bootle, *Cumb.* . . . 6 D2 54 17N 3 24W
Bootle, *Mersey.* . . 7 F2 53 28N 3 1W
Borders □ 5 C10 55 35N 2 50W
Borehamwood . . . 9 C8 51 40N 0 15W
Boroughbridge . . . 6 D6 54 6N 1 23W
Borth 10 C5 52 29N 4 3W
Boscastle 11 F4 50 42N 4 42W
Boston 7 G8 52 59N 0 2W
Bourne 7 G8 52 46N 0 22W
Bournemouth 8 E5 50 43N 1 53W
Bourton-on-the-
Water 8 C5 51 53N 1 45W
Bowland, Forest of 7 E3 54 0N 2 30W
Bowmore 4 C3 55 45N 6 18W
Bowness-on-
Windermere . . . 6 D3 54 22N 2 56W
Box Hill 9 D8 51 16N 0 16W
Boyle 12 D5 53 58N 8 19W
Boyne → 13 D9 53 43N 6 15W
Bracadale, L. . . . 2 H4 57 20N 6 30W
Brackley 8 B6 52 3N 1 9W
Bracknell 9 D7 51 24N 0 45W
Bradda Hd. 13 C12 54 6N 4 46W
Bradford 7 E5 53 47N 1 45W
Bradford on Avon . 8 D4 51 20N 2 15W
Bradwell-on-Sea . 9 C10 51 44N 0 55 E
Braemar 3 J11 57 0N 3 25W
Braeriach 3 H10 57 4N 3 44W
Braich-y-pwll 10 B4 52 47N 4 46W
Braintree . . . . . . 9 C10 51 53N 0 34 E
Brampton 6 C3 54 56N 2 43W
Branderburgh . . . 3 G11 57 43N 3 17W
Brandon, *Kilk.* . . . 15 C9 52 31N 6 58W
Brandon, *Durham* 6 C5 54 46N 1 37W
Brandon, *Suffolk* . 9 B10 52 27N 0 37 E
Brandon B. 14 D2 52 17N 10 8W
Brandon Mt. 14 D2 52 15N 10 15W
Brandon Pt. 14 D2 52 18N 10 10W
Braunton 11 E5 51 6N 4 9W
Bray 15 B10 53 12N 6 6W
Bray Hd., *Kerry* . . 14 E2 51 52N 10 26W
Bray Hd., *Wick.* . . 15 B10 53 12N 6 2W
Breadalbane 4 A7 56 30N 4 15W
Brechin 5 A10 56 44N 2 40W
Breckland . . . . . . 9 B10 52 30N 0 40 E
Brecon 10 D7 51 57N 3 23W
Brecon Beacons . 10 D7 51 53N 3 27W
Bredon Hill 8 B4 52 3N 2 2W
Brendon Hills 8 D2 51 6N 3 25W
Brenig, L. 10 A6 53 6N 3 30W
Brent 9 C8 51 33N 0 18W
Brentwood . . . . . . 9 C9 51 37N 0 19 E
Bressay Sd. 2 B15 60 8N 1 10W
Brianne, L. 10 C6 52 8N 3 45W
Bridge of Don . . . 3 H13 57 10N 2 8W
Bridgend 11 D6 51 30N 3 35W
Bridgnorth 7 G4 52 33N 2 25W
Bridgwater 8 D3 51 7N 3 0W
Bridlington 6 D8 54 6N 0 11W
Bridport 11 E3 50 43N 2 45W
Brierfield 7 E4 53 49N 2 15W
Brierley Hill 8 B4 52 29N 2 7W
Brigg 7 E8 53 33N 0 30W
Brighouse 7 E5 53 42N 1 47W
Brightlingsea . . . . 9 C11 51 49N 1 1 E
Brighton 9 E8 50 50N 0 9W
Bristol 8 D3 51 26N 2 35W
Bristol Channel . . 11 E4 51 18N 4 30W
Brixham 11 G6 50 24N 3 31W
Brize Norton 8 C5 51 46N 1 35W
Broad Bay 2 F5 58 14N 6 16W
Broad Haven 12 C2 54 20N 9 55W
Broad Law 5 C9 55 31N 3 22W
Broad Sd. 11 H1 49 56N 6 19W
Broadstairs . . . . . 9 D11 51 21N 1 28 E
Broadway 8 B5 52 2N 1 51W
Broadwindsor 8 E3 50 49N 2 49W
Brockenhurst 8 E5 50 49N 1 34W
Brodick 4 C5 55 34N 5 9W
Bromfield 8 B3 52 25N 2 45W
Bromley . . . . 9 D9 51 20N 0 5 E
Bromsgrove 8 B4 52 20N 2 3W
Bromyard 8 B4 52 12N 2 30W
Broom, L. 2 G7 57 55N 5 15W
Brora 3 F10 58 3N 3 50W
Brosna → 14 B7 53 8N 8 0W
Brotton 6 C7 54 34N 0 55W
Brough 6 C4 54 32N 2 19W
Brough Hd. 3 D11 59 8N 3 20W
Broughty Ferry . . . 5 B10 56 29N 2 50W
Brown Clee Hill . . 8 B3 52 28N 2 36W
Brown Willy 11 F4 50 35N 4 34W
Brownhills 7 G5 52 38N 1 57W
Broxburn 5 C9 55 56N 3 23W
Bruernish Pt. 2 J3 57 0N 7 22W
Bruton 8 D4 51 6N 2 28W
Brynmawr 10 D7 51 48N 3 11W
Buchan 3 G13 57 32N 2 8W
Buchan Ness 3 H14 57 29N 1 48W
Buckfastleigh 11 G6 50 28N 3 47W
Buckhaven 5 B9 56 10N 3 2W
Buckie 3 G12 57 40N 2 58W
Buckingham 9 C7 52 0N 0 59W
Buckinghamshire □ 9 C7 51 50N 0 55W
Buckley 10 A7 53 10N 3 5W
Buddon Ness 5 B10 56 29N 2 42W
Bude 11 F4 50 49N 4 33W
Budle B. 6 A5 55 37N 1 45W
Budleigh Salterton 11 F7 50 37N 3 19W
Buie, L. 4 B4 56 20N 5 55W
Builth Wells 10 C7 52 10N 3 26W
Bulkington 8 B6 52 29N 1 25W
Bunclody 15 C9 52 40N 6 40W
Buncrana 12 A7 55 8N 7 28W
Bundoran 12 C5 54 24N 8 17W
Bungay . . . . 9 B11 52 27N 1 26 E
Burford 8 C5 51 48N 1 38W
Burgess Hill 9 E8 50 57N 0 7W
Burghead B. 3 G10 57 40N 3 33W
Burnham 9 C7 51 32N 0 40W
Burnham Market . 9 A10 52 57N 0 43 E
Burnham-on-
Crouch . . . . 9 C10 51 37N 0 50 E
Burnham-on-Sea . 8 D3 51 14N 3 0W
Burnley 7 E4 53 47N 2 15W
Burntisland 5 B9 56 4N 3 14W
Burntwood 7 G5 52 41N 1 55W
Burrow Hd. 4 E7 54 40N 4 23W
Burry Port 10 D5 51 41N 4 17W
Burscough Bridge 7 E3 53 36N 2 52W
Burton Latimer . . . 9 B7 52 23N 0 41W
Burton upon Trent 7 G5 52 48N 1 39W
Bury 7 E4 53 36N 2 19W
Bury St. Edmunds 9 B10 52 15N 0 42 E
Bushey 9 C8 51 38N 0 20W
Bushmills 13 A8 55 14N 6 32W
Bute 4 C5 55 48N 5 2W
Bute, Kyles of . . . 4 C5 55 55N 5 10W
Bute, Sd. of 4 C5 55 43N 5 8W
Buttevant 14 D5 52 14N 8 40W
Buxton 7 F5 53 16N 1 54W
Byfleet 9 D7 51 20N 0 32W

C

Cader Idris 10 B6 52 43N 3 56W
Caernarfon 10 A5 53 8N 4 17W
Caernarfon B. . . . 10 A4 53 4N 4 40W
Caernarvon =
Caernarfon 10 A5 53 8N 4 17W
Caerphilly 11 D7 51 34N 3 13W
Caha Mts. 14 E3 51 45N 9 40W
Caher 14 D7 52 23N 7 56W
Cahirciveen 14 E2 51 57N 10 13W
Cahore Pt. 15 C10 52 34N 6 11W
Cairn Gorm 3 H10 57 7N 3 40W
Cairn Table 5 C7 55 30N 4 0W
Cairngorm Mts. . . 3 H10 57 6N 3 42W
Cairnsmore of Fleet 4 E7 54 59N 4 20W
Caister-on-Sea . . 9 A12 52 38N 1 43 E
Caithness 3 F10 58 25N 3 35W
Caithness, Ord of 3 F10 58 9N 3 37W
Calder → 7 E6 53 44N 1 21W
Caledonian Canal 2 J7 56 50N 5 6W
Caliach Pt. 4 A3 56 37N 6 20W
Callan 15 C8 52 33N 7 25W
Callander 4 B7 56 15N 4 14W
Calne 8 D5 51 26N 2 0W
Cam → . . . . 9 B9 52 21N 0 16 E
Camberley 9 D7 51 20N 0 44W
Camborne 11 G3 50 13N 5 18W
Cambrian Mts. . . . 10 C6 52 25N 3 52W
Cambridge . . . . . . 9 B9 52 13N 0 8 E
Cambridgeshire □ 9 B9 52 12N 0 7 E
Camden 9 C8 51 33N 0 10W
Camelford 11 F4 50 37N 4 41W
Campbeltown 4 D4 55 25N 5 36W
Canbane East . . . 13 D7 53 45N 7 6W
Canna, Sd. of . . . 2 H5 57 1N 6 30W
Cannock 7 G4 52 42N 2 2W
Cannock Chase . . 7 G5 52 43N 2 0W
Canterbury . . . . . 9 D11 51 17N 1 5 E
Canvey . . . . 9 C10 51 32N 0 35 E
Caolisport, L. 4 C4 55 54N 5 40W
Cardiff 8 E7 51 28N 3 11W
Cardigan 10 C4 52 6N 4 41W
Cardigan B. 10 B4 52 30N 4 30W
Carisbrooke 8 E6 50 42N 1 19W
Carlingford L. . . . 13 C9 54 2N 6 5W
Carlisle 6 C3 54 54N 2 55W
Carlow 15 C9 52 50N 6 58W
Carlow □ 15 C9 52 43N 6 50W
Carlton 7 G6 52 58N 1 6W
Carluke 5 C8 55 44N 3 50W
Carmarthen 10 D5 51 52N 4 20W
Carmarthen B. . . . 10 D4 51 40N 4 30W
Carmel Hd. 10 A4 53 24N 4 34W
Carn Ban 3 H9 57 6N 4 15W
Carn Eige 2 H7 57 17N 5 9W
Carn Glas-choire . 3 H10 57 20N 3 50W
Carn Mor 3 H11 57 14N 3 13W
Carn na
Saobhaidhe . . . 3 H9 57 12N 4 20W
Carndonagh 13 A7 55 15N 7 16W
Carnedd Llewelyn 10 A6 53 9N 3 58W
Carnforth 6 D3 54 8N 2 47W
Carnoustie 5 A10 56 30N 2 41W
Carnsore Pt. 15 D10 52 10N 6 20W
Carra, L. 12 D3 53 41N 9 12W
Carrauntoohill . . . 14 E3 52 0N 9 49W
Carrick 4 D6 55 12N 4 38W
Carrick-on-
Shannon 12 D5 53 57N 8 7W
Carrick-on-Suir . . 15 D8 52 22N 7 30W
Carrickfergus 13 B10 54 43N 5 50W
Carrickmacross . . 13 D8 53 58N 6 43W
Carrigan Hd. 12 B4 54 38N 8 40W
Carron → 2 H7 57 30N 5 30W
Carron, L. 2 H6 57 22N 5 35W
Carstairs 5 C8 55 42N 3 41W
Cashel 14 C7 52 31N 7 53W
Cashla B. 14 B3 53 12N 9 37W
Castle Cary 8 D3 51 5N 2 32W
Castle Donington . 7 G6 52 50N 1 20W
Castle Douglas . . 5 E8 54 57N 3 57W
Castlebar 12 D3 53 52N 9 17W
Castleblaney 13 C8 54 7N 6 44W
Castlederg 12 B6 54 43N 7 35W
Castleford 7 E6 53 43N 1 21W
Castleisland 14 D4 52 14N 9 28W
Castlemaine
Harbour 14 D3 52 8N 9 50W
Castlepollard 12 D7 53 40N 7 20W
Castlerea 12 D5 53 47N 8 30W
Castletown 13 C12 54 4N 4 40W
Castletown
Bearhaven 14 E3 51 40N 9 54W
Caterham 9 D8 51 16N 0 4W
Cavan 12 D7 54 0N 7 22W
Cavan □ 13 D7 53 58N 7 10W
Ceanannus Mor . . 13 D8 53 42N 6 53W
Cefn-mawr 10 B7 52 58N 3 3W
Cefnfford 10 D6 51 42N 3 39W
Celbridge 15 B9 53 20N 6 33W
Cellar Hd. 2 F5 58 25N 6 10W
Celyn, L. 10 B6 52 56N 3 42W
Cemaes Hd. 10 C4 52 7N 4 44W
Central □ 4 B7 56 10N 4 30W
Chadwell St. Mary 9 D9 51 28N 0 22 E
Chandler's Ford . . 8 E6 50 59N 1 23W
Channel Is. 11 J9 49 30N 2 40W
Chapel en le Frith 7 F5 53 19N 1 54W
Chard 8 E3 50 52N 2 59W
Charlbury 8 C6 51 52N 1 29W
Charlestown of
Aberlour 3 H11 57 27N 3 13W
Charleville = Rath
Luirc 14 D5 52 21N 8 40W
Charlton Kings . . . 8 C4 51 52N 2 3W
Charnwood Forest 7 G6 52 43N 1 18W
Chatham . . . . 9 D10 51 22N 0 32 E
Chatteris . . . . 9 B9 52 27N 0 3 E
Cheadle, *Gt. Man.* 7 F4 53 23N 2 14W
Cheadle, *Staffs.* . . 7 G5 52 59N 1 59W
Cheddar 8 D3 51 16N 2 47W
Chelmsford . . . . . 9 C9 51 44N 0 29 E
Cheltenham 8 C4 51 55N 2 5W
Chepstow 10 D8 51 38N 2 40W
Chertsey 9 D7 51 23N 0 30W
Cherwell → 8 C6 51 46N 1 18W
Chesham 9 C7 51 42N 0 36W
Cheshire □ 7 F3 53 14N 2 30W
Cheshunt 9 C8 51 42N 0 1W
Chesil Beach 11 F8 50 37N 2 33W
Chester 7 F3 53 12N 2 53W
Chester-le-Street . 6 C5 54 53N 1 34W
Chesterfield 7 F6 53 14N 1 26W
Cheviot Hills 6 B3 55 20N 2 30W
Chichester 9 E7 50 50N 0 47W
Chicken Hd. 2 F5 58 10N 6 15W
Chigwell . . . . 9 C9 51 37N 0 4 E
Chiltern Hills 9 C7 51 44N 0 42W
Chippenham 8 D4 51 27N 2 7W
Chipping Norton . . 8 C5 51 56N 1 32W
Chipping Ongar . . 9 C9 51 42N 0 11 E
Chipping Sodbury 8 C4 51 31N 2 23W
Chobham 9 D7 51 20N 0 36W
Chorley 7 E3 53 39N 2 39W
Chorleywood 9 C8 51 39N 0 29W
Christchurch 8 E5 50 44N 1 45W
Chulmleigh 11 F6 50 55N 3 52W
Church Stretton . . 8 A3 52 32N 2 49W
Churchdown 8 C4 51 53N 2 9W
Chwarel y Fan . . . 10 D7 51 56N 3 5W
Cill Chainnigh =
Kilkenny 15 C8 52 40N 7 17W
Cinderford 8 C3 51 49N 2 30W
Cirencester 8 C5 51 43N 1 59W
Clach Leathad . . . 4 A6 56 36N 4 52W
Clacton-on-Sea . . 9 C11 51 47N 1 10 E
Clara 15 B7 53 20N 7 38W
Clare □ 14 C4 52 45N 9 0W
Clare → 14 B4 53 22N 9 5W
Clare I. 12 D2 53 48N 10 0W
Clay Cross 7 F6 53 11N 1 26W
Clear, C. 14 F3 51 26N 9 30W
Cleator Moor 6 C2 54 31N 3 30W
Clee Hills 8 B3 52 26N 2 35W
Cleethorpes 7 E8 53 33N 0 2W
Cleeve Cloud 8 C5 51 56N 1 57W
Clent Hills 8 B4 52 25N 2 6W
Clevedon 8 D3 51 26N 2 52W
Cleveland □ 6 C6 54 35N 1 8W
Cleveland Hills . . . 6 D6 54 25N 1 11W
Cleveleys 7 E2 53 53N 3 3W
Clew B. 12 D2 53 54N 9 50W
Clifden 12 E1 53 30N 10 2W
Clifden B. 12 E1 53 29N 10 5W
Clift Sd. 2 B15 60 4N 1 17W
Clisham 2 G4 57 57N 6 50W
Clitheroe 7 E4 53 52N 2 23W
Clogher Hd. 13 D9 53 48N 6 15W
Clonakilty 14 E5 51 37N 8 53W
Clondalkin 15 B10 53 20N 6 25W
Clones 13 C7 54 10N 7 13W
Clonmel 15 D7 52 22N 7 42W
Clovelly 11 F5 51 0N 4 25W
Clun Forest 8 B2 52 27N 3 7W
Clwyd □ 7 F2 53 5N 3 20W
Clwyd → 10 A6 53 20N 3 30W
Clydach 10 D6 51 42N 3 54W
Clyde → 4 C7 55 56N 4 29W
Clyde, Firth of . . . 4 D6 55 20N 5 0W
Clydebank 4 C7 55 54N 4 25W
Clydesdale 5 C8 55 42N 3 50W
Clywedog, L. 10 C6 52 29N 3 40W
Cnoc Moy 4 D4 55 23N 5 44W
Coalisland 13 B8 54 33N 6 42W
Coalville 7 G6 52 43N 1 21W
Coatbridge 4 C7 55 52N 4 2W
Cóbh 14 E6 51 50N 8 18W
Cockenzie 5 C10 55 58N 2 59W
Cockermouth 6 C2 54 40N 3 22W
Cods Hd. 14 E2 51 40N 10 7W
Coigach 2 G7 57 55N 5 10W
Colchester . . . . . . 9 C10 51 54N 0 55 E
Cold Fell 6 C3 54 54N 2 40W
Coldstream 5 C11 55 39N 2 14W
Coleraine 13 A8 55 8N 6 40W
Coleshill 8 B5 52 30N 1 42W
Colgrave Sd. 2 A16 60 35N 1 0W
Colinton 5 C9 55 54N 3 15W
Coll 4 A2 56 40N 6 35W
Collier Law 6 C5 54 47N 1 59W
Collooney 12 C5 54 11N 8 28W
Colne 7 E4 53 51N 2 11W
Colonsay 4 B3 56 4N 6 12W
Colwyn Bay 10 A6 53 17N 3 44W
Combe Martin . . . 11 E5 51 12N 4 2W
Comber 13 B10 54 33N 5 45W
Comeragh Mts. . . 15 D7 52 17N 7 35W
Congleton 7 F4 53 10N 2 12W
Conisbrough 7 F6 53 29N 1 12W
Coniston 6 D2 54 22N 3 6W
Conn, L. 12 C3 54 3N 9 15W
Connacht 14 D4 53 45N 8 40W
Connah's Quay . . 10 A7 53 13N 3 6W
Connel 4 B5 56 27N 5 24W
Connemara 12 E2 53 29N 9 45W
Cononbridge 3 G9 57 32N 4 30W
Consett 6 C5 54 52N 1 50W
Conway = Conwy 10 A6 53 17N 3 50W
Conwy 10 A6 53 17N 3 50W
Conwy B. 10 A6 53 17N 3 57W
Cookstown 13 B8 54 40N 6 43W
Cootehill 13 C7 54 5N 7 5W
Coquet → 6 B5 55 18N 1 45W
Corbridge 6 C5 54 58N 2 0W
Corby 9 A7 52 30N 0 41W
Corby Glen 7 G7 52 49N 0 31W
Corcaigh = Cork . 14 E6 51 54N 8 30W
Corfe Castle 8 E4 50 37N 2 3W
Cork 14 E6 51 54N 8 30W
Cork □ 14 E5 51 50N 8 50W
Cork Harbour 14 E6 51 46N 8 16W
Corn Hill 12 D6 53 48N 7 43W
Cornwall □ 11 G4 50 26N 4 40W
Cornwall, C. 11 G2 50 8N 5 42W
Corrib, L. 14 B4 53 5N 9 10W
Corringham . . . . . 9 C10 51 30N 0 26 E
Corry Mt. 12 C5 54 8N 8 8W
Corryvreckan, G. of 4 B4 56 10N 5 44W
Corsewall Pt. . . . 4 E5 55 0N 5 10W
Corsham 8 D4 51 25N 2 11W
Coseley 7 G4 52 33N 2 6W
Cot Nab 7 D7 54 1N 0 45W
Cotswold Hills . . . 8 C4 51 42N 2 10W
Cottingham 7 E8 53 47N 0 23W
Coul Pt. 4 C2 55 50N 6 30W
Coupar Angus . . . 5 A9 56 33N 3 17W
Courtmacsherry B. 14 E5 51 37N 8 37W
Cove 4 B6 56 2N 4 50W
Coventry 8 B6 52 25N 1 28W
Cow Green Res. . . 6 C4 54 40N 2 20W
Cowal 4 B5 56 5N 5 8W
Cowdenbeath 5 B9 56 7N 3 20W
Cowes 8 E6 50 45N 1 18W
Craigavon 13 C9 54 28N 6 20W
Craignish, L. 4 B4 56 11N 5 32W
Crail 5 B10 56 16N 2 38W
Cramlington 6 B5 55 5N 1 36W
Cranborne Chase . 8 E4 50 56N 2 6W
Cranbrook . . . . . . 9 D10 51 6N 0 33 E
Cranfield Pt. 13 C9 54 1N 6 3W
Cranleigh 9 D8 51 8N 0 29W
Crawley 9 D8 51 7N 0 10W
Creag Meagaidh . . 3 J8 56 57N 4 38W
Crediton 11 F6 50 47N 3 39W
Cree → 4 E7 54 51N 4 24W
Creran, L. 4 A5 56 30N 5 20W
Crewe 7 F4 53 6N 2 28W
Crewkerne 8 E3 50 53N 2 48W
Criccieth 10 B5 52 55N 4 15W
Cricklade 8 C5 51 38N 1 50W
Crieff 5 B8 56 22N 3 50W
Criffell 5 E8 54 56N 3 38W
Crinan Canal 4 B5 56 4N 5 30W
Croagh Patrick . . . 12 D2 53 46N 9 40W
Croghan Mt. 15 C10 52 48N 6 20W
Crohy Hd. 12 B5 54 55N 8 28W
Cromarty 3 G9 57 40N 4 2W
Cromarty Firth . . . 3 G9 57 40N 4 15W
Cromdale, Hills of 3 H11 57 20N 3 28W
Cromer . . . . 9 A11 52 56N 1 18 E
Crook 6 C5 54 43N 1 45W
Crosby 7 E2 53 30N 3 2W
Cross Fell 6 C4 54 44N 2 29W
Crossfarnoge Pt. . 15 D9 52 10N 6 37W
Crosshaven 14 E6 51 48N 8 19W
Crossmaglen 13 C8 54 5N 6 37W
Crow Hd. 14 E2 51 34N 10 9W
Crow Sd. 11 H1 49 56N 6 16W
Crowborough . . . . 9 D9 51 3N 0 9 E
Crowthorne 9 D7 51 22N 0 50W
Croydon 9 D8 51 18N 0 5W
Cruden Bay 3 H14 57 25N 1 50W
Cuckfield 9 D8 51 1N 0 8W
Cuffley 9 C8 51 43N 0 9W
Cuilcagh 12 C6 54 12N 7 50W
Cuillin Hills 2 H5 57 14N 6 15W
Cuillin Sd. 2 H5 57 4N 6 20W
Cullen 3 G12 57 45N 2 50W
Cullin, L. 12 D3 53 58N 9 12W
Culloden 3 H9 57 29N 4 7W
Cullompton 11 F7 50 52N 3 23W
Culm → 11 F6 50 46N 3 31W
Culter Fell 5 C8 55 35N 3 30W
Cults 3 H13 57 8N 2 10W
Culvain 2 J7 56 55N 5 19W
Cumbernauld 5 C8 55 57N 3 58W
Cumbrae Is. 4 C6 55 46N 4 54W
Cumbria □ 6 C3 54 35N 2 55W
Cumbrian Mts. . . . 6 D2 54 30N 3 0W
Cumnock 4 D7 55 27N 4 18W
Cunninghame 4 C6 55 38N 4 35W
Cupar 5 B9 56 20N 3 3W
Cupidstown Hill . . 15 B9 53 15N 6 31W
Currane, L. 14 E2 51 50N 10 8W
Cwmbran 10 D7 51 39N 3 3W

D

Daingean 15 B8 53 18N 7 15W
Dalbeattie 5 E8 54 55N 3 50W
Dalkeith 5 C9 55 54N 3 5W
Dalmellington 4 D7 55 20N 4 25W
Dalry 4 C6 55 44N 4 42W

35
Dalton-in-Furness
Humber

Dalton-in-Furness 6 D2 54 9N 3 10W
Danbury 9 C10 51 43N 0 34 E
Darlington 6 C5 54 33N 1 33W
Dart → 11 G6 50 24N 3 36W
Dartford 9 D9 51 26N 0 15 E
Dartmoor 11 F6 50 36N 4 0W
Dartmouth 11 G6 50 21N 3 35W
Darton 7 E5 53 36N 1 32W
Darvel 4 C7 55 37N 4 20W
Darwen 7 E4 53 42N 2 29W
Daventry 8 B6 52 16N 1 10W
Dawlish 11 F7 50 34N 3 28W
Dawros Hd. 12 B4 54 48N 8 32W
Deal 9 D11 51 13N 1 25 E
Dean, Forest of 8 C3 51 50N 2 35W
Dearne 7 E6 53 32N 1 17W
Dee →, *Clwyd* 10 A7 53 15N 3 7W
Dee →, *Gramp.* 3 H13 57 4N 2 7W
Deer Sd. 3 E12 58 58N 2 50W
Denbigh 10 A7 53 12N 3 26W
Denby Dale 7 E5 53 35N 1 40W
Dennis Hd. 3 D13 59 23N 2 26W
Denny 5 B8 56 1N 3 55W
Denton 7 F4 53 26N 2 10W
Derby 7 G6 52 27N 1 28W
Derbyshire □ 7 F5 53 0N 1 30W
Derg, L. 14 C6 53 0N 8 20W
Derravaragh, L. 12 D7 53 38N 7 22W
Derry = Londonderry 12 B7 55 0N 7 23W
Derry → 15 C9 52 43N 6 35W
Derrynsaggart Mts. 14 E4 51 58N 9 15W
Derwent →, *Derby* 7 G6 52 53N 1 17W
Derwent →, *N. Yorks.* 7 E7 53 45N 0 57W
Desborough 9 B7 52 27N 0 50W
Deveron → 3 G12 57 40N 2 31W
Devilsbit 14 C7 52 50N 7 58W
Devizes 8 D5 51 21N 2 0W
Devon □ 8 F6 50 50N 3 40W
Devonport 11 G5 50 23N 4 11W
Dewsbury 7 E5 53 42N 1 38W
Didcot 8 C6 51 36N 1 14W
Dinas Hd. 10 C4 52 2N 4 56W
Dingle 14 D2 52 9N 10 17W
Dingle B. 14 D2 52 3N 10 20W
Dingwall 3 G9 57 36N 4 26W
Dinnington 7 F6 53 21N 1 12W
Diss 9 B11 52 23N 1 6 E
Ditchling Beacon 9 E8 50 49N 0 7W
Dizzard Pt. 11 F4 50 46N 4 38W
Dodman Pt. 11 G4 50 13N 4 49W
Dolgellau 10 B6 52 44N 3 53W
Dolgelley = Dolgellau 10 B6 52 44N 3 53W
Dollar 5 B8 56 9N 3 41W
Don →, *Gramp.* 3 H13 57 14N 2 5W
Don →, *S. Yorks.* 7 E7 53 41N 0 51W
Donaghadee 13 B10 54 38N 5 32W
Doncaster 7 E6 53 31N 1 9W
Donegal 12 B5 54 39N 8 8W
Donegal □ 12 B6 54 53N 8 0W
Donegal B. 12 B4 54 30N 8 35W
Donegal Harbour 12 B5 54 30N 8 15W
Donna Nook 7 F9 53 29N 0 9 E
Dooega Hd. 12 D1 53 54N 10 3W
Doon, L. 4 D7 55 15N 4 22W
Dorchester 11 E4 50 42N 2 28W
Dorking 9 D8 51 14N 0 20W
Dornoch 3 G9 57 52N 4 5W
Dornoch Firth 3 G10 57 52N 4 0W
Dorridge 8 B5 52 22N 1 45W
Dorset □ 8 E4 50 48N 2 25W
Douglas 13 C13 54 9N 4 29W
Doulus Hd. 14 E2 51 57N 10 19W
Doune 4 B7 56 12N 4 3W
Dounreay 3 E10 58 34N 3 44W
Dove → 7 G5 52 51N 1 36W
Dover 9 D11 51 7N 1 19 E
Dovey = Dyfi → 10 B6 52 32N 4 0W
Down □ 13 C10 54 20N 5 47W
Downham Market 9 A9 52 36N 0 22 E
Downpatrick 13 C10 54 20N 5 43W
Downpatrick Hd. 12 C3 54 20N 9 21W
Driffield 7 D8 54 1N 0 25W
Drogheda 13 D9 53 45N 6 20W
Droichead Atha = Drogheda 13 D9 53 45N 6 20W
Droichead Nua 15 B9 53 11N 6 50W
Droitwich 8 B4 52 16N 2 10W
Dromore 12 B7 54 31N 7 28W
Dronfield 7 F6 53 18N 1 29W
Druridge B. 6 B5 55 16N 1 32W
Drygarn Fawr 10 C6 52 13N 3 39W
Dublin 15 B10 53 20N 6 18W
Dublin □ 15 B10 53 24N 6 20W
Dudley 8 A4 52 30N 2 5W
Dufftown 3 H11 57 26N 3 9W
Dukinfield 7 F4 53 29N 2 5W
Dulas B. 10 A5 53 22N 4 16W
Dumbarton 4 C6 55 58N 4 35W
Dumfries 5 D8 55 4N 3 37W
Dumfries & Galloway □ 5 D8 55 5N 4 0W
Dún Dealgan = Dundalk 13 C9 54 1N 6 25W
Dun Laoghaire 15 B10 53 17N 6 9W
Dunaff Hd. 12 A6 55 18N 7 30W
Dunany Pt. 13 D9 53 51N 6 15W
Dunbar 5 C10 56 0N 2 32W
Dunblane 5 B8 56 10N 3 58W
Duncansby Hd. 3 E12 58 39N 3 0W
Dundalk 13 C9 54 1N 6 25W
Dundalk B. 13 D9 53 55N 6 15W
Dundee 5 B10 56 29N 3 0W
Dundrum 13 C10 54 17N 5 50W
Dunfermline 5 B9 56 5N 3 28W
Dungannon 13 B8 54 30N 6 47W
Dungarvan 15 D7 52 6N 7 40W
Dungarvan Harbour 15 D7 52 5N 7 35W
Dungeness 9 E10 50 54N 0 59 E
Dunipace 5 B8 56 4N 3 55W
Dunkeld 5 A8 56 34N 3 36W
Dunkery Beacon 8 D1 51 15N 3 37W
Dúnleary = Dun Laoghaire 15 B10 53 17N 6 9W
Dunmanway 14 E4 51 43N 9 8W
Dunnet B. 3 E11 58 37N 3 23W
Dunoon 4 C6 55 57N 4 56W
Duns 5 C11 55 47N 2 20W
Dunstable 9 C7 51 53N 0 31W
Dunster 8 D2 51 11N 3 28W
Dunvegan Hd. 2 G4 57 30N 6 42W
Durham 6 C5 54 47N 1 34W
Durham □ 6 C5 54 42N 1 45W
Durlston Hd. 8 E5 50 35N 1 58W
Durness 3 E8 58 34N 4 45W
Dursley 8 C4 51 41N 2 21W
Dury Voe 2 B15 60 20N 1 8W
Dyce 3 H13 57 12N 2 11W
Dyfed □ 10 D5 52 0N 4 30W
Dyfi → 10 B6 52 32N 4 0W
Dymchurch 9 D11 51 2N 1 0 E

E

Ealing 9 C8 51 30N 0 19W
Earadale Pt. 4 D4 55 24N 5 50W
Earby 7 E4 53 55N 2 8W
Earl Shilton 7 G6 52 35N 1 20W
Earlsferry 5 B10 56 11N 2 50W
Earn → 5 B9 56 20N 3 19W
Earn, L. 4 B7 56 23N 4 14W
Easington 6 C6 54 50N 1 24W
Easington Colliery 6 C6 54 49N 1 19W
East Cowes 8 E6 50 45N 1 17W
East Dereham 9 A10 52 40N 0 57 E
East Grinstead 9 D9 51 8N 0 0 E
East Kilbride 4 C7 55 46N 4 10W
East Linton 5 C10 56 0N 2 40W
East Retford = Retford 7 F7 53 19N 0 55W
East Sussex □ 9 E9 51 0N 0 20 E
East Wittering 9 E7 50 46N 0 53W
Eastbourne 9 E9 50 46N 0 18 E
Easter Ross 3 G8 57 50N 4 35W
Eastleigh 8 E6 50 58N 1 21W
Eastwood 7 F6 53 2N 1 17W
Eaval 2 G3 57 33N 7 12W
Ebbw Vale 10 D7 51 47N 3 12W
Eccleshall 7 G4 52 52N 2 14W
Eckington 7 F6 53 19N 1 21W
Eday Sd. 3 D12 59 12N 2 45W
Eddrachillis B. 2 F7 58 16N 5 10W
Eddystone 11 G5 50 11N 4 16W
Eden → 6 C2 54 57N 3 2W
Edenbridge 9 D9 51 12N 0 4 E
Edenderry 15 B8 53 21N 7 3W
Edge Hill 8 B6 52 7N 1 28W
Edinburgh 5 C9 55 57N 3 12W
Egham 9 D7 51 25N 0 33W
Egremont 6 D1 54 28N 3 33W
Eigg 2 J5 56 54N 6 10W
Eil, L. 2 J7 56 50N 5 15W
Eishort, L. 2 H6 57 9N 6 0W
Elan → 10 C6 52 17N 3 30W
Elan Valley Reservoirs 10 C6 52 12N 3 42W
Elgin 3 G11 57 39N 3 20W
Elie 5 B10 56 11N 2 50W
Elland 7 E5 53 41N 1 49W
Ellesmere Port 7 F3 53 17N 2 55W
Ellon 3 H13 57 21N 2 5W
Ely 9 B9 52 24N 0 16 E
Emsworth 9 E7 50 51N 0 56W
Enard B. 2 F7 58 5N 5 20W
Enfield 9 C8 51 39N 0 4W
Ennell, L. 12 E7 53 29N 7 25W
Ennis 14 C5 52 51N 8 59W
Enniscorthy 15 D9 52 30N 6 35W
Enniskillen 12 C6 54 20N 7 40W
Ennistimon 14 C4 52 56N 9 18W
Eport, L. 2 G3 57 33N 7 10W
Epping 9 C9 51 42N 0 8 E
Epsom 9 D8 51 19N 0 16W
Eriboll, L. 3 F8 58 28N 4 41W
Ericht, L. 3 J9 56 50N 4 25W
Eriskay, Sd. of 2 H3 57 5N 7 20W
Erisort L. 2 F4 58 5N 6 30W
Erne → 12 C5 54 30N 8 16W
Erne, Lower L. 12 C6 54 26N 7 46W
Erne, Upper L. 12 C7 54 14N 7 22W
Errigal 12 A5 55 2N 8 8W
Erris Hd. 12 C2 54 19N 10 0W
Erskine 4 C7 55 52N 4 27W
Esha Ness 2 A14 60 30N 1 36W
Esher 9 D8 51 21N 0 22W
Esk → 5 E9 54 58N 3 4W
Eskdale 5 D9 55 12N 3 4W
Essex □ 9 C9 51 55N 0 30 E
Eston 6 C6 54 33N 1 6W
Etive, L. 4 A5 56 30N 5 12W
Ettrick Water → 5 C10 55 31N 2 55W
Evesham 8 B5 52 6N 1 57W
Ewe, L. 2 G6 57 49N 5 38W
Ewell 9 D8 51 20N 0 15W
Exe → 11 F7 50 38N 3 27W
Exeter 11 F6 50 43N 3 31W
Exmoor 11 E6 51 10N 3 59W
Exmouth 11 F7 50 37N 3 26W
Eye, *Cambs.* 7 G8 52 36N 0 11W
Eye, *Suffolk* 9 B11 52 19N 1 9 E
Eye Pen. 2 F5 58 13N 6 10W
Eyemouth 5 C11 55 53N 2 5W
Eynhallow Sd. 3 D11 59 8N 3 7W
Eynort, L. 2 H3 57 13N 7 18W

F

Fair Hd. 13 A9 55 14N 6 10W
Fair Isle 2 C14 59 32N 1 36W
Fairford 8 C5 51 42N 1 48W
Fakenham 9 A10 52 50N 0 51 E
Faldingworth 7 F8 53 21N 0 22W
Falkirk 5 B8 56 1N 3 47W
Falkland 5 B9 56 15N 3 13W
Falmouth 11 G3 50 9N 5 5W
Fanad Hd. 12 A6 55 17N 7 40W
Faraid Hd. 3 E8 58 35N 4 48W
Fareham 8 E6 50 52N 1 11W
Faringdon 8 C5 51 39N 1 34W
Farnborough 9 D7 51 17N 0 46W
Farne Is. 6 A5 55 38N 1 37W
Farnham 9 D7 51 13N 0 49W
Farnworth 7 E4 53 33N 2 24W
Fauldhouse 5 C8 55 50N 3 44W
Faversham 9 D10 51 18N 0 54 E
Fawley 8 E6 50 49N 1 20W
Feale → 14 D3 52 26N 9 40W
Featherbed Moss 7 E5 53 31N 1 56W
Felixstowe 9 C11 51 58N 1 22 E
Felton 6 B5 55 18N 1 42W
Fergus → 14 C5 52 45N 9 0W
Fermanagh □ 12 C6 54 21N 7 40W
Fermoy 14 D6 52 4N 8 18W
Ferndown 8 E5 50 48N 1 53W
Ferryhill 6 C5 54 42N 1 32W
Fethaland, Pt. of 2 A15 60 39N 1 20W
Ffestiniog 10 B6 52 58N 3 56W
Fife □ 5 B9 56 13N 3 2W
Fife Ness 5 B10 56 17N 2 35W
Filey 6 D8 54 13N 0 18W
Filton 8 C3 51 30N 2 34W
Findhorn → 3 G10 57 38N 3 38W
Findochty 3 G12 57 42N 2 53W
Finn → 12 B6 54 50N 7 55W
Fionn L. 2 G7 57 46N 5 30W
Fishguard 10 D4 51 59N 4 59W
Fitful Hd. 2 C15 59 54N 1 20W
Five Sisters 2 H7 57 11N 5 21W
Flamborough Hd. 6 D8 54 8N 0 4W
Fleet 9 D7 51 16N 0 50W
Fleet, L. 3 G9 57 57N 4 2W
Fleetwood 7 E2 53 55N 3 1W
Flint 10 A7 53 15N 3 7W
Flitwick 9 C8 51 59N 0 30W
Flodden 6 A4 55 37N 2 8W
Foinaven 3 F8 58 30N 4 53W
Folkestone 9 D11 51 5N 1 11 E
Fordingbridge 8 E5 50 56N 1 48W
Foreland Pt. 11 E6 51 14N 3 47W
Forfar 5 A10 56 40N 2 53W
Formartine 3 H13 57 20N 2 15W
Formby 7 E2 53 33N 3 3W
Forres 3 G10 57 37N 3 38W
Fort Augustus 3 H8 57 9N 4 40W
Fort William 2 J7 56 48N 5 8W
Forth 5 B8 56 8N 3 48W
Forth, Firth of 5 B10 56 5N 2 55W
Fortrose 3 G9 57 35N 4 10W
Fortuneswell 11 F9 50 33N 2 26W
Foulness I. 9 C10 51 36N 0 55 E
Fowey 11 G4 50 20N 4 39W
Fowey → 11 G4 50 20N 4 39W
Foyle → 13 B7 55 0N 7 13W
Foyle, L. 13 A7 55 6N 7 8W
Foynes 14 C4 52 37N 9 5W
Framlingham 9 B11 52 14N 1 20 E
Fraserburgh 3 G13 57 41N 2 3W
Frimley 9 D7 51 18N 0 43W
Frinton-on-Sea 9 C11 51 50N 1 16 E
Frodsham 7 F3 53 17N 2 45W
Frome 8 D4 51 16N 2 17W
Frome → 8 E4 50 44N 2 5W
Frower Pt. 14 E6 51 40N 8 30W
Fulwood 7 E3 53 47N 2 41W
Furness 6 D2 54 14N 3 8W
Fyne, L. 4 C5 56 0N 5 20W

G

Gaillimh = Galway 14 B4 53 16N 9 4W
Gainsborough 7 F7 53 23N 0 46W
Gairloch 2 G6 57 42N 5 40W
Gairloch, L. 2 G6 57 43N 5 45W
Galashiels 5 C10 55 37N 2 50W
Gallan Hd. 2 F3 58 14N 7 2W
Galley Hd. 14 E5 51 32N 8 56W
Galloway 4 D7 55 1N 4 25W
Galloway, Mull of 4 E6 54 38N 4 50W
Galston 4 C7 55 36N 4 22W
Galty Mts. 14 D6 52 22N 8 10W
Galtymore 14 D6 52 22N 8 12W
Galway 14 B4 53 16N 9 4W
Galway □ 14 B4 53 16N 9 3W
Galway B. 14 B4 53 10N 9 20W
Gamlingay 9 B8 52 9N 0 11W
Gara, L. 12 D5 53 57N 8 26W
Garforth 7 E6 53 48N 1 22W
Garioch 3 H12 57 18N 2 40W
Garron Pt. 13 A10 55 3N 6 0W
Garry, L. 3 H8 57 5N 4 52W
Garstang 7 E3 53 53N 2 47W
Gatehouse of Fleet 4 E7 54 53N 4 10W
Gateshead 6 C5 54 57N 1 37W
Gatley 7 F4 53 25N 2 15W
Gerrans B. 11 G4 50 12N 4 57W
Gerrards Cross 9 C7 51 35N 0 32W
Giants Causeway 13 A8 55 15N 6 30W
Gibraltar Pt. 7 F9 53 6N 0 20 E
Gill, L. 12 C5 54 15N 8 25W
Gillingham, *Dorset* 8 D4 51 2N 2 15W
Gillingham, *Kent* 9 D10 51 23N 0 34 E
Girdle Ness 3 H13 57 9N 2 2W
Girvan 4 D6 55 15N 4 50W
Gisborough Moor 6 D7 54 30N 1 2W
Glanaruddery Mts. 14 D4 52 20N 9 27W
Glandore Harbour 14 E4 51 33N 9 8W
Glas Maol 3 J11 56 52N 3 20W
Glasgow 4 C7 55 52N 4 14W
Glastonbury 8 D3 51 9N 2 42W
Glen Affric 3 H8 57 15N 5 0W
Glen B. 12 B4 54 43N 8 45W
Glen Garry, *Highl.* 2 H7 57 3N 5 7W
Glen Garry, *Tayside* 3 J9 56 47N 4 5W
Glen Mor 3 H8 57 12N 4 37W
Glen Shiel 2 H7 57 8N 5 20W
Glencoe 4 A5 56 40N 5 6W
Gleneagles 5 B8 56 16N 3 44W
Glengad Hd. 13 A7 55 19N 7 11W
Glengarriff 14 E3 51 45N 9 33W
Glennamaddy 12 D4 53 37N 8 33W
Glenrothes 5 B9 56 12N 3 11W
Glenties 12 B5 54 48N 8 18W
Glossop 7 F5 53 27N 1 56W
Gloucester 8 C4 51 52N 2 15W
Gloucestershire □ 8 C4 51 44N 2 10W
Goat Fell 4 C5 55 37N 5 11W
Godalming 9 D7 51 12N 0 37W
Goil, L. 4 B6 56 8N 4 52W
Golden Vale 14 C6 52 33N 8 17W
Golspie 3 G10 57 58N 3 58W
Goodwick 10 C3 52 1N 5 0W
Goole 7 E7 53 42N 0 52W
Gorebridge 5 C9 55 51N 3 2W
Gorey 15 C10 52 41N 6 18W
Goring-by-Sea 9 E8 50 49N 0 26W
Gorleston 9 A12 52 35N 1 44 E
Gorseinon 10 D5 51 40N 4 2W
Gort 14 B5 53 4N 8 50W
Gosport 8 E6 50 48N 1 8W
Gourock 4 C6 55 58N 4 49W
Gower 11 D5 51 35N 4 10W
Grafham Water 9 B8 52 18N 0 17W
Gragareth 6 D4 54 12N 2 29W
Grampian □ 3 H12 57 20N 3 0W
Grampian Highlands = Grampian Mts. 3 J10 56 50N 4 0W
Grampian Mts. 3 J10 56 50N 4 0W
Granard 12 D6 53 47N 7 30W
Grand Union Canal 9 B7 52 5N 0 52W
Grange-over-Sands 6 D3 54 12N 2 55W
Grangemouth 5 B8 56 1N 3 43W
Grantham 7 G7 52 55N 0 39W
Grantown-on-Spey 3 H10 57 19N 3 36W
Grassington 6 D5 54 5N 2 0W
Gravesend 9 D9 51 25N 0 22 E
Grays 9 D9 51 28N 0 23 E
Great Blasket I. 14 D1 52 5N 10 30W
Great Driffield = Driffield 7 D8 54 1N 0 25W
Great Dunmow 9 C9 51 52N 0 22 E
Great Harwood 7 E4 53 47N 2 25W
Great I. 14 E6 51 52N 8 15W
Great Malvern 8 B4 52 7N 2 19W
Great Ormes Hd. 10 A6 53 20N 3 52W
Great Ouse → 9 A9 52 47N 0 22 E
Great Shunner Fell 6 D4 54 22N 2 16W
Great Stour = Stour → 9 D11 51 15N 1 20 E
Great Sugar Loaf 15 B10 53 10N 6 10W
Great Torrington 11 F5 50 57N 4 9W
Great Whernside 6 D5 54 9N 1 59W
Great Yarmouth 9 A12 52 40N 1 45 E
Greater London □ 9 C8 51 30N 0 5W
Greater Manchester □ 7 E4 53 30N 2 15W
Green Lowther 5 D8 55 22N 3 44W
Greenholm 4 C7 55 40N 4 20W
Greenock 4 C6 55 57N 4 46W
Greenore 13 C9 54 2N 6 8W
Greenore Pt. 15 D10 52 15N 6 20W
Greenstone Pt. 2 G6 57 55N 5 38W
Greenwich 9 D9 51 28N 0 0 E
Greian Hd. 2 H2 57 1N 7 30W
Gretna 5 E9 54 59N 3 4W
Gretna Green 5 E9 55 0N 3 3W
Greystones 15 B10 53 9N 6 4W
Griminish Pt. 2 G3 57 40N 7 29W
Grimsby 7 E8 53 35N 0 5W
Gruinard B. 2 G6 57 56N 5 35W
Gruinart, L. 4 C3 55 50N 6 20W
Gruting Voe 2 B14 60 12N 1 32W
Guernsey 11 J8 49 30N 2 35W
Guildford 9 D7 51 14N 0 34W
Guisborough 6 C6 54 32N 1 2W
Guiseley 7 E5 53 52N 1 43W
Gullane 5 B10 56 2N 2 50W
Gurnard's Hd. 11 G2 50 12N 5 37W
Gweebarra B. 12 B5 54 52N 8 21W
Gweedore 12 A5 55 4N 8 15W
Gwent □ 8 D8 51 45N 2 55W
Gwynedd □ 10 A6 53 0N 4 0W

H

Hackley Hd. 3 H14 57 19N 1 58W
Hackney 9 C8 51 33N 0 2W
Haddington 5 C10 55 57N 2 48W
Hadleigh, *Essex* 9 C10 51 33N 0 37 E
Hadleigh, *Suffolk* 9 B10 52 3N 0 58 E
Hags Hd. 14 C4 52 57N 9 28W
Hailsham 9 E9 50 52N 0 17 E
Halberry Hd. 3 F11 58 20N 3 11W
Halesowen 8 B4 52 27N 2 2W
Halesworth 9 B12 52 21N 1 31 E
Halifax 7 E5 53 43N 1 51W
Halkirk 3 E11 58 30N 3 30W
Halstead 9 C10 51 59N 0 39 E
Haltwhistle 6 C4 54 58N 2 27W
Hambleton Hills 6 D6 54 17N 1 12W
Hamilton 4 C7 55 47N 4 2W
Hammersmith and Fulham 9 D8 51 30N 0 15W
Hampshire □ 8 D6 51 3N 1 20W
Hampshire Downs 8 D6 51 10N 1 10W
Handa I. 2 F7 58 23N 5 10W
Haringey 9 C8 51 35N 0 7W
Harlech 10 B5 52 52N 4 7W
Harleston 9 B11 52 25N 1 18 E
Harlow 9 C9 51 47N 0 9 E
Harpenden 9 C8 51 48N 0 20W
Harris 2 G4 57 50N 6 55W
Harris, Sd. of 2 G3 57 44N 7 6W
Harrogate 7 E5 53 59N 1 32W
Harrow 9 C8 51 35N 0 15W
Hartland Pt. 11 E4 51 2N 4 32W
Hartlepool 6 C6 54 42N 1 11W
Harwich 9 C11 51 56N 1 18 E
Haslemere 9 D7 51 5N 0 41W
Haslingden 7 E4 53 43N 2 20W
Hastings 9 E10 50 51N 0 36 E
Hatfield, *Herts.* 9 C8 51 46N 0 11W
Hatfield, *S. Yorks.* 7 E7 53 34N 0 59W
Havant 9 E7 50 51N 0 59W
Haverfordwest 10 D4 51 48N 4 59W
Haverhill 9 B9 52 6N 0 27 E
Havering 9 C9 51 33N 0 20 E
Haweswater 6 C3 54 32N 2 48W
Hawick 5 D10 55 25N 2 48W
Hawkhurst 9 D10 51 2N 0 31 E
Hay-on-Wye 10 C7 52 4N 3 9W
Hayle 11 G3 50 12N 5 25W
Haywards Heath 9 D8 51 1N 0 6W
Hazel Grove 7 F4 53 23N 2 7W
Healaval Bheag 2 H4 57 24N 6 41W
Heanor 7 F6 53 1N 1 20W
Heathfield 9 E9 50 58N 0 18 E
Heaval 2 J3 56 58N 7 30W
Hebburn 6 C5 54 59N 1 30W
Hebden Bridge 7 E5 53 45N 2 0W
Hecla 2 H3 57 18N 7 15W
Hednesford 7 G5 52 43N 2 0W
Hedon 7 E8 53 44N 0 11W
Helensburgh 4 B6 56 1N 4 44W
Helli Ness 2 B15 60 3N 1 10W
Helmsdale 3 F10 58 8N 3 43W
Helmsley 6 D6 54 15N 1 2W
Helston 11 G3 50 7N 5 17W
Helvellyn 6 C2 54 31N 3 1W
Helvick Hd. 15 D7 52 3N 7 33W
Hemel Hempstead 9 C8 51 45N 0 28W
Hemsworth 7 E6 53 37N 1 21W
Henfield 9 E8 50 56N 0 17W
Hengoed 10 D7 51 39N 3 14W
Henley-on-Thames 9 C7 51 32N 0 53W
Hereford 8 B3 52 4N 2 42W
Hereford and Worcester □ 8 B3 52 10N 2 30W
Herma Ness 2 A16 60 50N 0 54W
Herne Bay 9 D11 51 22N 1 8 E
Hertford 9 C8 51 47N 0 4W
Hertfordshire □ 9 C8 51 51N 0 5W
Hessle 7 E8 53 44N 0 28W
Heswall 7 F2 53 19N 3 6W
Hetton-le-Hole 6 C6 54 49N 1 26W
Hexham 6 C4 54 58N 2 7W
Heysham 6 D3 54 5N 2 53W
Heywood 7 E4 53 35N 2 13W
High Pike 6 C2 54 43N 3 4W
High Willhays 11 F6 50 41N 3 59W
High Wycombe 9 C7 51 37N 0 45W
Higham Ferrers 9 B7 52 18N 0 36W
Highbridge 8 D3 51 13N 2 59W
Highland □ 3 H7 57 30N 5 0W
Highworth 8 C5 51 38N 1 42W
Hillingdon 9 C8 51 33N 0 29W
Hilpsford Pt. 6 D2 54 4N 3 12W
Hinckley 7 G6 52 33N 1 21W
Hindley 7 E3 53 32N 2 35W
Hinkley Pt. 8 D2 51 13N 3 9W
Hitchin 9 C8 51 57N 0 16W
Hockley 9 C10 51 35N 0 39 E
Hoddesdon 9 C8 51 45N 0 1W
Hog's Back 9 D7 51 13N 0 40W
Hogs Hd. 14 E2 51 46N 10 13W
Holbeach 7 G9 52 48N 0 1 E
Holborn Hd. 3 E10 58 37N 3 30W
Holderness 7 E8 53 45N 0 5W
Holmfirth 7 E5 53 34N 1 48W
Holsworthy 11 F5 50 48N 4 21W
Holt 9 A11 52 55N 1 4 E
Holy I., *Gwynedd* 10 A4 53 17N 4 37W
Holy I., *Northumb.* 6 A5 55 42N 1 48W
Holyhead 10 A4 53 18N 4 38W
Holywell 10 A7 53 16N 3 14W
Honiton 11 F7 50 48N 3 11W
Hook 9 D7 51 17N 0 55W
Hook Hd. 15 D9 52 8N 6 57W
Horden 6 C6 54 45N 1 17W
Horley 9 D8 51 10N 0 10W
Horn Hd. 12 A6 55 13N 8 0W
Horncastle 7 F8 53 13N 0 8W
Horndean 9 E6 50 50N 1 0W
Hornsea 7 E8 53 55N 0 10W
Horsforth 7 E5 53 50N 1 39W
Horsham 9 D8 51 4N 0 20W
Horwich 7 E3 53 37N 2 33W
Houghton-le-Spring 6 C6 54 51N 1 28W
Houghton Regis 9 C7 51 54N 0 32W
Hounslow 9 D8 51 29N 0 20W
Hourn, L. 2 H6 57 7N 5 35W
Hove 9 E8 50 50N 0 10W
Howden 7 E7 53 45N 0 52W
Howth Hd. 15 B10 53 21N 6 3W
Hoy Sd. 3 E11 58 57N 3 20W
Hoylake 7 F2 53 24N 3 11W
Hucknall 7 F6 53 3N 1 12W
Huddersfield 7 E5 53 38N 1 49W
Hull = Kingston upon Hull 7 E8 53 45N 0 20W
Humber → 7 E8 53 40N 0 10W

37

Naas

Slieve Beagh

N

Naas **15 B9** 53 12N 6 40W
Nagles Mts. **14 D5** 52 8N 8 30W
Nailsea **8 D3** 51 25N 2 44W
Nailsworth **8 C4** 51 41N 2 12W
Nairn **3 G10** 57 35N 3 54W
Nairn → **3 G10** 57 32N 3 58W
Nantwich **7 F3** 53 5N 2 31W
Narberth **10 D4** 51 48N 4 45W
Narrows **2 H5** 57 20N 6 5W
Nash Pt. **8 E6** 51 24N 3 34W
Navan = An Uaimh **13 D8** 53 39N 6 40W
Naver → **3 E9** 58 34N 4 15W
Neagh, L. **13 B9** 54 35N 6 25W
Neath **10 D6** 51 39N 3 49W
Neath → **10 D6** 51 38N 3 35W
Neist Pt. **2 H4** 57 24N 6 48W
Nelson **7 E4** 53 50N 2 14W
Nenagh **14 C6** 52 52N 8 11W
Nenagh → **14 C6** 52 56N 8 16W
Nene → **9 A9** 52 38N 0 13 E
Nephin **12 C3** 54 1N 9 21W
Nephin Beg Range **12 D2** 54 0N 9 40W
Ness **2 F5** 58 27N 6 20W
Ness, L. **3 H8** 57 15N 4 30W
Neston **7 F2** 53 17N 3 3W
Nevis, L. **2 J6** 57 0N 5 43W
New Alresford **8 D6** 51 6N 1 10W
New Bedford R. → **9 A9** 52 34N 0 20 E
New Forest **8 E5** 50 53N 1 40W
New Galloway **4 D7** 55 4N 4 10W
New Holland **7 E8** 53 42N 0 22W
New Mills **7 F5** 53 22N 2 0W
New Milton **8 E5** 50 45N 1 40W
New Quay **10 C5** 52 13N 4 21W
New Radnor **10 C7** 52 15N 3 10W
New Romney **9 E10** 50 59N 0 57 E
New Ross **15 D9** 52 24N 6 58W
New Rossington **7 F6** 53 30N 1 4W
New Scone **5 B9** 56 25N 3 26W
New Tredegar **10 D7** 51 43N 3 15W
Newark-on-Trent **7 F7** 53 6N 0 48W
Newbiggin-by-the-Sea **6 B5** 55 12N 1 31W
Newbridge = Droichead Nua **15 B9** 53 11N 6 50W
Newburgh **5 B9** 56 21N 3 15W
Newburn **6 C5** 54 57N 1 45W
Newbury **8 D6** 51 24N 1 19W
Newcastle **13 C10** 54 13N 5 54W
Newcastle Emlyn **10 C5** 52 2N 4 29W
Newcastle-under-Lyme **7 F4** 53 2N 2 15W
Newcastle-upon-Tyne **6 C5** 54 59N 1 37W
Newcastle West **14 D4** 52 27N 9 3W
Newham **9 C9** 51 31N 0 2 E
Newhaven **9 E9** 50 47N 0 4 E
Newlyn **11 G2** 50 6N 5 33W
Newmarket, *Ireland* **14 D5** 52 13N 9 0W
Newmarket, *Suffolk* **9 B9** 52 15N 0 23 E
Newmilns **4 C7** 55 36N 4 20W
Newport, *Mayo* **12 D2** 53 53N 9 31W
Newport, *Gwent* **11 D8** 51 35N 3 0W
Newport, *I. of W.* **8 E6** 50 42N 1 18W
Newport, *Shrops.* **7 G4** 52 47N 2 22W
Newport B. **12 D2** 53 52N 9 38W
Newport-on-Tay **5 B10** 56 27N 2 56W
Newport Pagnell **9 B7** 52 5N 0 42W
Newquay **11 G3** 50 24N 5 6W
Newry **13 C9** 54 10N 6 20W
Newton Abbot **11 F6** 50 32N 3 37W
Newton Aycliffe **6 C5** 54 36N 1 33W
Newton le Willows **7 F3** 53 28N 2 40W
Newton Stewart **4 E6** 54 57N 4 30W
Newtongrange **5 C9** 55 52N 3 4W
Newtonmore **3 H9** 57 4N 4 7W
Newtown **10 B7** 52 31N 3 19W
Newtownabbey **13 B10** 54 40N 5 55W
Newtownards **13 B10** 54 37N 5 40W
Newtownbarry = Bunclody **15 C9** 52 40N 6 40W
Newtownstewart **12 B7** 54 43N 7 22W
Neyland **10 D4** 51 43N 4 58W
Nidd → **7 E6** 53 58N 1 28W
Nidderdale **6 D5** 54 5N 1 46W
Nigg B. **3 G9** 57 41N 4 5W
Nith → **5 D8** 55 20N 3 5W
Nithsdale **5 D8** 55 14N 3 50W
Nore → **15 D9** 52 24N 6 58W
Norfolk □ **9 A11** 52 39N 1 0 E
Norfolk Broads Nat. Park **9 A11** 52 45N 1 30 E
Normanton **7 E6** 53 41N 1 26W
North Berwick **5 B10** 56 4N 2 44W
North Channel **4 D4** 55 0N 5 30W
North Dorset Downs **8 E3** 50 50N 2 30W
North Downs **9 D9** 51 17N 0 30 E
North Esk → **5 A11** 56 44N 2 25W
North Foreland **9 D11** 51 22N 1 28 E
North Harris **2 G4** 58 0N 6 55W
North Minch **2 F6** 58 5N 5 55W
North Roe **2 A15** 60 40N 1 22W
North Sd. **14 B3** 53 10N 9 48W
North Tyne → **6 C4** 54 59N 2 7W
North Uist **2 G3** 57 40N 7 15W
North Walsham **9 A11** 52 49N 1 22 E
North West Highlands **2 G8** 57 35N 5 0W
North York Moors **6 D7** 54 25N 0 50W
North Yorkshire □ **6 D6** 54 15N 1 25W
Northallerton **6 D6** 54 20N 1 26W
Northampton **9 B7** 52 14N 0 54W
Northamptonshire □ **9 B7** 52 16N 0 55W
Northern Ireland □ **13 B8** 54 45N 7 0W
Northfleet **9 D9** 51 26N 0 20 E
Northumberland □ **6 B5** 55 12N 2 0W
Northwich **7 F3** 53 16N 2 31W
Norton **6 D7** 54 9N 0 48W
Norwich **9 A11** 52 38N 1 17 E
Noss Hd. **3 F11** 58 29N 3 4W
Nottingham **7 G6** 52 57N 1 10W
Nottinghamshire □ **7 F7** 53 10N 1 0W
Noup Hd. **3 D11** 59 20N 3 2W
Nowen Hill **14 E4** 51 42N 9 15W
Nuneaton **8 A6** 52 32N 1 29W

O

Oa, Mull of **4 C3** 55 35N 6 20W
Oadby **7 G6** 52 37N 1 7W
Oakengates **7 G4** 52 42N 2 29W
Oakham **7 G7** 52 40N 0 43W
Oban **4 B5** 56 25N 5 30W
Ochil Hills **5 B8** 56 14N 3 40W
Offaly □ **15 B7** 53 15N 7 30W
Okehampton **11 F5** 50 44N 4 1W
Old Bedford R. → **9 A9** 52 36N 0 20 E
Old Fletton **7 G8** 52 34N 0 13W
Old Man of Hoy **3 E11** 58 53N 3 25W
Oldbury **8 C3** 51 38N 2 30W
Oldcastle **13 D7** 53 46N 7 10W
Oldham **7 E4** 53 33N 2 8W
Oldmeldrum **3 H13** 57 20N 2 19W
Olney **9 B7** 52 9N 0 42W
Omagh **12 B7** 54 36N 7 20W
Orford Ness **9 B12** 52 6N 1 31 E
Orkney □ **3 D11** 59 0N 3 0W
Ormskirk **7 E3** 53 35N 2 53W
Oronsay, Passage of **4 C3** 56 0N 6 10W
Orwell → **9 B11** 52 2N 1 12 E
Ossett **7 E5** 53 40N 1 35W
Oswaldtwistle **7 E4** 53 44N 2 27W
Oswestry **7 G2** 52 52N 3 3W
Otley **7 E5** 53 54N 1 41W
Ottery St. Mary **11 F7** 50 45N 3 16W
Oughter, L. **12 C7** 54 2N 7 30W
Oughterard **14 B4** 53 26N 9 20W
Oundle **9 B8** 52 28N 0 28W
Ouse → **7 E7** 53 33N 0 44W
Outer Hebrides **2 J2** 57 30N 7 40W
Owel, L. **12 D7** 53 34N 7 24W
Oxford **8 C6** 51 45N 1 15W
Oxfordshire □ **8 C6** 51 45N 1 15W
Oxted **9 D9** 51 15N 0 0E
Oxwich Pt. **11 D5** 51 33N 4 8W
Oykel → **3 G9** 57 55N 4 26W

P

Pabbay, Sd. of **2 G3** 57 45N 7 4W
Paddock Wood **9 D9** 51 13N 0 24 E
Padiham **7 E4** 53 48N 2 20W
Padstow **11 F4** 50 33N 4 57W
Paignton **11 G6** 50 26N 3 33W
Painshawfield **6 C5** 54 56N 1 54W
Paisley **4 C7** 55 51N 4 27W
Papa, Sd. of **2 B14** 60 19N 1 40W
Papa Sd. **3 D12** 59 20N 2 56W
Parrett → **8 D3** 51 7N 3 0W
Partry Mts. **12 D3** 53 40N 9 28W
Parys Mt. **10 A5** 53 23N 4 18W
Passage West **14 E6** 51 52N 8 20W
Patna **4 D6** 55 21N 4 30W
Peak District Nat. Park **7 F5** 58 21N 1 6W
Peebles **5 C9** 55 40N 3 12W
Peel **13 C12** 54 13N 4 41W
Peel Fell **6 B3** 55 17N 2 35W
Pegwell B. **9 D11** 51 18N 1 22 E
Pembroke **10 D4** 51 41N 4 57W
Pen-y-Ghent **6 D4** 54 10N 2 15W
Penarth **8 E7** 51 26N 3 11W
Pendle Hill **7 E4** 53 53N 2 18W
Penicuik **5 C9** 55 50N 3 14W
Penistone **7 E5** 53 31N 1 38W
Penkridge **7 G4** 52 44N 2 8W
Penmaenmawr **10 A6** 53 16N 3 55W
Pennines **6 C4** 54 50N 2 20W
Penrith **6 C3** 54 40N 2 45W
Penryn **11 G3** 50 10N 5 7W
Pentire Pt. **11 F4** 50 35N 4 57W
Pentland Firth **3 E11** 58 43N 3 10W
Pentland Hills **5 C9** 55 48N 3 25W
Penzance **11 G2** 50 7N 5 32W
Perranporth **11 G3** 50 21N 5 9W
Pershore **8 B4** 52 7N 2 4W
Perth **5 B9** 56 24N 3 27W
Peterborough **7 G8** 52 35N 0 14W
Peterculter **3 H13** 57 5N 2 18W
Peterhead **3 G14** 57 30N 1 49W
Peterlee **6 C6** 54 45N 1 18W
Petersfield **9 D7** 51 0N 0 56W
Petworth **9 E7** 50 59N 0 37W
Pewsey, Vale of **8 D5** 51 20N 1 46W
Pickering **6 D7** 54 15N 0 46W
Pickering, Vale of **6 D7** 54 14N 0 45W
Pilsdon Pen **8 E3** 50 49N 2 51W
Pitlochry **5 A8** 56 43N 3 43W
Pittenweem **5 B10** 56 13N 2 43W
Plymouth **11 G5** 50 23N 4 9W
Plympton **11 G5** 50 24N 4 2W
Plymstock **11 G5** 50 22N 4 6W
Plynlimon = Pumlumon Fawr **10 C6** 52 29N 3 47W
Pocklington **7 E7** 53 56N 0 48W
Polegate **9 E9** 50 49N 0 15 E
Polperro **11 G4** 50 19N 4 31W
Pontardawe **10 D6** 51 43N 3 51W
Pontardulais **10 D5** 51 42N 4 3W
Pontefract **7 E6** 53 42N 1 19W
Ponteland **6 B5** 55 7N 1 45W
Pontypool **10 D7** 51 42N 3 1W
Pontypridd **11 D7** 51 36N 3 21W
Poole **8 E5** 50 42N 1 58W
Poole Harbour **8 E5** 50 41N 2 0W
Port Bannatyne **4 C5** 55 51N 5 4W
Port Ellen **4 C3** 55 38N 6 10W
Port Erin **13 C12** 54 5N 4 45W
Port Eynon Pt. **11 D5** 51 32N 4 12W
Port Glasgow **4 C6** 55 57N 4 40W
Port Isaac B. **11 F4** 50 36N 4 50W
Port Lairge = Waterford **15 D8** 52 16N 7 8W
Port Laoise **15 B8** 53 2N 7 20W
Port Talbot **11 D6** 51 35N 3 48W
Portadown **13 C9** 54 27N 6 26W
Portaferry **13 C10** 54 23N 5 32W
Portarlington **15 B8** 53 10N 7 10W
Porth Neigwl **10 B4** 52 48N 4 33W
Porthcawl **11 E6** 51 28N 3 42W
Porthleven **11 G3** 50 5N 5 19W
Porthmadog **10 B5** 52 55N 4 13W
Portishead **8 D3** 51 29N 2 46W
Portknockie **3 G12** 57 40N 2 52W
Portland, I. of **11 F9** 50 32N 2 25W
Portland Bill **11 F9** 50 31N 2 27W
Portmadoc = Porthmadog **10 B5** 52 55N 4 13W
Portpatrick **4 E5** 54 50N 5 7W
Portree **2 H5** 57 25N 6 11W
Portrush **13 A8** 55 13N 6 40W
Portslade **9 E8** 50 50N 0 11W
Portsmouth **8 E6** 50 48N 1 6W
Portsoy **3 G12** 57 41N 2 41W
Portstewart **13 A8** 55 12N 6 43W
Portumna **14 B6** 53 5N 8 12W
Potters Bar **9 C8** 51 42N 0 11W
Poulaphouca Res. **15 B10** 53 8N 6 30W
Poulton le Fylde **7 E3** 53 51N 2 59W
Powys □ **8 C7** 52 20N 3 20W
Prawle Pt. **11 G6** 50 13N 3 41W
Prestatyn **10 A7** 53 20N 3 24W
Prestbury **8 C4** 51 54N 2 2W
Presteigne **10 C7** 52 17N 3 0W
Preston **7 E3** 53 46N 2 42W
Prestonpans **5 C10** 55 58N 2 58W
Prestwich **7 E4** 53 32N 2 18W
Prestwick **4 D6** 55 30N 4 38W
Princes Risborough **9 C7** 51 43N 0 50W
Prudhoe **6 C5** 54 57N 1 52W
Pudsey **7 E5** 53 47N 1 40W
Pulborough **9 E8** 50 58N 0 30W
Pumlumon Fawr **10 C6** 52 29N 3 47W
Purbeck, I. of **8 E4** 50 40N 2 5W
Purfleet **9 D9** 51 29N 0 15 E
Pwllheli **10 B5** 52 54N 4 26W

Q

Quantock Hills **8 D2** 51 8N 3 10W
Queenborough **9 D10** 51 24N 0 46 E
Queensbury **7 E5** 53 46N 1 50W
Quendale, B. of **2 C15** 59 53N 1 20W
Quinag **2 F7** 58 13N 5 5W
Quoich, L. **2 H7** 57 4N 5 20W

R

Raasay **2 H5** 57 25N 6 4W
Radcliffe **7 E4** 53 35N 2 19W
Radcliffe-on-Trent **7 G6** 52 57N 1 3W
Radlett **9 C8** 51 41N 0 19W
Radnor Forest **10 C7** 52 17N 3 10W
Radstock **8 D4** 51 17N 2 25W
Rainham **9 D10** 51 22N 0 36 E
Rame Hd. **11 G5** 50 19N 4 14W
Ramsbottom **7 E4** 53 36N 2 20W
Ramsey, *Cambs.* **9 B8** 52 27N 0 6W
Ramsey, *I. of M.* **13 C13** 54 20N 4 21W
Ramsgate **9 D11** 51 20N 1 25 E
Randalstown **13 B9** 54 45N 6 20W
Rannoch **4 A7** 56 40N 4 20W
Rannoch, L. **4 A7** 56 41N 4 20W
Rannoch Moor **4 A6** 56 38N 4 48W
Rath Luirc **14 D5** 52 21N 8 40W
Rathdrum **15 C10** 52 57N 6 13W
Rathkeale **14 C5** 52 32N 8 57W
Rathlin I. **13 A9** 55 18N 6 14W
Rathmelton **12 A6** 55 3N 7 35W
Rattray **5 A9** 56 36N 3 20W
Rattray Hd. **3 G14** 57 38N 1 50W
Raunds **9 B7** 52 20N 0 32W
Ravenshead **7 F6** 53 5N 1 10W
Rawmarsh **7 F6** 53 27N 1 20W
Rawtenstall **7 E4** 53 42N 2 18W
Rayleigh **9 C10** 51 36N 0 38 E
Reading **9 D7** 51 27N 0 57W
Red B. **13 A9** 55 4N 6 2W
Red Wharf B. **10 A5** 53 18N 4 10W
Redbridge **9 C9** 51 35N 0 7 E
Redcar **6 C6** 54 37N 1 4W
Redditch **8 B5** 52 18N 1 57W
Redhill **9 D8** 51 14N 0 10W
Redruth **11 G3** 50 14N 5 14W
Ree, L. **12 D6** 53 35N 8 0W
Reigate **9 D8** 51 14N 0 11W
Renfrew **4 C7** 55 52N 4 24W
Renish Pt. **2 G4** 57 44N 6 59W
Retford **7 F7** 53 19N 0 55W
Rhayader **10 C7** 52 19N 3 30W
Rhinns Pt. **4 C3** 55 40N 6 29W
Rhois-Bheinn **2 J6** 56 50N 5 40W
Rhondda **10 D6** 51 39N 3 30W
Rhosllanerchrugog **10 A7** 53 3N 3 4W
Rhossili B. **11 D5** 51 33N 4 15W
Rhum **2 J5** 57 0N 6 20W
Rhum, Sd. of **2 J5** 56 54N 6 14W
Rhyl **10 A7** 53 19N 3 29W
Rhymney **10 D7** 51 45N 3 17W
Ribble → **6 E3** 53 46N 2 42W
Richmond **6 D5** 54 24N 1 43W
Richmond-upon-Thames **9 D8** 51 28N 0 18W
Rickmansworth **9 C8** 51 38N 0 28W
Ringwood **8 E5** 50 50N 1 48W
Ripley **7 F6** 53 3N 1 24W
Ripon **6 D5** 54 8N 1 31W
Risca **11 D7** 51 36N 3 6W
Rishton **7 E4** 53 46N 2 26W
Roag, L. **2 F4** 58 10N 6 55W
Roaringwater B. **14 F3** 51 30N 9 30W
Robin Hood's Bay **6 D7** 54 26N 0 31W
Rochdale **7 E4** 53 36N 2 10W
Rochester **9 D10** 51 22N 0 30 E
Rochford **9 C10** 51 36N 0 42 E
Rockingham Forest **9 B7** 52 28N 0 42W
Roe → **13 A8** 55 10N 6 59W
Rogans Seat **6 D4** 54 25N 2 10W
Romney Marsh **9 D10** 51 4N 0 58 E
Romsey **8 E6** 51 0N 1 29W
Ronas Hill **2 A15** 60 33N 1 25W
Rora Hd. **3 E11** 58 51N 3 21W
Roscommon **12 D5** 53 38N 8 11W
Roscommon □ **12 D5** 53 40N 8 15W
Roscrea **14 C7** 52 58N 7 50W
Rose Ness **3 E12** 58 52N 2 50W
Ross-on-Wye **8 C3** 51 55N 2 34W
Rossall Pt. **7 E2** 53 55N 3 2W
Rossan Pt. **12 B4** 54 42N 8 47W
Rosscarbery B. **14 E5** 51 32N 9 0W
Rosses B. **12 A5** 55 2N 8 30W
Rosslare **15 D10** 52 17N 6 23W
Rosyth **5 B9** 56 2N 3 26W
Rotherham **7 F6** 53 26N 1 21W
Rothes **3 G11** 57 31N 3 12W
Rothesay **4 C5** 55 50N 5 3W
Rothwell, *Northants.* **9 B7** 52 25N 0 48W
Rothwell, *W. Yorks.* **7 E6** 53 46N 1 29W
Rottingdean **9 E8** 50 48N 0 3W
Rough Pt. **14 D2** 52 19N 10 2W
Royal Leamington Spa **8 B5** 52 18N 1 32W
Royal Tunbridge Wells **9 D9** 51 7N 0 16 E
Royston, *Herts.* **9 B8** 52 3N 0 1W
Royston, *S. Yorks.* **7 E6** 53 36N 1 27W
Royton **7 E4** 53 34N 2 7W
Rubh a' Mhail **4 C3** 55 55N 6 10W
Rubha Ardvule **2 H3** 57 17N 7 29W
Rubha Coigeach **2 F7** 58 6N 5 27W
Rubha Hunish **2 G5** 57 42N 6 20W
Rubha Robhanais = Lewis, Butt of **2 E5** 58 30N 6 12W
Rubh'an Dunain **2 H5** 57 10N 6 20W
Rugby **8 B6** 52 23N 1 16W
Rugeley **7 G5** 52 47N 1 56W
Runabay Hd. **13 A9** 55 10N 6 2W
Runcorn **7 F3** 53 20N 2 44W
Rush **13 D9** 53 31N 6 7W
Rushden **9 B7** 52 17N 0 37W
Rutherglen **4 C7** 55 50N 4 11W
Ruthin **10 A7** 53 7N 3 20W
Rutland Water **7 G7** 52 38N 0 38W
Ryan, L. **4 E5** 55 0N 5 2W
Ryde **8 E6** 50 44N 1 9W
Rye **9 E10** 50 57N 0 46 E

S

Sacquoy Hd. **3 D11** 59 12N 3 5W
Saddle Hd. **12 C1** 54 1N 10 10W
Saffron Walden **9 B9** 52 2N 0 15 E
St. Abb's Hd. **5 C11** 55 55N 2 10W
St. Agnes Hd. **11 G3** 50 19N 5 14W
St. Albans **9 C8** 51 44N 0 19W
St. Alban's Hd. **8 E4** 50 34N 2 3W
St. Andrews **5 B10** 56 20N 2 48W
St. Ann's Hd. **10 D3** 51 41N 5 11W
St. Asaph **10 A7** 53 15N 3 27W
St. Austell **11 G4** 50 20N 4 48W
St. Bee's Hd. **6 C1** 54 30N 3 38W
St. Brides B. **10 D3** 51 48N 5 15W
St. Catherine's Hill **8 E6** 50 36N 1 18W
St. Catherine's Pt. **8 E6** 50 34N 1 18W
St. David's **10 D3** 51 54N 5 16W
St. David's Hd. **10 D3** 51 55N 5 16W
St. Finan's B. **14 E2** 51 50N 10 22W
St. George's Channel **15 D11** 52 0N 6 0W
St. Govan's Hd. **11 D4** 51 35N 4 56W
St. Helens **7 F3** 53 28N 2 44W
St. Helier **11 J9** 49 11N 2 6W
St. Ives, *Cambs.* **9 B8** 52 20N 0 5W
St. Ives, *Corn.* **11 G3** 50 13N 5 29W
St. Ives B. **11 G3** 50 15N 5 27W
St. John's Pt., *Ireland* **12 B5** 54 35N 8 26W
St. John's Pt., *Down* **13 C10** 54 14N 5 40W
St. Just **11 G2** 50 7N 5 41W
St. Leonards **9 E10** 50 51N 0 33 E
St. Magnus B. **2 B14** 60 25N 1 35W
St. Mary's Sd. **11 H1** 49 53N 6 19W
St. Mawes **11 G3** 50 10N 5 1W
St. Michael's Mount **11 G3** 50 7N 5 30W
St. Monance **5 B10** 56 13N 2 46W
St. Neots **9 B8** 52 14N 0 16W
St. Ouens B. **11 J9** 49 13N 2 14W
St. Peter Port **11 J8** 49 27N 2 31W
Saintfield **13 C10** 54 28N 5 50W
Salcombe **11 G6** 50 14N 3 47W
Sale **7 F4** 53 26N 2 19W
Salford **7 F4** 53 30N 2 17W
Salisbury **8 D5** 51 4N 1 48W
Salisbury Plain **8 D5** 51 13N 1 50W
Saltash **11 G5** 50 25N 4 13W
Saltburn by the Sea **6 C7** 54 35N 0 58W
Saltcoats **4 C6** 55 38N 4 47W
Sanday Sd. **3 D12** 59 11N 2 31W
Sandbach **7 F4** 53 9N 2 23W
Sandgate **9 D11** 51 5N 1 9 E
Sandness **2 B14** 60 18N 1 38W
Sandown **8 E6** 50 39N 1 9W
Sandringham **9 A10** 52 50N 0 30 E
Sandwich **9 D11** 51 16N 1 21 E
Sandy **9 B8** 52 8N 0 18W
Sanquhar **5 D8** 55 21N 3 56W
Sawbridgeworth **9 C9** 51 49N 0 10 E
Sawel **13 B7** 54 48N 7 5W
Saxmundham **9 B12** 52 13N 1 31 E
Scafell Pike **6 D2** 54 26N 3 14W
Scalby **6 D8** 54 18N 0 26W
Scalloway **2 B15** 60 9N 1 16W
Scalpay **2 H6** 57 18N 6 0W
Scapa Flow **3 E11** 58 52N 3 6W
Scarborough **6 D8** 54 17N 0 24W
Scavaig, L. **2 H5** 57 8N 6 10W
Schiehallion **4 A7** 56 40N 4 6W
Scilly, Isles of **11 H1** 49 55N 6 15W
Score Hd. **2 B15** 60 12N 1 5W
Scotch Corner **6 D5** 54 27N 1 40W
Scridain, L. **4 B3** 56 23N 6 7W
Scunthorpe **7 E7** 53 35N 0 38W
Seaford **9 E9** 50 46N 0 8 E
Seaforth, L. **2 G4** 57 52N 6 36W
Seaham **6 C6** 54 51N 1 20W
Seahouses **6 A5** 55 35N 1 39W
Seascale **6 D2** 54 24N 3 29W
Seaton **11 F7** 50 42N 3 3W
Sedbergh **6 D3** 54 20N 2 31W
Selby **7 E6** 53 47N 1 5W
Selkirk **5 C10** 55 33N 2 50W
Selsey **9 E7** 50 44N 0 47W
Selsey Bill **9 E7** 50 44N 0 47W
Settle **6 D4** 54 5N 2 18W
Seven Heads **14 E5** 51 35N 8 43W
Sevenoaks **9 D9** 51 16N 0 11 E
Severn → **8 C3** 51 35N 2 38W
Sgurr a' Choire Ghlais **3 H8** 57 30N 4 56W
Sgurr Mor **3 G7** 57 42N 5 0W
Sgurr na Ciche **2 H7** 57 0N 5 29W
Sgurr na Lapaich **2 H7** 57 23N 5 5W
Shaftesbury **8 E4** 51 0N 2 12W
Shanklin **8 E6** 50 39N 1 9W
Shannon → **14 C3** 52 35N 9 38W
Shannon Airport **14 C5** 52 42N 8 57W
Shapinsay Sd. **3 D12** 59 0N 2 51W
Sheelin, L. **12 D7** 53 48N 7 20W
Sheep Haven **12 A6** 55 12N 7 55W
Sheeps Hd. **14 E3** 51 32N 9 50W
Sheerness **9 D10** 51 26N 0 47 E
Sheffield **7 F6** 53 23N 1 28W
Shehy Mts. **14 E4** 51 47N 9 15W
Shell, L. **2 F5** 58 0N 6 28W
Shenfield **9 C9** 51 39N 0 21 E
Sheppey, I. of **9 D10** 51 23N 0 50 E
Shepshed **7 G6** 52 47N 1 18W
Shepton Mallet **8 D3** 51 11N 2 31W
Sherborne **8 E3** 50 56N 2 31W
Sheringham **9 A11** 52 56N 1 11 E
Sherwood Forest **7 F6** 53 5N 1 5W
Shetland □ **2 B15** 60 30N 1 30W
Shiant, Sd. of **2 G5** 57 54N 6 30W
Shiel, L. **2 J6** 56 48N 5 32W
Shildon **6 C5** 54 37N 1 39W
Shillelagh **15 C9** 52 46N 6 32W
Shin → **3 G9** 57 58N 4 26W
Shin, L. **3 F8** 58 7N 4 30W
Shining Tor **7 F4** 53 15N 2 0W
Shipley **7 E5** 53 50N 1 47W
Shipston-on-Stour **8 B5** 52 4N 1 38W
Shirebrook **7 F6** 53 13N 1 11W
Shoeburyness **9 C10** 51 31N 0 49 E
Shoreham by Sea **9 E8** 50 50N 0 17W
Shotts **5 C8** 55 49N 3 47W
Shrewsbury **7 G3** 52 42N 2 45W
Shropshire □ **7 G3** 52 36N 2 45W
Sidlaw Hills **5 A9** 56 32N 3 10W
Sidmouth **11 F7** 50 40N 3 13W
Sighty Crag **6 B3** 55 8N 2 37W
Silloth **5 E9** 54 53N 3 25W
Silsden **7 E5** 53 55N 1 55W
Silvermine Mts. **14 C6** 52 47N 8 15W
Simonside **6 B5** 55 17N 1 58W
Sinclair's B. **3 E11** 58 30N 3 0W
Sion Mills **12 B7** 54 47N 7 29W
Sittingbourne **9 D10** 51 20N 0 43 E
Sixmilebridge **14 C5** 52 45N 8 46W
Sizewell **9 B12** 52 13N 1 38 E
Skaw Taing **2 B16** 60 23N 0 57W
Skegness **7 F9** 53 9N 0 20 E
Skelmersdale **7 E3** 53 34N 2 49W
Skelmorlie **4 C6** 55 52N 4 53W
Skelton **6 C7** 54 33N 0 59W
Skibbereen **14 E4** 51 33N 9 16W
Skiddaw **6 C2** 54 39N 3 9W
Skipton **7 E4** 53 57N 2 1W
Skokholm I. **10 D3** 51 42N 5 16W
Skomer I. **10 D3** 51 44N 5 19W
Skull **14 E3** 51 32N 9 40W
Skye **2 H5** 57 15N 6 10W
Slaney → **15 D10** 52 20N 6 30W
Slea Hd. **14 D2** 52 7N 10 30W
Sleaford **7 F8** 53 1N 0 22W
Sleat, Pt. of **2 H5** 57 1N 6 0W
Sleat, Sd. of **2 H6** 57 5N 5 47W
Slieve Anierin **12 C6** 54 5N 7 58W
Slieve Aughty **14 B5** 53 4N 8 30W
Slieve Beagh **13 C7** 54 20N 7 12W

Slieve Bernagh   **Youghal**

WORLD MAPS

EUROPE 4-15, ASIA 16-25, AFRICA 26-33, AUSTRALIA AND OCEANIA 34-37,
NORTH AMERICA 38-45, SOUTH AMERICA 46-47

───── SETTLEMENTS ─────

◷ PARIS ■ Berne ◉ Livorno ◉ Brugge ◎ Algeciras ○ Frejus ○ Oberammergau ○ Thira

Settlement symbols and type styles vary according to the scale of each map and indicate the importance
of towns on the map rather than specific population figures

∴ Ruins or Archæological Sites ⌣ Wells in Desert

───── ADMINISTRATION ─────

──────── International Boundaries

─ ─ ─ International Boundaries
(Undefined or Disputed)

············ Internal Boundaries

National Parks

Country Names

NICARAGUA

Administrative
Area Names

K E N T

CALABRIA

International boundaries show the *de facto* situation where there are rival claims to territory

───── COMMUNICATIONS ─────

──────── Principal Roads

⌒ Other Roads

-·-·-· Trails and Seasonal Roads

≍ Passes

✿ Airfields

⌒ Principal Railways

----- Railways
Under Construction

⌒ Other Railways

⌐---⌐ Railway Tunnels

············· Principal Canals

───── PHYSICAL FEATURES ─────

⌒ Perennial Streams

------- Intermittent Streams

⌷ Perennial Lakes

⌁ Intermittent Lakes

Swamps and Marshes

Permanent Ice
and Glaciers

▲ 8848 Elevations in metres

▼ 8050 Sea Depths in metres

1134 Height of Lake Surface
Above Sea Level
in metres

───── ELEVATION AND DEPTH TINTS ─────

| Height of Land Above Sea Level | Land Below Sea Level | Depth of Sea |

in metres 6000 4000 3000 2000 1500 1000 400 200 0
in feet 18 000 12 000 9000 6000 4500 3000 1200 600

6000 12 000 15 000 18 000 24 000 in feet
0 200 2000 4000 5000 6000 8000 in metres

Some of the maps have different contours to highlight and clarify the principal relief features

1:80 000 000

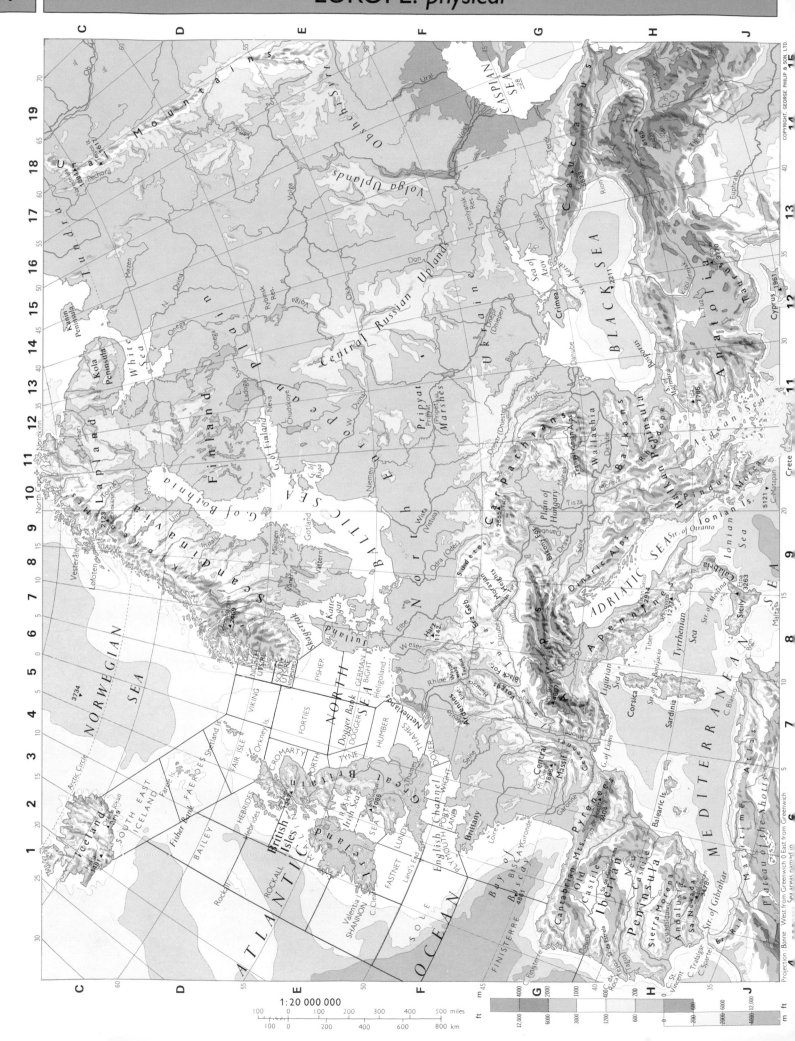

1:20 000 000

Projection: Bonne   West from Greenwich 0 East from Greenwich   Sea areas named in

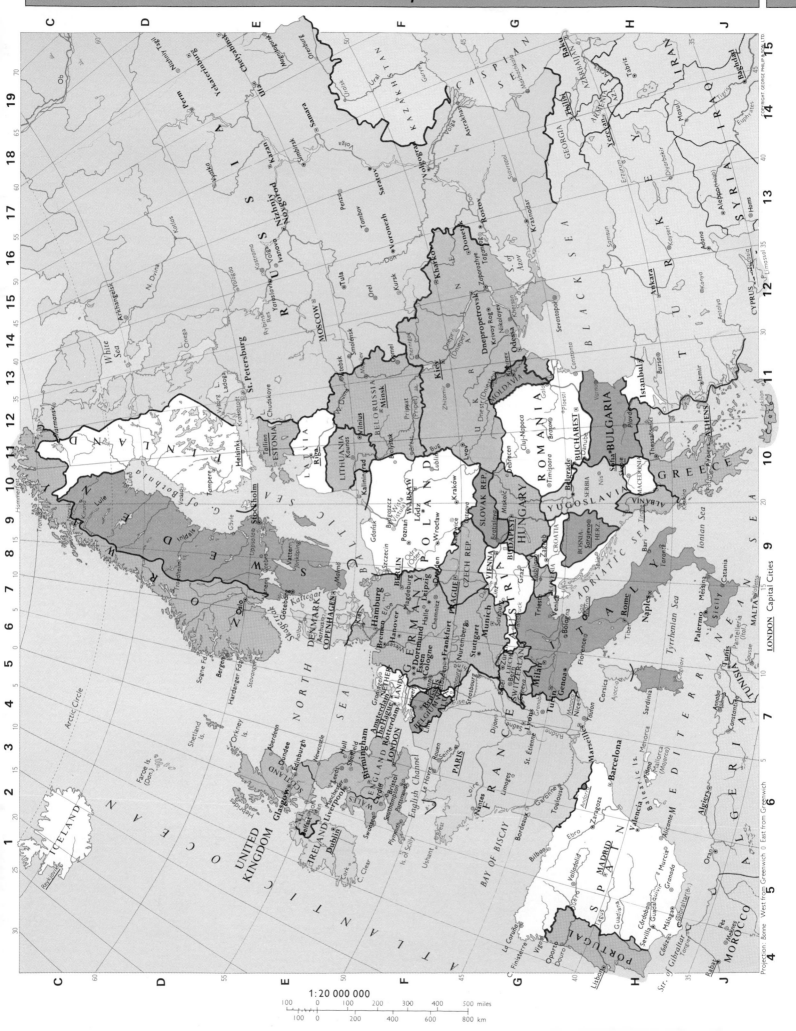

1:20 000 000

Projection: Bonne   West from Greenwich 0 East from Greenwich

ICELAND
On the same scale West from Greenwich

Projection: Conical with two standard parallels

East from Greenwich

1:10 000 000

COPYRIGHT. GEORGE PHILIP & SON. LTD.

Projection: Conical with two standard parallels

1 : 4 000 000

COPYRIGHT. GEORGE PHILIP & SON, LTD.

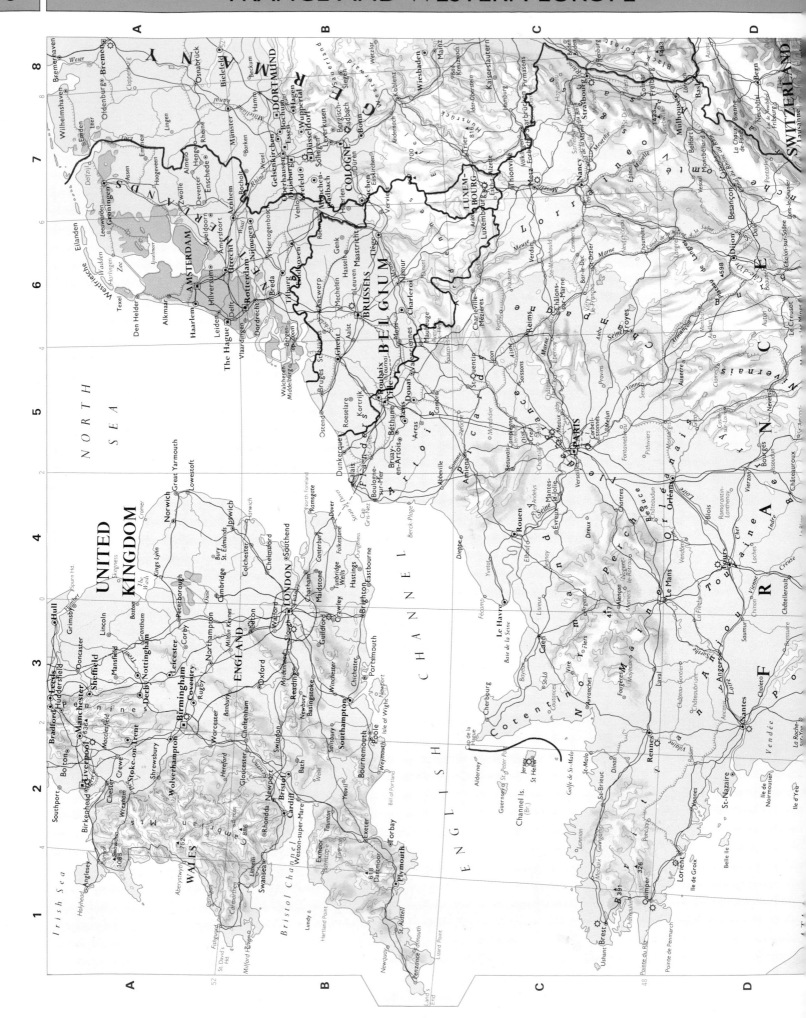

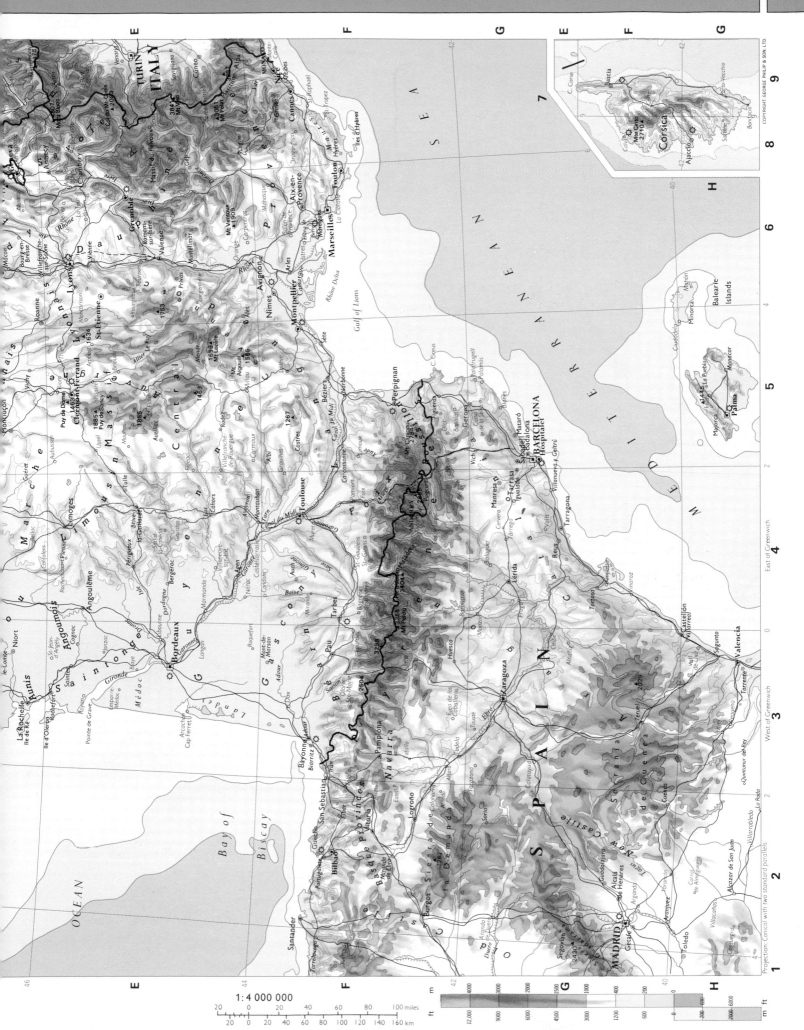

1 : 4 000 000

Projection: Conical with two standard parallels

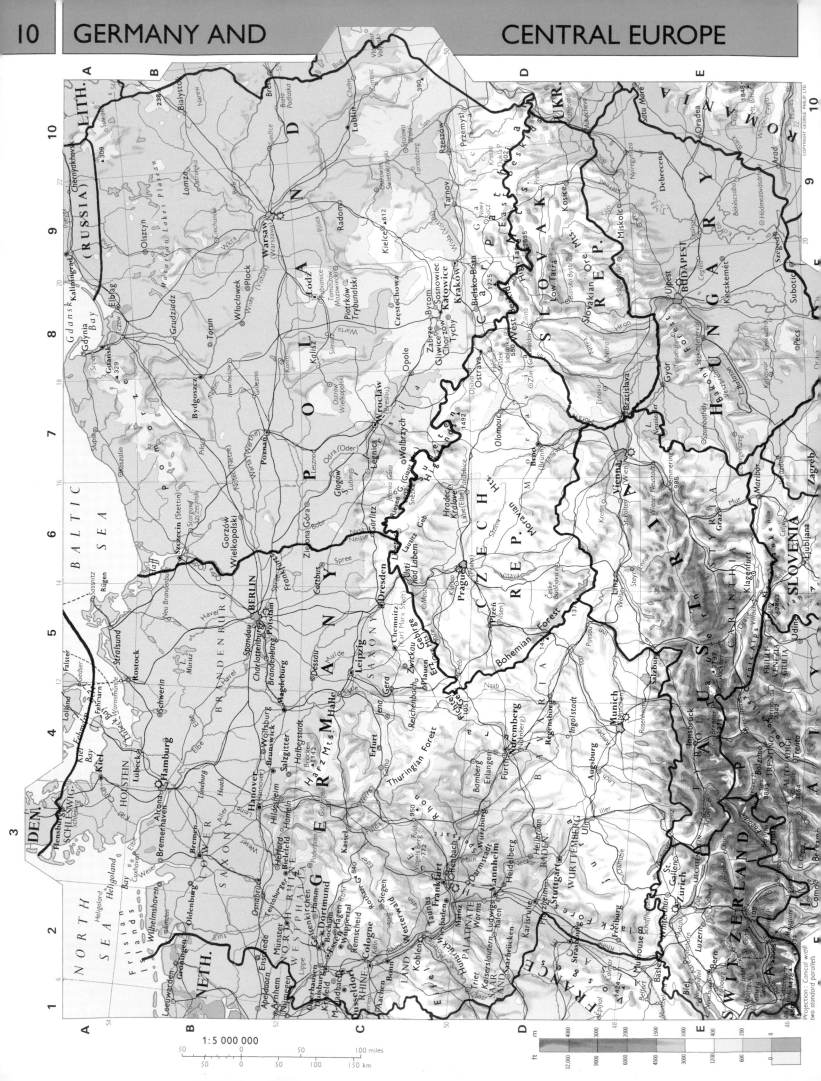

1 : 5 000 000

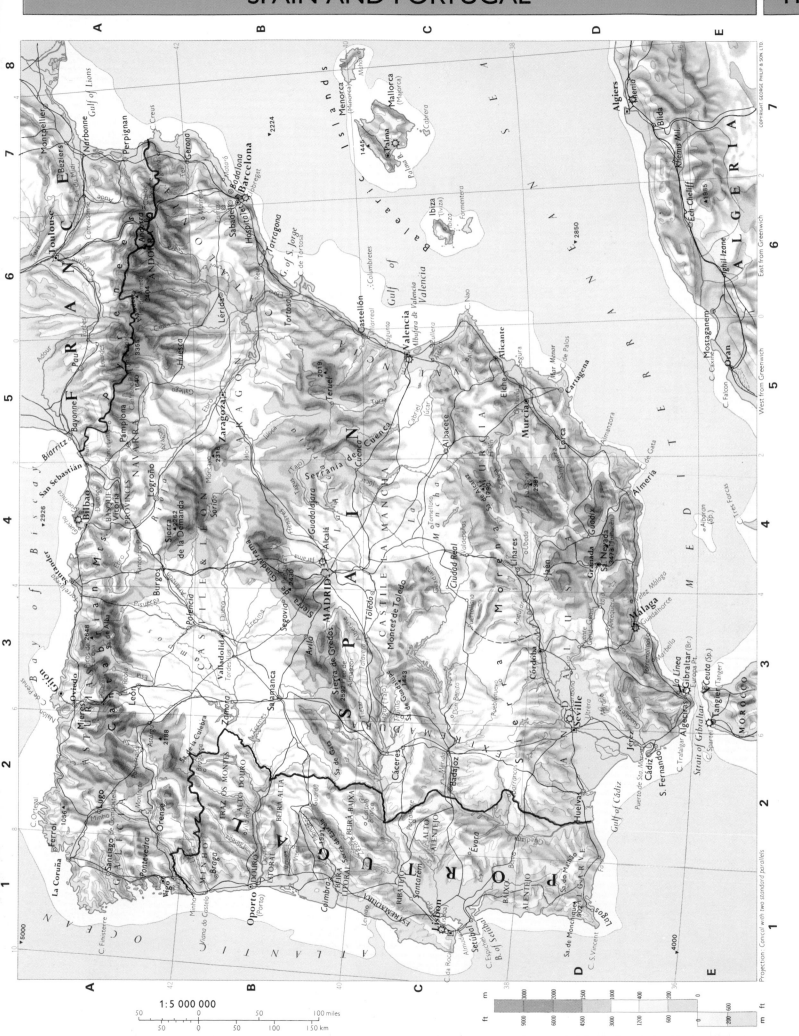

1:5 000 000

Projection: Conical with two standard parallels

1 2 3 4 5 6 7

46

SWITZERLAND

Lyons
Geneva
Annecy
Genève

St. Gotthard P.
Brenner P.

Maribor
Klagenfurt
Villach
Drava
Varaždin

Grenoble
Mt. Pelvoux 4103
Mt. Cenis P. 2183

Turin
Torino
PIEDMONT
Mt. Viso 3841

LOMBARDY
Como
Bergamo
Brescia
Novara
Vercelli
Milan (Milano)
Pavia

Bolzano
TRENTINO ALTO ADIGE
Trento
Stelvio P. 3899

FRIULI VENEZIA GIULIA
Udine
Pordenone
Belluno
Trieste

Ljubljana
SLOVENIA
Sava
Zagreb
CROATIA

FRANCE
Avignon
Montélimar
Valence
Vienne

PROVENCE
Aix
Marseilles
Toulon
Nice
Cannes
Grasse
Monaco & Monte Carlo
Imperia

DAUPHINÉ

44

Cuneo
Savona
RIVIERA
Riv. di Ponente
Riv. di Levante
Genoa (Genova)
G. of Genoa
La Spezia

Alessandria
Asti
Piacenza
Parma
Reggio
Modena
EMILIA ROMAGNA
Bologna
Mte. Cimone 2165
Ferrara
Rovigo

Vicenza
Verona
Padua (Padova)
Venice (Venezia)
Gulf of Venice
VENETO

Pula (Pola)
Rijeka
Istra
Cres
Lošinj
Krk
Karlovac
Kupa
Unac

HER...

LIGURIAN SEA
Iles d'Hyères
St. Tropez
C. Corse

Leghorn (Livorno)
Pisa
Lucca
Pistoia
Prato
Florence (Firenze)
Arno

Ravenna
Forlì
Cesena
Rimini
Rubicone
Pesaro
San Marino
MARCHES
Ancona
Macerata

Dugi Otok
Zadar
Šibenik
Split
Brač
Hvar
Korčula
Lastovo
Vis

ADRIATIC

C

42

Capraia
Portoferraio
Calvi
Bastia
CORSICA
Mte. Cinto 2710
Elba
Aleria
Ajaccio

TUSCANY
Siena
Arezzo
Grosseto
L. Trasimeno
Chiusi
Amiata 1738
L. Bolsena
Viterbo
Perugia
UMBRIA
Terni
Rieti
Ascoli Piceno
Teramo 2914
Gran Sasso
L'Aquila
Pescara
Chieti
Mt. Amaro 2795
ABRUZZI

Mte. Argentario
Fiora
Bracciano
Ostia
ROME (Roma)

Bonifacio
Str.
Capreta

D

Asinara
G. of Asinara
C. Falcone
2855
Sassari
Alghero
Coghinas
Olbia (Terranova)

Anzio
Latina
Frosinone
MOLISE
Campobasso
Mt. Gargano 1056
Foggia
G. of Manfredonia
Cerignola
Barletta
Andria
Bari
Benevento
Caserta
Avellino
CAMPANIA
APULIA

40

SARDINIA
Nuoro
Tirso
Mt. Gennargentu 1834
C. Mte. Santo
G. of Oristano
Oristano
Iglesias
Cagliari
Carbonia
G. of Cagliari
G. of Palmas
C. Carbonara
C. Spartivento

3719
Gaigliano
Volturno
Pontine Is.
Naples (Napoli)
Capri
Salerno
Sele
Potenza
BASILICATA
Matera
Taranto
G. of Taranto
Agri

TYRRHENIAN SEA

Cosenza 1929
CALABRIA

E

38

M E D I T E R...

Ustica
Stromboli
Lipari Is.
Salina
Lipari
Vulcano

Catanzaro
C. Rizzuto
Palermo
Trapani
Erice
Egadi Is.
Termini
C. Peloro
Milazzo
Messina
Str. of Messina
Reggio
C. Spartivento

F

Skikda
Annaba
Bizerte
Galite Is.
SICILY
Marsala
Castelvetrano
Sciacca
Caltanissetta
Enna
Etna 3340
Nebrodi Mts.
Paternò
Catánia
Giarre
Lentini

Béja
Constantine
ALGERIA
TUNISIA
Tunis
G. de Tunis
C. Bon
Nabeul
Agrigento
Favara
Licata
Platani
Gela
Ragusa
Vittória
Siracusa (Syracuse)
Augusta
Pozzallo
C. Passero

G

Khenchela
Tebessa
Kairouan
Sousse
G. de Hammamet
Pantelleria (Ital.)
1730
Lampedusa (Ital.)
Gozo
Mdina
Valletta
MALTA

ft m
12,000 4000
9000 3000
6000 2000
4500 1500
3000 1000
1200 400
600 200
0 0
200 600
m ft

1 2 3 4 5 6 7

1:10 000 000

50   0   50   100   150   200   250 miles

50   0   50   100   150   200   250   300   350   400 km

Projection: Conical with two standard parallels

Division between Greeks and Turks
in Cyprus, Turks to the North

East from Greenwich

COPYRIGHT. GEORGE PHILIP & SON, LTD.

1 Kabardino-Balkar Rep.
2 North Ossetian Rep.
3 Nakhichevan Rep. (Azer.)
4 Checheno-Ingush Rep.
Karagiye Depression

1:50 000 000

Projection: Bonne

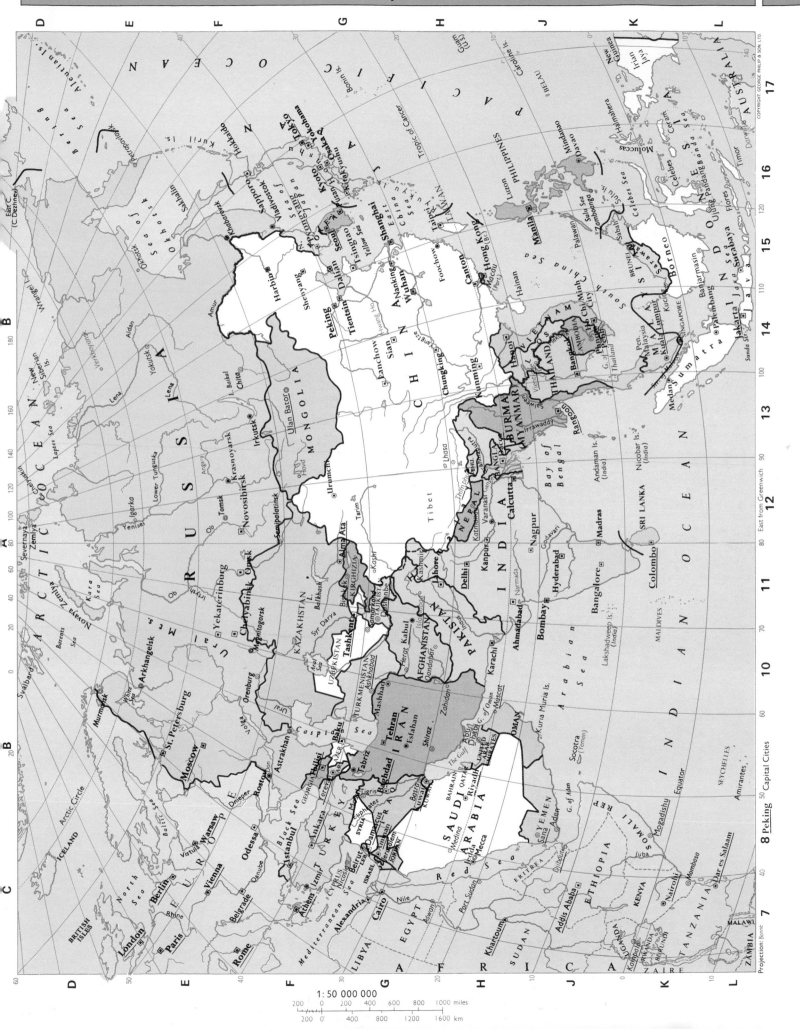

1:50 000 000

| 200 | 0 | 200 | 400 | 600 | 800 | 1000 miles |

| 200 | 0 | 400 | 800 | 1200 | 1600 km |

Projection: Bonne

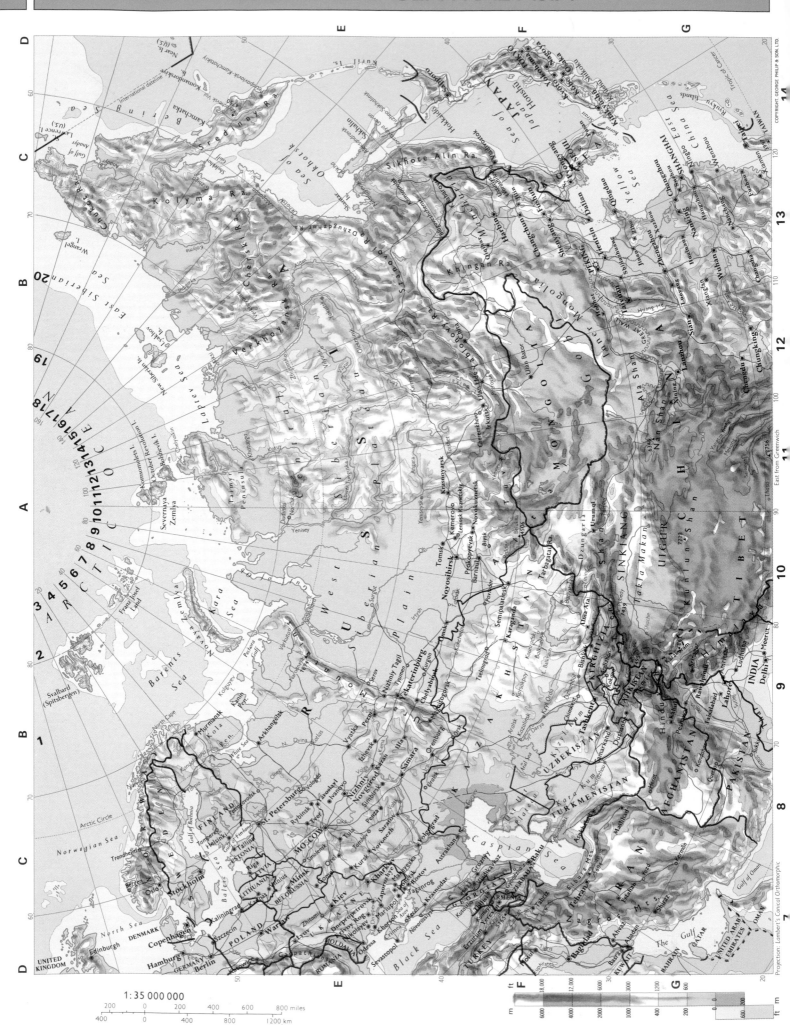

1:35 000 000

Projection: Lambert's Conical Orthomorphic

SOUTHERN HONSHU,
KYUSHU AND SHIKOKU

JAPAN

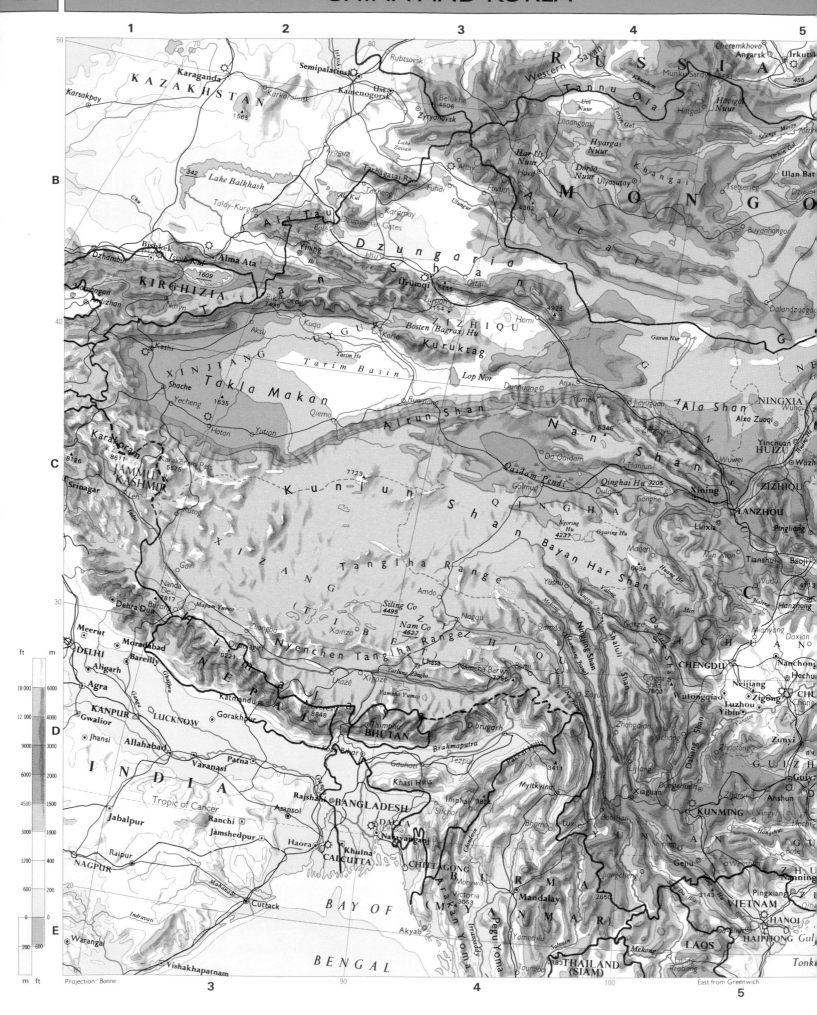

SEA OF JAPAN

YELLOW SEA

EAST CHINA SEA

SOUTH CHINA SEA

PACIFIC OCEAN

Ryukyu Islands

Sakhalin

Hokkaido

SAPPORO

TAIWAN

HONG KONG (Br.)

Macau (Port.)

CANTON (Guangzhou)

1:15 000 000

100   0   100   200   300   400 miles
100 0 100 200 300 400 500 600 km

Tropic of Cancer

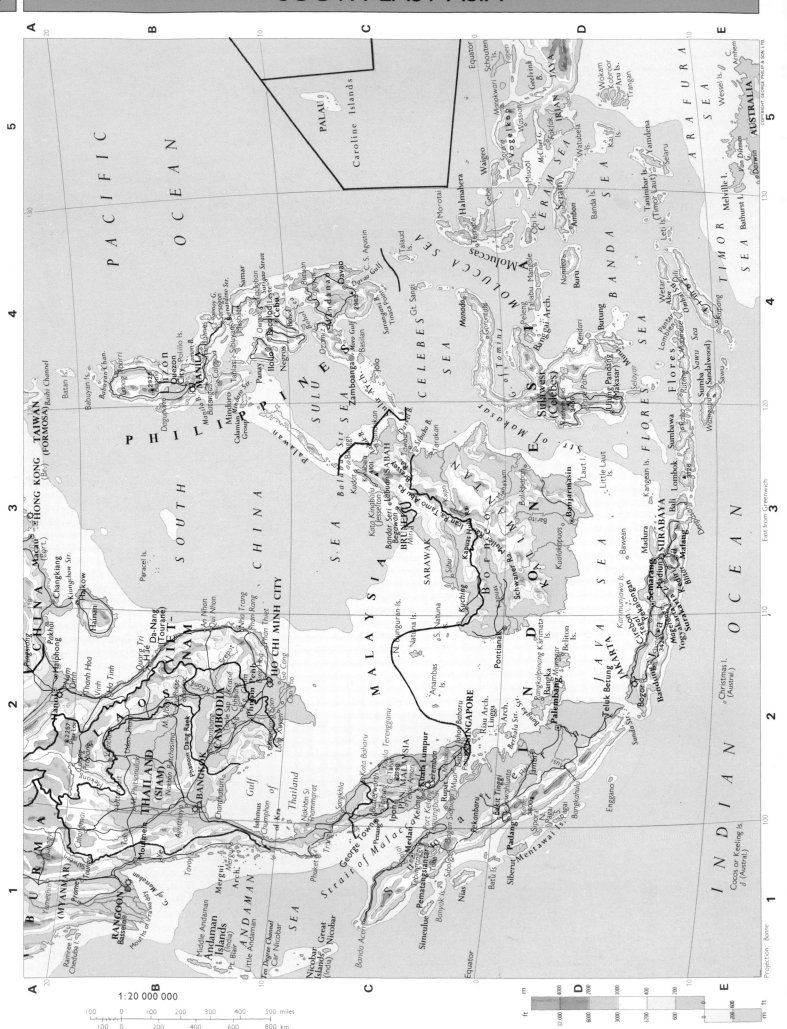

1:20 000 000

100   0   100   200   300   400   500 miles

100   0   200   400   600   800 km

Projection: Bonne

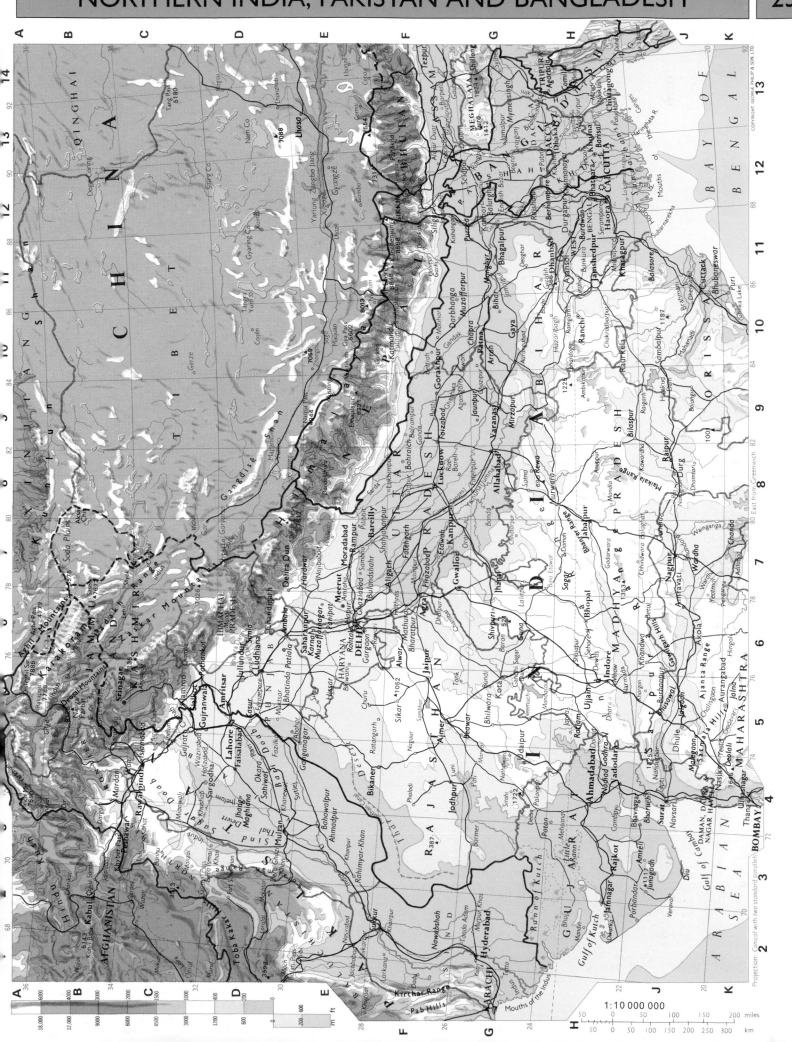

1:10 000 000

Projection: Conical with two standard parallels

Projection : Alber's Equal Area with two standard parallels

East from Greenwich

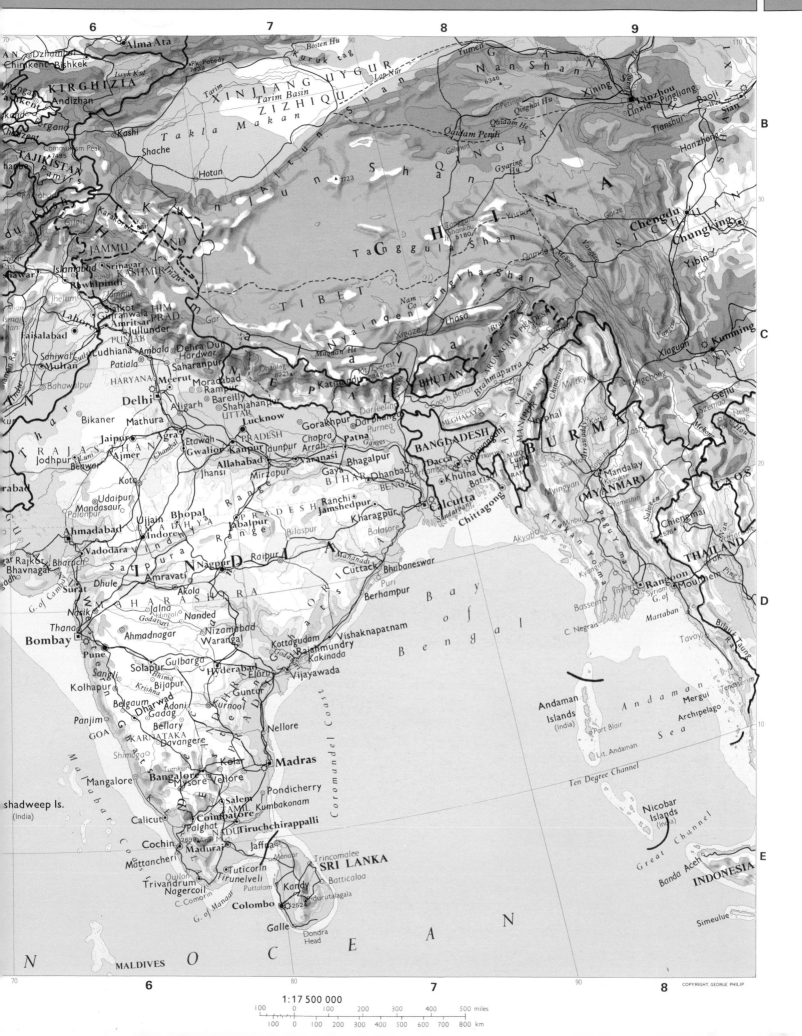

1:17 500 000

COPYRIGHT. GEORGE PHILIP

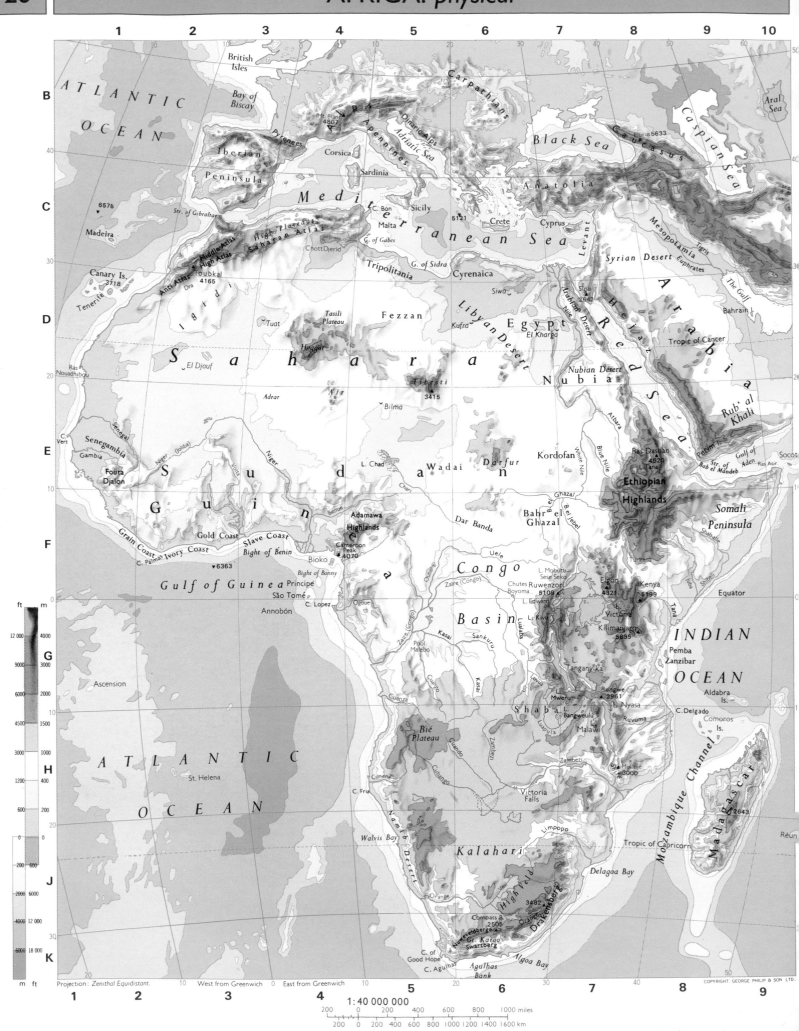

Projection: Zenithal Equidistant.

1 : 40 000 000

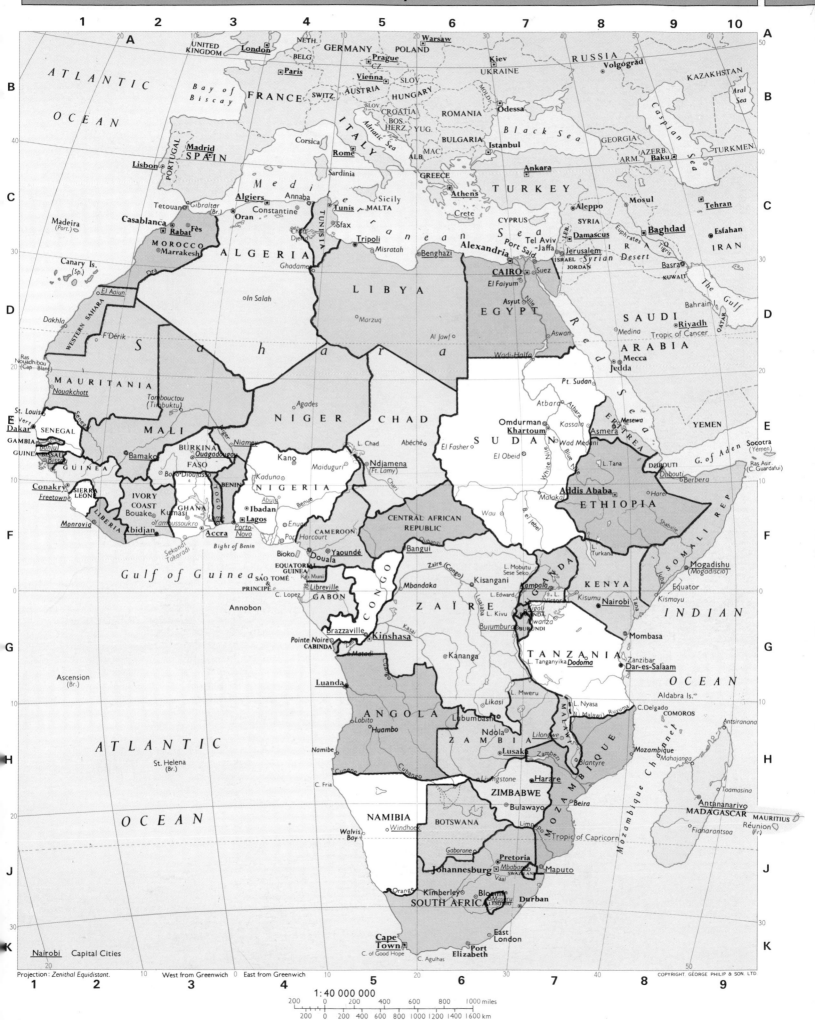

AFRICA: political

Projection: Zenithal Equidistant.   West from Greenwich | East from Greenwich   COPYRIGHT GEORGE PHILIP & SON LTD

Nairobi Capital Cities

1:40 000 000

200 0 200 400 600 800 1000 miles
200 0 200 400 600 800 1000 1200 1400 1600 km

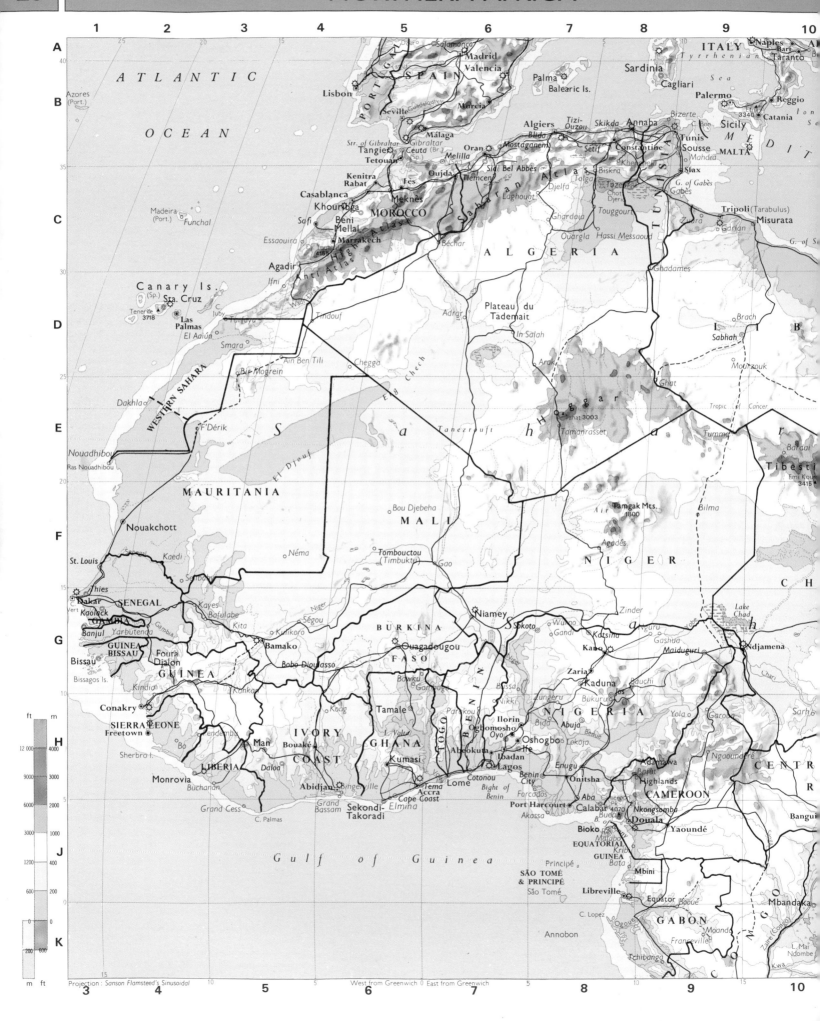

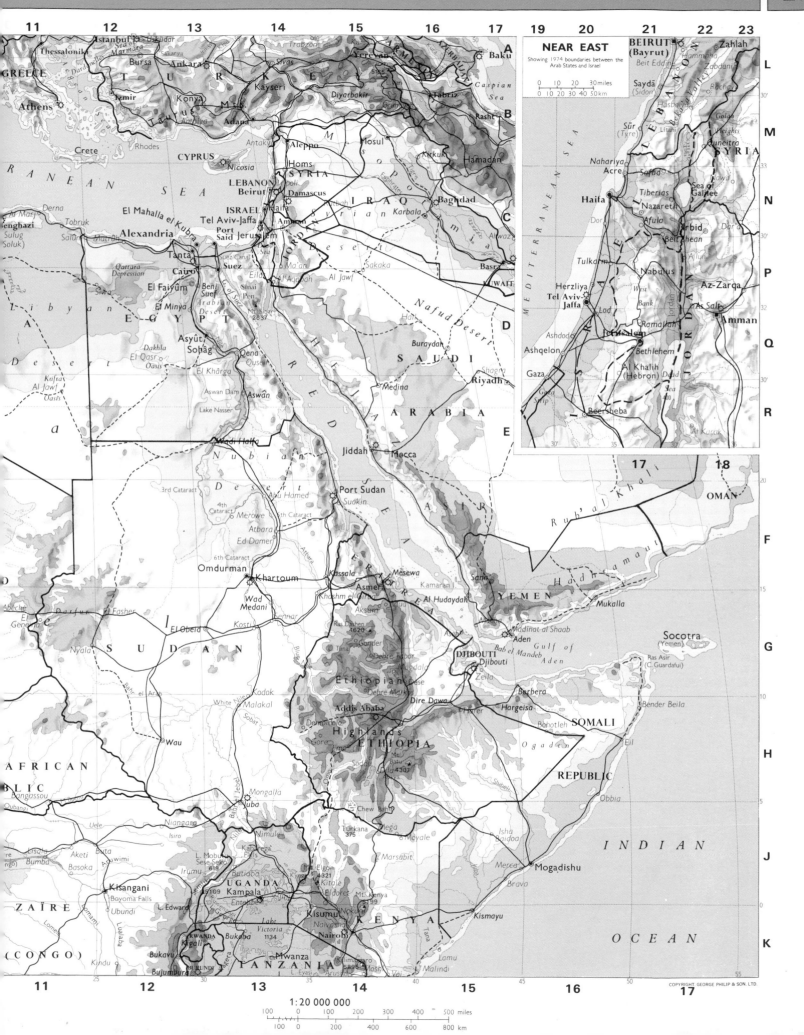

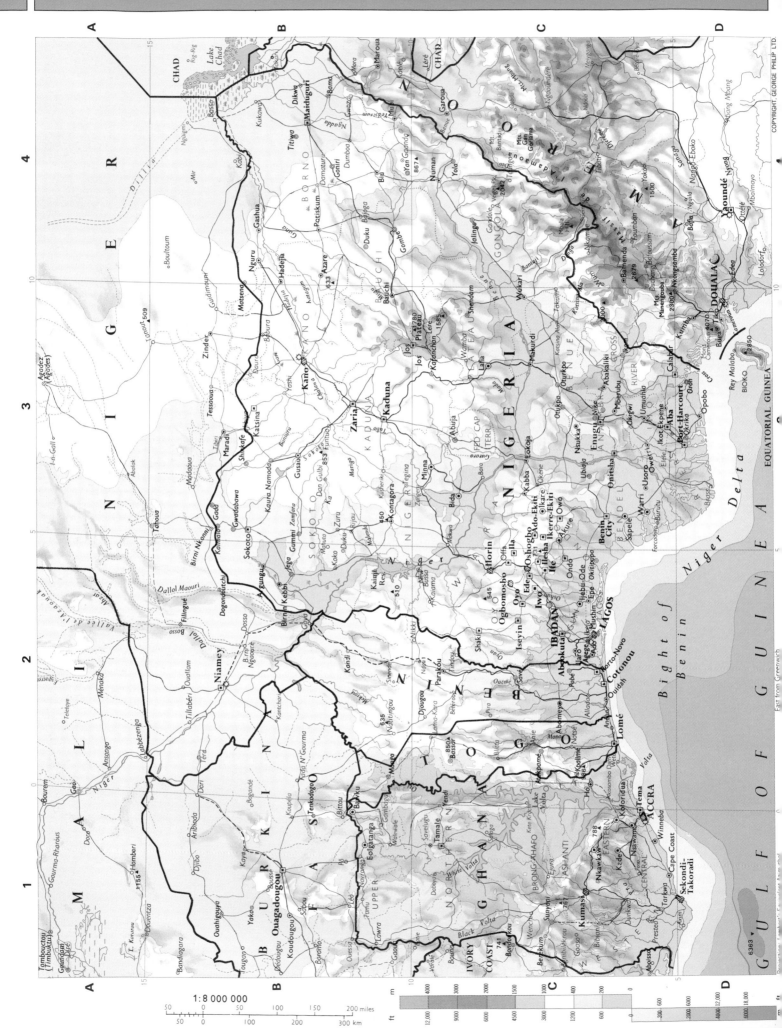

1:8 000 000

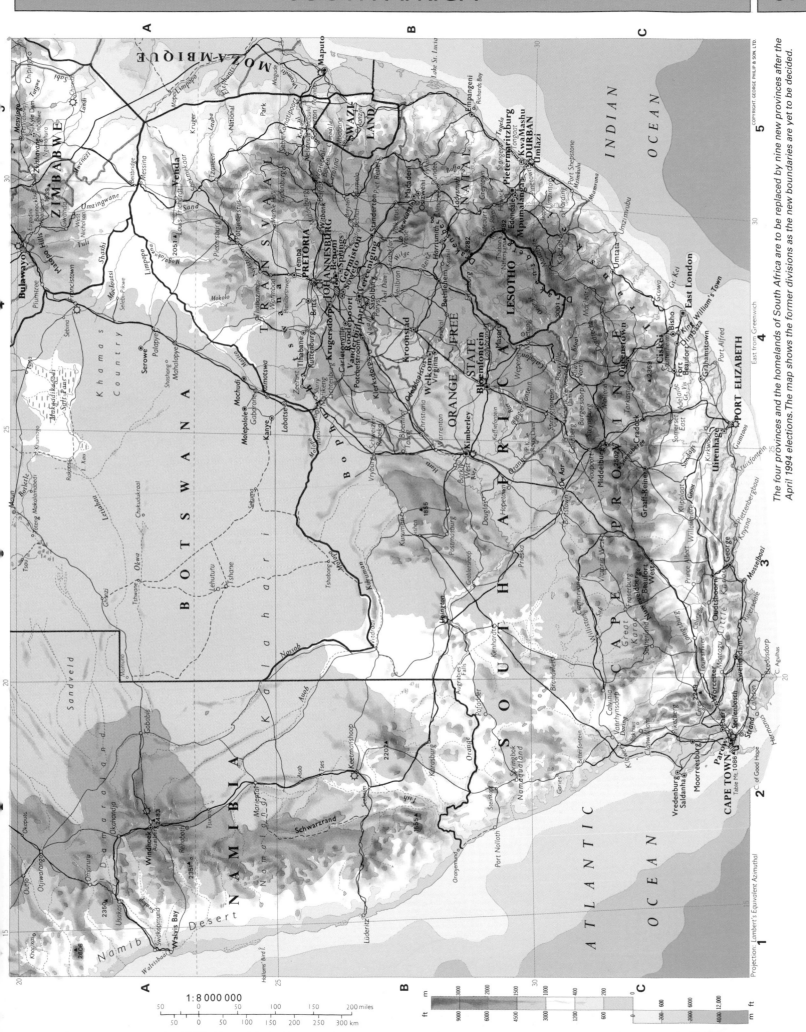

The four provinces and the homelands of South Africa are to be replaced by nine new provinces after the April 1994 elections. The map shows the former divisions as the new boundaries are yet to be decided.

1:8 000 000

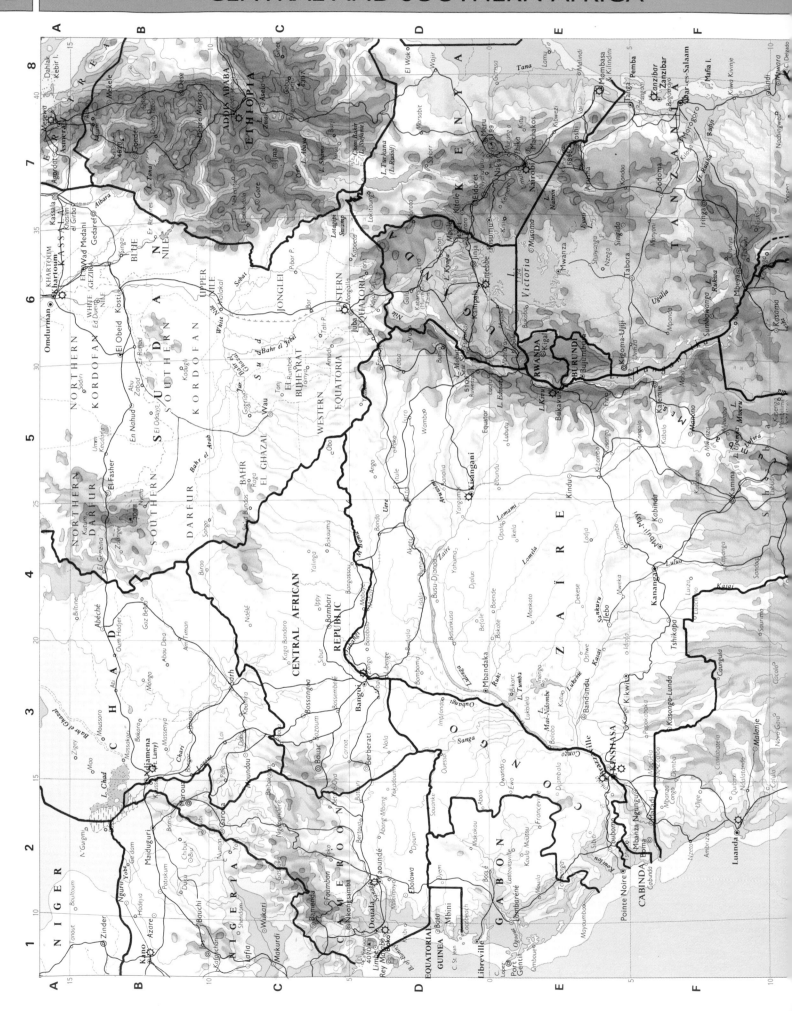

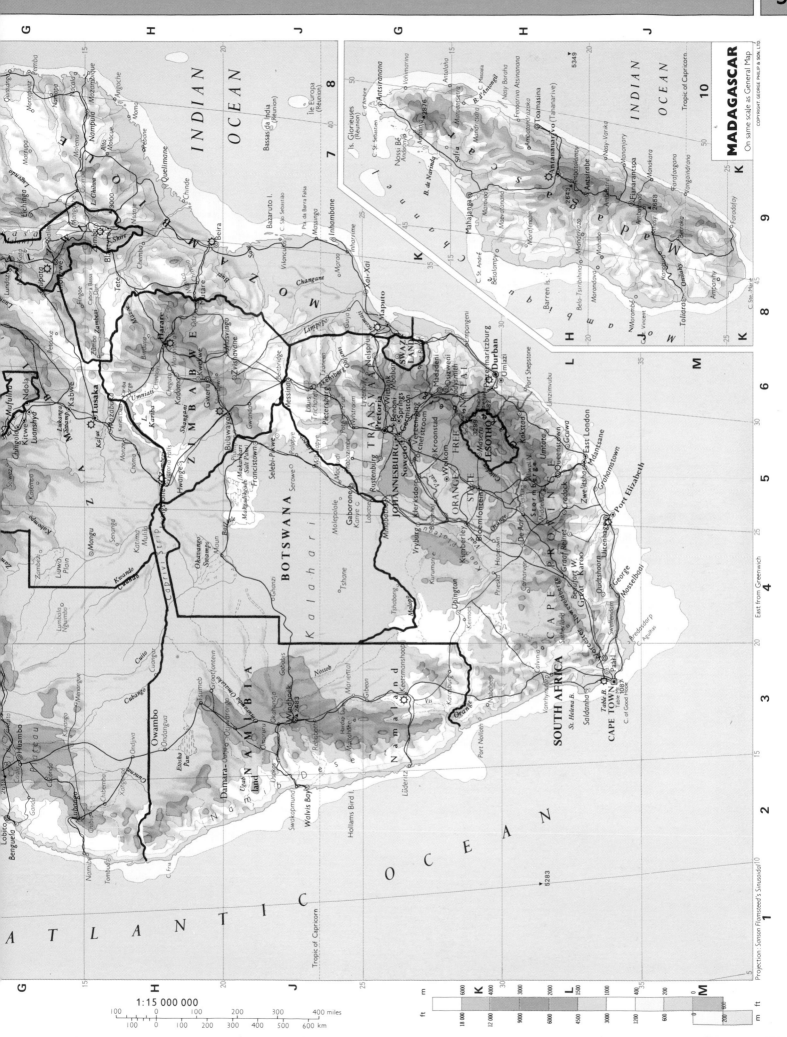

MADAGASCAR
On same scale as General Map

COPYRIGHT GEORGE PHILIP & SON, LTD.

Projection: Sanson Flamsteed's Sinusoidal

1:15 000 000

100   0   100   200   300   400 miles
100   0   100   200   300   400   500   600 km

East from Greenwich

Projection : Lambert's Equivalent Azimuthal   East from Greenwich

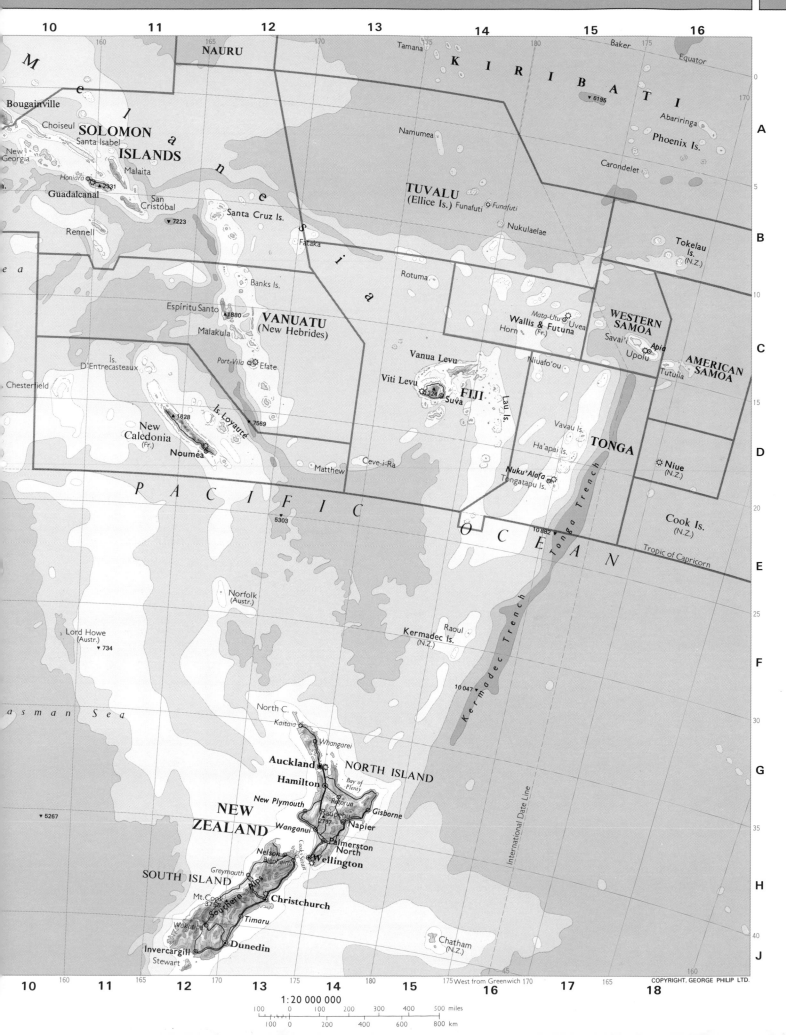

1:20 000 000

COPYRIGHT, GEORGE PHILIP LTD.

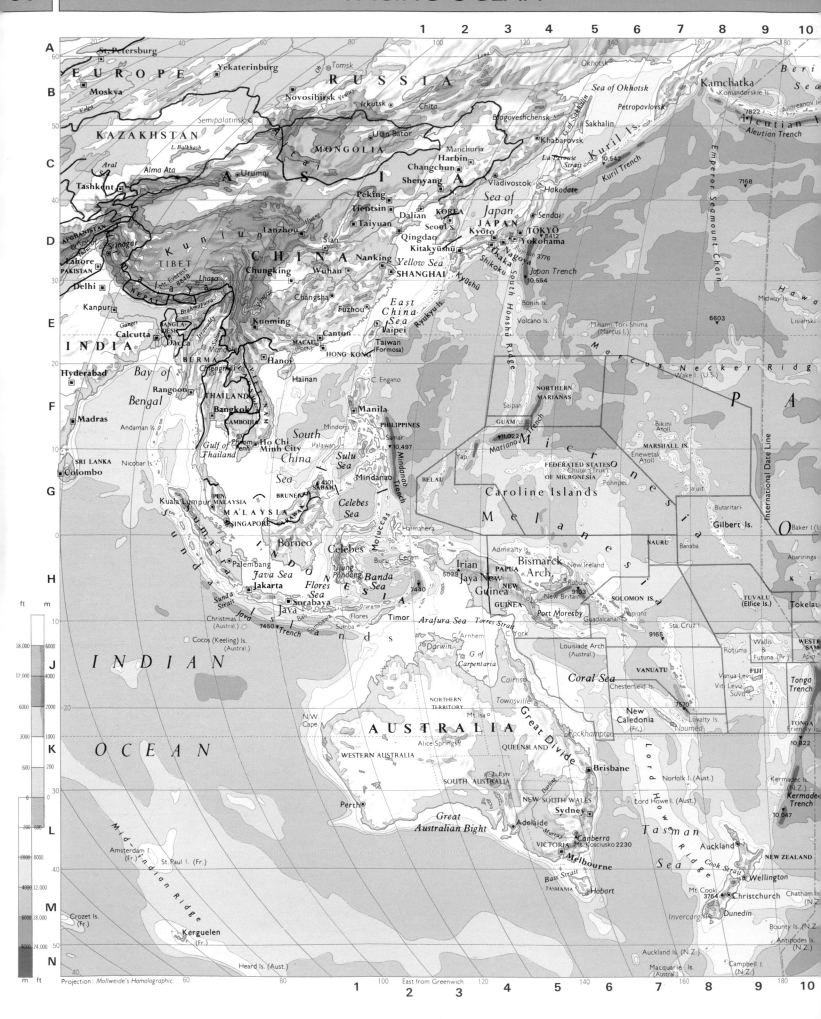

Projection: Mollweide's Homolographic
East from Greenwich

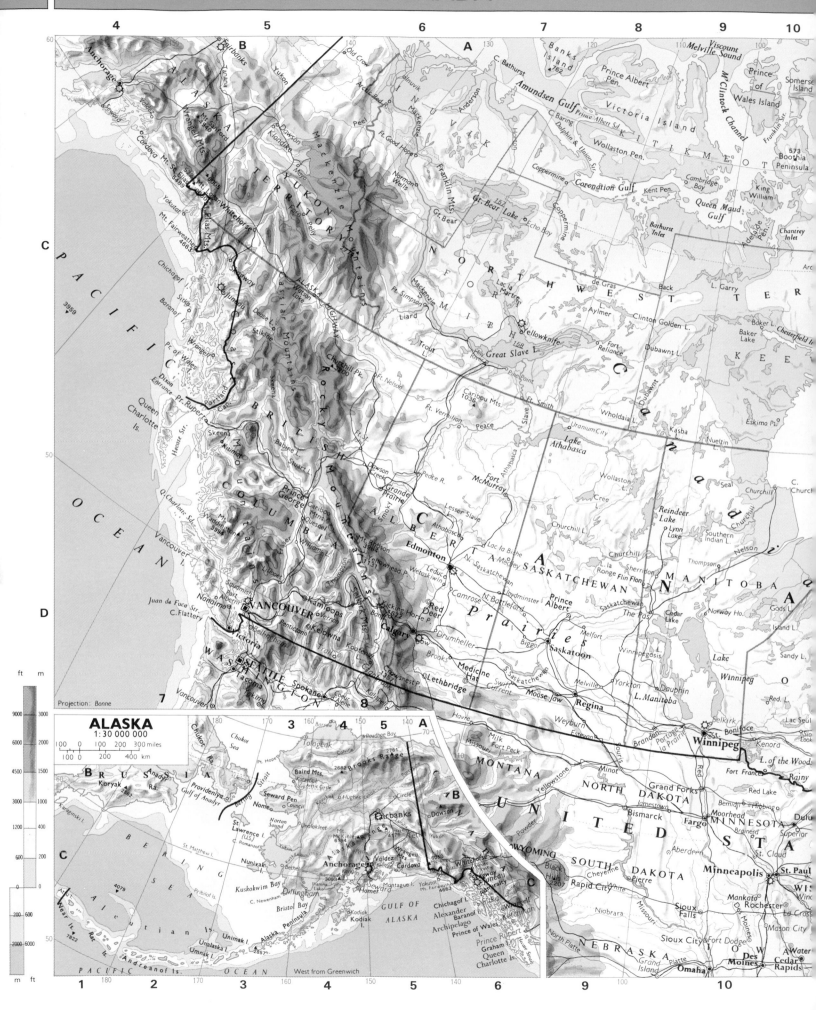

ft   m

9000   3000

6000   2000

4500   1500

3000   1000

1200   400

600   200

0   0

600   200

6000   2000

m   ft

Projection: Bonne

ALASKA
1:30 000 000

100   0   100   200   300 miles

100   0   200   400 km

PACIFIC OCEAN

West from Greenwich

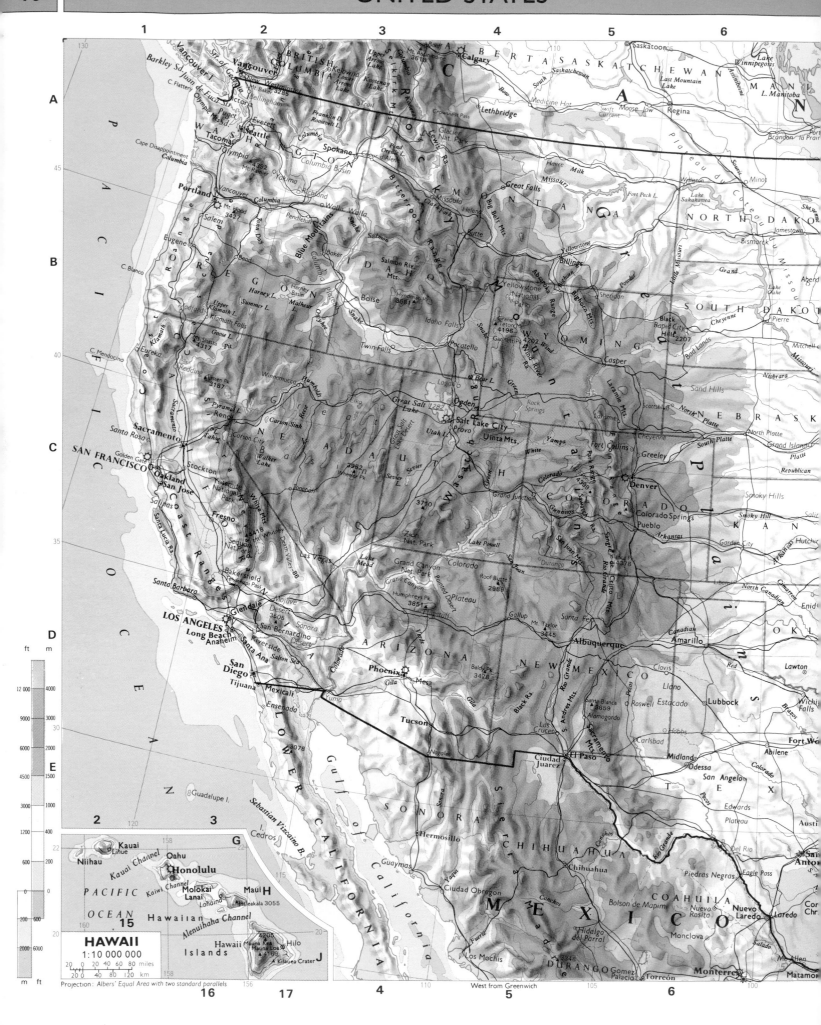

HAWAII
1:10 000 000

Projection: Albers' Equal Area with two standard parallels

1:12 000 000

50   0   50   100   150   200   250   300 miles

50   0 50 100 150 200 250 300 350 400 450 500 km

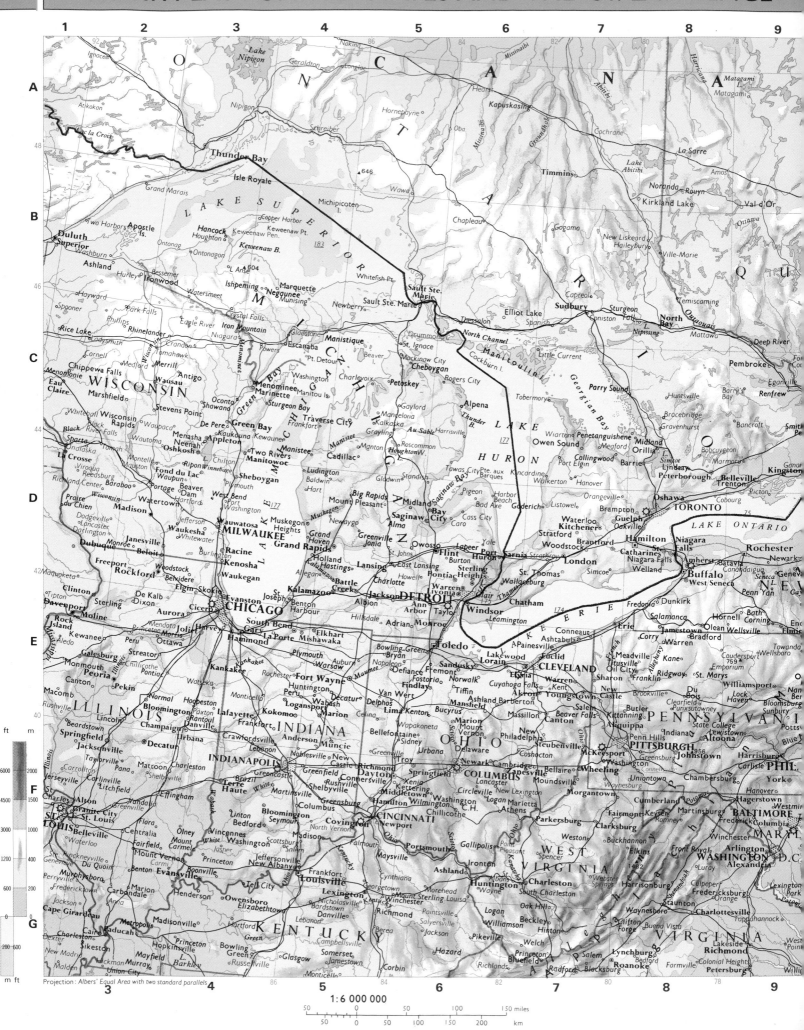

Projection: Albers' Equal Area with two standard parallels

1:6 000 000

50   0   50   100   150 miles

50 0 50 100 150 200 km

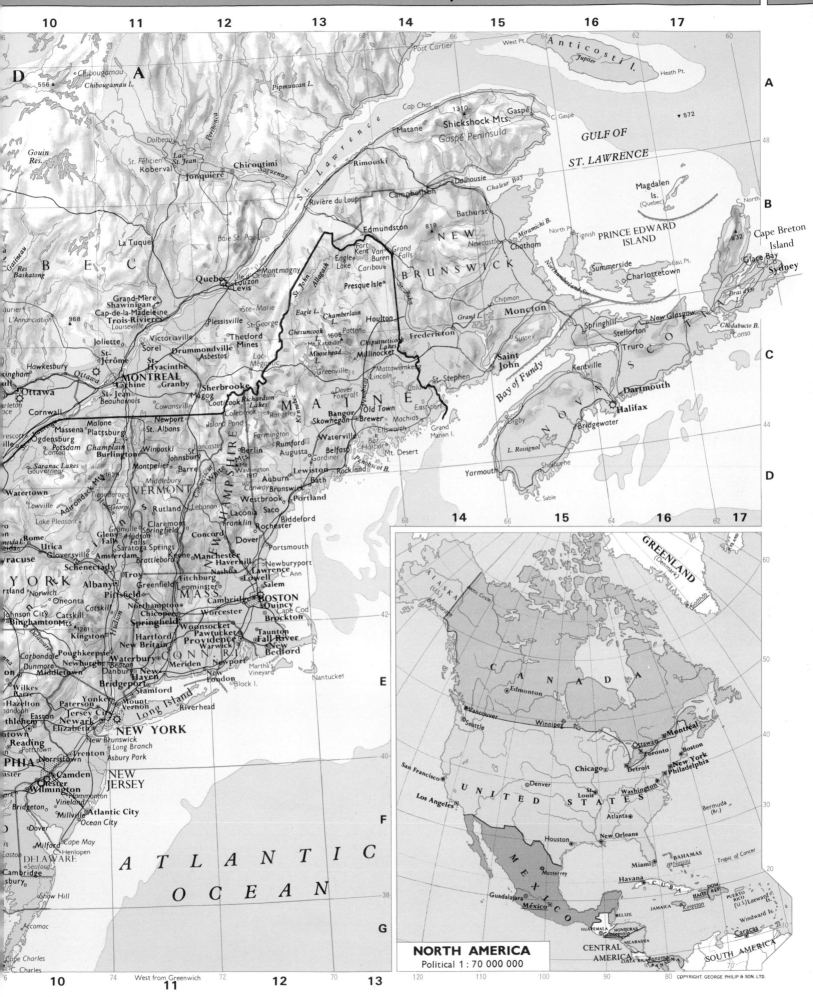

NORTH AMERICA
Political 1 : 70 000 000

PANAMA CANAL
1 : 1 000 000

JAMAICA
1 : 5 000 000

TRINIDAD
AND TOBAGO
1 : 5 000 000

LEEWARD
ISLANDS
1 : 5 000 000

WINDWARD
ISLANDS
1 : 5 000 000

ATLANTIC OCEAN

CARIBBEAN SEA

COLOMBIA

VENEZUELA

BRAZIL

West from Greenwich

1:15 000 000

COPYRIGHT. GEORGE PHILIP & SON. LTD.

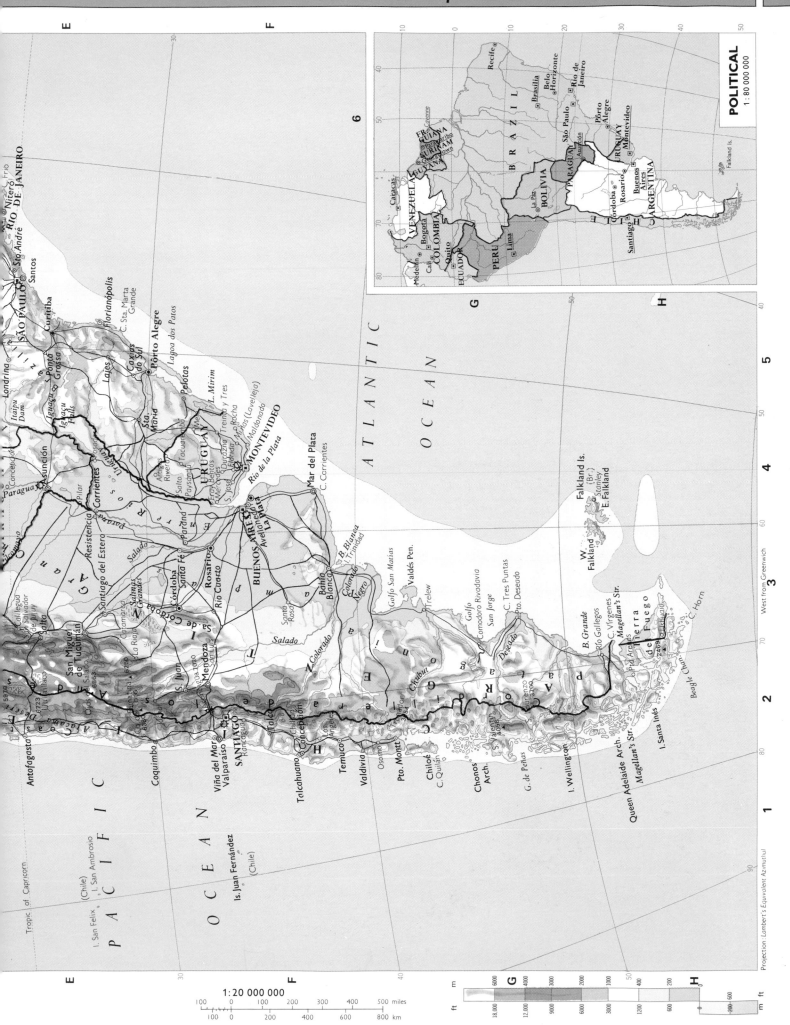

POLITICAL
1 : 80 000 000

Projection: Lambert's Equivalent Azimuthal

1 : 20 000 000

100   0   100   200   300   400   500 miles

100   0   200   400   600   800 km

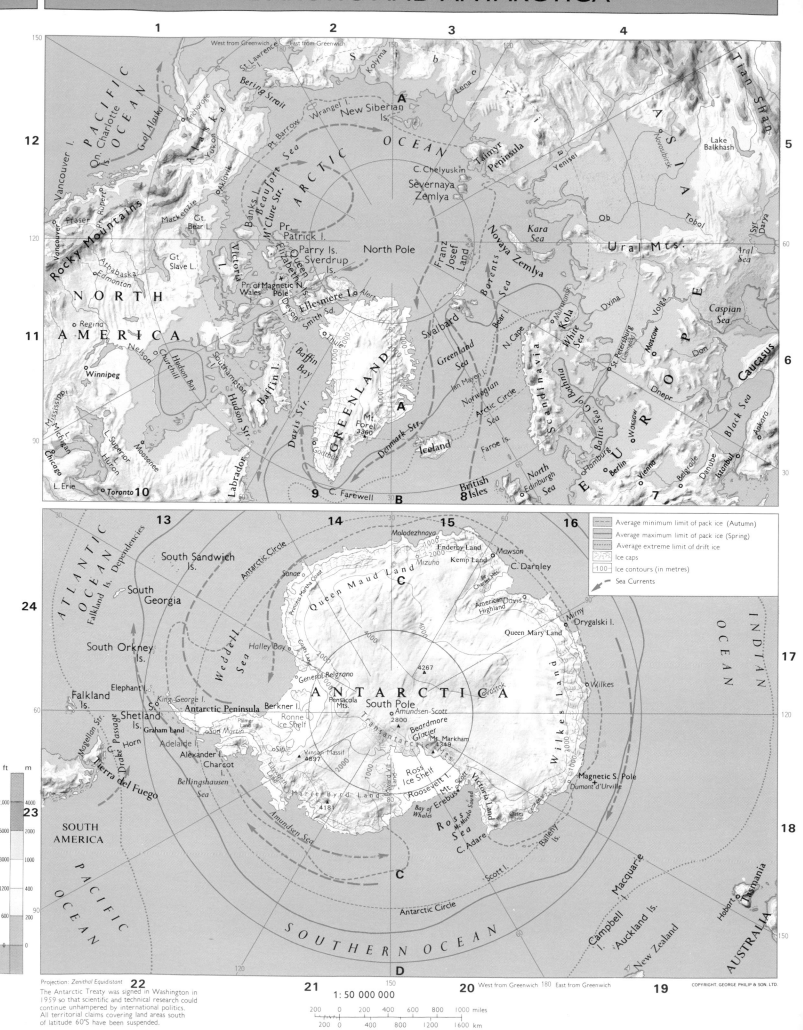

Projection: *Zenithal Equidistant*

The Antarctic Treaty was signed in Washington in 1959 so that scientific and technical research could continue unhampered by international politics. All territorial claims covering land areas south of latitude 60°S have been suspended.

1 : 50 000 000

200   0   200   400   600   800   1000 miles
200   0   400   800   1200   1600 km

WORLD THEMATIC MAPS

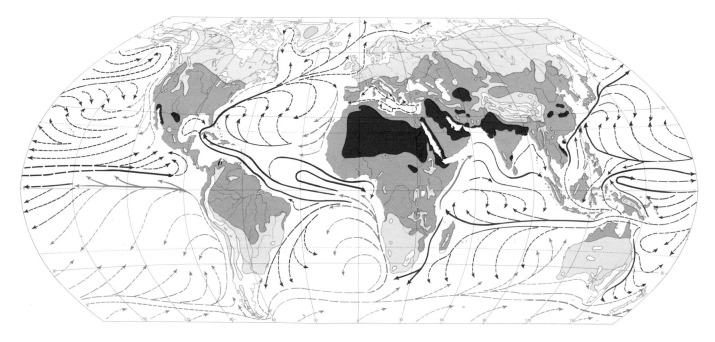

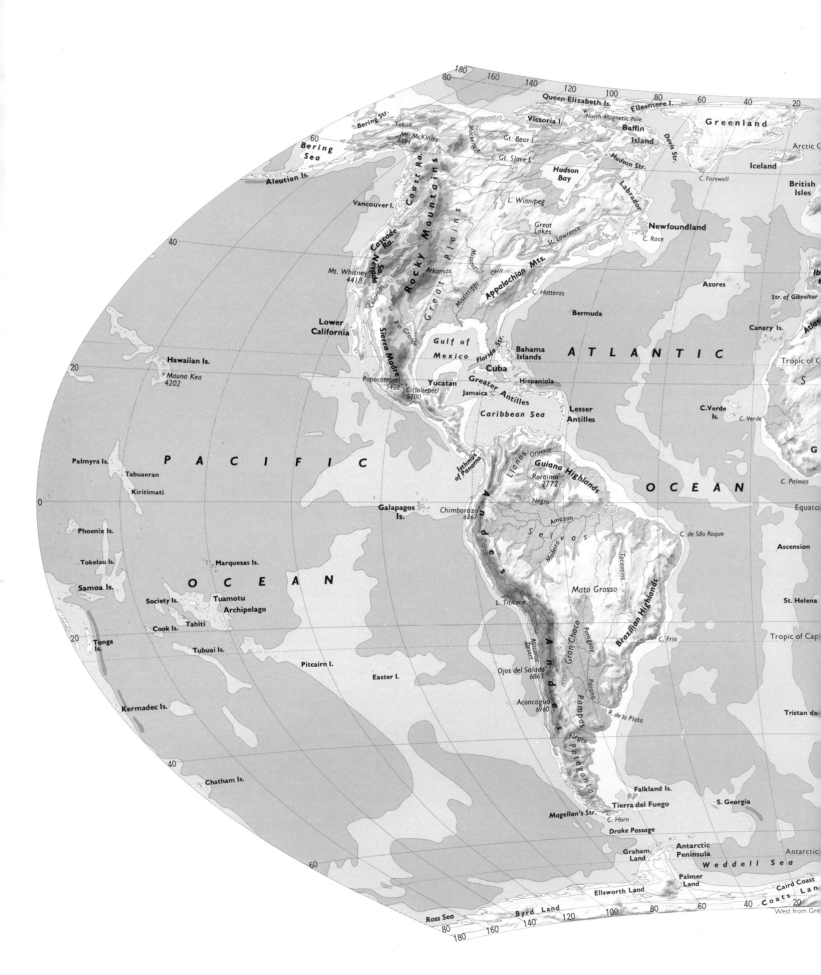

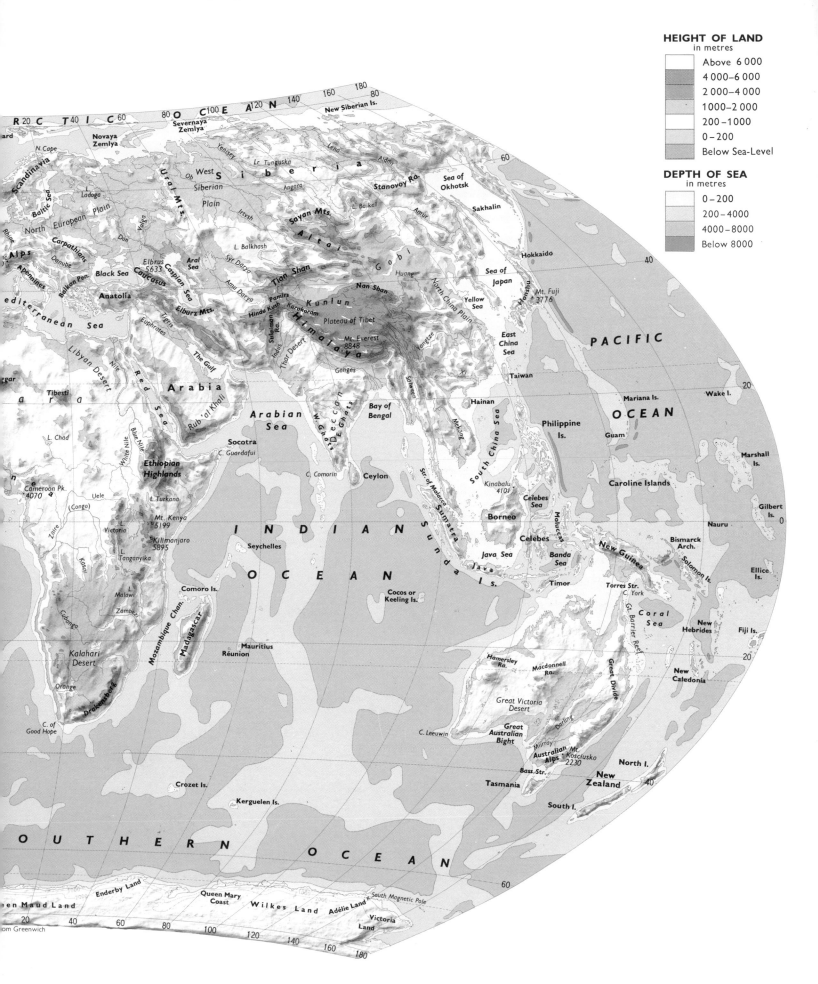

HEIGHT OF LAND
in metres

Above 6 000
4 000–6 000
2 000–4 000
1 000–2 000
200–1 000
0–200
Below Sea-Level

DEPTH OF SEA
in metres

0–200
200–4 000
4 000–8 000
Below 8 000

1:80 000 000

STRUCTURE

1: 95 000 000

Structural Regions of the Land

- Pre-Cambrian shields
- Sedimentary cover on Pre-Cambrian shields
- Palæozoic (Caledonian and Hercynian) folding
- Sedimentary cover on Palæozoic folding
- Mesozoic folding
- Sedimentary cover on Mesozoic folding
- Cainozoic folding
- Sedimentary cover on Cainozoic folding
- Intensive Mesozoic and Cainozoic vulcanism
- Oceanic-type crust raised above sea level

Structural Regions of the Oceans

- Regions of continental-type crust
- Limit of continental shelf
- Oceanic marginal troughs
- Mid-oceanic volcanic ridges
- Rift valleys in mid-oceanic ridges
- Principal faults
- Frontal line of overthrust folds

GEOLOGICAL TIME SCALE

Era	System	Orogeny	Millions of years before present
Cainozoic (Tertiary, Quaternary)	Quaternary	ALPINE FOLDING	
	Pliocene		
	Miocene		
	Oligocene		
	Eocene		50
	Paleocene	LARAMIDE FOLDING	
Mesozoic (Secondary)	Cretaceous		100
	Jurassic		150
	Triassic		200
Palæozoic (Primary) Upper	Permian		250
	Carboniferous	HERCYNIAN FOLDING	300
	Devonian	CALEDONIAN FOLDING	350
	Silurian		400
Palæozoic (Primary) Lower	Ordovician		450
	Cambrian		500
			550
Pre-Cambrian	Pre-Cambrian		600

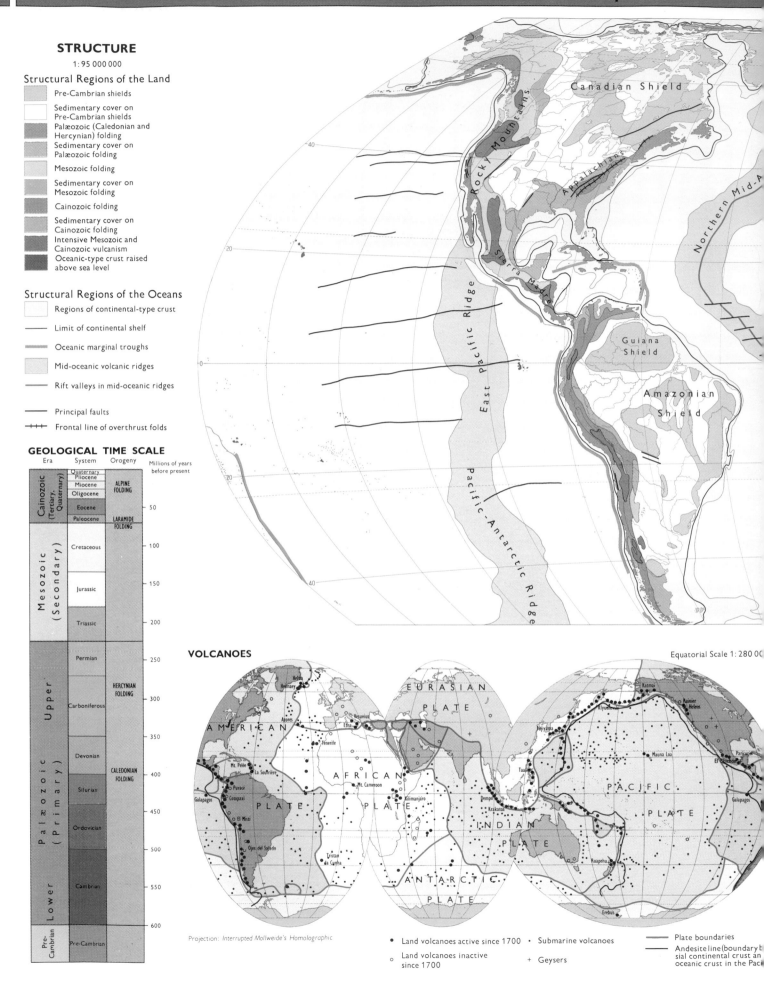

VOLCANOES

Equatorial Scale 1: 280 00

Projection: *Interrupted Mollweide's Homolographic*

- ● Land volcanoes active since 1700
- ○ Land volcanoes inactive since 1700
- • Submarine volcanoes
- + Geysers
- — Plate boundaries
- — Andesite line (boundary b sial continental crust an oceanic crust in the Pac

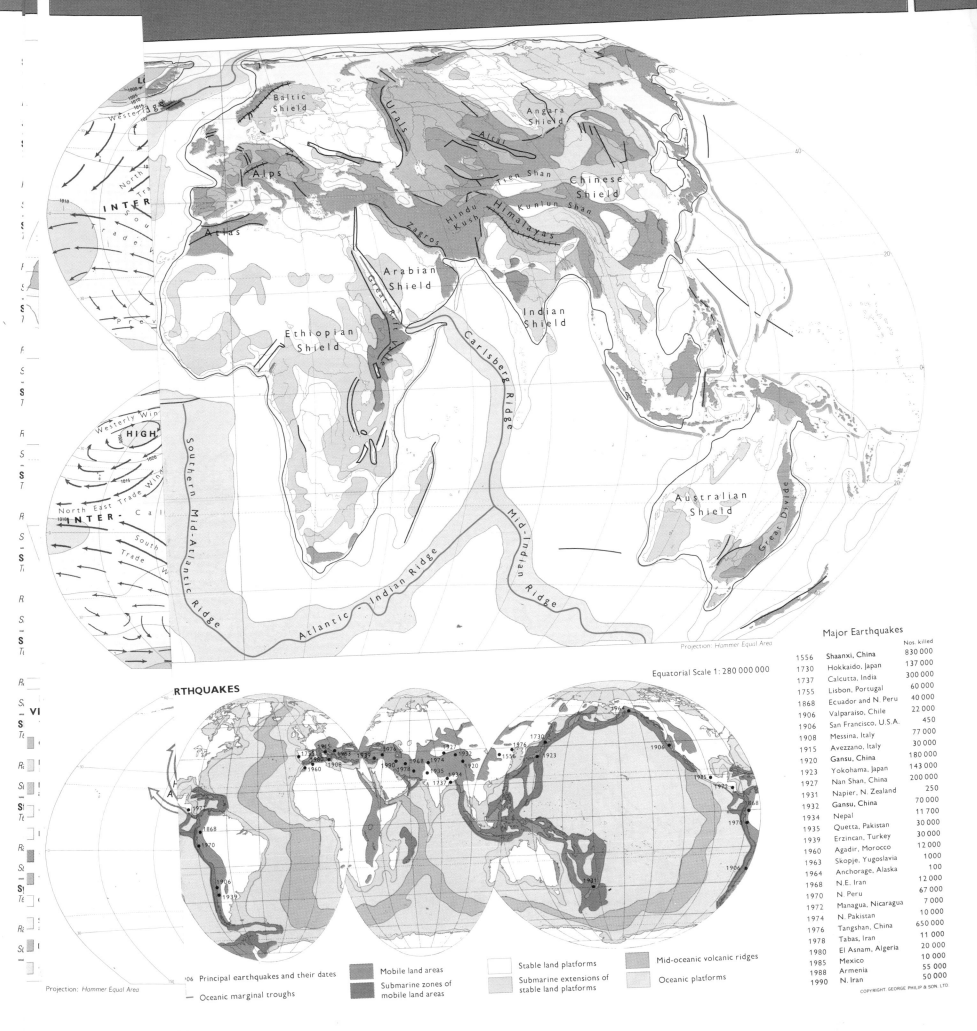

Baltic Shield

Urals

Angara Shield

Altai

Alps

Tien Shan

Chinese Shield

Atlas

Hindu Kush

Kunlun Shan

Himalayas

Zagros

Arabian Shield

Great Rift

Indian Shield

Ethiopian Shield

Carlsberg Ridge

Australian Shield

Great Dividing

Southern Mid-Atlantic Ridge

Atlantic - Indian Ridge

Mid-Indian Ridge

INTER-

North Trade

Trade W

Prev

Westerly Win

HIGH

North East Trade

INTER-

Calm

South Trade W

Westerly

Projection: *Hammer Equal Area*

Equatorial Scale 1: 280 000 000

RTHQUAKES

Projection: *Hammer Equal Area*

1906 Principal earthquakes and their dates

— Oceanic marginal troughs

Mobile land areas

Submarine zones of mobile land areas

Stable land platforms

Submarine extensions of stable land platforms

Mid-oceanic volcanic ridges

Oceanic platforms

Major Earthquakes

		Nos. killed
1556	Shaanxi, China	830 000
1730	Hokkaido, Japan	137 000
1737	Calcutta, India	300 000
1755	Lisbon, Portugal	60 000
1868	Ecuador and N. Peru	40 000
1906	Valparaiso, Chile	22 000
1906	San Francisco, U.S.A.	450
1908	Messina, Italy	77 000
1915	Avezzano, Italy	30 000
1920	Gansu, China	180 000
1923	Yokohama, Japan	143 000
1927	Nan Shan, China	200 000
1931	Napier, N. Zealand	250
1932	Gansu, China	70 000
1934	Nepal	11 700
1935	Quetta, Pakistan	30 000
1939	Erzincan, Turkey	30 000
1960	Agadir, Morocco	12 000
1963	Skopje, Yugoslavia	1000
1964	Anchorage, Alaska	100
1968	N.E. Iran	12 000
1970	N. Peru	67 000
1972	Managua, Nicaragua	7 000
1974	N. Pakistan	10 000
1976	Tangshan, China	650 000
1978	Tabas, Iran	11 000
1980	El Asnam, Algeria	20 000
1985	Mexico	10 000
1988	Armenia	55 000
1990	N. Iran	50 000

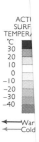
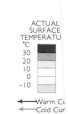

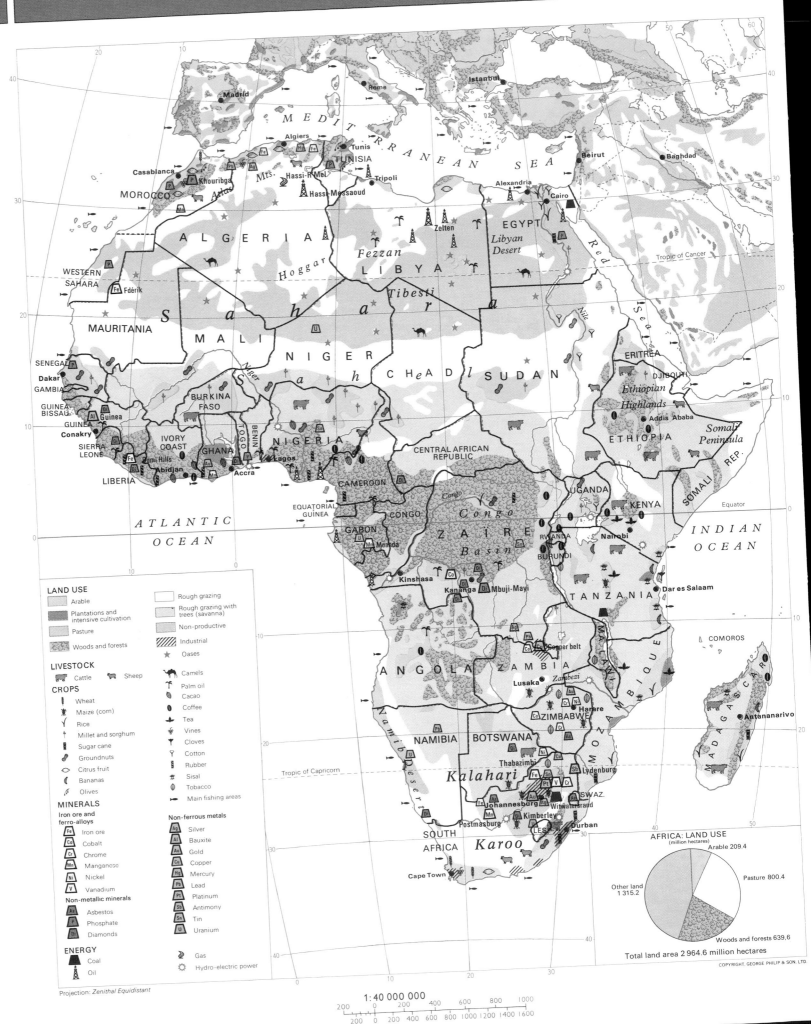

LAND USE
- Arable
- Plantations and intensive cultivation
- Pasture
- Woods and forests
- Rough grazing
- Rough grazing with trees (savanna)
- Non-productive
- Industrial
- ★ Oases

LIVESTOCK
- Cattle
- Sheep

CROPS
- Wheat
- Maize (corn)
- Rice
- Millet and sorghum
- Sugar cane
- Groundnuts
- Citrus fruit
- Bananas
- Olives
- Camels
- Palm oil
- Cacao
- Coffee
- Tea
- Vines
- Cloves
- Cotton
- Rubber
- Sisal
- Tobacco
- Main fishing areas

MINERALS
Iron ore and ferro-alloys
- Fe Iron ore
- Co Cobalt
- Cr Chrome
- Mn Manganese
- Ni Nickel
- V Vanadium

Non-metallic minerals
- As Asbestos
- P Phosphate
- Di Diamonds

Non-ferrous metals
- Ag Silver
- Al Bauxite
- Au Gold
- Cu Copper
- Hg Mercury
- Pb Lead
- Pt Platinum
- Sb Antimony
- Sn Tin
- U Uranium

ENERGY
- Coal
- Oil
- Gas
- Hydro-electric power

AFRICA: LAND USE
(million hectares)
Arable 209.4
Pasture 800.4
Woods and forests 639.6
Other land 1 315.2
Total land area 2 964.6 million hectares

COPYRIGHT. GEORGE PHILIP & SON. LTD

Projection: Zenithal Equidistant

1:40 000 000

The annual range of temperature is the difference in degrees between the warmest and coldest months of the year.

Projection: Hammer Equal Area

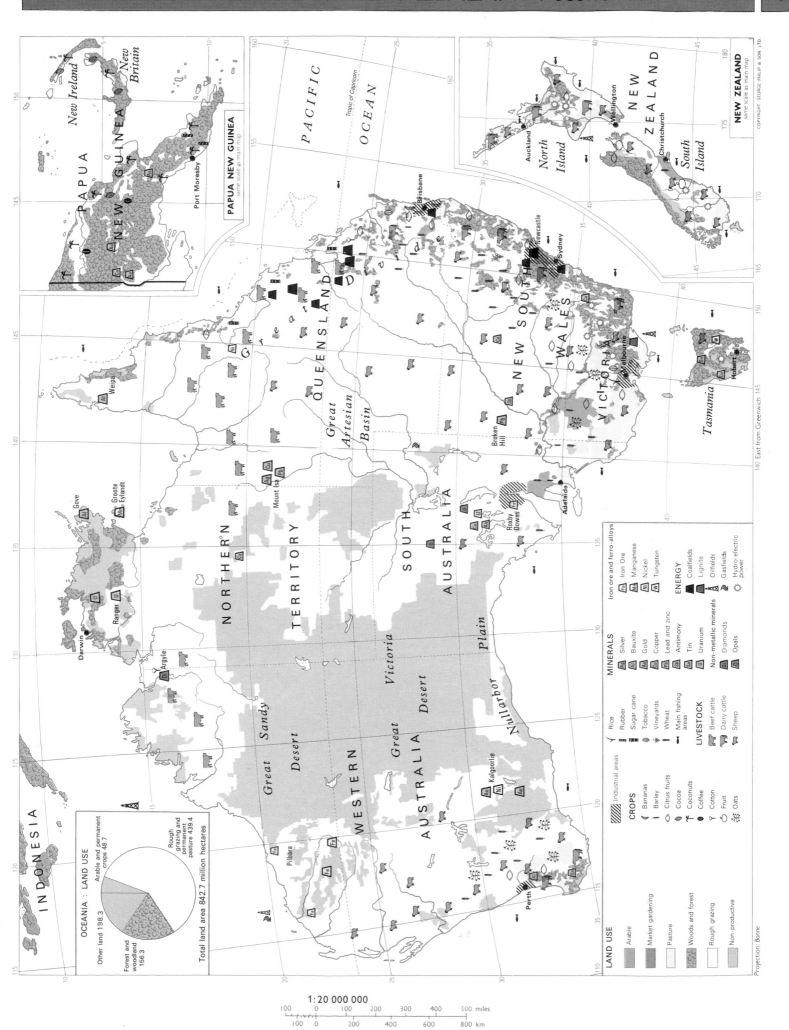

PACIFIC

OCEAN

Tropic of Capricorn

PAPUA NEW GUINEA
same scale as main map

New Ireland

New Britain

PAPUA

NEW GUINEA

Port Moresby

NEW ZEALAND
same scale as main map

COPYRIGHT GEORGE PHILIP & SON, LTD.

Auckland

North Island

Wellington

NEW ZEALAND

Christchurch

South Island

Brisbane

Newcastle

Sydney

QUEENSLAND

NEW SOUTH WALES

VICTORIA

Melbourne

Broken Hill

Tasmania

Hobart

Adelaide

Roxby Downs

SOUTH AUSTRALIA

Weipa

Gove

Groote Eylandt

Mount Isa

NORTHERN TERRITORY

Darwin

Ranger

Argyle

WESTERN AUSTRALIA

Great Sandy Desert

Great Victoria Desert

Nullarbor Plain

Great Artesian Basin

Kalgoorlie

Perth

Pilbara

INDONESIA

140 East from Greenwich 145

OCEANIA : LAND USE

Other land 198.3

Arable and permanent crops 48.7

Rough grazing and permanent pasture 439.4

Forest and woodland 156.3

Total land area 842.7 million hectares

LAND USE

Arable

Market gardening

Pasture

Woods and forest

Rough grazing

Non-productive

CROPS

Bananas	Rice	Rubber
Barley	Sugar cane	
Citrus fruits	Tobacco	
Cocoa	Vineyards	
Coconuts	Wheat	
Coffee	Main fishing areas	
Cotton		
Fruit	**LIVESTOCK**	
Oats	Beef cattle	
	Dairy cattle	
	Sheep	

Industrial areas

MINERALS

Silver	Antimony
Bauxite	Tin
Gold	Uranium
Copper	Non-metallic minerals
Lead and zinc	Diamonds
	Opals

Iron ore and ferro-alloys

Iron Ore, Manganese, Nickel, Tungsten

ENERGY

Coalfields, Lignite, Oilfields, Gasfields, Hydro-electric power

Projection: Bonne

1:20 000 000

100   0   100   200   300   400   500 miles

100   0   200   400   600   800 km

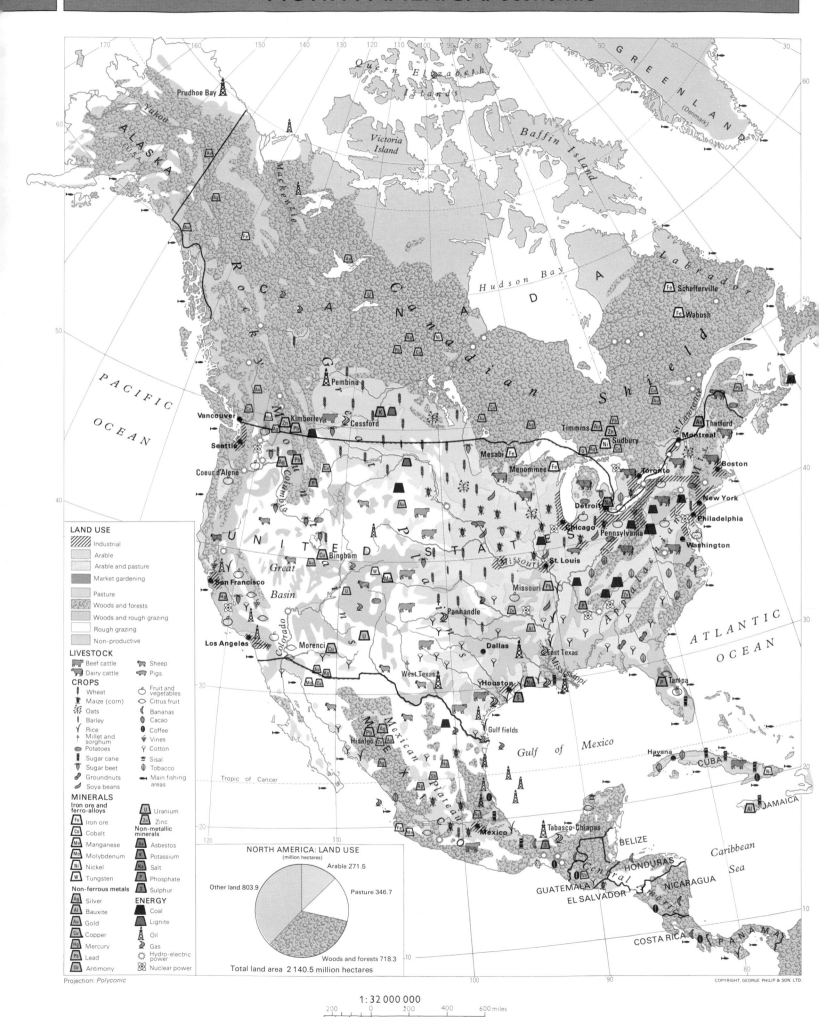

LAND USE
- Industrial
- Arable
- Arable and pasture
- Market gardening
- Pasture
- Woods and forests
- Woods and rough grazing
- Rough grazing
- Non-productive

LIVESTOCK
- Beef cattle
- Dairy cattle
- Sheep
- Pigs

CROPS
- Wheat
- Maize (corn)
- Oats
- Barley
- Rice
- Millet and sorghum
- Potatoes
- Sugar cane
- Sugar beet
- Groundnuts
- Soya beans
- Fruit and vegetables
- Citrus fruit
- Bananas
- Cacao
- Coffee
- Vines
- Cotton
- Sisal
- Tobacco
- Main fishing areas

MINERALS
Iron ore and ferro-alloys
- Fe Iron ore
- Co Cobalt
- Mn Manganese
- Mo Molybdenum
- Ni Nickel
- W Tungsten
- U Uranium
- Zn Zinc

Non-metallic minerals
- As Asbestos
- P Potassium
- Sa Salt
- P Phosphate
- S Sulphur

Non-ferrous metals
- Ag Silver
- Al Bauxite
- Au Gold
- Cu Copper
- Hg Mercury
- Pb Lead
- Sb Antimony

ENERGY
- Coal
- Lignite
- Oil
- Gas
- Hydro-electric power
- Nuclear power

NORTH AMERICA: LAND USE
(million hectares)

- Arable 271.5
- Pasture 346.7
- Woods and forests 718.3
- Other land 803.9

Total land area 2 140.5 million hectares

Projection: *Polyconic*

COPYRIGHT. GEORGE PHILIP & SON. LTD.

1:32 000 000

200   0   200   400   600 miles
400   0   400   800 km

SOUTH AMERICA: LAND USE
(million hectares)

Arable 104.1

Other land 283.5

Pasture 441.8

Woods and forests 924.3

Total land area 1 753.7 million hectares

LAND USE

Industrial

Arable

Market gardening and plantations

Pasture

Woods and forests

Rough grazing

Non-productive

LIVESTOCK

Beef cattle — Sheep

Dairy cattle — Pigs

CROPS

Wheat — Coconut palms

Maize (corn) — Cacao

Rice — Coffee

Millet and sorghum — Tea

Potatoes — Vines

Sugar cane — Cotton

Groundnuts — Rubber

Fruit and vegetables — Tobacco

Citrus fruit — Main fishing areas

Bananas

MINERALS

Iron ore and ferro-alloys

Fe Iron ore

Cr Chrome

Mn Manganese

Mo Molybdenum

W Tungsten

Non-metallic minerals

Saltpetre

Non-ferrous metals

Ag Silver

Al Bauxite

Au Gold

Cu Copper

Pb Lead

Sb Antimony

Sn Tin

Zn Zinc

ENERGY

Coal

Oil

Nuclear power

Gas

Hydro-electric power

Projection: Lambert's Equivalent Azimuthal

COPYRIGHT GEORGE PHILIP & SON LTD

1:30 000 000

200   0   200   400   600 miles

200 0 200 400 600 800 km

Wheat

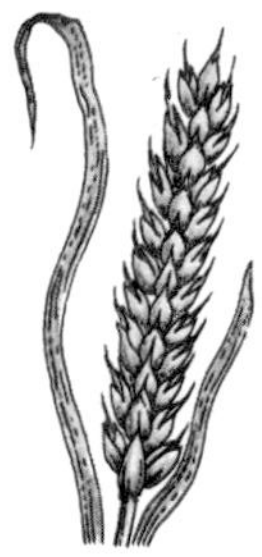

The most important grain crop in the temperate regions though it is also grown in a variety of climates e.g. in Monsoon lands as a winter crop.

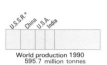

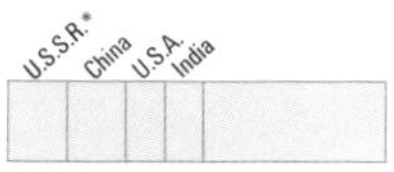
U.S.S.R.*
China
U.S.A.
India

World production 1990
595.7 million tonnes

Oats

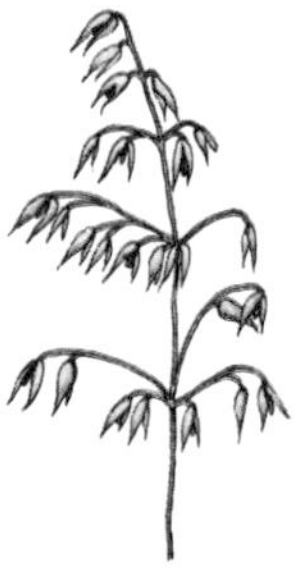

Widely grown in temperate regions with the limit fixed by early autumn frosts. Mainly fed to cattle. The best quality oats are used for oatmeal, porridge and breakfast foods.

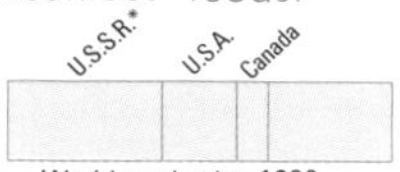
U.S.S.R.*
U.S.A.
Canada

World production 1990
43.8 million tonnes

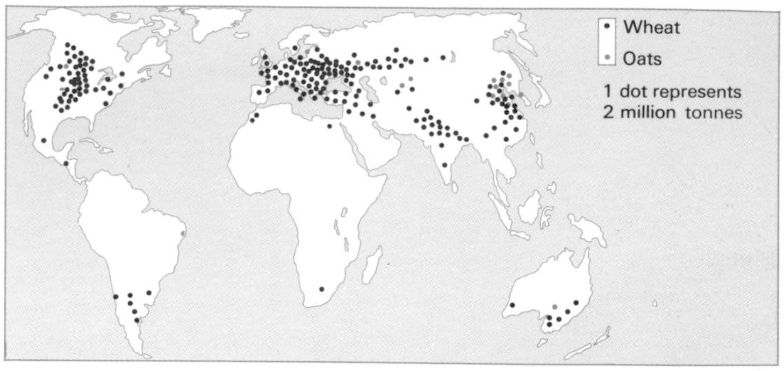
Wheat
Oats
1 dot represents
2 million tonnes

Rye

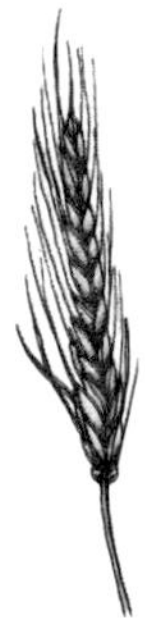

The hardiest of cereals and more resistant to cold, pests and disease than wheat. An important foodstuff in Central and E. Europe.

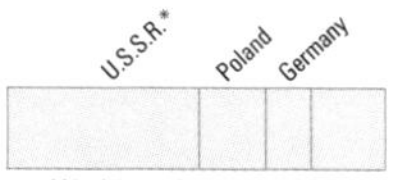
U.S.S.R.*
Poland
Germany

World production 1990
36.6 million tonnes

Maize (or Corn)

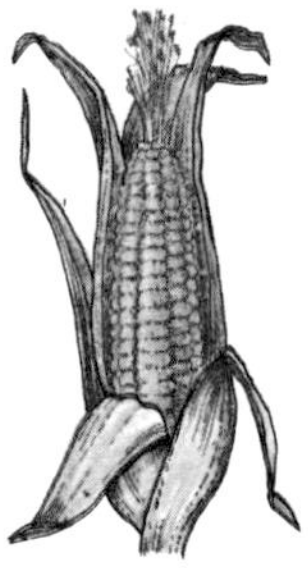

Needs plenty of sunshine, summer rain or irrigation and frost free for 6 months. Important as animal feed and for human food in Africa, Latin America and as a vegetable and breakfast cereal.

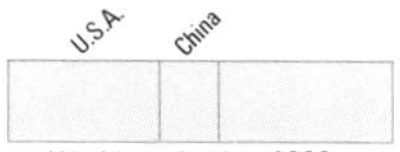
U.S.A.
China

World production 1990
468.8 million tonnes

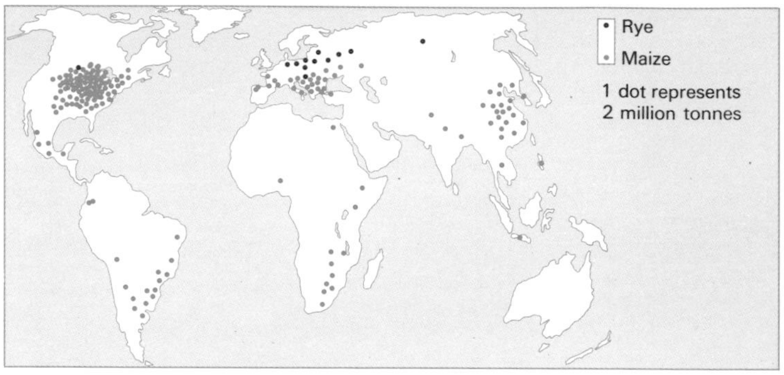
Rye
Maize
1 dot represents
2 million tonnes

Barley

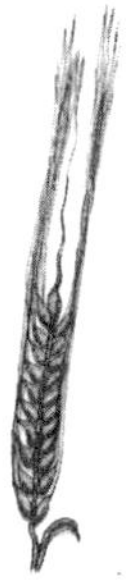

Has the widest range of cultivation requiring only 8 weeks between seed time and harvest. Used mainly as animal-feed and by the malting industry.

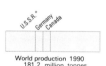

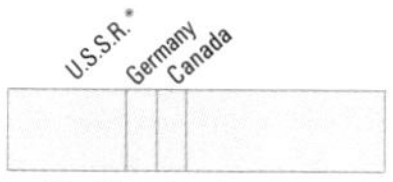
U.S.S.R.*
Germany
Canada

World production 1990
181.2 million tonnes

Rice

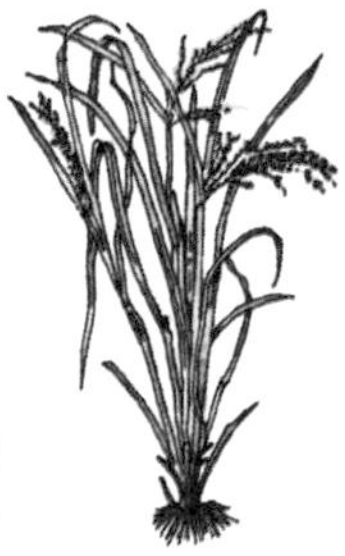

The staple food of half the human race. The main producing areas are the flood plains and hill terraces of S. and E. Asia where water is abundant in the growing season.

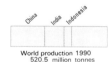

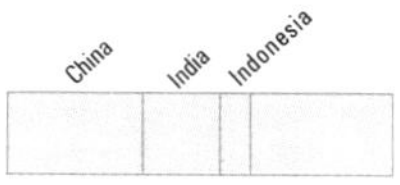
China
India
Indonesia

World production 1990
520.5 million tonnes

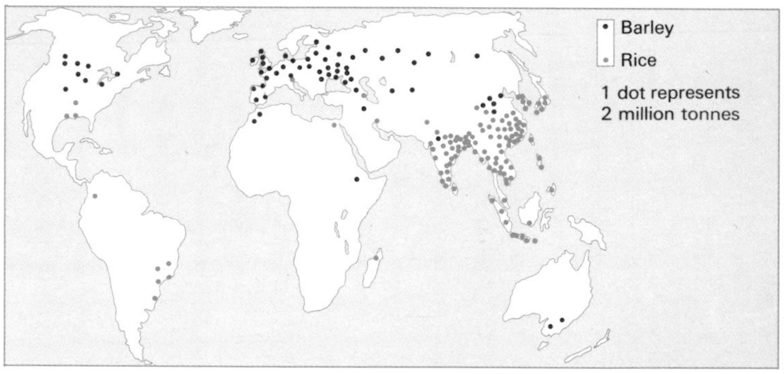
Barley
Rice
1 dot represents
2 million tonnes

Millets

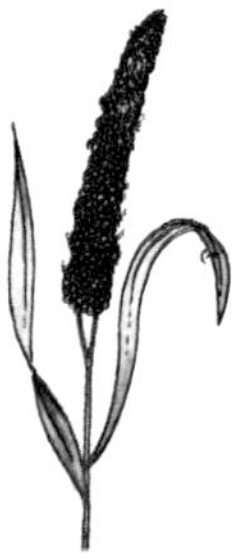

The name given to a number of related members of the grass family, of which sorghum is one of the most important. They provide nutritious grain.

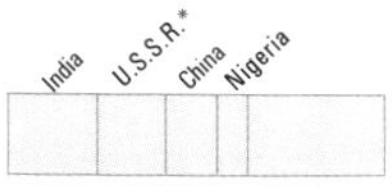
India
U.S.S.R.*
China
Nigeria

World production 1990
89.2 million tonnes

Potatoes

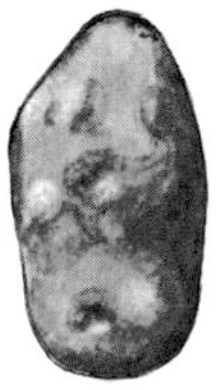

An important food crop though less nutritious weight for weight than grain crops. Requires a temperate climate with a regular and plentiful supply of rain.

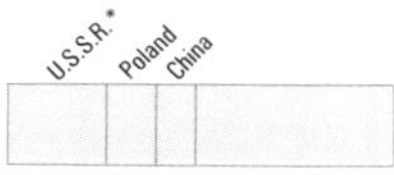
U.S.S.R.*
Poland
China

World production 1990
268.4 million tonnes

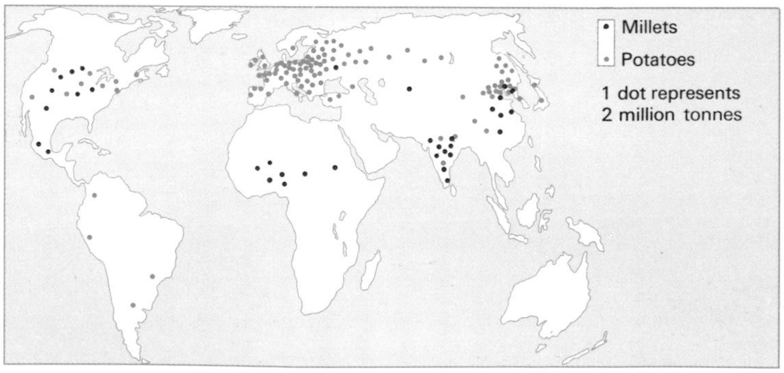
Millets
Potatoes
1 dot represents
2 million tonnes

Vegetable oilseeds and oils

Despite the increasing use of synthetic chemical products and animal and marine fats, vegetable oils extracted from these crops grow in quantity, value and importance. Food is the major use- in margarine and cooking fats.

Groundnuts are also a valuable subsistence crop and the meal is used as animal feed. Soya-bean meal is a growing source of protein for humans and animals. The Mediterranean lands are the prime source of olive oil.

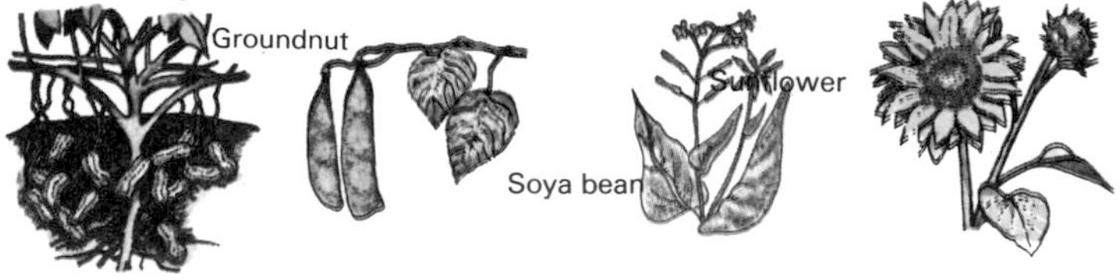
Groundnut
Soya bean
Sunflower

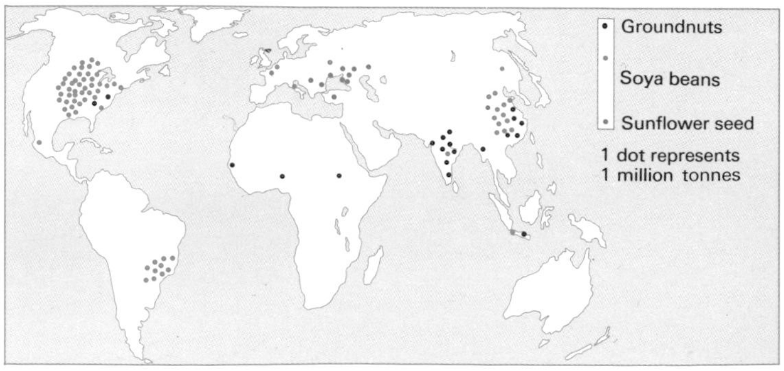
Groundnuts
Soya beans
Sunflower seed
1 dot represents
1 million tonnes

* *Statistics for each of the new republics of the former U.S.S.R., Czechoslovakia and Yugoslavia are not yet available.*

Tea and cacao

Tea requires plentiful rainfall and well-drained, sloping ground, whereas cacao prefers a moist heavy soil. Both are grown mainly for export.

Coffee

Prefers a hot climate, wet and dry seasons and an elevated location. It is very susceptible to frost, drought and market fluctuations.

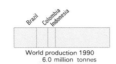

World production 1990
6.0 million tonnes

- Tea
- Cacao
- Coffee

1 dot represents
100 000 tonnes

Sugar beet

Requires a deep, rich soil and a temperate climate. Europe produces over 90 % of the world's beets mainly for domestic consumption.

World production 1990
307.7 million tonnes

Sugar cane

Also requires deep and rich soil but a tropical climate. It produces a much higher yield per hectare than beet and is grown primarily for export.

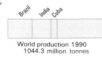

World production 1990
1044.3 million tonnes

- Sugar beet
- Sugar cane

1 dot represents
10 million tonnes

Fruit

With the improvements in canning, drying and freezing, and in transport and marketing, the international trade and consumption of deciduous and soft fruits, citrus fruits and tropical fruits has greatly increased. Recent developments in the use of the peel will give added value to some of the fruit crops.

Fish

Commercial fishing requires large shoals of fish of one species within reach of markets. Freshwater fishing is also important. A rich source of protein, fish will become an increasingly valuable food source.

World catch 1988
98.0 million tonnes

- Temperate fruit
- Citrus fruit
- Principal fishing grounds

Beef cattle

Australia, New Zealand and Argentina provide the major part of international beef exports. Western U.S.A. and Europe have considerable production of beef for their local high demand.

World production 1989
49.4 million tonnes of meat

Dairy cattle

The need of herds for a rich diet and for nearby markets result in dairying being characteristic of densely-populated areas of the temperate zones - U.S.A., N.W. Europe, and S.E. Australia.

World production 1989
474.0 million tonnes of milk

- Cattle

1 dot represents
10 million head

- Dairy produce

Sheep

Raised mostly for wool and meat, their skins and the cheese from their milk are important products in some countries. The merino yields a fine wool and crossbreeds are best for meat.

World production 1990
6.5 million tonnes of meat

Pigs

Can be reared in most climates from monsoon to cool temperate. They are abundant in China, the Corn Belt of the U.S.A. N.W. and C. Europe, Brazil and Russia.

World production 1990
67.1 million tonnes of meat

- Sheep
- Pigs

1 dot represents
10 million head

COPYRIGHT. GEORGE PHILIP & SON. LTD.

*Statistics for each of the new republics of the former U.S.S.R., Czechoslovakia and Yugoslavia are not yet available.

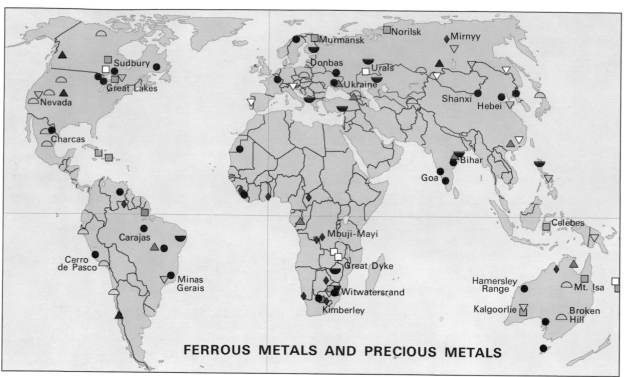

FERROUS METALS AND PRECIOUS METALS

Precious Metals

▽**Gold**
World total (1990)
1,750 tonnes

South Africa	34.9%
U.S.A.	16.9%
U.S.S.R.	16.0%
Australia	13.8%
Canada	9.4%

⌒**Silver**
World total (1990)
14,654 tonnes

Mexico	15.7%
U.S.A.	13.7%
Peru	12.6%
U.S.S.R.	10.2%
Canada	8.9%

◆**Diamonds**
World total (1990)
108,000,000 carats

Australia	33.3%
Zaire	22.2%
Botswana	16.0%
U.S.S.R.	13.9%
South Africa	7.9%

● Iron Ore	▣ Nickel	◗ Chrome	▲ Manganese	▢ Cobalt	▲ Molybdenum	▽ Tungsten
World total (1990)	World total (1990)	World total (1990)	World total (1990)	World total (1988)	World total (1988)	World total (1990)
962,000,000 tonnes	865,000 tonnes	12,000 tonnes	24,000 tonnes	43,900 tonnes	94,700 tonnes	45,000 tonnes
U.S.S.R. 14.8%	U.S.S.R. 24.3%	South Africa 35.0%	U.S.S.R. 37.5%	Zaire 57.9%	U.S.A. 45.4%	China 44.4%
Brazil 10.9%	Canada 23.5%	U.S.S.R. 31.7%	South Africa 15.8%	Zambia 15.3%	Chile 18.0%	U.S.S.R. 15.6%
China 8.8%	New Caledonia 11.1%	India 6.3%	China 11.3%	U.S.S.R. 6.6%	Canada 13.1%	Mongolia 3.3%
Australia 7.3%	Australia 7.5%	Albania 5.8%	Australia 9.6%	Canada 5.7%	U.S.S.R. 12.1%	Austria 3.1%
U.S.A. 3.6%	Indonesia 6.9%	Turkey 5.0%	Gabon 9.2%	New Caledonia 4.8%	Mexico 4.5%	Portugal 3.1%

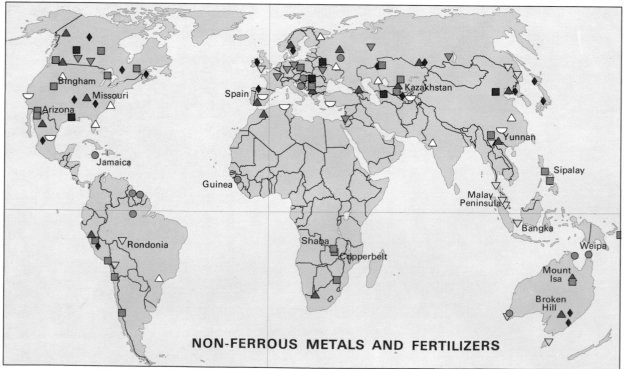

NON-FERROUS METALS AND FERTILIZERS

Fertilizers

■**Nitrates**
World total (1989)
85,151,000 tonnes

U.S.S.R.	18.3%
China	16.4%
U.S.A.	14.9%
Hungary	7.9%
Canada	3.2%

△**Phosphates**
World total (1989)
41,532,000 tonnes

U.S.A.	22.9%
U.S.S.R.	22.0%
China	9.1%
India	5.5%
Brazil	3.4%

▽**Potash**
World total (1989)
31,151,000 tonnes

U.S.S.R.	36.3%
Canada	26.0%
Germany	18.5%
France	4.5%
Israel	3.9%

▣ Copper	▲ Lead	● Bauxite	▽ Tin	◆ Zinc	⌒ Mercury
World total (1989)	World total (1989)	World total (1989)	World total (1989)	World total (1989)	World total (1990)
9,129,000 tonnes	3,341,000 tonnes	106,560,000 tonnes	223,000 tonnes	7,138,000 tonnes	5,541 tonnes
Chile 17.6%	U.S.S.R. 15.0%	Australia 36.2%	Brazil 22.5%	Canada 17.0%	U.S.S.R. 45.1%
U.S.A. 17.3%	Australia 14.8%	Guinea 16.4%	China 14.8%	U.S.S.R. 13.2%	China 18.8%
U.S.S.R. 10.4%	U.S.A. 12.5%	Jamaica 8.8%	Malaysia 14.3%	Australia 11.2%	Spain 12.9%
Canada 8.0%	China 10.2%	Brazil 7.4%	Indonesia 14.0%	China 8.7%	Algeria 12.6%
Zambia 5.5%	Canada 8.2%	U.S.S.R. 5.4%	Bolivia 7.1%	Peru 8.4%	Mexico 3.5%

Some countries are highly dependent upon minerals. The following are dependent on metals and minerals for over 50% of the value of their exports:
Zambia 93%,
New Caledonia 81%,
Zaire 55%.

Projection: *Modified Hammer Equal Area*

Statistics for each of the new republics of the former U.S.S.R., Czechoslovakia and Yugoslavia are not yet available.

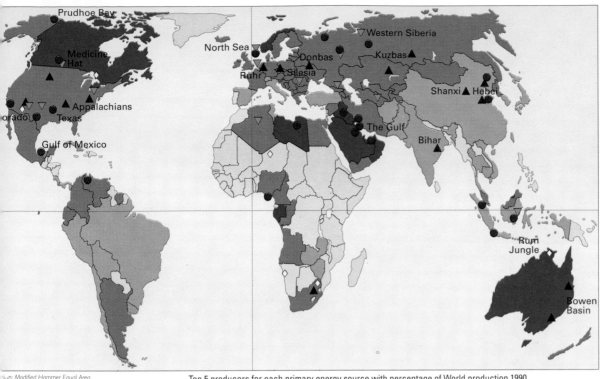

ENERGY PRODUCTION

Primary energy production
expressed in kilograms
of coal equivalent per
person 1989

- Over 10 000 kg per person
- 1 000-10 000 kg per person
- 100-1 000 kg per person
- 10-100 kg per person
- Under 10 kg per person

● Oil

▽ Natural gas

▲ Coal and lignite

◇ Uranium (the fuel used to
generate nuclear power)

*In developing countries
traditional fuels are still very
important. Sometimes called
biomass fuels, they include
wood, charcoal and dried dung.
The pie graph for Nigeria at the
foot of the page shows their
importance.*

Projection: Modified Hammer Equal Area

Top 5 producers for each primary energy source with percentage of World production 1990

Oil		Natural Gas		Coal (bituminous)		Brown Coal (lignite)		Uranium		Nuclear Power		Hydro-Electric Power	
World total (1990) 000 000 tonnes		World total (1990) 3 007 075 tonnes		World total (1990) 3 562 000 000 tonnes		World total (1990) 1 176 000 000 tonnes		World total (1990) 37 000 tonnes		World total (1990) 461 100 000 tonnes of oil equivalent		World total (1990) 540 600 000 tonnes of oil equivalent	
S.R.	18,1%	U.S.S.R.	37,2%	China	29,5%	Germany	30,4%	Canada	23,0%	U.S.A.	33,8%	U.S.A.	13,3%
A.	13,2%	U.S.A.	25,2%	U.S.A.	24,2%	U.S.S.R.	13,4%	U.S.S.R.	12,5%	France	13,3%	Canada	11,8%
di Arabia	10,4%	Canada	5,0%	U.S.S.R.	13,3%	Czechoslovakia	7,3%	Germany	11,8%	Japan	10,6%	U.S.S.R.	10,3%
	4,9%	Netherlands	3,1%	India	5,6%	U.S.A.	7,0%	U.S.A.	10,4%	U.S.S.R.	9,4%	Brazil	8,8%
a	4,4%	U.K.	2,3%	South Africa	5,1%	China	9,6%	Australia	7,4%	Germany	7,2%	China	5,8%

ENERGY CONSUMPTION

Primary energy consumption
expressed in kilograms
of coal equivalent per
person 1989

- Over 10 000 kg per person
- 5 000-10 000 kg per person
- 1 000-5 000 kg per person
- 100-1 000 kg per person
- Under 100 kg per person

Energy Consumption by Continent 1990

		Change 1989-90
Europe*	38,5%	(-2,6%)
North America	27,6%	(-0,2%)
Asia	23,9%	(+4,9%)
South America	5,9%	(+3,7%)
Africa	2,8%	(+2,6%)
Australasia	1,3%	(+2,7%)

*includes U.S.S.R.

TYPE OF ENERGY CONSUMED BY SELECTED COUNTRIES

- Coal and Lignite
- Oil
- Natural Gas
- Hydro-electricity
- Nuclear electricity
- Traditional Fuels

NIGERIA

CHINA

JAPAN

FRANCE

U.S.A.

NORWAY

*Statistics for each of the new republics of the former U.S.S.R.,
Czechoslovakia and Yugoslavia are not yet available.*

AGE DISTRIBUTION PYRAMIDS

The bars represent the percentage of the total population (males plus females) in the age group shown.

Developed countries such as the U.K. have populations evenly spread across age groups and usually a growing percentage of elderly people. Developing countries such as Kenya have the great majority of their people in the younger age groups, about to enter their most fertile years.

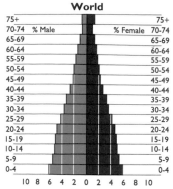

World

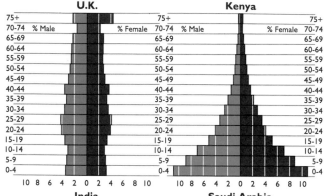

U.K.   Kenya

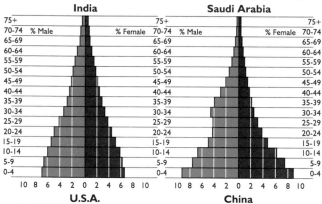

India   Saudi Arabia

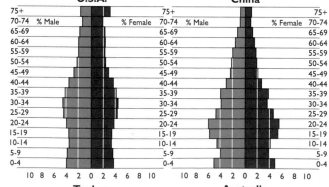

U.S.A.   China

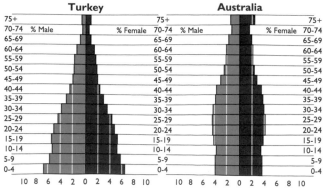

Turkey   Australia

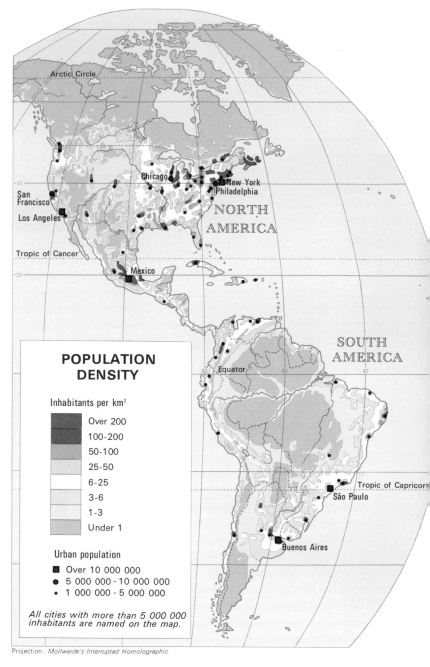

POPULATION DENSITY

Inhabitants per km²

	Over 200
	100-200
	50-100
	25-50
	6-25
	3-6
	1-3
	Under 1

Urban population

- ■ Over 10 000 000
- ● 5 000 000 - 10 000 000
- • 1 000 000 - 5 000 000

All cities with more than 5 000 000 inhabitants are named on the map.

Projection : *Mollweide's Interrupted Homolographic*

POPULATION CHANGE 1930-2020   Population totals are in millions

Figures in italics represent the percentage average annual increase for the period sho

	1930	1930-1960	1960	1960-1990	1990	1990-2020	2020
World	2013	*1.4%*	3019	*1.9%*	5292	*1.4%*	8062
Africa	155	*2.0%*	281	*2.8%*	648	*2.7%*	1441
North America	135	*1.3%*	199	*1.1%*	276	*0.6%*	327
Latin America*	129	*1.8%*	218	*2.4%*	448	*1.6%*	719
Asia	1073	*1.5%*	1669	*2.1%*	3108	*1.4%*	4680
Europe	355	*0.6%*	425	*0.5%*	498	*0.1%*	514
Oceania	10	*1.4%*	16	*1.7%*	27	*1.1%*	37
C.I.S. †	176	*0.7%*	214	*1.0%*	288	*0.6%*	343

* South America plus Central America, Mexico and the West Indies
† Commonwealth of Independent States, formerly the U.S.S.R.

1 : 105 000 000

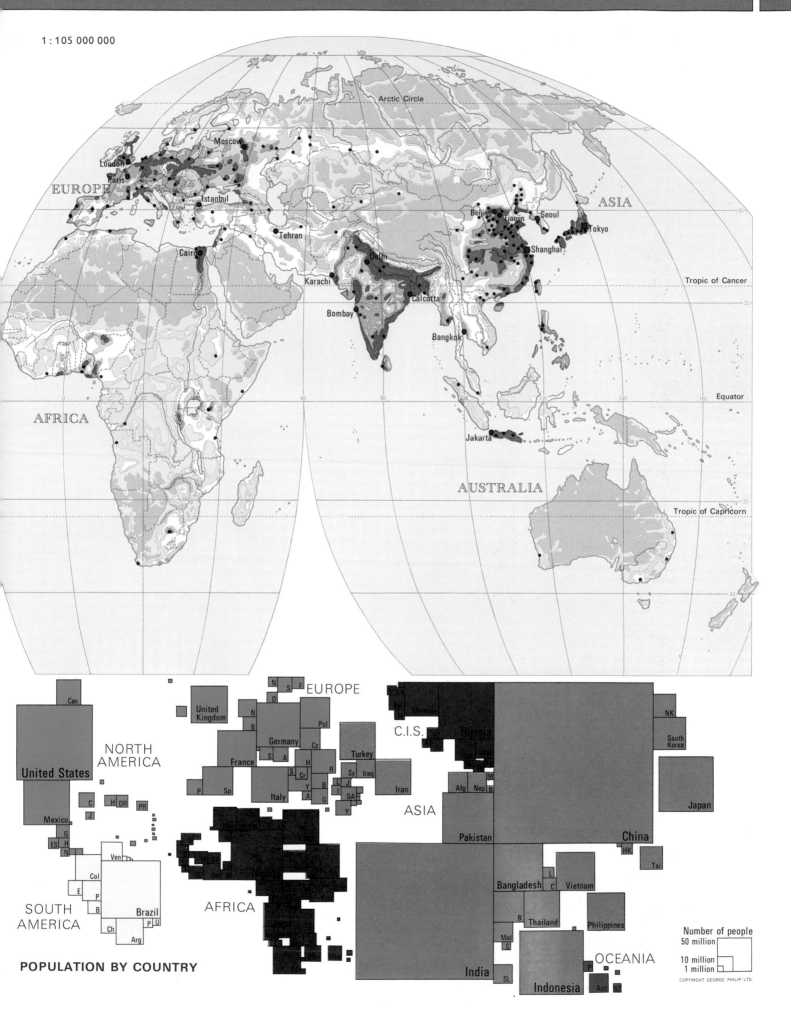

Arctic Circle

60

EUROPE

Moscow

London

Paris

Istanbul

ASIA

Tehran

Beijing Tianjin Seoul

Tokyo

Cairo

Shanghai

Delhi

Tropic of Cancer

Karachi

Calcutta

20

Bombay

Bangkok

AFRICA

Jakarta

Equator

AUSTRALIA

Tropic of Capricorn

20

40

POPULATION BY COUNTRY

Can

EUROPE

N   S   F

D

United
Kingdom

N

Pol

C.I.S.

NK

NORTH
AMERICA

B

Germany

Cz

Turkey

Russia

South
Korea

United States

France

S   A

H
Cr
R

Sy   Iraq

ASIA

Japan

P   Sp

Italy

B
Y
A
G

J   J
I   SA
Y

Iran

Afg Nep

China

Mexico

C   H DR   PR

Pakistan

HK

G
ES H
N

J

Ven

Tai

L
C

SOUTH
AMERICA

Col

E
P
B

Brazil

Bangladesh

Vietnam

B   Thailand

Philippines

Ch

P U

AFRICA

Mal
S

OCEANIA

Arg

India

SL

Indonesia

Aus

Number of people
50 million
10 million
1 million

COPYRIGHT GEORGE PHILIP LTD.

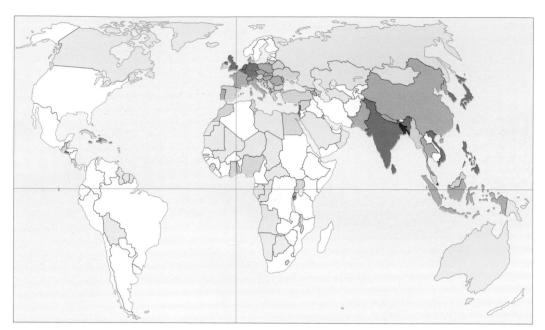

POPULATION DENSITY BY COUNTRY

Density of people per square kilometre 1991

Over 500 people per km²

200-500 people per km²

100-200 people per km²

50-100 people per km²

10-50 people per km²

Under 10 people per km²

Top 5 countries		Bottom 5 countries	
Macau	24 850 per km²	Mauritania	2.0 per km²
Hong Kong	5 960 per km²	Mongolia	1.5 per km²
Singapore	4 667 per km²	French Guiana	1.1 per km²
Gibraltar	3 000 per km²	Congo	0.7 per km²
Malta	1 333 per km²	Greenland	0.2 per km²

U.K. 238 per km²

POPULATION CHANGE 1990-2000

Expected percentage population change between 1990 and 2000*

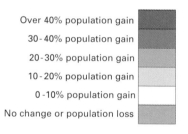

Over 40% population gain

30- 40% population gain

20- 30% population gain

10- 20% population gain

0- 10% population gain

No change or population loss

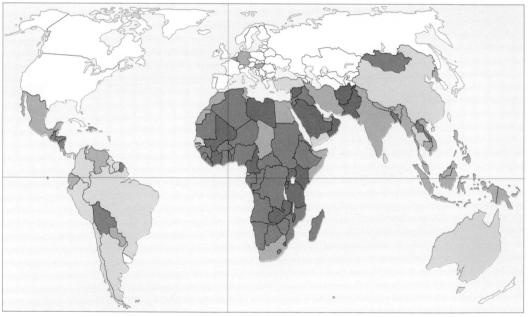

Top 5 countries		Bottom 5 countries	
Afghanistan	+60%	Hungary	-0.2%
Mali	+56%	Singapore	-0.2%
Tanzania	+55%	Grenada	-2.4%
Ivory Coast	+47%	Tonga	-3.2%
Saudi Arabia	+46%	Germany	-3.2%

U.K. +2.0%

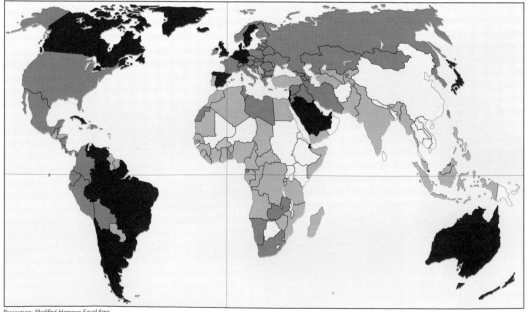

URBAN POPULATION

Percentage of total population living in towns and cities 1990

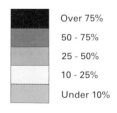

Over 75%

50 - 75%

25 - 50%

10 - 25%

Under 10%

Most urbanized		Least urbanized	
Singapore	100%	Bhutan	5%
Belgium	97%	Burundi	7%
Kuwait	96%	Rwanda	8%
Hong Kong	93%	Burkina Faso	9%
U.K.	93%	Nepal	10%

Projection: Modified Hammer Equal Area

*Statistics for the new republics of the former U.S.S.R., Czechoslovakia and Yugoslavia are not yet available. The map shows the statistics for the entire U.S.S.R., Czechoslovakia and Yugoslavia.

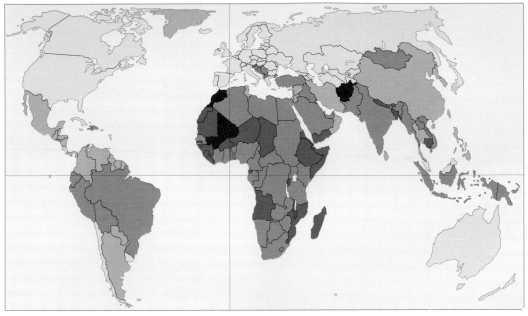

CHILD MORTALITY

The number of babies who will die under the age of one, per 1 000 births (average 1990-95)*

- Over 150 deaths per 1 000 births
- 100-150 deaths per 1 000 births
- 50-100 deaths per 1 000 births
- 20-50 deaths per 1 000 births
- 10-20 deaths per 1 000 births
- Under 10 deaths per 1 000 births

Highest child mortality		Lowest child mortality	
Afghanistan	162 deaths	Hong Kong	6 deaths
Mali	159 deaths	Denmark	6 deaths
Sierra Leone	143 deaths	Japan	5 deaths
Guinea-Bissau	140 deaths	Iceland	5 deaths
Malawi	138 deaths	Finland	5 deaths
		U.K.	8 deaths

LIFE EXPECTANCY

Average expected lifespan in years of babies born in the period 1990-95*

- Over 75 years
- 70-75 years
- 65-70 years
- 60-65 years
- 55-60 years
- 50-55 years
- Under 50 years

Highest life expectancy		Lowest life expectancy	
Japan	79 years	Gambia	45 years
Iceland	78 years	Guinea	45 years
Sweden	78 years	Afghanistan	44 years
Hong Kong	78 years	Guinea-Bissau	44 years
Switzerland	78 years	Sierra Leone	43 years
		U.K.	76 years

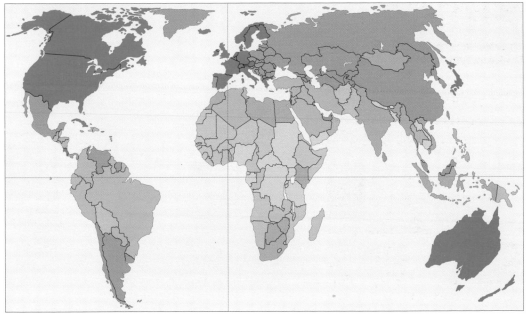

FAMILY SIZE

The average number of children a woman can expect to bear during her lifetime 1991

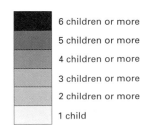

- 6 children or more
- 5 children or more
- 4 children or more
- 3 children or more
- 2 children or more
- 1 child

In the U.K. the average family size is 1.8 children per family, whilst in Kenya the average size is 6.8 children.

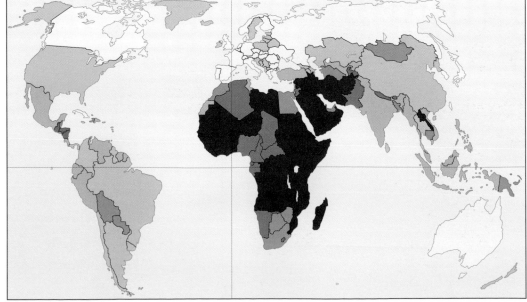

Projection: *Modified Hammer Equal Area*

Statistics for the new republics of the former U.S.S.R., Czechoslovakia and Yugoslavia are not yet available. The map shows the statistics for the entire U.S.S.R., Czechoslovakia and Yugoslavia.

CARTOGRAPHY BY PHILIP'S. COPYRIGHT REED INTERNATIONAL BOOKS LTD

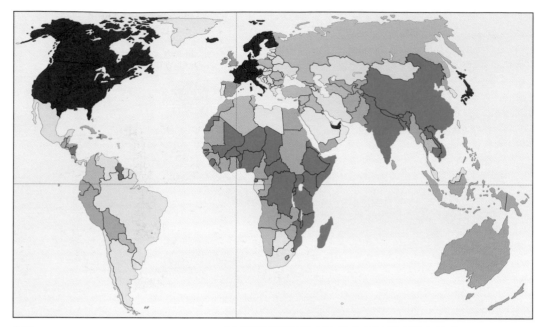

WEALTH

The value of total production in 1991 divided by the population.
(The Gross National Product per capita)

- Over 400% of world average
- 200 - 400% of world average
- 100 - 200% of world average

World average wealth per person $4 210

- 50 - 100% of world average
- 25 - 50% of world average
- 10 - 25% of world average
- Under 10% of world average

Top 5 countries		Bottom 5 countries	
Switzerland	$33 510	Mozambique	$70
Luxembourg	$31 080	Tanzania	$100
Japan	$26 920	Ethiopia	$120
Sweden	$25 490	Somalia	$150
Bermuda	$25 000	Uganda	$160
		U.K. $16 750	

AID

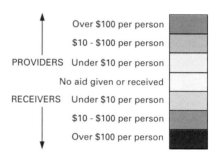

Aid provided or received, divided by the total population 1990*

	Over $100 per person
	$10 - $100 per person
PROVIDERS	Under $10 per person
	No aid given or received
RECEIVERS	Under $10 per person
	$10 - $100 per person
	Over $100 per person

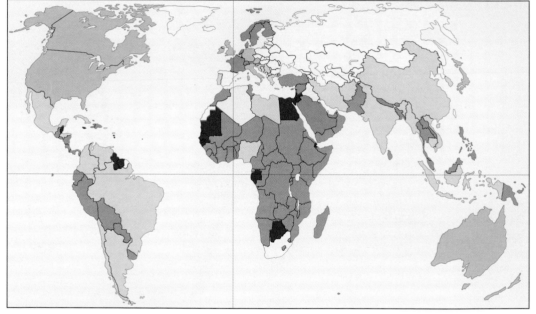

Top 5 providers		Top 5 receivers	
Kuwait	$793	Israel	$295
U.A.E.	$555	Djibouti	$293
Norway	$287	Jordan	$221
Saudi Arabia	$248	Dominica	$185
Sweden	$234	Surinam	$135
U.K. $46			

ILLITERACY

Percentage of the total population unable to read or write (latest available year)*

- Over 75% of population illiterate
- 50 - 75% of population illiterate
- 25 - 50% of population illiterate
- 10 - 25% of population illiterate
- Under 10% of population illiterate

Educational expenditure per person (latest available year)

Top 5 countries		Bottom 5 countries	
Sweden	$997	Chad	$2
Qatar	$989	Bangladesh	$3
Canada	$983	Ethiopia	$3
Norway	$971	Nepal	$4
Switzerland	$796	Somalia	$4
		U.K. $447	

Projection: *Modified Hammer Equal Area*

*Statistics for the new republics of the former U.S.S.R., Czechoslovakia and Yugoslavia are not yet available.
The map shows the statistics for the entire U.S.S.R., Czechoslovakia and Yugoslavia.

THE IMPORTANCE OF AGRICULTURE

The percentage of the total population who depend on agriculture 1991

Over 75% dependent

50 - 75% dependent

25 - 50% dependent

10 - 25% dependent

Under 10% dependent

Top 5 countries		Bottom 5 countries	
Nepal	92%	Singapore	0.9%
Rwanda	91%	Hong Kong	1.2%
Burundi	91%	Bahrain	1.7%
Bhutan	91%	Belgium	1.7%
Niger	87%	U.K.	1.9%

DAILY FOOD CONSUMPTION

Average daily food intake in calories per person 1989*

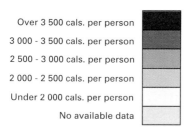

Over 3 500 cals. per person

3 000 - 3 500 cals. per person

2 500 - 3 000 cals. per person

2 000 - 2 500 cals. per person

Under 2 000 cals. per person

No available data

Top 5 countries		Bottom 5 countries	
Belgium	3 902	Ethiopia	1 666
Greece	3 825	Mozambique	1 679
Ireland	3 778	Chad	1 742
Bulgaria	3 707	Sierra Leone	1 799
U.S.A.	3 670	Angola	1 806
		U.K.	3 148

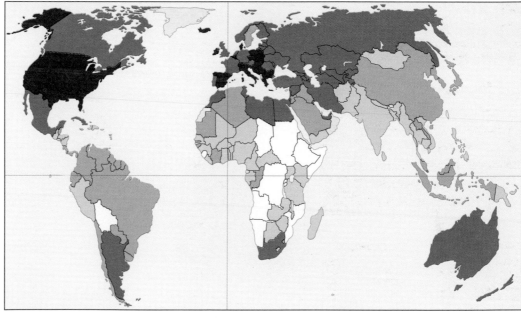

HEALTH CARE

Number of people per doctor (latest available year)*

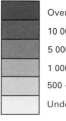

Over 25 000 people per doctor

10 000 - 25 000 people per doctor

5 000 - 10 000 people per doctor

1 000 - 5 000 people per doctor

500 - 1 000 people per doctor

Under 500 people per doctor

Most people per doctor		Least people per doctor	
Ethiopia	78 740	Russia	235
Equatorial Guinea	62 000	Austria	256
Mozambique	50 817	Hungary	304
Chad	47 640	Spain	316
Burkina Faso	42 128	Belgium	342
		U.K.	668

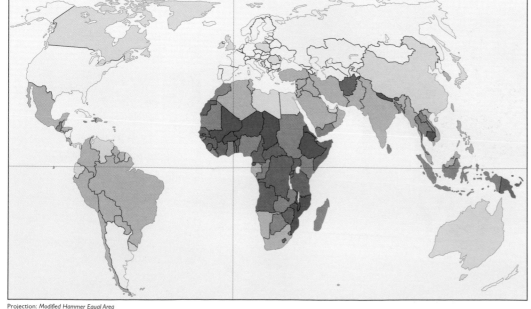

Projection: *Modified Hammer Equal Area*

Statistics for the new republics of the former U.S.S.R., Czechoslovakia and Yugoslavia are not yet available. The map shows the statistics for the entire U.S.S.R., Czechoslovakia and Yugoslavia.

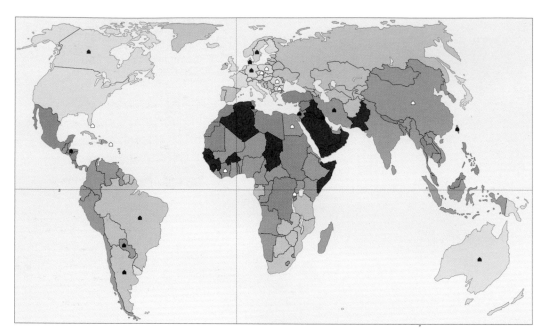

HOUSING

Number of people per household
(latest available year)*

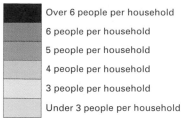

- Over 6 people per household
- 6 people per household
- 5 people per household
- 4 people per household
- 3 people per household
- Under 3 people per household

Expenditure on housing and energy as a
percentage of total consumer spending

- ▲   Over 20% spent
- △   Under 5% spent

WATER SUPPLY

Percentage of total population
with access to safe drinking water
(latest available year)*

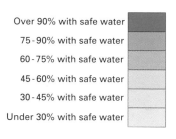

- Over 90% with safe water
- 75 - 90% with safe water
- 60 - 75% with safe water
- 45 - 60% with safe water
- 30 - 45% with safe water
- Under 30% with safe water

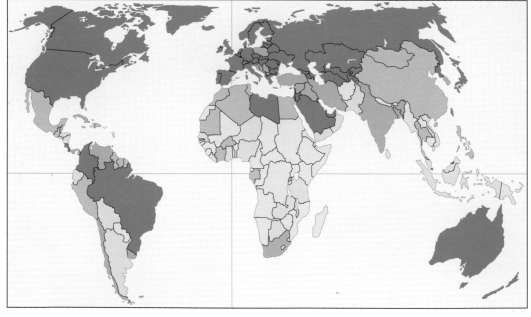

Least well provided countries

Cambodia	3%	Afghanistan	21%
Central Africa	12%	Congo	21%
Ethiopia	19%	Guinea Bissau	21%
Uganda	20%	Sudan	21%

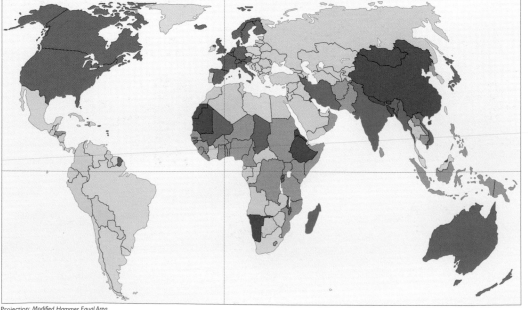

CAR OWNERSHIP

Number of people per car
(latest available year)*

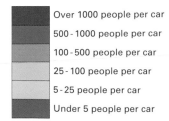

- Over 1000 people per car
- 500 - 1000 people per car
- 100 - 500 people per car
- 25 - 100 people per car
- 5 - 25 people per car
- Under 5 people per car

Most people per car		Most cars (millions)	
China	4300	U.S.A.	140.7
Mauritania	3400	Japan	30.8
Bangladesh	2053	Germany	29.2
Nepal	2000	France	27.0
Togo	1237	Italy	23.5

Projection: *Modified Hammer Equal Area*

*Statistics for the new republics of the former U.S.S.R., Czechoslovakia and Yugoslavia are not yet available.
The map shows the statistics for the entire U.S.S.R., Czechoslovakia and Yugoslavia.*

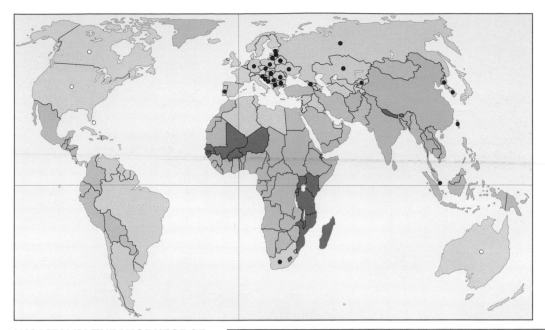

TYPE OF WORK

Percentage of total workforce
employed in agriculture†,
(latest available year)*

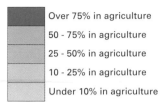

Over 75% in agriculture

50 - 75% in agriculture

25 - 50% in agriculture

10 - 25% in agriculture

Under 10% in agriculture

● Over 25% of total workforce
employed in manufacturing

○ Over 75% of total workforce
employed in service industries
(work in offices, shops, tourism,
transport, construction and
government)

†Includes forestry and fishing

WOMEN IN THE WORKFORCE

Working women as a percentage of
the total workforce (latest available year)

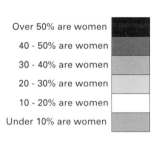

Over 50% are women

40 - 50% are women

30 - 40% are women

20 - 30% are women

10 - 20% are women

Under 10% are women

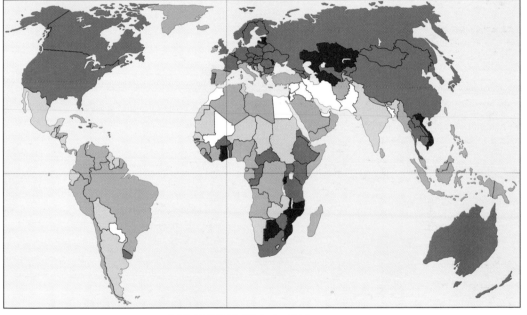

Most women in the workforce		Fewest women in the workforce	
Kazakhstan	54%	Guinea Bissau	3%
Rwanda	54%	Oman	6%
Botswana	53%	Afghanistan	8%
Burundi	53%	Libya	8%
Mozambique	52%	Algeria	9%
U.K.	43%		

SELF SUFFICIENCY IN FOOD

Balance of trade in food products as
a percentage of total trade in food
products 1988*

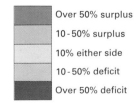

Over 50% surplus

10 - 50% surplus

10% either side

10 - 50% deficit

Over 50% deficit

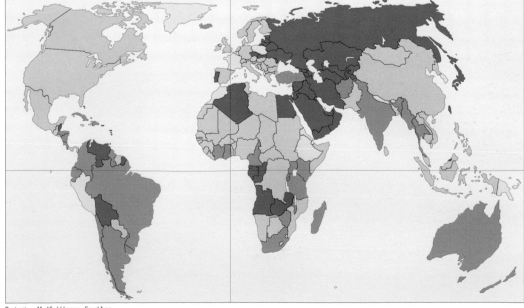

Projection: *Modified Hammer Equal Area*

CARTOGRAPHY BY PHILIP'S. COPYRIGHT REED INTERNATIONAL BOOKS LTD

*Statistics for the new republics of the former U.S.S.R., Czechoslovakia and Yugoslavia are not yet available.
The map shows the statistics for the entire U.S.S.R., Czechoslovakia and Yugoslavia.

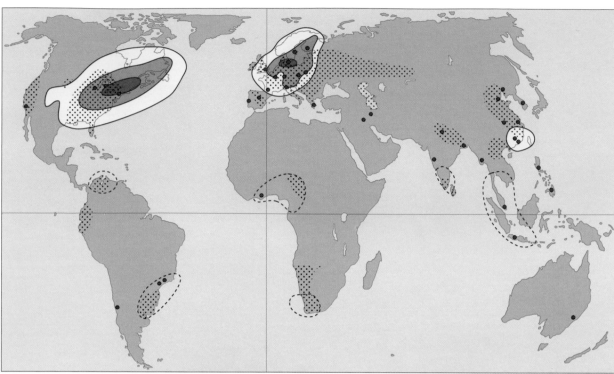

ACID RAIN

Acid rain is caused by high levels of sulphur and nitrogen in the atmosphere. They combine with water vapour and oxygen to form acids (H_2SO_4 and HNO_3) which fall as precipitation.

 Main areas of sulphur and nitrogen emission (from the burning of fossil fuels)

 Major cities with high levels of air pollution (including sulphur and nitrogen emissions)

Areas of acid deposition

(pH numbers measure acidity: normal rain is pH 5.6)

pH less than 4.0 (most acidic)

pH 4.0 - 4.5

pH 4.5 - 5.0

Potential problem areas

GLOBAL WARMING

Global warming is caused by high levels of carbon dioxide and other gases in the atmosphere (the Greenhouse Effect). It is estimated that by 2020 the world could be approximately 1.3°C warmer than now.

Carbon dioxide (CO_2) emissions in tonnes per person per year*

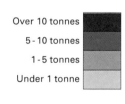

Over 10 tonnes

5 - 10 tonnes

1 - 5 tonnes

Under 1 tonne

Coastal areas vulnerable to rising sea levels caused by global warming

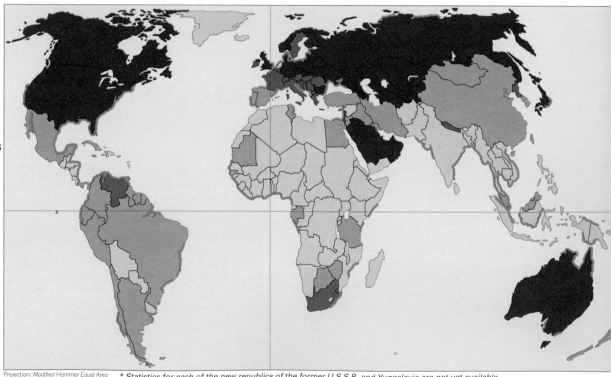

Projection: Modified Hammer Equal Area

* Statistics for each of the new republics of the former U.S.S.R. and Yugoslavia are not yet available. The map shows the statistics for the entire U.S.S.R. and Yugoslavia.

THE GREENHOUSE EFFECT

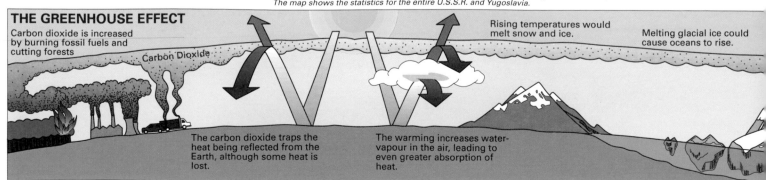

Carbon dioxide is increased by burning fossil fuels and cutting forests

Carbon Dioxide

Rising temperatures would melt snow and ice.

Melting glacial ice could cause oceans to rise.

The carbon dioxide traps the heat being reflected from the Earth, although some heat is lost.

The warming increases water-vapour in the air, leading to even greater absorption of heat.

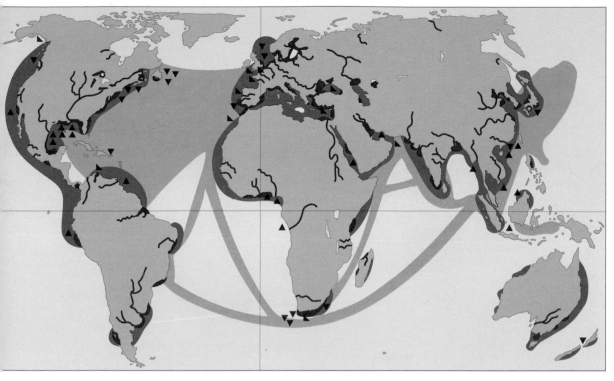

WATER POLLUTION

	Severely polluted sea areas and lakes
	Other polluted sea areas and lakes
	Sea areas of frequent oil pollution from shipping

 Major oil tanker spills

▲ Major oil rig blow-outs

▼ Offshore dumpsites for industrial and municipal waste

── Severely polluted rivers

DESERTIFICATION

	Existing deserts
	Areas with a high risk of desertification
	Areas with a moderate risk of desertification

DEFORESTATION IN THE TROPICS

| | Former areas of rainforest |
| | Existing rainforest |

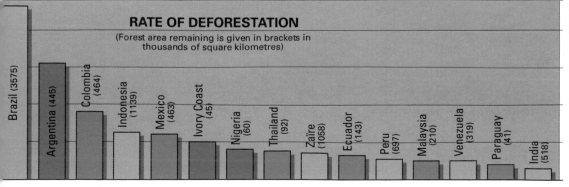

RATE OF DEFORESTATION

(Forest area remaining is given in brackets in thousands of square kilometres)

Brazil (3575), Argentina (445), Colombia (464), Indonesia (1139), Mexico (463), Ivory Coast (45), Nigeria (60), Thailand (92), Zaïre (1058), Ecuador (143), Peru (697), Malaysia (210), Venezuela (319), Paraguay (41), India (518)

Forest area lost each year in the 1980s
20 000km²
15 000km²
10 000km²
5 000km²

Rate of deforestation (% each year)

Over 2.5%
1.0 - 2.5%
0 - 1.0%

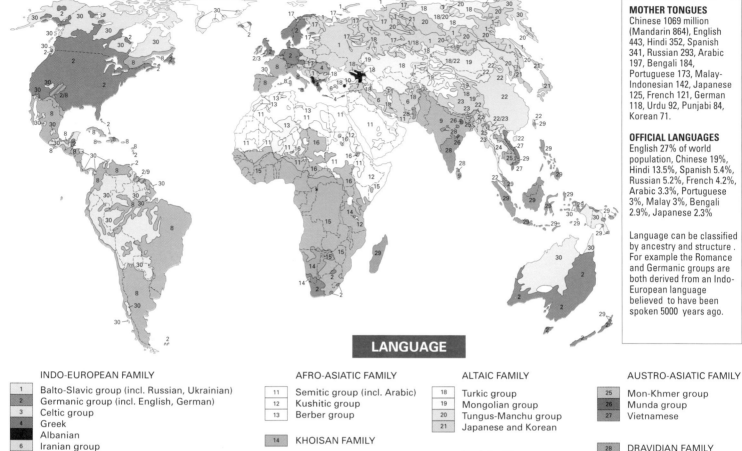

MOTHER TONGUES
Chinese 1069 million
(Mandarin 864), English
443, Hindi 352, Spanish
341, Russian 293, Arabic
197, Bengali 184,
Portuguese 173, Malay-
Indonesian 142, Japanese
125, French 121, German
118, Urdu 92, Punjabi 84,
Korean 71.

OFFICIAL LANGUAGES
English 27% of world
population, Chinese 19%,
Hindi 13.5%, Spanish 5.4%,
Russian 5.2%, French 4.2%,
Arabic 3.3%, Portuguese
3%, Malay 3%, Bengali
2.9%, Japanese 2.3%

Language can be classified
by ancestry and structure .
For example the Romance
and Germanic groups are
both derived from an Indo-
European language
believed to have been
spoken 5000 years ago.

LANGUAGE

INDO-EUROPEAN FAMILY

- 1 Balto-Slavic group (incl. Russian, Ukrainian)
- 2 Germanic group (incl. English, German)
- 3 Celtic group
- 4 Greek
- 5 Albanian
- 6 Iranian group
- 7 Armenian
- 8 Romance group (incl. Spanish, Portuguese, French, Italian)
- 9 Indo-Aryan group (incl. Hindi, Bengali, Urdu, Punjabi, Marathi)
- 10 CAUCASIAN FAMILY

AFRO-ASIATIC FAMILY

- 11 Semitic group (incl. Arabic)
- 12 Kushitic group
- 13 Berber group
- 14 KHOISAN FAMILY
- 15 NIGER-CONGO FAMILY
- 16 NILO-SAHARAN FAMILY
- 17 URALIC FAMILY

ALTAIC FAMILY

- 18 Turkic group
- 19 Mongolian group
- 20 Tungus-Manchu group
- 21 Japanese and Korean

SINO-TIBETAN FAMILY

- 22 Sinitic (Chinese) languages
- 23 Tibetic-Burmic languages
- 24 TAI FAMILY

AUSTRO-ASIATIC FAMILY

- 25 Mon-Khmer group
- 26 Munda group
- 27 Vietnamese
- 28 DRAVIDIAN FAMILY (incl. Telugu, Tamil)
- 29 AUSTRONESIAN FAMILY (incl. Malay-Indonesian)
- 30 OTHER LANGUAGES

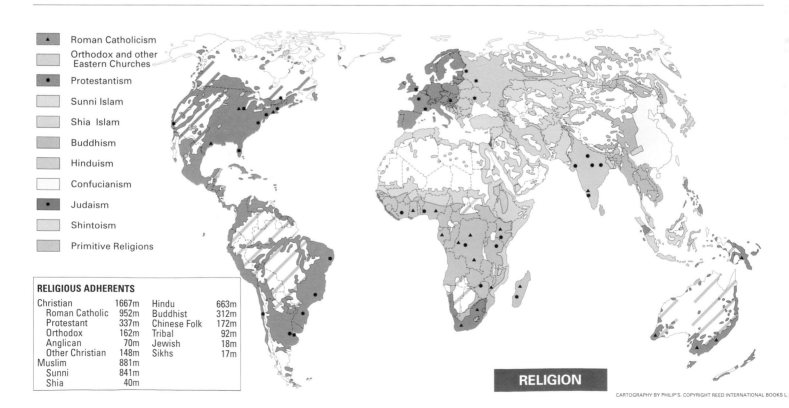

- ▲ Roman Catholicism
- Orthodox and other Eastern Churches
- • Protestantism
- Sunni Islam
- Shia Islam
- Buddhism
- Hinduism
- Confucianism
- • Judaism
- Shintoism
- Primitive Religions

RELIGIOUS ADHERENTS

Christian	1667m	Hindu	663m
Roman Catholic	952m	Buddhist	312m
Protestant	337m	Chinese Folk	172m
Orthodox	162m	Tribal	92m
Anglican	70m	Jewish	18m
Other Christian	148m	Sikhs	17m
Muslim	881m		
Sunni	841m		
Shia	40m		

RELIGION

UNITED NATIONS

Created in 1945 to promote peace and co-operation and based in New York, the United Nations is the world's largest international organization, with 184 members and an annual budget of US $2.6 billion (1994–95). Each member of the General Assembly has one vote, while the permanent members of the 15-nation Security Council – USA, Russia, China, UK and France – hold a veto. The 54 members of the Economic and Social Council are responsible for economic, social, cultural, educational, health and related matters. The Secretariat is the UN's principal administrative arm; the only territory now administered by the Trusteeship Council is Belau (by the USA). The UN has 16 specialized agencies – based in Canada, France, Switzerland and Italy as well as the USA – which help members in fields such as education (UNESCO), agriculture (FAO), medicine (WHO) and finance (IFC).

[The International Court of Justice is based in The Hague]

Members of UN
Year of joining

- 1940s
- 1950s
- 1960s
- 1970s
- 1980s
- 1990s
- Non members

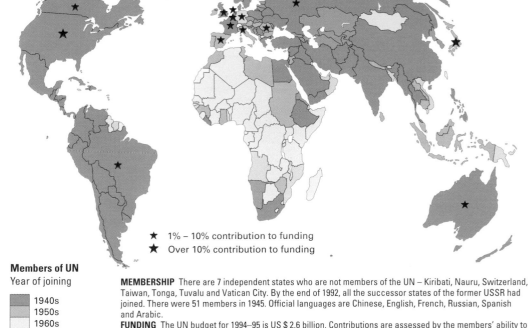

★ 1% – 10% contribution to funding
★ Over 10% contribution to funding

MEMBERSHIP There are 7 independent states who are not members of the UN – Kiribati, Nauru, Switzerland, Taiwan, Tonga, Tuvalu and Vatican City. By the end of 1992, all the successor states of the former USSR had joined. There were 51 members in 1945. Official languages are Chinese, English, French, Russian, Spanish and Arabic.

FUNDING The UN budget for 1994–95 is US $ 2.6 billion. Contributions are assessed by the members' ability to pay, with the maximum 25% of the total, the minimum 0.01%. Contributions for 1992–94 were: USA 25%, Japan 12.45%, Germany 8.93%, Russia 6.71%, France 6%, UK 5.02%, Italy 4.29%, Canada 3.11% (others 28.49%).

PEACEKEEPING The UN has been involved in 33 peacekeeping operations worldwide since 1948 and there are currently 17 areas of UN patrol. In July 1993 there were 80,146 'blue berets' from 74 countries.

EC As from December 1993 the European Union (EU) refers to matters of foreign policy, security and justice. The European Community (EC) refers to all other matters. The 12 members – Belgium, Denmark, France, Germany, Greece, Ireland, Italy, Luxembourg, Netherlands, Portugal, Spain and the UK – aim to integrate economies, co-ordinate social developments and bring about political union. These members of what is now the world's biggest market share agricultural and industrial policies and tariffs on trade.

EFTA European Free Trade Association (formed in 1960). Portugal left the 'Seven' in 1989 to join the EC.

ACP African-Caribbean-Pacific (1963).

NATO North Atlantic Treaty Organization (formed in 1949). It continues after 1991 despite the winding up of the Warsaw Pact.

OAS Organization of American States (1949). It aims to promote social and economic co-operation between developed countries of North America and developing nations of Latin America.

ASEAN Association of South-east Asian Nations (1967).

OAU Organization of African Unity (1963). Its 52 members represent over 90% of Africa's population.

LAIA Latin American Integration Association (1980).

OECD Organization for Economic Co-operation and Development (1961). The 24 major Western free-market economies. 'G7' is its 'inner group' of USA, Canada, Japan, UK, Germany, Italy and France.

COMMONWEALTH The Commonwealth of Nations evolved from the British Empire; it comprises 18 nations recognizing the British monarch as head of state and 32 with their own heads of state.

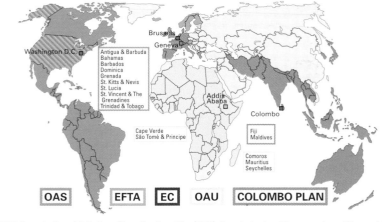

OAS   EFTA   EC   OAU   COLOMBO PLAN

OPEC Organization of Petroleum Exporting Countries (1960). It controls about three-quarters of the world's oil supply.

ARAB LEAGUE (1945) The League's aim is to promote economic, social, political and military co-operation.

COLOMBO PLAN (1951) Its 26 members aim to promote economic and social development in Asia and the Pacific.

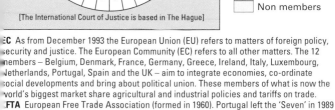

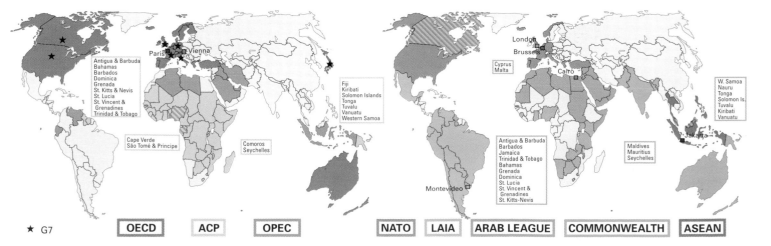

★ G7   OECD   ACP   OPEC   NATO   LAIA   ARAB LEAGUE   COMMONWEALTH   ASEAN

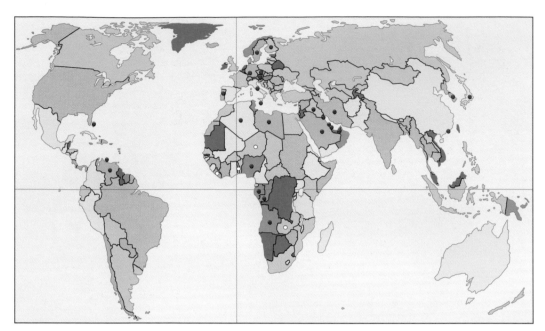

DEPENDENCE ON TRADE

Value of exports as a percentage of G.D.P. (Gross Domestic Product) 1989

Over 50% G.D.P.

40 - 50% G.D.P.

30 - 40% G.D.P.

20 - 30% G.D.P.

10 - 20% G.D.P.

Under 10% G.D.P.

● Most dependent on industrial exports (over 75% of total exports)

● Most dependent on fuel exports (over 75% of total exports)

○ Most dependent on metal and mineral exports (over 75% of total exports)

BALANCE OF TRADE

Value of exports in proportion to the value of imports (latest available year)

Exports exceed imports by:

More than 40%

10 - 40%

10% either side

10 - 40%

More than 40%

Imports exceed exports by:

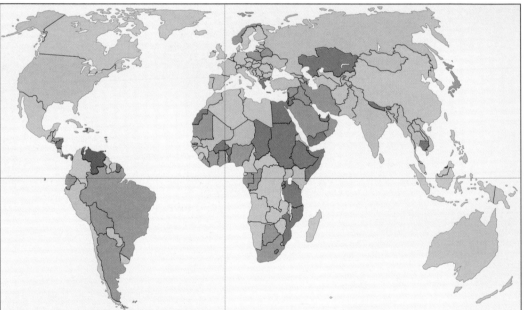

SHARE OF WORLD TRADE

Percentage share of total world exports by value 1990*

Over 10% of world trade

5 - 10% of world trade

1 - 5% of world trade

0.5 - 1% of world trade

0.25 - 0.5% of world trade

Under 0.25% of world trade

Projection: *Modified Hammer Equal Area*

*Statistics for the new republics of the former U.S.S.R., Czechoslovakia and Yugoslavia are not yet available. The map shows the statistics for the entire U.S.S.R., Czechoslovakia and Yugoslavia.

SHIPPING

Freight unloaded in
millions of tonnes
(latest available year)*

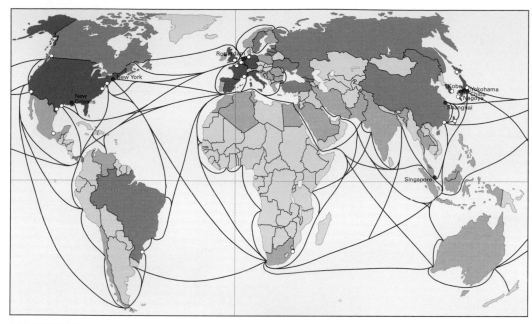

Over 100 million tonnes

50 - 100 million tonnes

10 - 50 million tonnes

5 - 10 million tonnes

Under 5 million tonnes

Land-locked countries

Major Seaports

● Handling over 100 million
tonnes p.a.

○ Handling 50 - 100 million
tonnes p.a.

AIR TRAVEL

Passenger kilometres flown
(latest available year)

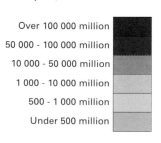

Over 100 000 million

50 000 - 100 000 million

10 000 - 50 000 million

1 000 - 10 000 million

500 - 1 000 million

Under 500 million

Major airports (handling over ○
20 million passengers in 1991)

Passenger kilometres are the number of
passengers (international and domestic)
multiplied by the distance flown by each
passenger from the airport of origin.

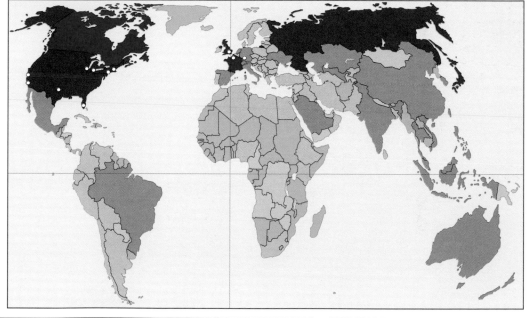

TOURISM

Tourism receipts as a percentage of
G.N.P. (Gross National Product) 1990*

Over 10% of G.N.P. from tourism

5 - 10% of G.N.P. from tourism

2.5 - 5% of G.N.P. from tourism

1 - 2.5% of G.N.P. from tourism

0.5 - 1% of G.N.P. from tourism

Under 0.5% of G.N.P. from tourism

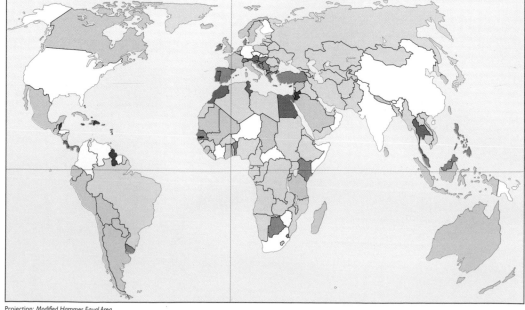

Largest percentage share of total world spending on tourism 1991		Largest percentage share of total world receipts from tourism 1991	
U.S.A.	16%	U.S.A.	16%
Germany	13%	France	8%
Japan	10%	Italy	8%
U.K.	7%	Spain	7%
Italy	6%	U.K.	6%

Projection: *Modified Hammer Equal Area*

*Statistics for the new republics of the former U.S.S.R., Czechoslovakia and Yugoslavia are not yet available.
The map shows the statistics for the entire U.S.S.R., Czechoslovakia and Yugoslavia.*

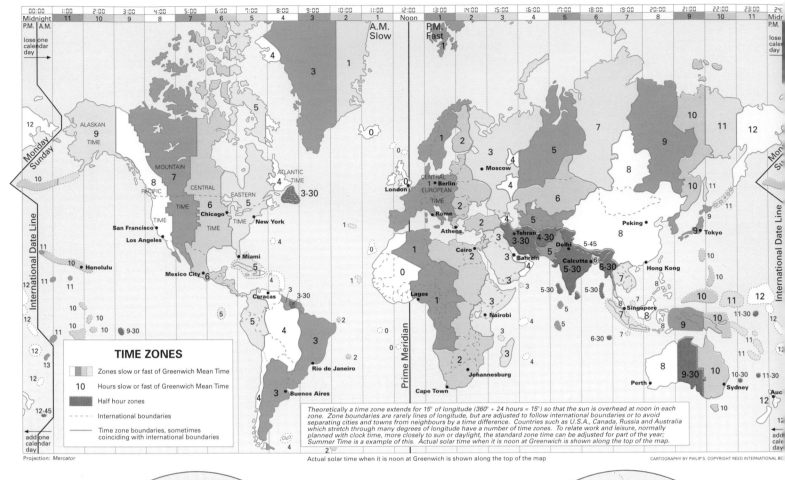

00:00	1:00	2:00	3:00	4:00	5:00	6:00	7:00	8:00	9:00	10:00	11:00	12:00	13:00	14:00	15:00	16:00	17:00	18:00	19:00	20:00	21:00	22:00	23:00	24:
Midnight	11	10	9	8	7	6	5	4	3	2	1	Noon	1	2	3	4	5	6	7	8	9	10	11	Midr
P.M.	A.M.																							P.M.

A.M. Slow   P.M. Fast

TIME ZONES

Zones slow or fast of Greenwich Mean Time

10 Hours slow or fast of Greenwich Mean Time

Half hour zones

--- International boundaries

— Time zone boundaries, sometimes coinciding with international boundaries

Theoretically a time zone extends for 15° of longitude (360° ÷ 24 hours = 15°) so that the sun is overhead at noon in each zone. Zone boundaries are rarely lines of longitude, but are adjusted to follow international boundaries or to avoid separating cities and towns from neighbours by a time difference. Countries such as U.S.A., Canada, Russia and Australia which stretch through many degrees of longitude have a number of time zones. To relate work and leisure, normally planned with clock time, more closely to sun or daylight, the standard zone time can be adjusted for part of the year; Summer Time is a example of this. Actual solar time when it is noon at Greenwich is shown along the top of the map.

Projection: *Mercator*

Actual solar time when it is noon at Greenwich is shown along the top of the map

CARTOGRAPHY BY PHILIP'S. COPYRIGHT REED INTERNATIONAL BC

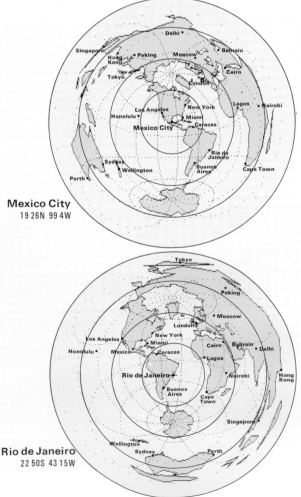

Mexico City
19 26N 99 4W

Rio de Janeiro
22 50S 43 15W

These circular maps are drawn on an Azimuthal Equidistant projection with its origin, its centre, at the city shown. The whole world is shown and so there are some strange distortions of the coastline at the edges, for example, in that of Singapore. The principal property of the projection is that all distances measured through the centre of the circle are true to scale, and so a straight line passing from the centre to any other point is a great circle and shows the shortest distance between the cities. Also that line is correct for direction/bearing and shows the great circle flight path.

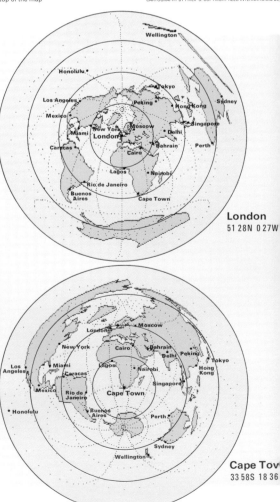

London
51 28N 0 27W

Cape Tov
33 58S 18 36

	Bahrain	Buenos Aires	Cairo	Cape Town	Caracas	Delhi	Hong Kong	Honolulu	Lagos	London	Los Angeles	Mexico	Miami	Moscow	Nairobi	New York	Peking	Perth	Rio de Janeiro	Singapore	Sydney	Tokyo
Buenos Aires	13 291																					
Cairo	1 927	11 845																				
Cape Town	7 496	6 880	7 246																			
Caracas	12 121	5 124	10 200	10 254																		
Delhi	2 618	15 784	4 400	9 278	14 186																	
Hong Kong	6 387	18 442	8 121	11 852	16 340	3 768																
Honolulu	13 882	12 158	14 195	18 555	9 671	11 984	8 911															
Lagos	5 454	7 932	3 926	4 783	7 722	8 071	11 832	16 286														
London	5 089	11 128	3 528	9 672	7 465	6 726	9 637	11 617	4 998													
Los Angeles	13 210	9 854	12 206	16 067	5 813	12 863	11 634	4 105	12 408	8 752												
Mexico	13 962	7 391	12 360	13 701	3 572	14 651	12 121	6 096	11 043	8 898	2 498											
Miami	12 182	7 113	10 441	12 334	2 190	13 495	14 430	7 806	9 045	7 102	3 759	2 050										
Moscow	3 466	13 488	2 909	10 150	9 900	4 359	7 148	11 289	6 250	2 505	9 748	10 682	9 191									
Nairobi	3 398	10 413	3 542	4 096	11 545	5 413	8 750	17 255	3 828	6 835	15 560	14 812	12 771	6 365								
New York	10 613	8 526	9 009	12 551	3 402	11 747	12 956	8 000	8 437	5 535	3 968	3 361	1 751	7 476	11 828							
Peking	6 180	19 273	7 526	12 956	14 356	3 804	1 985	8 124	11 452	8 146	10 030	12 426	12 475	5 789	9 217	10 971						
Perth	9 467	12 562	11 256	8 684	17 610	7 874	6 030	10 886	12 517	14 495	14 986	16 247	18 281	12 236	8 889	18 699	8 000					
Rio de Janeiro	11 462	1 990	9 897	6 080	4 522	14 054	17 688	13 330	6 022	9 248	10 132	7 659	6 713	11 528	8 937	7 724	17 306	13 527				
Singapore	6 319	15 860	8 246	9 650	18 332	4 148	2 581	10 789	11 149	10 867	14 099	16 593	16 951	8 437	7 446	15 330	4 489	3 909	15 729			
Sydney	12 502	11 760	14 391	10 982	15 341	10 424	7 370	8 163	15 514	17 005	12 052	12 973	15 012	14 501	12 125	16 001	8 956	3 274	13 512	6 294		
Tokyo	8 271	18 338	9 552	14 710	14 154	5 852	2 874	6 185	13 475	9 584	8 806	11 304	11 991	7 487	11 243	10 869	2 089	7 896	18 557	5 300	7 809	
Wellington	14 678	9 943	16 503	11 287	13 119	12 647	9 424	7 508	16 047	18 816	10 787	11 099	13 054	16 547	13 643	14 406	10 782	5 246	11 865	8 521	2 226	9 258

These distances are in kilometres and are the great circle distances between the cities (international airports). Great circle distances are the shortest distances between two points on the globe. They are the normal flight paths for aircraft where they are free from the restrictions of air corridors or national airspace.

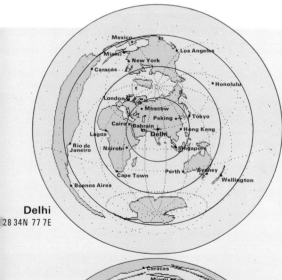

Delhi
28 34N 77 7E

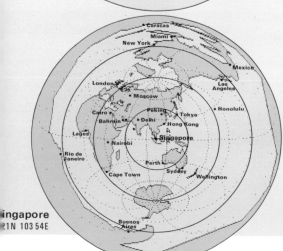

Singapore
1 21N 103 54E

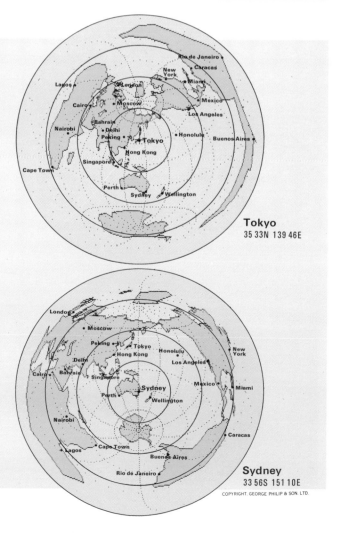

Tokyo
35 33N 139 46E

Sydney
33 56S 151 10E

The three circles are drawn at radius 5 000, 10 000 and 15 000 km from the central city

• Cities shown on the distance table

The co-ordinates given are for the airport of each city

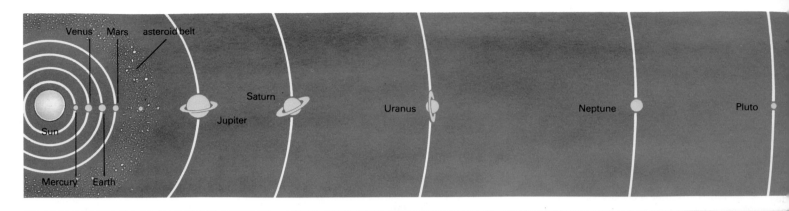

THE SOLAR SYSTEM

A minute part of one of the billions of galaxies (collections of stars) that comprise the Universe, the Solar System lies some 27,000 light-years from the centre of our own galaxy, the 'Milky Way'. Thought to be over 4,700 million years old, it consists of a central sun with nine planets and their moons revolving around it, attracted by its gravitational pull. The planets orbit the Sun in the same direction – anti-clockwise when viewed from the Northern Heavens – and almost in the same plane. Their orbital paths, however, vary enormously.

The Sun's diameter is 109 times that of Earth, and the temperature at its core – caused by continuous thermonuclear fusions of hydrogen into helium – is estimated to be 15 million degrees Celsius. It is the Solar System's only source of light and heat.

PROFILE OF THE PLANETS

	Mean distance from Sun (million km)	Mass (Earth = 1)	Period of orbit	Period of rotation (in days)	Diameter (km)	Number of known satellites
Mercury	58.3	0.06	88 days	58.67	4,878	0
Venus	107.7	0.8	224.7 days	243.0	12,104	0
Earth	149.6	1.0	365.24 days	0.99	12,756	1
Mars	227.3	0.1	1.88 years	1.02	6,794	2
Jupiter	777.9	317.8	11.86 years	0.41	142,800	16
Saturn	1427.1	95.2	29.63 years	0.42	120,000	17
Uranus	2872.3	14.5	83.97 years	0.45	52,000	15
Neptune	4502.7	17.2	164.8 years	0.67	48,400	8
Pluto	5894.2	0.002	248.63 years	6.38	2,400	1

All planetary orbits are elliptical in form, but only Pluto and Mercury follow paths that deviate noticeably from a circular one. Near Perihelion - its closest approach to the Sun - Pluto actually passes inside the orbit of Neptune, an event that last occurred in 1983. Pluto will not regain its station as outermost planet until February 1999.

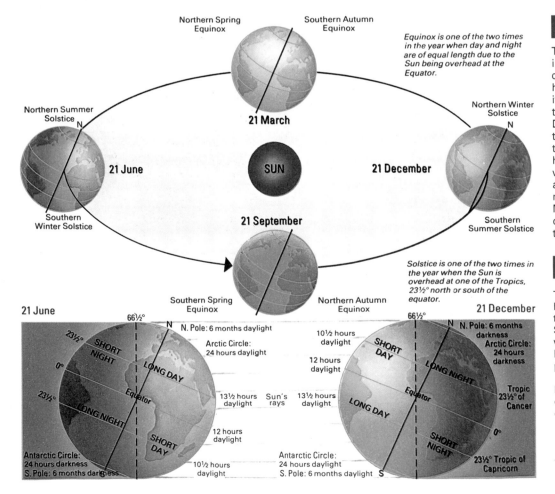

THE SEASONS

The Earth revolves around the Sun once a year in an 'anti-clockwise' direction, tilted at a constant angle 66½°. In June, the northern hemisphere is tilted towards the Sun: as a result it receives more hours of sunshine in a day and therefore has its warmest season, summer. In December, the Earth has rotated halfway round the Sun so that the southern hemisphere is tilted towards the Sun and has its summer; the hemisphere that is tilted away from the Sun has winter. On 21 June the Sun is directly overhead at the Tropic of Cancer (23½° N), and this is midsummer in the northern hemisphere. Midsummer in the southern hemisphere occurs on 21 December, when the Sun is overhead at the Tropic of Capricorn (23½° S).

DAY & NIGHT

The Sun appears to rise in the east, reach its highest point at noon, and then set in the west to be followed by night. In reality it is not the Sun that is moving but the Earth revolving from west to east. Due to the tilting of the Earth the length of day and night varies from place to place and month to month.

At the summer solstice in the northern hemisphere (21 June), the Arctic has total daylight and the Antarctic total darkness. The opposite occurs at the winter solstice (21 December). At the equator, the length of day and night are almost equal all year, at latitude 30° the length of day varies from about 14 hours to 10 hours, and at latitude 50° from about hours to about 8 hours.

TIME

r: the time taken by the Earth to revolve around
Sun, or 365.24 days.

nth: the approximate time taken by the Moon to
lve around the Earth. The 12 months of the
r in fact vary from 28 (29 in a Leap Year) to 31
s.

k: an artificial period of 7 days, not based on
onomical time.

: the time taken by the Earth to complete one
tion on its axis.

r: 24 hours make one day. Usually the day is
ded into hours AM (ante meridiem or before
n) and PM (post meridiem or after noon),
ough most timetables now use the 24-hour
em, from midnight to midnight.

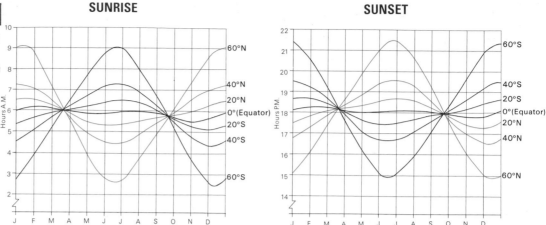

SUNRISE

SUNSET

THE MOON

Distance from Earth: 356,410 km - 406,685 km; Mean diameter: 3,475.1 km; Mass: approx. 1/81 that of Earth;
Surface gravity: one sixth of Earth's; Daily range of temperature at lunar equator: 200°C; Average orbital speed: 3,683 km/h

PHASES OF THE MOON

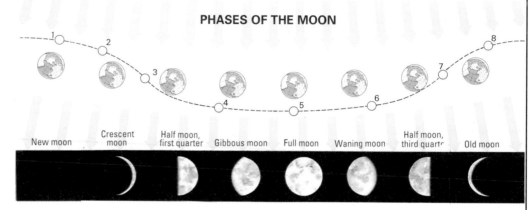

| New moon | Crescent moon | Half moon, first quarter | Gibbous moon | Full moon | Waning moon | Half moon, third quarter | Old moon |

e Moon rotates more slowly than the Earth, making
e complete turn on its axis in just over 27 days.
ce this corresponds to its period of revolution
und the Earth, the Moon always presents the

same hemisphere or face to us, and we never see 'the
dark side'. The interval between one full Moon and
the next (and between new Moons) is about 29½
days - a lunar month. The apparent changes in the

shape of the Moon are caused by its changing
position in relation to the Earth; like the planets, it
produces no light of its own and shines only by
reflecting the rays of the Sun.

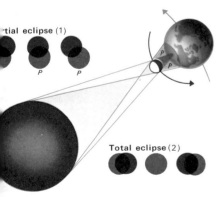

tial eclipse (1)

Total eclipse (2)

Lunar eclipse

ECLIPSES

When the Moon passes between the Sun and the
Earth it causes a partial eclipse of the Sun (1) if the
Earth passes through the Moon's outer shadow
(P), or a total eclipse (2) if the inner cone shadow
crosses the Earth's surface. In a lunar eclipse, the
Earth's shadow crosses the Moon and, again,
provides either a partial or total eclipse. Eclipses
of the Sun and the Moon do not occur every
month because of the 5° difference between the
plane of the Moon's orbit and the plane in which
the Earth moves. In the 1990s only 14 lunar
eclipses are possible, for example, seven partial
and seven total; each is visible only from certain,
and variable, parts of the world. The same period
witnesses 13 solar eclipses - six partial (or
annular) and seven total.

TIDES

daily rise and fall of the ocean's tides are the
ult of the gravitational pull of the Moon and
of the Sun, though the effect of the latter is
46.6% as strong as that of the Moon. This
ct is greatest on the hemisphere facing the
on and causes a tidal 'bulge'. When lunar and
r forces pull together, with Sun, Earth and
on in line (near new and full Moons), higher
ing tides' (and lower low tides) occur; when
r and solar forces are least coincidental with
Sun and Moon at an angle (near the Moon's
and third quarters), 'neap tides' occur, which
e a small tidal range.

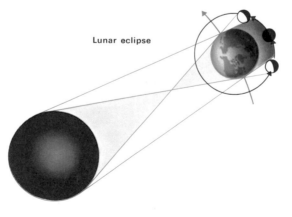

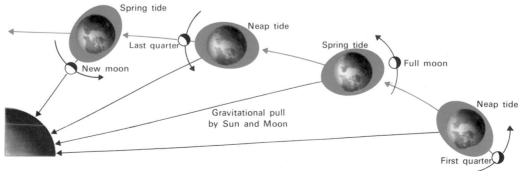

Spring tide

Neap tide

Last quarter

Spring tide

New moon

Full moon

Gravitational pull
by Sun and Moon

Neap tide

First quarter

MAP PROJECTIONS

A map projection is the systematic depiction on a plane surface of the imaginary lines of latitude or longitude from a globe of the earth. This network of lines is called the graticule and forms the framework upon which an accurate depiction of the earth is made. The map graticule, which is the basis of any map, is constructed sometimes by graphical means, but often by using mathematical formulae to give the intersections of the graticule plotted as x and y co-ordinates. The choice between projections is based upon which properties the cartographer wishes the map to possess, the map scale and also the extent of the area to be mapped. Since the globe is three dimensional, it is not possible to depict its surface on a two dimensional plane without distortion. Preservation of one of the basic properties listed below can only be secured at the expense of the others and the choice of projection is often a compromise solution.

Correct Area

In these projections the areas from the globe are to scale on the map. For example, if you look at the diagram at the top right, areas of 10° x 10° are shown from the equator to the poles. The proportion of this area at the extremities are approximately 11:1. An equal area projection will retain that proportion in its portrayal of those areas. This is particularly useful in the mapping of densities and distributions. Projections with this property are termed **Equal Area, Equivalent or Homolographic.**

Correct Distance

In these projections the scale is correct along the meridians, or in the case of the Azimuthal Equidistant scale is true along any line drawn from the centre of the projection. They are called **Equidistant.**

Correct Shape

This property can only be true within small areas as it is achieved only by having a uniform scale distortion along both x and y axes of the projection. The projections are called **Conformal** or **Orthomorphic.**

In order to minimise the distortions at the edges of some projections, central portions of them are often selected for atlas maps. Below are listed some of the major types of projection.

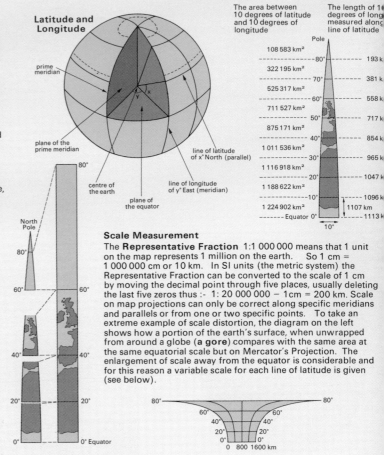

Latitude and Longitude

prime meridian

plane of the prime meridian

centre of the earth

plane of the equator

line of latitude of x° North (parallel)

line of longitude of y° East (meridian)

The area between 10 degrees of latitude and 10 degrees of longitude		The length of 10 degrees of long measured along line of latitude
	Pole	
108 583 km²	—80°	193 k
322 195 km²	—70°	381 k
525 317 km²	—60°	558 k
711 527 km²	—50°	717 k
875 171 km²	—40°	854 k
1 011 536 km²	—30°	965 k
1 116 918 km²	—20°	1047 k
1 188 622 km²	—10°	1096 k
1 224 902 km²		1107 km
	Equator 0°	1113 k
	10°	

Scale Measurement

The **Representative Fraction** 1:1 000 000 means that 1 unit on the map represents 1 million on the earth. So 1 cm = 1 000 000 cm or 10 km. In SI units (the metric system) the Representative Fraction can be converted to the scale of 1 cm by moving the decimal point through five places, usually deleting the last five zeros thus :- 1: 20 000 000 – 1cm = 200 km. Scale on map projections can only be correct along specific meridians and parallels or from one or two specific points. To take an extreme example of scale distortion, the diagram on the left shows how a portion of the earth's surface, when unwrapped from around a globe (**a gore**) compares with the same area at the same equatorial scale but on Mercator's Projection. The enlargement of scale away from the equator is considerable and for this reason a variable scale for each line of latitude is given (see below).

0   800 1600 km

AZIMUTHAL OR ZENITHAL PROJECTIONS

These are constructed by the projection of part of the graticule from the globe onto a plane tangential to any single point on it. This plane may be tangential to the equator (**equatorial case**), the poles (**polar case**) or any other point (**oblique case**). Any straight line drawn from the point at which the plane touches the globe is the shortest distance from that point and is known as a **great circle**. In its Gnomonic construction *any* straight line on the map is a great circle, but there is great exaggeration towards the edges and this reduces its general uses. There are five different ways of transferring the graticule onto the plane and these are shown on the right. The central diagram below shows how the graticules vary, using the polar case as the example.

Equidistant | Equal-Area | Orthographic | Gnomonic | Stereographic (conformal)

Oblique Case

The plane touches the globe at any point between the equator and poles. The oblique orthographic uses the distortion in azimuthal projections away from the centre to give a graphic depiction of the earth as seen from any desired point in space. It can also be used in both Polar and Equatorial cases. It is used not only for the earth but also for the moon and planets.

Polar Case

The polar case is the simplest to construct and the diagram below shows the differing effects of all five methods of construction comparing their coverage, distortion etc., using North America as the example.

Equatorial Case

The example shown here is Lambert's Equivalent Azimuth. It is the only projection which is both equal area and where bearing is true from the centre

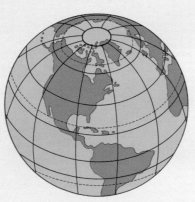

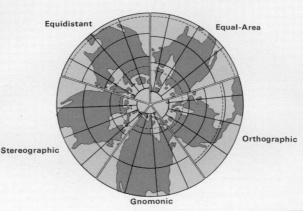

Equidistant

Equal-Area

Stereographic

Orthographic

Gnomonic

CONICAL PROJECTIONS

These use the projection of the graticule from the globe onto a cone which is tangential to a line of latitude (termed the **standard parallel**). This line is always an arc and scale is always true along it. Because of its method of construction it is used mainly for depicting the temperate latitudes around the standard parallel i.e. where there is least distortion. To reduce the distortion and include a larger range of latitudes, the projection may be constructed with the cone bisecting the surface of the globe so that there are two standard parallels each of which is true to scale. The distortion is thus spread more evenly between the two chosen parallels.

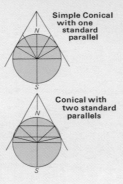

Simple Conical with one standard parallel

Conical with two standard parallels

Bonne

This is a modification of the simple conic whereby the true scale along the meridians is sacrificed to enable the accurate representation of areas. However scale is true along each parallel but shapes are distorted at the edges.

Simple Conic

Scale is correct not only along the standard parallel but also along all meridians. The selection of the standard parallel used is crucial because of the distortion away from it. The projection is usually used to portray regions or continents at small scales.

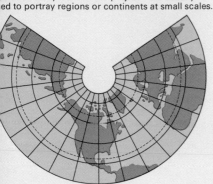

Lambert's Conformal Conic

This projection uses two standard parallels but instead of being equal area as Albers, it is Conformal. Because it has comparatively small distortion, direction and distances can be readily measured and it is therefore used for some navigational charts.

Albers Conical Equal Area

This projection uses two standard parallels and once again the selection of the two specific ones relative to the land area to be mapped is very important. It is equal area and is especially useful for large land masses oriented East-West, for example the U.S.A.

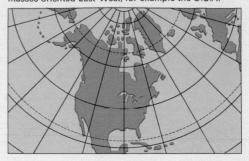

CYLINDRICAL AND OTHER WORLD PROJECTIONS

This group of projections are those which permit the whole of the Earth's surface to be depicted on one map. They are a very large group of projections and the following are only a few of them. Cylindrical projections are constructed by the projection of the graticule from the globe onto a cylinder tangential to the globe. In the examples shown here the cylinder touches the equator, but it can be moved through 90° so it touches the poles - this is called the **Transverse Aspect**. If the cylinder is twisted so that it touches anywhere between the equator and poles it is called the **Oblique Aspect**. Although cylindrical projections can depict all the main land masses, there is considerable distortion of shape and area towards the poles. One cylindrical projection, **Mercator** overcomes this shortcoming by possessing the unique navigational property that any straight drawn on it is a line of constant bearing (**loxodrome**), i.e. a straight line route on the globe crosses the parallels and meridians on the map at the same angles as on the globe. It is used for maps and charts between 15° either side of the equator. Beyond this enlargement of area is a serious drawback, although it is used for navigational charts at all latitudes.

Cylindrical with two standard parallels

Simple Cylindrical

Mercator

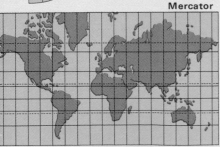

Mollweide

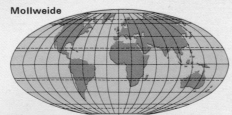

Sanson-Flamsteed

Aitoff / Hammer

This is not a cylindrical projection, but is developed from the Lambert Azimuthal Equal Area by doubling the East-West distances along the parallels from the central meridian. Like both Sanson–Flamsteed and Mollweide it is distorted towards its edges but uses curved parallels to lessen the distortion.

Mollweide and Sanson-Flamsteed

Both of these projections are termed **pseudo-cylindrical**. They are basically cylindrical projections where parallels have been progressively shortened and drawn to scale towards the poles. This allows them to overcome the gross distortions exhibited by the ordinary cylindrical projections and they are in fact Equal Area, Mollweide's giving a slightly better shape. To improve the shape of the continents still further they, like some other projections can be **Interrupted** as can be seen below, but this is at the expense of contiguous sea areas. These projections can have any central meridian and so can be 'centred' on the Atlantic, Pacific, Asia, America etc. In this form both projections are suitable for any form of mapping statistical distributions.

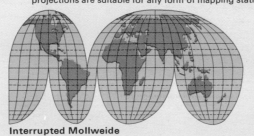

Interrupted Mollweide

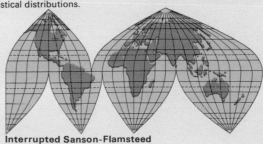

Interrupted Sanson-Flamsteed

	Population									Land and Agriculture					Energy	Trade	
	Population Total 1991	Population Density 1991	Change 1970-80	Change 1980-90	Birth Rate	Death Rate	Fertility Rate	Life Expectancy	Urban Population	Land Area	Arable and Permanent Crops	Permanent grassland	Forest	Agric. Population	Comm. Consumpt. 1989	Imports per capita	Exports per capita
	millions	persons per km²	%	%	births per thousand	deaths per thousand	children	years	%	thousand km²	% of land area	% of land area	% of land area	% of active pop.	gigajoules	US $	US $
Afghanistan	17.7	27	18	3	52	22	6.8	44	22	652	12	46	3	55	7	58	15
Albania	3.3	122	25	21	22	6	2.7	73	35	27	26	15	38	48	37	...	...
Algeria	25.7	11	36	33	35	7	4.9	66	45	2,382	3	13	2	24	27	313	345
Angola	10.3	8.3	38	30	47	10	6.3	47	28	1,247	3	23	42	70	3	48	233
Argentina	32.7	12	18	14	20	9	2.8	71	86	2,737	13	52	22	10	57	126	380
Australia	17.1	2.2	17	15	14	8	1.8	77	86	7,618	6	55	14	5	211	2,223	2,410
Austria	7.6	93	1	0	12	12	1.5	75	58	82	19	24	39	6	117	6,488	5,254
Bahamas	0.26	26	23	20	19	5	2.2	69	59	10	1	0	32	6	76	12,004	11,144
Bangladesh	119	914	32	31	41	14	5.1	53	14	130	71	5	15	69	2	27	13
Barbados	0.26	593	4	2	16	9	1.8	75	45	0.43	77	9	0	7	47	2,692	804
Belgium	9.8	321	2	0	12	12	1.7	76	97	31	25	21	21	2	168	11,875	11,602
Benin	4.9	44	28	34	49	18	7.1	48	42	111	17	4	32	61	1	103	20
Bolivia	7.6	7.0	29	31	41	12	5.8	56	51	1,084	3	25	51	42	11	124	113
Botswana	1.4	2.5	45	45	44	10	6.4	61	24	567	2	58	19	63	...	...	...
Brazil	153	18	27	24	26	8	3.2	66	77	8,457	9	20	65	24	23	134	209
Bulgaria	9	81	4	2	12	12	1.8	73	70	111	38	18	35	12	144	1,434	1,485
Burkina Faso	9.3	34	25	29	47	17	6.5	49	9	274	13	37	24	84	1	57	17
Burma	42.6	65	27	20	30	9	3.7	63	25	658	15	1	49	47	2	14	10
Burundi	5.6	218	17	32	47	16	6.8	50	7	26	52	36	3	91	1	43	14
Cambodia	8.5	48	-8	29	37	15	4.4	51	12	177	17	3	76	70	1	...	...
Cameroon	12.2	26	31	37	47	13	6.9	55	49	465	15	18	53	61	7	115	84
Canada	26.7	2.9	13	10	13	8	1.7	77	76	9,221	5	4	39	3	321	4,376	4,699
Central Africa	3.1	5.0	25	31	45	16	6.2	51	47	623	3	5	57	63	1	51	45
Chad	5.8	4.6	23	27	43	18	5.8	48	33	1,259	3	36	10	75	1	78	26
Chile	13.4	18	17	18	23	6	2.7	72	86	749	6	18	12	13	35	552	652
China	1,131	121	20	14	21	7	2.3	71	21	9,326	10	34	14	68	23	55	63
Colombia	33.6	32	26	23	26	6	2.9	69	70	1,039	5	39	49	27	24	169	205
Congo	2.3	6.73	32	36	46	13	6.3	55	42	342	0	29	62	60	10	238	414
Costa Rica	3.1	61	32	32	26	4	3.0	75	54	51	10	45	32	24	16	684	466
Cuba	10.7	97	14	10	17	7	1.9	76	75	110	30	27	25	19	45	728	530
Cyprus	0.71	77	2	11	17	8	2.2	77	53	9.2	17	1	13	21	74	3,664	1,356
Czechoslovakia	15.7	126	7	2	14	11	2.0	72	69	125	41	13	37	9	175	837	759
Denmark	5.1	121	4	0	11	11	1.5	76	86	42	60	5	12	5	130	6,276	6,967
Dominican Republic	7.3	152	29	26	26	6	3.3	68	60	48	30	43	13	36	12	249	102
Ecuador	10.9	39	34	30	31	7	3.9	67	57	277	10	18	40	30	19	249	295
Egypt	53.6	54	24	30	31	9	4.0	62	49	995	3	0	0	41	22	173	49
El Salvador	5.4	270	26	16	36	7	4.5	66	44	20	35	29	5	37	7	172	79
Ethiopia	50.7	46	27	27	48	18	6.8	47	13	1,101	13	41	25	75	1	21	6
Finland	5	16	4	4	12	10	1.7	76	68	305	8	0	76	8	169	4,257	4,532
France	56.3	102	6	4	13	10	1.8	77	74	550	35	21	27	5	115	4,075	3,767
Gabon	1.2	4.7	60	45	43	16	5.3	54	46	258	2	18	78	68	37	691	1,215
Gambia	0.88	88	38	34	45	20	6.2	45	23	10	18	9	16	81	4	233	48
Germany	79.5	228	1	2	11	12	1.5	75	84	349	35	16	30	5	200	4,734	4,849
Ghana	15.5	67	25	40	44	12	6.3	56	33	230	12	22	35	50	3	64	72
Greece	10.1	77	10	4	12	10	1.7	77	63	131	30	40	20	24	91	1,954	792
Guatemala	9.5	88	32	33	39	8	5.4	65	42	108	17	13	35	51	6	177	130
Guinea	5.9	24	14	29	51	20	7.0	45	26	246	3	25	60	74	3	...	...
Guinea-Bissau	0.98	35	51	21	43	21	5.8	44	20	28	12	38	38	79	2	69	14
Guyana	0.80	4.1	7	5	24	7	2.4	65	34	197	3	6	83	22	11	640	319
Haiti	6.6	244	18	21	35	12	4.8	57	30	27	33	18	1	64	2	56	16
Honduras	5.3	47	39	40	37	7	4.9	66	44	112	16	23	30	55	5	198	184
Hong Kong	5.9	5,960	28	16	12	6	1.4	78	93	0.99	7	1	12	1	58	16,992	16,708
Hungary	10.5	114	4	-1	12	13	1.8	72	60	92	57	13	18	12	107	831	920
Iceland	0.26	2.6	12	11	15	7	1.9	78	91	100	0	23	1	7	165	6,615	5,977
India	871	293	24	20	31	10	4.1	60	28	2,973	57	4	22	67	9	28	22
Indonesia	188	104	26	19	27	9	3.1	63	29	1,812	12	7	63	49	8	122	143
Iran	55.8	34	37	40	33	7	4.7	67	55	1,636	9	27	11	28	45	306	353
Iraq	19.6	45	42	42	41	7	5.9	66	74	437	12	9	4	21	31	670	2,021

Wealth							Social Indicators						Aid		
GNP 1990	GNP per capita 1990	Rate of change 1980-90	GDP share agriculture	GDP share industry	GDP share services	Real GDP per capita 1989	Human Development Index	Food Intake	Population per doctor 1984	% of GNP spent on education 1989	% of age-group in secondary education	Adult Illiteracy	Per capita 1989	% of GNP 1990	
million US $	US $	%	%	%	%	US $		calories per day	persons	%	%	%	US $	%	
7,200	450	2.6	65	20	15	710	0.065	2,000	5,200	1.8	8	71	10	...	Afghanistan
3,255	1,000	1.8	60	28	12	4,270	0.791	2,500	1,230	...	...	15	3	...	Albania
51,585	2,060	-0.3	16	44	40	3,088	0.533	2,818	2,340	9.4	61	43	9	0.3	Algeria
6,207	620	6.1	75	10	15	1,225	0.169	2,000	17,790	3.4	11	58	21	3.5	Angola
76,491	2,370	-1.8	14	33	53	4,310	0.833	3,110	370	1.5	74	5	6.7	0.4	Argentina
290,522	17,080	1.7	4	32	64	15,266	0.971	3,186	440	5.7	79	1	*59.6	*0.38	Australia
147,016	19,240	2	3	37	60	13,063	0.95	3,496	390	6	...	1	*37.2	*0.23	Austria
2,913	11,510	1.7	...	...	...	11,293	0.875	2,791	1,100	6.2	...	1	12	0.1	Bahamas
22,579	200	1	44	14	42	820	0.185	1,996	6,730	2.2	17	65	16.2	8.9	Bangladesh
1,680	6,540	1.4	7	15	78	8,351	0.927	3,247	1,150	6.9	93	1	12	0.2	Barbados
154,688	15,440	1.2	2	31	67	13,313	0.95	3,947	330	5.4	89	1	*71.7	*0.46	Belgium
1,716	360	-1	46	12	42	1,030	0.111	2,245	15,940	3.5	16	77	53.8	14.7	Benin
4,526	620	-2.6	24	30	46	1,531	0.394	1,968	1,540	2.3	34	22	60.8	9.6	Bolivia
2,561	2,040	6.3	3	57	40	3,180	0.534	2,368	6,900	8.2	37	26	116	6.5	Botswana
402,788	2,680	0.6	9	43	48	4,951	0.739	2,722	1,080	3.7	38	19	1.3	0.05	Brazil
19,875	2,210	2.3	11	59	30	5,064	0.865	3,683	280	3.5	59	7	...	...	Bulgaria
2,955	330	1.4	32	26	42	617	0.074	2,286	57,220	2.3	7	82	32.4	11.1	Burkina Faso
20,805	500	2.1	51	10	39	595	0.385	2,474	3,740	2.2	24	19	5.4	1.1	Burma
1,151	210	1.3	56	15	29	611	0.165	1,995	21,120	3.2	4	50	37.3	18.6	Burundi
2,475	300	2.5	75	10	15	1,000	0.178	2,500	...	...	...	65	4	...	Cambodia
11,233	940	-0.3	27	27	46	1,699	0.313	2,195	14,000	3.3	26	46	40.7	4.2	Cameroon
542,774	20,450	2.4	3	21	76	18,635	0.982	3,462	510	7.2	93	1	*86.9	*0.44	Canada
1,194	390	-1.3	42	15	43	770	0.159	2,004	23,530	2.9	11	62	75	17.1	Central Africa
1,074	190	3.3	36	20	44	582	0.088	1,800	38,360	2	7	70	55	30.3	Chad
25,504	1,940	1.1	8	30	62	4,987	0.863	2,553	1,230	3.6	75	7	7	0.2	Chile
415,884	370	7.9	32	48	20	2,656	0.612	2,634	1,000	2.4	44	27	2	0.5	China
40,805	1,240	1.1	17	36	47	4,068	0.758	2,571	1,240	2.9	52	13	3	0.2	Colombia
2,296	1,010	-0.2	14	35	51	2,382	0.372	2,603	8,320	5.1	...	43	92	10.2	Congo
5,342	1,910	0.6	18	27	56	4,413	0.842	2,791	960	4.4	41	7	76	4.3	Costa Rica
21,250	2,000	1.1	12	36	52	2,500	0.732	3,153	560	6.6	89	6	3	0.1	Cuba
5,633	8,040	4.9	7	27	66	9,368	0.912	3,250	1,100	3.6	88	6	49	0.7	Cyprus
49,225	3,140	1.3	6	57	37	7,420	0.897	3,609	280	4	86	1	...	...	Czechoslovakia
113,515	22,090	2.1	5	29	66	13,751	0.953	3,622	400	7.3	84	1	*183.7	*0.94	Denmark
5,847	820	-0.4	15	26	59	2,537	0.595	2,342	1,760	1.5	74	17	13	2.1	Dominican Republic
10,112	960	-0.8	15	39	46	3,012	0.641	2,518	820	2.6	56	14	15.7	1.6	Ecuador
31,381	600	2.1	19	30	51	1,934	0.385	3,326	770	6.8	81	52	107	17.2	Egypt
5,767	1,100	-0.6	21	21	58	1,897	0.498	2,200	2,830	2	26	27	65	7.6	El Salvador
6,041	120	-1.2	42	16	42	392	0.173	1,750	60,000	4.4	15	34	18	11.6	Ethiopia
129,823	26,070	3.1	7	36	57	14,598	0.953	3,144	440	5.7	83	1	*141.2	*0.63	Finland
1,099,750	19,480	1.7	4	29	67	14,164	0.969	3,449	320	6.6	83	1	*132.3	*0.78	France
3,654	3,220	-2.6	11	47	42	4,735	0.545	2,500	2,790	5.6	...	39	121.3	3.9	Gabon
229	260	-0.3	34	12	54	886	0.083	2,351	11,600	4	16	73	109	48	Gambia
1,468,871	22,730	2.2	3	37	60	14,507	0.955	3,650	380	4.5	85	1	*62.3	*0.41	Germany
5,824	390	-0.6	50	17	33	1,005	0.31	2,246	14,890	3.4	39	40	37.6	10.3	Ghana
60,245	6,000	0.8	16	29	55	6,764	0.901	3,793	350	3.1	85	7	3.3	0.1	Greece
8,309	900	-2.1	18	26	56	2,531	0.485	2,229	2,180	1.8	21	45	21	3.1	Guatemala
2,756	480	2.5	30	33	37	602	0.052	2,193	46,420	3	9	76	48	12.6	Guinea
176	180	1.7	47	16	37	820	0.088	2,500	7,500	2.8	7	63	122	68.2	Guinea-Bissau
293	370	-3.2	25	31	44	1,453	0.539	2,736	6,200	8.8	64	4	133	42.7	Guyana
2,400	370	-2.3	31	38	31	962	0.276	2,011	7,180	1.8	19	47	31.1	8.4	Haiti
3,023	590	-1.2	21	25	54	1,504	0.473	2,229	1,510	4.9	32	27	87	9.9	Honduras
66,666	11,540	5.5	0	28	72	15,180	0.913	2,817	1,070	2.8	73	10	8	0.03	Hong Kong
30,047	2,780	1.5	14	36	50	6,245	0.893	3,638	310	4	73	3	...	...	Hungary
5,456	21,150	1.2	10	15	75	14,210	0.958	3,518	460	3.7	85	1	...	...	Iceland
294,816	350	3.2	32	29	39	910	0.297	2,196	2,520	3.2	43	52	2.3	0.7	India
101,151	560	4.1	24	37	39	2,034	0.491	2,708	9,460	0.9	47	23	10.3	1.9	Indonesia
139,120	2,450	-0.8	25	15	60	3,120	0.547	3,300	2,690	3.1	53	46	1.7	0.1	Iran
37,828	2,000	3.6	25	20	55	3,510	0.589	3,000	1,740	3.7	47	40	3	0.01	Iraq

Left-margin partial column (Wealth — GNP 1990, million US $):

GNP 1990 million US $
12,404
132,660
2,779
79,044
1,474
4,458
11,592
91,742
3,814
1,435,000
923,959
5,445,825
7,929
50,574
19,942
6,432
72,800
8,117
3,391
6,313

Left-margin partial country list:

American, Andorra, Anguilla, Antigua, Armenia, Aruba, Ascension, Azerbaija, Bahrain, Belize, Beloruss, Bermuda, Bhutan, Bosnia-H, Brunei, Cape Ve, Cayman, Cocos Is, Comoros, Cook Is., Croatia, Czech Re, Djibouti, Dominica, Equatoria, Eritrea, Estonia, Ethiopia, Falkland, Faroe Is., Fiji, French G, French P

This list shows the principal cities with more than 500,000 inhabitants (for Brazil, China, India, Japan and USA only cities with more than 1 million are included). The figures are taken from the most recent census or estimate available, and as far as possible are the population of the metropolitan area, eg greater New York, Mexico or London. All the figures are in thousands. The top 20 world cities are indicated with their rank in brackets following the name.

Population in Thousands

Afghanistan
Kabul 1,127
Algeria
Algiers 1,722
Oran 664
Angola
Luanda 1,200
Argentina
Buenos Aires [8] 10,728
Cordoba 1,055
Rosario 1,016
Mendoza 668
La Plata 611
San Miguel de Tucuman 571
Armenia
Yerevan 1,199
Australia
Sydney 3,531
Melbourne 2,965
Brisbane 1,215
Perth 1,083
Adelaide 1,013
Austria
Vienna 1,483
Azerbaijan
Baku 1,757
Bangladesh
Dacca 4,770
Chittagong 1,840
Khulna 860
Rajshahi 430
Belgium
Brussels 970
Antwerp 500
Belorussia
Minsk 1,589
Gomel 500
Bolivia
La Paz 993
Brazil
São Paulo [3] 16,832
Rio de Janeiro [7] 11,141
Belo Horizonte 3,446
Recife 2,945
Pôrto Alegre 2,924
Salvador 2,362
Fortaleza 2,169
Çuritiba 1,926
Brasilia 1,557
Nova Iguaçu 1,325
Belem 1,296
Santos 1,200
Bulgaria
Sofia 1,129
Burma
Rangoon 2,459
Mandalay 533
Cambodia
Phnom Penh 500
Cameroon
Douala 1,030
Yaoundé 654
Central African Rep.
Bangui 597
Chad
Ndjamena 512
Canada
Toronto 3,427
Montréal 2,921
Vancouver 1,381
Ottawa-Hull 819
Edmonton 785
Calgary 671
Winnipeg 623
Québec 603
Hamilton 557
Chile
Santiago 4,858
China
Shanghai [5] 12,320

Peking [10] 9,750
Tientsin 5,459
Shenyang 4,285
Wuhan 3,493
Canton 3,359
Chungking 2,832
Harbin 2,668
Chengdu 2,642
Sian 2,387
Zibo 2,329
Nanking 2,290
Nanchang 2,289
Lupanshui 2,247
Taiyuan 1,929
Changchun 1,908
Dalian 1,682
Zhaozhuang 1,612
Zhengzhou 1,610
Kunming 1,516
Jinan 1,464
Tangshan 1,410
Guiyang 1,403
Lanzhou 1,391
Linyi 1,385
Pingxiang 1,305
Qiqihar 1,301
Anshan 1,298
Qingdao 1,273
Xintao 1,272
Hangzhou 1,271
Fushun 1,270
Yangcheng 1,265
Yulin 1,255
Dongguang 1,230
Chao'an 1,227
Xiaogan 1,219
Fuzhou 1,205
Suining 1,195
Changsha 1,193
Shijiazhuang 1,187
Jilin 1,169
Xintai 1,167
Puyang 1,125
Baotou 1,119
Bozhou 1,112
Zhongshan 1,073
Luoyang 1,063
Laiwu 1,054
Leshan 1,039
Urumqi 1,038
Ningbo 1,033
Datong 1,020
Huainan 1,019
Heze 1,017
Handan 1,014
Linhai 1,012
Macheng 1,010
Changshu 1,004
Colombia
Bogotá 4,185
Medellin 1,506
Cali 1,397
Barranquilla 920
Cartagena 560
Congo
Brazzaville 596
Croatia
Zagreb 1,175
Cuba
Havana 2,059
Czech Republic
Prague 1,194
Denmark
Copenhagen 1,339
Dominican Rep.
Santo Domingo 1,313
Ecuador
Guayaquil 1,301
Quito 1,110
Egypt
Cairo [18] 6,325
Alexandria 2,893

El Giza 1,858
Shubra el Kheima 711
El Salvador
San Salvador 973
Ethiopia
Addis Ababa 1,686
Finland
Helsinki 987
France
Paris [13] 8,510
Lyons 1,170
Marseilles 1,080
Lille 935
Bordeaux 628
Toulouse 523
Georgia
Tbilisi 1,194
Germany
Berlin 3,301
Hamburg 1,594
Munich 1,189
Cologne 928
Essen 623
Frankfurt 619
Dortmund 584
Düsseldorf 563
Stuttgart 552
Leipzig 545
Bremen 533
Duisburg 525
Dresden 518
Hanover 500
Ghana
Accra 965
Greece
Athens 3,027
Thessalonika 872
Guatemala
Guatemala 2,000
Guinea
Conakry 705
Haiti
Port-au-Prince 1,144
Honduras
Tegucigalpa 605
Hong Kong
Kowloon 2,302
Hong Kong 1,176
Tsuen Wan 690
Hungary
Budapest 2,115
India
Calcutta [11] 9,194
Bombay [14] 8,243
Delhi 5,729
Madras 4,289
Bangalore 2,922
Ahmadabad 2,548
Hyderabad 2,546
Poona 1,686
Kanpur 1,639
Nagpur 1,302
Jaipur 1,015
Lucknow 1,008
Indonesia
Jakarta [17] 7,348
Surabaya 2,224
Medan 1,806
Bandung 1,567
Semarang 1,026
Palembang 787
Ujung Pandang 709
Malang 512
Iran
Tehran [19] 6,043
Mashhad 1,464
Esfahan 987
Tabriz 971
Shiraz 848
Ahvaz 580
Bakhtaran 561
Qom 543

Iraq
Baghdad 4,649
Basra 617
Mosul 571
Ireland
Dublin 921
Italy
Rome 2,817
Milan 1,464
Naples 1,203
Turin 1,012
Palermo 731
Genoa 712
Ivory Coast
Abidjan 1,850
Bouaké 640
Jamaica
Kingston 525
Japan
Tokyo [6] 11,829
Yokohama 2,993
Osaka 2,636
Nagoya 2,116
Sapporo 1,543
Kyoto 1,479
Kobe 1,411
Fukuoka 1,160
Kawasaki 1,089
Kitakyushu 1,056
Hiroshima 1,044
Jordan
Amman 1,160
Irbid 680
Kazakhstan
Alma Ata 1,108
Karaganda 614
Astrakhan 509
Kenya
Nairobi 1,429
Mombasa 500
Kirghizia
Bishkek 616
Korea, North
Pyongyang 2,639
Hamhung 775
Chongjin 754
Chinnampo 691
Sinuiju 500
Korea, South
Seoul [9] 10,513
Pusan 3,754
Taegu 2,206
Inchon 1,604
Kwangju 1,165
Taejon 866
Ulsan 551
Latvia
Riga 915
Lebanon
Beirut 702
Libya
Tripoli 980
Benghazi 650
Lithuania
Vilnius 582
Macedonia
Skopje 505
Madagascar
Antananarivo 703
Malaysia
Kuala Lumpur 1,103
Mali
Bamako 646
Mauritania
Nouakchott 500
Mexico
Mexico City [1] 18,748
Guadalajara 2,587
Monterrey 2,335
Puebla 1,218
León 947
Torreón 730

San Luis Potosi 602
Ciudad Juárez 596
Mérida 580
Culiacán Rosales 560
Mexicali 511
Moldavia
Kishinev 565
Mongolia
Ulan Bator 500
Morocco
Casablanca 2,158
Rabat-Salé 893
Fès 548
Mozambique
Maputo 1,070
Netherlands
Rotterdam 1,040
Amsterdam 1,038
The Hague 684
Utrecht 526
New Zealand
Auckland 851
Nicaragua
Managua 682
Nigeria
Lagos 1,097
Ibadan 1,060
Ogbomosho 527
Norway
Oslo 643
Pakistan
Karachi 5,208
Lahore 2,953
Faisalabad 1,104
Rawalpindi 795
Hyderabad 752
Multan 722
Gujranwala 659
Peshawar 556
Panama
Panama City 625
Paraguay
Asunción 708
Peru
Lima-Callao 4,605
Arequipa 592
Philippines
Manila 1,728
Quezon City 1,326
Cebu 552
Caloocan 524
Poland
Warsaw 1,671
Lodz 852
Krakow 744
Wroclaw 640
Poznan 586
Portugal
Lisbon 1,612
Oporto 1,315
Puerto Rico
San Juan 1,816
Romania
Bucharest 2,014
Russia
Moscow [12] 8,967
St Petersburg 5,020
Nizhniy Novgorod 1,438
Novosibirsk 1,436
Yekaterinburg 1,367
Samara 1,257
Chelyabinsk 1,179
Omsk 1,148
Kazan 1,094
Perm 1,091
Ufa 1,083
Rostov 1,020
Volgograd 999
Krasnoyarsk 912
Saratov 905
Voronezh 887
Vladivostok 648

Izhevsk 635
Yaroslavl 633
Togliatti 630
Irkutsk 626
Simbirsk 625
Krasnodar 620
Barnaul 602
Khaborovsk 601
Novokuznetsk 600
Orenburg 547
Penza 543
Tula 540
Kemerovo 520
Ryazan 515
Tomsk 502
Naberezhniye-Chelni 501
Saudi Arabia
Riyadh 2,000
Jedda 1,400
Mecca 618
Medina 500
Senegal
Dakar 1,382
Serbia
Belgrade 1,470
Singapore
Singapore 2,600
Somali Rep.
Mogadishu 1,000
South Africa
Cape Town 1,912
Johannesburg 1,762
East Rand 1,038
Durban 982
Pretoria 823
Port Elizabeth 652
West Rand 647
Vereeniging 540
Spain
Madrid 3,123
Barcelona 1,694
Valencia 739
Seville 668
Zaragoza 596
Malaga 595
Sri Lanka
Colombo 1,412
Sudan
Omdurman 600
Khartoum 510
Sweden
Stockholm 1,471
Gothenburg 720
Malmö 500
Switzerland
Zurich 839
Syria
Damascus 1,361
Aleppo 1,308
Taiwan
Taipei 2,680
Kaohsiung 1,343
Taichung 715
Tainan 657
Panchiao 506
Tajikistan
Dushanbe 595
Tanzania
Dar es Salaam 1,100
Thailand
Bangkok 5,609
Tunisia
Tunis 774
Turkey
Istanbul 5,495
Ankara 2,252
Izmir 1,490
Adana 776
Bursa 614
Uganda
Kampala 500

Ukraine
Kiev 2,587
Kharkhov 1,611
Dnepropetrovsk 1,179
Odessa 1,115
Donetsk 1,110
Zaporozhye 884
Lvov 790
Krivoy Rog 713
Mariupol 529
Lugansk 509
Nikolayev 503
United Kingdom
London [17] 6,378
Manchester 1,669
Birmingham 1,400
Liverpool 1,060
Glasgow 730
Newcastle 617
Uruguay
Montevideo 1,248
United States
New York [2] 18,120
Los Angeles [4] 13,770
Chicago [15] 8,181
San Francisco [20] 6,042
Philadelphia 5,963
Detroit 4,620
Dallas 3,766
Boston 3,736
Washington 3,734
Houston 3,642
Miami 3,001
Cleveland 2,769
Atlanta 2,737
Saint Louis 2,467
Seattle 2,421
Minneapolis-SP. 2,388
San Diego 2,370
Baltimore 2,343
Pittsburgh 2,284
Phoenix 2,030
Tampa 1,995
Denver 1,858
Cincinnati 1,729
Kansas City 1,575
Milwaukee 1,572
Portland 1,414
Sacramento 1,385
Norfolk 1,380
Columbus 1,344
San Antonio 1,323
New Orleans 1,307
Indianapolis 1,237
Buffalo 1,176
Providence 1,118
Charlotte 1,112
Hartford 1,108
Salt Lake City 1,065
Uzbekistan
Tashkent 2,073
Venezuela
Caracas 3,247
Maracaibo 1,295
Valencia 1,135
Maracay 857
Barquisimeto 718
Vietnam
Ho Chi Minh 3,900
Hanoi 3,100
Haiphong 1,279
Da-Nang 500
Yemen
San'a 500
Zaïre
Kinshasa 2,654
Lubumbashi 543
Zambia
Lusaka 900
Zimbabwe
Harare 681
Bulawayo 500

INDEX TO
WORLD MAPS

The index contains the names of all the principal places and features shown on the World Maps. Each name is followed by an additional entry in italics giving the country or region within which it is located. The alphabetical order of names composed of two or more words is governed primarily by the first word and then by the second. This is an example of the rule:

New South Wales □, *Australia*.. **34 G8**   33 0S   146 0E
New York □, *U.S.A.* **43 D10** 42 40N   76 0W
New York City, *U.S.A.* **43 E11** 40 45N   74 0W
New Zealand ■, *Oceania*............. **35 J13** 40 0S   176 0E
Newark, *U.S.A.* **43 F10** 39 42N 75 45W

Physical features composed of a proper name (Erie) and a description (Lake) are positioned alphabetically by the proper name. The description is positioned after the proper name and is usually abbreviated:

Erie, L., *N. Amer.* **42 D7**   42 15N   81 0W

Where a description forms part of a settlement or administrative name, however, it is always written in full and put in its true alphabetical position:

Mount Isa, *Australia*...................... **34 E6**   20 42S   139 26E

Names beginning with M' and Mc are indexed as if they were spelt Mac. Names beginning St. are alphabetized under Saint, but Santa and San are all spelt in full and are alphabetized accordingly. If the same placename occurs two or more times in the index and all are in the same country, each is followed by the name of the administrative subdivision in which it is located. The names are placed in the alphabetical order of the subdivision. For example:

Columbus, Ga., *U.S.A.* **41 D10** 32 30N 84 58W
Columbus, Ind., *U.S.A.* **42 F5**   39 14N 85 55W
Columbus, Ohio, *U.S.A.* **42 F6**   39 57N   83 1W

The number in bold type which follows each name in the index refers to the number of the map page where that feature or place will be found. This is usually the largest scale at which the place or feature appears.

The letter and figure which are in bold type immediately after the page number give the grid square on the map page, within which the feature is situated. The letter represents the latitude and the figure the longitude. In some cases the feature itself may fall within the specified square, while the name is outside.

For a more precise location, the geographical co-ordinates which follow the letter-figure references give the latitude and the longitude of each place. The first set of figures represent the latitude, which is the distance north or south of the Equator measured as an angle at the centre of the Earth. The Equator is latitude 0°, the North Pole is 90°N, and the South Pole 90°S.

The second set of figures represent the longitude, which is the distance east or west of the prime meridian, which runs through Greenwich, England. Longitude is also measured as an angle at the centre of the Earth and is given east or west of the prime meridian, from 0° to 180° in either direction.

The unit of measurement for latitude and longitude is the degree, which is subdivided into 60 minutes. Each index entry states the position of a place in degrees and minutes, a space being left between the degrees and the minutes. The latitude is followed by N(orth) or S(outh) and the longitude by E(ast) or W(est).

Rivers are indexed to their mouths or confluences, and carry the symbol ~→ after their names. A solid square ■ follows the name of a country, while an open square □ refers to a first order administrative area.

ABBREVIATIONS USED IN THE INDEX

Afghan. – Afghanistan	Conn. – Connecticut	Isla, Island, Isle(s)	Mo. – Missouri	Nebr. – Nebraska	Provincial	Sib. – Siberia
Ala. – Alabama	Cord. – Cordillera	Ill. – Illinois	Mont. – Montana	Neths. – Netherlands	Pt. – Point	St. – Saint, Sankt, Sint
Alta. – Alberta	Cr. – Creek	Ind. – Indiana	Mozam.– Mozambique	Nev. – Nevada	Pta. – Ponta, Punta	Str. – Strait, Stretto
Amer. – America(n)	D.C. – District of	Ind. Oc. – Indian Ocean	Mt.(s).– Mont, Monte,	Nfld. – Newfoundland	Pte. – Pointe	Switz. – Switzerland
Arch. – Archipelago	Columbia	Ivory C. – Ivory Coast	Monti, Montaña,	Nic. – Nicaragua	Qué. – Québec	Tas. – Tasmania
Ariz. – Arizona	Del. – Delaware	Kans. – Kansas	Mountain	O.F.S. – Orange Free	Queens. – Queensland	Tenn. – Tennessee
Ark. – Arkansas	Domin. – Dominica	Ky. – Kentucky	N. – Nord, Norte, North,	State	R. – Rio, River	Tex. – Texas
Atl. Oc. – Atlantic Ocean	Dom. Rep. – Dominican	L. – Lac, Lacul, Lago,	Northern	Okla. – Oklahoma	R.I. – Rhode Island	Trin. & Tob. – Trinidad
B. – Baie, Bahia, Bay,	Republic	Lagoa, Lake, Limni,	N.B. – New Brunswick	Ont. – Ontario	Ra.(s). – Range(s)	& Tobago
Bucht, Bugt	E. – East	Loch, Lough	N.C. – North Carolina	Oreg. – Oregon	Reg. – Region	U.A.E. – United Arab
B.C. – British Columbia	El Salv. – El Salvador	La. – Louisiana	N. Cal. – New Caledonia	P.E.I. – Prince Edward	Rep. – Republic	Emirates
Bangla. – Bangladesh	Eq. Guin. – Equatorial	Lux. – Luxembourg	N. Dak. – North Dakota	Island	Res. – Reserve,	U.K. – United Kingdom
C. – Cabo, Cap, Cape,	Guinea	Madag. – Madagascar	N.H. – New Hampshire	Pa. – Pennsylvania	Reservoir	U.S.A. – United States
Coast	Fla. – Florida	Man. – Manitoba	N.J. – New Jersey	Pac. Oc. – Pacific Ocean	S. – San, South	of America
C.A.R. – Central African	Falk. Is. – Falkland Is.	Mass.– Massachusetts	N. Mex. – New Mexico	Papua N.G. – Papua	Si. Arabia – Saudi Arabia	Va. – Virginia
Republic	G. – Golfe, Golfo, Gulf	Md. – Maryland	N.S. – Nova Scotia	New Guinea	S.C. – South Carolina	Vic. – Victoria
C. Prov. – Cape	Ga. – Georgia	Me. – Maine	N.S.W. – New South	Pen. – Peninsula,	S. Dak. – South Dakota	Vol. – Volcano
Province	Guinea–Biss. –	Medit. S. –	Wales	Peninsule	S. Leone – Sierra Leone	Vt. – Vermont
Calif. – California	Guinea–Bissau	Mediterranean Sea	N.W.T. – North West	Phil. – Philippines	Sa. – Serra, Sierra	W. – West
Cent. – Central	Hd. – Head	Mich. – Michigan	Territory	Pk. – Park, Peak	Sask. – Saskatchewan	W. Va. – West Virginia
Chan. – Channel	Hts. – Heights	Minn. – Minnesota	N.Y. – New York	Plat. – Plateau	Scot. – Scotland	Wash. – Washington
Colo. – Colorado	I.(s). – Ile, Ilha, Insel,	Miss. – Mississippi	N.Z. – New Zealand	Prov. – Province,	Sd. – Sound	Wis. – Wisconsin

106 INDEX TO WORLD MAPS

Aachen — Balkhash, L.

A

Aachen, *Germany* .... **10 C2** 50 47N 6 4 E
Aalborg, *Denmark* .... **6 G9** 57 2N 9 54 E
Aalst, *Belgium* .... **8 B6** 50 56N 4 2 E
Aarau, *Switz.* .... **10 E3** 47 23N 8 4 E
Aare →, *Switz.* ..... **10 E3** 47 33N 8 14 E
Aarhus, *Denmark* ..... **6 G10** 56 8N 10 11 E
Abadan, *Iran* .... **24 B3** 30 22N 48 20 E
Abbeville, *France* ..... **8 B4** 50 6N 1 49 E
Abéché, *Chad* .... **29 G11** 13 50N 20 35 E
Abeokuta, *Nigeria* .... **30 C2** 7 3N 3 19 E
Aberdeen, *U.K.* **7 D5** 57 9N 2 6W
Aberystwyth, *U.K.* **7 F4** 52 25N 4 6W
Abidjan, *Ivory C.* **28 H6** 5 26N 3 58W
Abitibi, L., *Canada* **42 A8** 48 40N 79 40W
Abkhaz Republic □, *Georgia* .... **15 F7** 43 0N 41 0 E
Abohar, *India* .... **23 D5** 30 10N 74 10 E
Abu Dhabi, *U.A.E.* ..... **24 C4** 24 28N 54 22 E
Abuja, *Nigeria* .... **30 C3** 9 16N 7 2 E
Acapulco, *Mexico* **44 D5** 16 51N 99 56W
Accomac, *U.S.A.* **43 G10** 37 43N 75 40W
Accra, *Ghana* **30 C1** 5 35N 0 6W
Achill I., *Ireland* **7 F1** 53 58N 10 5W
Acklins I., *Bahamas* ... **45 C10** 22 30N 74 0W
Aconcagua, *Argentina* . **47 F3** 32 39S 70 0W
Acre, *Israel* .... **29 N21** 32 55N 35 4 E
Acre □, *Brazil* **46 C2** 9 1S 71 0W
Adamawa Highlands, *Cameroon* .... **28 H9** 7 20N 12 20 E
Adana, *Turkey* .... **15 G6** 37 0N 35 16 E
Adapazarı, *Turkey* ..... **15 F5** 40 48N 30 25 E
Adare, C., *Antarctica* .. **48 C19** 71 0S 171 0 E
Addis Ababa, *Ethiopia* . **29 H14** 9 2N 38 42 E
Adelaide, *Australia* .... **34 G6** 34 52S 138 30 E
Adelaide, *S. Africa* .... **31 C4** 32 42S 26 20 E
Adelaide I., *Antarctica* . **48 C23** 67 15S 68 30W
Adélie Land, *Antarctica* **48 C18** 68 0S 140 0 E
Aden, *Yemen* .... **24 D3** 12 45N 45 0 E
Aden, G. of, *Asia* ..... **24 D3** 12 30N 47 30 E
Adirondack Mts., *U.S.A.* **43 D10** 44 0N 74 15W
Admiralty Is., *Papua N. G.* .... **36 H6** 2 0S 147 0 E
Ado Ekiti, *Nigeria* ..... **30 C3** 7 38N 5 12 E
Adoni, *India* .... **25 D6** 15 33N 77 18 E
Adour →, *France* **9 F3** 43 32N 1 32W
Adrar, *Algeria* **28 D6** 27 51N 0 11W
Adrian, *U.S.A.* **42 E5** 41 55N 84 5W
Adriatic Sea, *Europe* ... **12 C6** 43 0N 16 0 E
Adzhar Republic □, *Georgia* .... **15 F7** 41 30N 42 0 E
Ægean Sea, *Europe* ... **13 E11** 38 30N 25 0 E
Afghanistan ■, *Asia* ... **24 B5** 33 0N 65 0 E
'Afif, *Si. Arabia* .... **24 C3** 23 53N 42 56 E
Agadès, *Niger* .... **30 A3** 16 58N 7 59 E
Agadir, *Morocco* **28 C5** 30 28N 9 55W
Agartala, *India* .... **23 H13** 23 50N 91 23 E
Agen, *France* .... **9 E4** 44 12N 0 38 E
Agra, *India* .... **23 F6** 27 17N 77 58 E
Agrigento, *Italy* .... **12 F5** 37 19N 13 33 E
Aguascalientes, *Mexico* **44 C4** 21 53N 102 12W
Agulhas, C., *S. Africa* . **31 C3** 34 52S 20 0 E
Ahmadabad, *India* .... **23 H4** 23 0N 72 40 E
Ahmadnagar, *India* ... **25 D6** 19 7N 74 46 E
Ahmadpur, *Pakistan* ... **23 E3** 29 12N 71 10 E
Ahvaz, *Iran* .... **24 B3** 31 20N 48 40 E
Ahvenanmaa Is., *Finland* **6 F11** 60 15N 20 0 E
Aigoual, Mt., *France* .. **9 E5** 44 8N 3 35 E
Ain →, *France* ...... **9 E6** 45 45N 5 11 E
Aïr, *Niger* .... **28 F8** 18 30N 8 0 E
Aisne →, *France* .... **8 C5** 49 26N 2 50 E
Aix-en-Provence, *France* **9 F6** 43 32N 5 27 E
Aix-les-Bains, *France* . **9 E6** 45 41N 5 53 E
Ajaccio, *France* ...... **9 G8** 41 55N 8 40 E
Ajanta Ra., *India* ..... **23 J5** 20 28N 75 50 E
Ajmer, *India* .... **23 F5** 26 28N 74 37 E
Akashi, *Japan* .... **19 B4** 34 45N 134 58 E
Akita, *Japan* .... **19 G12** 39 45N 140 7 E
Akola, *India* .... **23 J6** 20 42N 77 2 E
Akranes, *Iceland* **6 B2** 64 19N 22 5W
Akron, *U.S.A.* **42 E7** 41 7N 81 31W
Aksai Chih, *India* ..... **23 B7** 35 15N 79 55 E
Aktyubinsk, *Kazakhstan* **15 D10** 50 17N 57 10 E
Akure, *Nigeria* .... **30 C3** 7 15N 5 5 E
Akureyri, *Iceland* **6 B4** 65 40N 18 6W
Akyab, *Burma* .... **25 C8** 20 18N 92 45 E
Al Ḥudaydah, *Yemen* .. **24 D3** 14 50N 43 0 E
Al Hufūf, *Si. Arabia* .... **24 C3** 25 25N 49 45 E
Al Jawf, *Si. Arabia* .... **24 C2** 29 55N 39 40 E
Al Kut, *Iraq* .... **24 B3** 32 30N 46 0 E
Al Qatif, *Si. Arabia* .... **24 C3** 26 35N 50 0 E
Al 'Ula, *Si. Arabia* .... **24 C2** 26 35N 38 0 E
Alabama □, *U.S.A.* **41 D9** 33 0N 87 0W
Aland Is., *Sweden* ..... **6 G11** 60 0N 19 30 E
Alaska □, *U.S.A.* **38 B5** 65 0N 150 0W
Alaska, G. of, *Pac. Oc.* **38 C5** 58 0N 145 0W
Alaska Pen., *U.S.A.* ... **38 C4** 56 0N 160 0W
Alaska Range, *U.S.A.* . **38 B4** 62 50N 151 0W
Alba Iulia, *Romania* ... **13 A10** 46 8N 23 39 E
Albacete, *Spain* **11 C5** 39 0N 1 50W
Albania ■, *Europe* .... **13 D9** 41 0N 20 0 E
Albany, *Australia* ..... **34 H2** 35 1S 117 58 E
Albany, *Ga., U.S.A.* ... **41 D10** 31 40N 84 10W
Albany, *N.Y., U.S.A.* ... **43 D11** 42 35N 73 47W
Albany →, *Canada* .. **39 C11** 52 17N 81 31W
Alberta □, *Canada* ... **38 C8** 54 40N 115 0W
Albertville, *France* .... **9 E7** 45 40N 6 22 E
Albi, *France* .... **9 F5** 43 56N 2 9 E
Albion, *U.S.A.* **42 D5** 42 15N 84 45W
Albuquerque, *U.S.A.* .. **40 C5** 35 5N 106 47W
Albury, *Australia* ..... **34 H8** 36 3S 146 56 E
Alcalá de Henares, *Spain* **11 B4** 40 28N 3 22W
Aldabra Is., *Seychelles* **27 G8** 9 22S 46 28 E
Aldan →, *Russia* .... **18 C14** 63 28N 129 35 E
Alderney, *Chan. Is.* ... **8 C2** 49 42N 2 12W
Aleksandrovsk-Sakhalinskiy, *Russia* **18 D16** 50 50N 142 20 E
Alençon, *France* ..... **8 C4** 48 27N 0 4 E
Aleppo, *Syria* .... **24 B2** 36 10N 37 15 E
Alès, *France* .... **9 E6** 44 9N 4 5 E
Alessandria, *Italy* ..... **12 B3** 44 54N 8 37 E
Ålesund, *Norway* ..... **6 F9** 62 28N 6 12 E
Aleutian Is., *Pac. Oc.* . **36 B10** 52 0N 175 0W
Alexander Arch., *U.S.A.* **38 C6** 57 0N 135 0W
Alexander I., *Antarctica* **48 C23** 69 0S 70 0W
Alexandria, *Egypt* .... **29 C13** 31 0N 30 0 E
Alexandria, *La., U.S.A.* **41 D8** 31 20N 92 30W
Alexandria, *Va., U.S.A.* **42 F9** 38 47N 77 1W
Algarve, *Portugal* **11 D1** 36 58N 8 20W
Algeciras, *Spain* **11 D3** 36 9N 5 28W
Algeria ■, *Africa* ..... **28 D7** 28 30N 2 0 E
Algiers, *Algeria* .... **28 B7** 36 42N 3 8 E
Alicante, *Spain* **11 C5** 38 23N 0 30W
Alice Springs, *Australia* **34 E5** 23 40S 133 50 E
Aligarh, *India* .... **23 F7** 27 55N 78 10 E
Alipur Duar, *India* .... **23 F12** 26 30N 89 35 E
Aliquippa, *U.S.A.* **42 E7** 40 38N 80 18W
Aliwal North, *S. Africa* . **31 C4** 30 45S 26 45 E
Alkmaar, *Neths.* ...... **8 A6** 52 37N 4 45 E
Allahabad, *India* ...... **23 G8** 25 25N 81 58 E
Allegan, *U.S.A.* **42 D5** 42 32N 85 52W
Allegheny →, *U.S.A.* . **42 E8** 40 27N 80 0W
Allegheny Plateau, *U.S.A.* **42 G7** 38 0N 80 0W
Allentown, *U.S.A.* **43 E10** 40 36N 75 30W
Alleppey, *India* .... **25 E6** 9 30N 76 28 E
Allier →, *France* .... **8 D5** 46 57N 3 4 E
Alma, *U.S.A.* **42 D5** 43 25N 84 40W
Alma Ata, *Kazakhstan* . **18 E9** 43 15N 76 57 E
Almelo, *Neths.* .... **8 A7** 52 22N 6 42 E
Almería, *Spain* **11 D4** 36 52N 2 27W
Alor, *Indonesia* .... **22 D4** 8 15S 124 30 E
Alpena, *U.S.A.* **42 C6** 45 6N 83 24W
Alps, *Europe* .... **4 F7** 46 30N 9 30 E
Alsace, *France* .... **8 C7** 48 15N 7 25 E
Altai, *Mongolia* .... **20 B4** 46 40N 92 45 E
Altay, *China* .... **20 B3** 47 48N 88 10 E
Altoona, *U.S.A.* **42 E8** 40 32N 78 24W
Altun Shan, *China* .... **20 C3** 38 30N 88 0 E
Alwar, *India* .... **23 F6** 27 38N 76 34 E
Amadjuak L., *Canada* . **39 B12** 65 0N 71 8W
Amagasaki, *Japan* .... **19 B4** 34 42N 135 20 E
Amarillo, *U.S.A.* **40 C6** 35 14N 101 46W
Amazon →, *S. Amer.* . **46 C5** 0 5S 50 0W
Ambala, *India* .... **23 D6** 30 23N 76 56 E
Ambert, *France* ...... **9 E5** 45 33N 3 44 E
Ambikapur, *India* ..... **23 H9** 23 15N 83 15 E
Ambon, *Indonesia* .... **22 D4** 3 35S 128 20 E
American Highland, *Antarctica* .... **48 C16** 73 0S 75 0 E
American Samoa ■, *Pac. Oc.* **35 C17** 14 20S 170 40W
Amersfoort, *Neths.* ... **8 A6** 52 9N 5 23 E
Amiens, *France* ...... **8 C5** 49 54N 2 16 E
Amman, *Jordan* ...... **24 B2** 31 57N 35 52 E
Amos, *Canada* **42 A8** 48 35N 78 5W
Amravati, *India* ...... **23 J6** 20 55N 77 45 E
Amreli, *India* .... **23 J3** 21 35N 71 17 E
Amritsar, *India* .... **23 D5** 31 35N 74 57 E
Amroha, *India* .... **23 E7** 28 53N 78 30 E
Amsterdam, *Neths.* ... **8 A6** 52 23N 4 54 E
Amsterdam, *U.S.A.* ... **43 D10** 42 58N 74 10W
Amu Darya →, *Uzbekistan* .... **18 E7** 43 40N 59 0 E
Amundsen Gulf, *Canada* **38 A7** 71 0N 124 0W
Amundsen Sea, *Antarctica* **48 C22** 72 0S 115 0W
Amur →, *Russia* ..... **18 D16** 52 56N 141 10 E
An Najaf, *Iraq* .... **24 B3** 32 3N 44 15 E
An Nasiriyah, *Iraq* .... **24 B3** 31 0N 46 15 E
An Nhon, *Vietnam* .... **22 B2** 13 55N 109 7 E
Anadyr, *Russia* ...... **18 C19** 64 35N 177 20 E
Anadyr, G. of, *Russia* . **18 C20** 64 0N 180 0 E
Anaheim, *U.S.A.* **40 D3** 33 50N 118 0W
Anambas Is., *Indonesia* **22 C2** 3 20N 106 30 E
Anantnag, *India* ...... **23 C5** 33 45N 75 10 E
Anar, *Iran* .... **24 B4** 30 55N 55 13 E
Anatolia, *Turkey* ..... **15 G5** 39 0N 30 0 E
Ancenis, *France* **8 D3** 47 21N 1 10W
Anchorage, *U.S.A.* ... **38 B5** 61 10N 149 50W
Ancona, *Italy* .... **12 C5** 43 37N 13 30 E
Anda, *China* .... **21 B7** 46 24N 125 19 E
Andalusia □, *Spain* ... **11 D3** 37 35N 5 0W
Andaman Is., *Ind. Oc.* . **25 D8** 12 30N 92 30 E
Anderson, *U.S.A.* **42 E5** 40 5N 85 40W
Andes, *S. Amer.* **46 E3** 20 0S 68 0W
Andhra Pradesh □, *India* .... **25 D6** 18 0N 79 0 E
Andorra ■, *Europe* ... **11 A6** 42 30N 1 30 E
Andreanof Is., *U.S.A.* .. **38 C2** 52 0N 178 0W
Andria, *Italy* .... **12 D7** 41 13N 16 17 E
Andros I., *Bahamas* ... **45 C9** 24 30N 78 0W
Angara →, *Russia* ... **18 D11** 58 5N 94 20 E
Ånge, *Sweden* .... **6 F11** 62 31N 15 35 E
Angel Falls, *Venezuela* **46 B3** 5 57N 62 30W
Angerman →, *Sweden* **6 F11** 62 40N 18 0 E
Angers, *France* **8 D3** 47 30N 0 35W
Anglesey, *U.K.* **7 F4** 53 17N 4 20W
Angola ■, *Africa* ..... **33 G3** 12 0S 18 0 E
Angoulême, *France* ... **9 E4** 45 39N 0 10 E
Angoumois, *France* ... **9 E4** 45 50N 0 25 E
Anguilla, *W. Indies* **44 J18** 18 14N 63 5W
Anhui □, *China* ...... **21 C6** 32 0N 117 0 E
Anjou, *France* **8 D3** 47 20N 0 15W
Ankara, *Turkey* ...... **15 G5** 39 57N 32 54 E
Ann, C., *U.S.A.* **43 D12** 42 39N 70 37W
Ann Arbor, *U.S.A.* **42 D6** 42 17N 83 45W
Annaba, *Algeria* ...... **28 B8** 36 50N 7 46 E
Annapolis, *U.S.A.* **42 F9** 39 0N 76 30W
Annecy, *France* ...... **9 E7** 45 55N 6 8 E
Annemasse, *France* ... **9 D7** 46 12N 6 16 E
Annobón, *Atl. Oc.* .... **28 K8** 1 25S 5 36 E
Anshan, *China* .... **21 B7** 41 5N 122 58 E
Anshun, *China* .... **20 D5** 26 18N 105 57 E
Antalya, *Turkey* ...... **15 G5** 36 52N 30 45 E
Antananarivo, *Madag.* . **33 H9** 18 55S 47 31 E
Antarctic Pen., *Antarctica* **48 C24** 67 0S 60 0W
Antarctica .... **48 C24** 90 0S 0 0 E
Antibes, *France* ...... **9 F7** 43 34N 7 6 E
Anticosti I., *Canada* ... **43 A16** 49 30N 63 0W
Antigua & Barbuda ■, *W. Indies* **44 K20** 17 20N 61 48W
Antofagasta, *Chile* **47 E2** 23 50S 70 30W
Antrim, *U.K.* **7 E3** 54 43N 6 13W
Antrim, Mts. of, *U.K.* .. **7 E3** 54 57N 6 8W
Antsiranana, *Madag.* .. **33 G9** 12 25S 49 20 E
Antwerp, *Belgium* .... **8 B6** 51 13N 4 25 E
Anyang, *China* .... **21 C6** 36 5N 114 21 E
Aomori, *Japan* .... **19 F12** 40 45N 140 45 E
Aparri, *Phil.* .... **22 B4** 18 22N 121 38 E
Apeldoorn, *Neths.* .... **8 A6** 52 13N 5 57 E
Apennines, *Italy* ...... **12 C4** 44 0N 10 0 E
Apia, *W. Samoa* **35 C16** 13 50S 171 50W
Appalachian Mts., *U.S.A.* **42 G7** 38 0N 80 0W
Appleton, *U.S.A.* **42 C3** 44 17N 88 25W
Ar Ramadi, *Iraq* ...... **24 B3** 33 25N 43 20 E
Arabia, *Asia* .... **16 G8** 25 0N 45 0 E
Arabian Gulf = Gulf, The, *Asia* .... **24 C4** 27 0N 50 0 E
Arabian Sea, *Ind. Oc.* . **24 D5** 16 0N 65 0 E
Aracaju, *Brazil* **46 D6** 10 55S 37 4W
Arad, *Romania* .... **10 E9** 46 10N 21 20 E
Arafura Sea, *E. Indies* . **22 D5** 9 0S 135 0 E
Aragón □, *Spain* **11 B5** 41 25N 0 40W
Araguaia →, *Brazil* ... **46 C5** 5 21S 48 41W
Arakan Yoma, *Burma* . **25 C8** 20 0N 94 40 E
Aral Sea, *Asia* .... **18 E8** 44 30N 60 0 E
Aralsk, *Kazakhstan* ... **18 E8** 46 50N 61 20 E
Aran I., *Ireland* **7 E2** 55 0N 8 30W
Araq, *Iran* .... **24 B3** 34 0N 49 40 E
Arbroath, *U.K.* **7 D5** 56 34N 2 35W
Arcachon, *France* **9 E3** 44 40N 1 10W
Archangel = Arkhangelsk, *Russia* **14 B7** 64 40N 41 0 E
Arctic Ocean, *Arctic* .. **48 A1** 78 0N 160 0W
Arctic Red River, *Canada* **38 B6** 67 15N 134 0W
Ardebil, *Iran* .... **24 B3** 38 15N 48 18 E
Ardennes, *Belgium* ... **8 C6** 49 50N 5 5 E
Arendal, *Norway* ..... **6 G9** 58 28N 8 46 E
Arequipa, *Peru* **46 D2** 16 20S 71 30W
Argentan, *France* **8 C3** 48 45N 0 1W
Argentina ■, *S. Amer.* . **47 F3** 35 0S 66 0W
Arima, *Trin. & Tob.* ... **44 S20** 10 38N 61 17W
Arizona □, *U.S.A.* **40 D4** 34 20N 111 30W
Arkansas □, *U.S.A.* ... **41 D8** 35 0N 92 30W
Arkansas →, *U.S.A.* . **41 D8** 33 48N 91 4W
Arkhangelsk, *Russia* .. **14 B7** 64 40N 41 0 E
Arklow, *Ireland* **7 F3** 52 48N 6 10W
Arlberg Pass, *Austria* .. **10 E4** 47 9N 10 12 E
Arles, *France* .... **9 F6** 43 41N 4 40 E
Arlington, *U.S.A.* **42 F9** 38 52N 77 5W
Arlon, *Belgium* .... **8 C6** 49 42N 5 49 E
Armagh, *U.K.* **7 E3** 54 22N 6 40W
Armançon →, *France* **8 D5** 47 59N 3 30 E
Armenia ■, *Asia* ..... **15 F7** 40 20N 45 0 E
Arnhem, *Neths.* ...... **8 B6** 51 58N 5 55 E
Arnhem Land, *Australia* **34 C5** 13 10S 134 30 E
Arnprior, *Canada* **42 C9** 45 26N 76 21W
Arrah, *India* .... **23 G10** 25 35N 84 32 E
Arran, *U.K.* **7 E4** 55 34N 5 12W
Arras, *France* .... **8 B5** 50 17N 2 46 E
Artois, *France* .... **8 B5** 50 20N 2 30 E
Aru Is., *Indonesia* .... **22 D5** 6 0S 134 30 E
Arunachal Pradesh □, *India* .... **25 C8** 28 0N 95 0 E
Arusha, *Tanzania* ..... **32 E7** 3 20S 36 40 E
As Salt, *Jordan* ...... **29 P22** 32 2N 35 43 E
Asab, *Namibia* .... **31 B2** 25 30S 18 0 E
Asahigawa, *Japan* .... **19 F12** 43 46N 142 22 E
Asansol, *India* .... **23 H11** 23 40N 87 1 E
Asbestos, *Canada* **43 C12** 45 47N 71 58W
Asbury Park, *U.S.A.* ... **43 E10** 40 15N 74 1W
Ascension I., *Atl. Oc.* .. **2 E9** 8 0S 14 15W
Ashford, *U.K.* .... **7 G7** 51 8N 0 53 E
Ashkhabad, *Turkmenistan* ...... **18 F7** 38 0N 57 50 E
Ashland, *Ky., U.S.A.* ... **42 F6** 38 25N 82 40W
Ashland, *Ohio, U.S.A.* . **42 E6** 40 52N 82 20W
Ashqelon, *Israel* ...... **29 Q20** 31 42N 34 35 E
Ashtabula, *U.S.A.* **42 E7** 41 52N 80 50W
Asifabad, *India* .... **23 K7** 19 20N 79 24 E
Asir □, *Si. Arabia* .... **29 F15** 18 40N 42 30 E
Asir, Ras, *Somali Rep.* **29 G17** 11 55N 51 10 E
Asmara, *Eritrea* ...... **29 F14** 15 19N 38 55 E
Assam □, *India* ...... **23 F13** 26 0N 93 0 E
Assen, *Neths.* .... **8 A7** 53 0N 6 35 E
Asti, *Italy* .... **12 B3** 44 54N 8 11 E
Astrakhan, *Russia* .... **15 E8** 46 25N 48 5 E
Asturias □, *Spain* **11 A2** 43 15N 6 0W
Asunción, *Paraguay* .. **47 E4** 25 10S 57 30W
Aswân, *Egypt* .... **29 E13** 24 4N 32 57 E
Atacama Desert, *Chile* **47 E3** 24 0S 69 20W
Atbara →, *Sudan* .... **29 F13** 17 40N 33 56 E
Athabasca, L., *Canada* **38 C9** 59 15N 109 15W
Athens, *Greece* ...... **13 F10** 37 58N 23 46 E
Athens, *U.S.A.* **42 F6** 39 25N 82 6W
Athlone, *Ireland* **7 F3** 53 26N 7 57W
Atikokan, *Canada* **42 A2** 48 45N 91 37W
Atlanta, *U.S.A.* **41 D10** 33 50N 84 24W
Atlantic City, *U.S.A.* ... **43 F10** 39 25N 74 25W
Atlantic Ocean **2 E9** 0 0 20 0W
Au Sable →, *U.S.A.* . **42 C6** 44 25N 83 20W
Aube →, *France* ..... **8 C5** 48 34N 3 43 E
Auburn, *Ind., U.S.A.* .. **42 E5** 41 20N 85 5W
Auburn, *N.Y., U.S.A.* .. **42 D9** 42 57N 76 39W
Aubusson, *France* .... **9 E5** 45 57N 2 11 E
Auch, *France* .... **9 F4** 43 39N 0 36 E
Auckland, *N.Z.* .... **35 H13** 36 52S 174 46 E
Aude →, *France* ..... **9 F5** 43 13N 3 14 E
Augrabies Falls, *S. Africa* .... **31 B3** 28 35S 20 20 E
Augsburg, *Germany* .. **10 D4** 48 22N 10 54 E
Augusta, *Ga., U.S.A.* .. **41 D10** 33 29N 81 59W
Augusta, *Maine, U.S.A.* **43 C13** 44 20N 69 46W
Aunis, *France* **9 D3** 46 5N 0 50W
Aurangabad, *Bihar, India* **23 G10** 24 45N 84 18 E
Aurangabad, *Maharashtra, India* .. **23 K5** 19 50N 75 23 E
Aurillac, *France* ...... **9 E5** 44 55N 2 26 E
Aurora, *U.S.A.* **42 E3** 41 42N 88 12W
Austin, *U.S.A.* **40 D7** 30 20N 97 45W
Australia ■, *Oceania* .. **34 E5** 23 0S 135 0 E
Australian Alps, *Australia* .... **34 H8** 36 30S 148 30 E
Australian Capital Territory □, *Australia* **34 H8** 35 30S 149 0 E
Austria ■, *Europe* .... **10 E6** 47 0N 14 0 E
Autun, *France* .... **8 D6** 46 58N 4 17 E
Auvergne, *France* .... **9 E5** 45 20N 3 15 E
Auxerre, *France* ...... **8 D5** 47 48N 3 32 E
Avallon, *France* ...... **8 D5** 47 30N 3 53 E
Avellino, *Italy* .... **12 D6** 40 54N 14 46 E
Avesnes-sur-Helpe, *France* .... **8 B5** 50 8N 3 55 E
Aveyron →, *France* .. **9 E4** 44 5N 1 16 E
Avignon, *France* ..... **9 F6** 43 57N 4 50 E
Ávila, *Spain* **11 B3** 40 39N 4 43W
Avranches, *France* ... **8 C3** 48 40N 1 20W
Ayers Rock, *Australia* . **34 F5** 25 23S 131 5 E
Aylesbury, *U.K.* **7 G6** 51 48N 0 49W
Ayr, *U.K.* **7 E4** 55 28N 4 37W
Azamgarh, *India* ..... **23 F9** 26 5N 83 13 E
Azerbaijan ■, *Asia* .... **15 F8** 40 20N 48 0 E
Azores, *Atl. Oc.* **28 B1** 38 44N 29 0W
Azov, Sea of, *Europe* . **15 E6** 46 0N 36 30 E
Azuero, Pen., *Panama* . **45 F8** 7 30N 80 30W

B

Babol, *Iran* .... **24 B4** 36 40N 52 50 E
Babuyan Chan., *Phil.* .. **22 B4** 18 40N 121 30 E
Bacolod, *Phil.* .... **22 B4** 10 40N 122 57 E
Bad Axe, *U.S.A.* **42 D6** 43 48N 82 59W
Badajoz, *Spain* **11 C2** 38 50N 6 59W
Badalona, *Spain* ..... **11 B7** 41 26N 2 15 E
Baden-Württemberg □, *Germany* .... **10 D3** 48 40N 9 0 E
Baffin B., *Canada* **48 A10** 72 0N 64 0W
Baffin I., *Canada* **39 B12** 68 0N 75 0W
Baghdad, *Iraq* .... **24 B3** 33 20N 44 30 E
Bagnères-de-Bigorre, *France* .... **9 F4** 43 5N 0 9 E
Baguio, *Phil.* .... **22 B4** 16 26N 120 34 E
Bahamas ■, *N. Amer.* . **45 C10** 24 0N 75 0W
Bahawalpur, *Pakistan* . **23 E3** 29 24N 71 40 E
Bahía = Salvador, *Brazil* **46 D6** 13 0S 38 30W
Bahía □, *Brazil* **46 D5** 12 0S 42 0W
Bahía Blanca, *Argentina* **47 F3** 38 35S 62 13W
Bahraich, *India* ...... **23 F8** 27 38N 81 37 E
Bahrain ■, *Asia* ..... **24 C4** 26 0N 50 35 E
Baie-St-Paul, *Canada* . **43 B12** 47 28N 70 32W
Baikal, L., *Russia* .... **18 D12** 53 0N 108 0 E
Baile Atha Cliath = Dublin, *Ireland* **7 F3** 53 20N 6 18W
Baja California = Lower California, *Mexico* .. **44 B2** 31 10N 115 12W
Bakersfield, *U.S.A.* ... **40 C3** 35 25N 119 0W
Bakhtaran, *Iran* ...... **24 B3** 34 23N 47 0 E
Bakony Forest, *Hungary* **10 E7** 47 10N 17 30 E
Baku, *Azerbaijan* .... **15 F8** 40 25N 49 45 E
Balabac Str., *E. Indies* . **22 C3** 7 53N 117 5 E
Balaghat, *India* ...... **23 J8** 21 49N 80 12 E
Balasore, *India* ...... **23 J11** 21 35N 87 3 E
Balaton, L., *Hungary* .. **10 E7** 46 50N 17 40 E
Balboa, *Panama* **44 H14** 9 0N 79 30W
Baldwin, *U.S.A.* **42 D5** 43 54N 85 53W
Balearic Is., *Spain* .... **11 C7** 39 30N 3 0 E
Bali, *Indonesia* ...... **22 D3** 8 20S 115 0 E
Balıkeşir, *Turkey* ..... **15 G4** 39 35N 27 58 E
Balikpapan, *Indonesia* . **22 D3** 1 10S 116 55 E
Balkan Mts., *Bulgaria* . **13 C10** 43 15N 23 0 E
Balkan Peninsula, *Europe* .... **4 G10** 42 0N 23 0 E
Balkhash, *Kazakhstan* . **18 E9** 46 50N 74 50 E
Balkhash, L., *Kazakhstan* ...... **18 E9** 46 0N 74 50 E

Ballarat   **Bruce, Mt.**

Bruges

Colorado Springs

109
Columbia Eleuthera

Columbia, *U.S.A.* 41 D10 34 0N 81 0W
Columbia →, *N. Amer.* 40 A2 46 15N 124 5W
Columbia, District of □, *U.S.A.* 42 F9 38 55N 77 0W
Columbus, *Ga., U.S.A.* 41 D10 32 30N 84 58W
Columbus, *Ind., U.S.A.* 42 F5 39 14N 85 55W
Columbus, *Ohio, U.S.A.* 42 F6 39 57N 83 1W
Comilla, *Bangla.* 23 H13 23 28N 91 10 E
Commercy, *France* 8 C6 48 43N 5 34 E
Commonwealth of Independent States ■, *Eurasia* 18 C11 60 0N 100 0 E
Communism Pk., *Tajikistan* 18 F9 39 0N 72 2 E
Como, *Italy* 12 B3 45 48N 9 5 E
Como, L., *Italy* 12 A3 46 5N 9 17 E
Comodoro Rivadavia, *Argentina* 47 G3 45 50S 67 40W
Comorin, C., *India* 25 E6 8 3N 77 40 E
Comoro Is. ■, *Ind. Oc.* 27 H8 12 10S 44 15 E
Compiègne, *France* 8 C5 49 24N 2 50 E
Conakry, *Guinea* 28 H4 9 29N 13 49W
Concepción, *Chile* 47 F2 36 50S 73 0W
Conchos →, *Mexico* 44 B4 29 32N 105 0W
Concord, *U.S.A.* 43 D12 43 12N 71 30W
Condom, *France* 9 F4 43 57N 0 22 E
Confolens, *France* 9 D4 46 2N 0 40 E
Congo ■, *Africa* 32 E3 1 0S 16 0 E
Congo = Zaïre →, *Africa* 32 F2 6 4S 12 24 E
Congo Basin, *Africa* 26 G6 0 10S 24 30 E
Coniston, *Canada* 42 B7 46 29N 80 51W
Conn, L., *Ireland* 7 E2 54 3N 9 15W
Conneaut, *U.S.A.* 42 E7 41 55N 80 32W
Connecticut □, *U.S.A.* 43 E11 41 40N 72 40W
Connecticut →, *U.S.A.* 43 E11 41 17N 72 21W
Connellsville, *U.S.A.* 42 E8 40 3N 79 32W
Connemara, *Ireland* 7 F2 53 29N 9 45W
Connersville, *U.S.A.* 42 F5 39 40N 85 10W
Constance, L., *Europe* 10 E3 47 35N 9 25 E
Constanţa, *Romania* 13 B13 44 14N 28 38 E
Constantine, *Algeria* 28 B8 36 25N 6 42 E
Conway, *U.S.A.* 43 D12 43 58N 71 8W
Cooch Behar, *India* 23 F12 26 22N 89 29 E
Cook, Mt., *N.Z.* 35 J13 43 36S 170 9 E
Cook Is., *Pac. Oc.* 35 D18 17 0S 160 0W
Cook Strait, *N.Z.* 35 J13 41 15S 174 29 E
Copenhagen, *Denmark* 6 G10 55 41N 12 34 E
Copper Harbor, *U.S.A.* 42 B4 47 31N 87 55W
Coppermine, *Canada* 38 B8 67 50N 115 5W
Coppermine →, *Canada* 38 B8 67 49N 116 4W
Coral Sea, *Pac. Oc.* 36 J7 15 0S 150 0 E
Corbeil-Essonnes, *France* 8 C5 48 36N 2 26 E
Corbin, *U.S.A.* 42 G5 37 0N 84 3W
Corby, *U.K.* 7 F6 52 29N 0 41W
Córdoba, *Argentina* 47 F3 31 20S 64 10W
Córdoba, *Spain* 11 D3 37 50N 4 50W
Cordova, *U.S.A.* 38 B5 60 36N 145 45W
Corfu = Kérkira, *Greece* 13 E8 39 38N 19 50 E
Corinth, G. of, *Greece* 13 E10 38 16N 22 30 E
Cork, *Ireland* 7 G2 51 54N 8 30W
Corner Brook, *Canada* 39 D14 48 57N 57 58W
Corning, *U.S.A.* 42 D9 42 10N 77 3W
Cornwall, *Canada* 43 C10 45 2N 74 44W
Coromandel Coast, *India* 25 D7 12 30N 81 0 E
Coronation Gulf, *Canada* 38 B8 68 25N 110 0W
Corpus Christi, *U.S.A.* 40 E7 27 50N 97 28W
Corrib, L., *Ireland* 7 F2 53 5N 9 10W
Corrientes, *Argentina* 47 E4 27 30S 58 45W
Corry, *U.S.A.* 42 E8 41 55N 79 39W
Corse, C., *France* 9 E9 43 1N 9 25 E
Corsica, *France* 9 F8 42 0N 9 0 E
Corte, *France* 9 F9 42 19N 9 11 E
Cortland, *U.S.A.* 43 D9 42 35N 76 11W
Cosenza, *Italy* 12 E7 39 17N 16 14 E
Coshocton, *U.S.A.* 42 E7 40 17N 81 51W
Cosne-sur-Loire, *France* 8 D5 47 24N 2 54 E
Costa Rica ■, *Cent. Amer.* 45 F8 10 0N 84 0W
Côte-d'Ivoire = Ivory Coast ■, *Africa* 28 H6 7 30N 5 0W
Côte d'Or, *France* 8 D6 47 10N 4 50 E
Cotentin, *France* 8 C3 49 15N 1 30W
Cotonou, *Benin* 30 C2 6 20N 2 25 E
Cotopaxi, *Ecuador* 46 C2 0 40S 78 30W
Cotswold Hills, *U.K.* 7 G5 51 42N 2 10W
Cottbus, *Germany* 10 C6 51 44N 14 20 E
Coudersport, *U.S.A.* 42 E8 41 45N 78 1W
Council Bluffs, *U.S.A.* 41 B7 41 20N 95 50W
Coutances, *France* 8 C3 49 3N 1 28W
Coventry, *U.K.* 7 F6 52 25N 1 31W
Covington, *U.S.A.* 42 F5 39 5N 84 30W
Cox's Bazar, *Bangla.* 23 J13 21 26N 91 59 E
Cradock, *S. Africa* 31 C4 32 8S 25 36 E
Craiova, *Romania* 13 B10 44 21N 23 48 E
Cranbrook, *Canada* 38 D8 49 30N 115 46W
Crawfordsville, *U.S.A.* 42 E4 40 2N 86 51W
Creil, *France* 8 C5 49 15N 2 29 E
Cremona, *Italy* 12 B4 45 8N 10 2 E
Crete, *Greece* 13 G11 35 15N 25 0 E
Creuse →, *France* 9 D4 47 0N 0 34 E
Crewe, *U.K.* 7 F5 53 6N 2 28W
Crimea, *Ukraine* 15 E5 45 0N 34 0 E
Crişu, Black →, *Romania* 10 E9 46 42N 21 16 E
Crişu, White →, *Romania* 10 E9 46 42N 21 17 E
Croatia ■, *Europe* 12 B7 45 20N 16 0 E
Crocodile →, *Mozam.* 31 B5 25 14S 32 18 E
Crystal Falls, *U.S.A.* 42 B3 46 9N 88 11W
Cuba ■, *W. Indies* 45 C9 22 0N 79 0W
Cúcuta, *Colombia* 46 B2 7 54N 72 31W
Cuenca, *Ecuador* 46 C2 2 50S 79 9W
Cuenca, *Spain* 11 B4 40 5N 2 10W
Cuernavaca, *Mexico* 44 D5 18 55N 99 15W
Cuiabá, *Brazil* 46 D4 15 30S 56 0W
Culiacán, *Mexico* 44 C3 24 50N 107 23W
Culpeper, *U.S.A.* 42 F9 38 29N 77 59W
Cumberland, *U.S.A.* 42 F8 39 40N 78 43W
Cumberland Plateau, *U.S.A.* 41 C10 36 0N 84 30W
Cumbrian Mts., *U.K.* 7 E5 54 30N 3 0W
Cuneo, *Italy* 12 B2 44 23N 7 31 E
Cupar, *U.K.* 7 D5 56 20N 3 3W
Curitiba, *Brazil* 47 E5 25 20S 49 10W
Cuttack, *India* 23 J10 20 25N 85 57 E
Cuxhaven, *Germany* 10 B3 53 51N 8 41 E
Cuyahoga Falls, *U.S.A.* 42 E7 41 8N 81 30W
Cuzco, *Peru* 46 D2 13 32S 72 0W
Cyclades = Kikládhes, *Greece* 13 F11 37 20N 24 30 E
Cynthiana, *U.S.A.* 42 F5 38 23N 84 10W
Cyprus ■, *Medit. S.* 24 B2 35 0N 33 0 E
Czech Rep. ■, *Europe* 10 D6 50 0N 15 0 E
Częstochowa, *Poland* 10 C8 50 49N 19 7 E

D

Da Nang, *Vietnam* 22 B2 16 4N 108 13 E
Dacca, *Bangla.* 23 H13 23 43N 90 26 E
Dacca □, *Bangla.* 23 G13 24 25N 90 25 E
Dadra and Nagar Haveli □, *India* 23 J4 20 5N 73 0 E
Dadu, *Pakistan* 23 F1 26 45N 67 45 E
Dagestan Republic □, *Russia* 15 F8 42 30N 47 0 E
Dagupan, *Phil.* 22 B4 16 3N 120 20 E
Dahod, *India* 23 H5 22 50N 74 15 E
Dakar, *Senegal* 28 G3 14 34N 17 29W
Dakhla, *W. Sahara* 28 E3 23 50N 15 53W
Dalhousie, *Canada* 43 A14 48 5N 66 26W
Dalian, *China* 21 C7 38 50N 121 40 E
Dallas, *U.S.A.* 41 D7 32 50N 96 50W
Dalmatia □, *Croatia* 12 C7 43 20N 17 0 E
Daloa, *Ivory C.* 28 H5 7 0N 6 30W
Damaraland, *Namibia* 31 A2 21 0S 17 0 E
Damascus, *Syria* 24 B2 33 30N 36 18 E
Dammam, *Si. Arabia* 24 C4 26 20N 50 5 E
Dampier, *Australia* 34 E2 20 41S 116 42 E
Danbury, *U.S.A.* 43 E11 41 23N 73 29W
Dandeldhura, *Nepal* 23 E8 29 20N 80 35 E
Dandong, *China* 21 B7 40 10N 124 20 E
Dannemora, *Sweden* 6 F11 60 12N 17 51 E
Danube →, *Europe* 13 B13 45 20N 29 40 E
Danville, *Ill., U.S.A.* 42 E4 40 10N 87 40W
Danville, *Ky., U.S.A.* 42 G5 37 40N 84 45W
Dar-es-Salaam, *Tanzania* 32 F7 6 50S 39 12 E
Dar'ā, *Syria* 29 C14 32 36N 36 7 E
Darbhanga, *India* 23 F10 26 15N 85 55 E
Dardanelles, *Turkey* 13 D12 40 17N 26 32 E
Dargai, *Pakistan* 23 B3 34 25N 71 55 E
Darjeeling, *India* 23 F12 27 3N 88 18 E
Darling →, *Australia* 34 G7 34 4S 141 54 E
Darling Ra., *Australia* 34 G2 32 30S 116 0 E
Darlington, *U.K.* 7 E6 54 33N 1 33W
Darmstadt, *Germany* 10 D3 49 51N 8 40 E
Darnley, C., *Antarctica* 48 C16 68 0S 69 0 E
Dartmoor, *U.K.* 7 G5 50 36N 4 0W
Dartmouth, *Canada* 43 C16 44 40N 63 30W
Darwin, *Australia* 34 C5 12 25S 130 51 E
Dasht →, *Pakistan* 24 C5 25 10N 61 40 E
Dasht-e Lūt, *Iran* 24 B4 31 30N 58 0 E
Datong, *China* 21 B6 40 6N 113 18 E
Daulpur, *India* 23 F6 26 45N 77 59 E
Dauphin, *Canada* 38 C9 51 9N 100 5W
Dauphiné, *France* 9 E6 45 15N 5 25 E
Davao, *Phil.* 22 C4 7 0N 125 40 E
Davao G., *Phil.* 22 C4 6 30N 125 48 E
Davenport, *U.S.A.* 41 B8 41 30N 90 40W
David, *Panama* 45 F8 8 30N 82 30W
Davis Str., *N. Amer.* 39 B14 65 0N 58 0W
Dawson, *Canada* 38 B6 64 10N 139 30W
Dawson Creek, *Canada* 38 C7 55 45N 120 15W
Dax, *France* 9 F3 43 44N 1 3W
Dayton, *U.S.A.* 42 F5 39 45N 84 10W
De Aar, *S. Africa* 31 C3 30 39S 24 0 E
De Pere, *U.S.A.* 42 C3 44 28N 88 1W
Dead Sea, *Asia* 29 Q21 31 30N 35 30 E
Dease Lake, *Canada* 38 C6 58 25N 130 6W
Death Valley, *U.S.A.* 40 C3 36 19N 116 52W
Debrecen, *Hungary* 10 E9 47 33N 21 42 E
Decatur, *U.S.A.* 42 E5 40 50N 84 56W
Deccan, *India* 25 D6 18 0N 79 0 E
Dee →, *Clwyd, U.K.* 7 F5 53 15N 3 7W
Dee →, *Gramp., U.K.* 7 D5 57 4N 2 7W
Defiance, *U.S.A.* 42 E5 41 20N 84 20W
Dehra Dun, *India* 23 D7 30 20N 78 4 E
Delaware, *U.S.A.* 42 E6 40 20N 83 5W
Delaware □, *U.S.A.* 43 F10 39 0N 75 40W
Delaware →, *U.S.A.* 43 F10 39 20N 75 25W
Delft, *Neths.* 8 A6 52 1N 4 22 E
Delfzijl, *Neths.* 8 A7 53 20N 6 55 E
Delhi, *India* 23 E6 28 38N 77 17 E
Delphos, *U.S.A.* 42 E5 40 51N 84 17W
Demavand, *Iran* 24 B4 35 47N 52 0 E
Den Haag = The Hague, *Neths.* 8 A6 52 7N 4 17 E
Den Helder, *Neths.* 8 A6 52 57N 4 45 E
Denizli, *Turkey* 15 G4 37 42N 29 2 E
Denmark ■, *Europe* 6 G9 55 30N 9 0 E
Denmark Str., *Atl. Oc.* 48 A8 66 0N 30 0W
Denpasar, *Indonesia* 22 D3 8 45S 115 14 E
Denver, *U.S.A.* 40 C5 39 45N 105 0W
Deoghar, *India* 23 G11 24 30N 86 42 E
Deolali, *India* 23 K4 19 58N 73 50 E
Deosai Mts., *Pakistan* 23 B5 35 40N 75 0 E
Dera Ghazi Khan, *Pakistan* 23 D3 30 5N 70 43 E
Dera Ismail Khan, *Pakistan* 23 D3 31 50N 70 50 E
Derby, *U.K.* 7 F6 52 55N 1 28W
Derg, L., *Ireland* 7 F2 53 0N 8 20W
Derryveagh Mts., *Ireland* 7 E2 55 0N 8 4W
Des Moines, *U.S.A.* 41 B8 41 35N 93 37W
Des Moines →, *U.S.A.* 41 B8 40 23N 91 25W
Dessau, *Germany* 10 C5 51 49N 12 15 E
Detour, Pt., *U.S.A.* 42 C4 45 37N 86 35W
Detroit, *U.S.A.* 42 D6 42 23N 83 5W
Deventer, *Neths.* 8 A7 52 15N 6 10 E
Devon I., *Canada* 48 A10 75 10N 85 0W
Dewas, *India* 23 H6 22 59N 76 3 E
Dhamtari, *India* 23 J8 20 42N 81 35 E
Dhanbad, *India* 23 H11 23 50N 86 30 E
Dhankuta, *Nepal* 23 F11 26 55N 87 40 E
Dhar, *India* 23 H5 22 35N 75 26 E
Dharwad, *India* 25 D6 15 22N 75 15 E
Dhaulagiri, *Nepal* 23 E9 28 39N 83 28 E
Dhenkanal, *India* 23 J10 20 45N 85 35 E
Dhuburi, *India* 23 F12 26 2N 89 59 E
Dhule, *India* 23 J5 20 58N 74 50 E
Diamantina →, *Australia* 34 F6 26 45S 139 10 E
Dieppe, *France* 8 C4 49 54N 1 4 E
Digby, *Canada* 43 C15 44 38N 65 50W
Digne, *France* 9 E7 44 5N 6 12 E
Dijon, *France* 8 D6 47 20N 5 3 E
Dili, *Indonesia* 22 D4 8 39S 125 34 E
Dillingham, *U.S.A.* 38 C4 59 5N 158 30W
Dimbaza, *S. Africa* 31 C4 32 50S 27 14 E
Dinajpur, *Bangla.* 23 G12 25 33N 88 43 E
Dinan, *France* 8 C2 48 28N 2 2W
Dinant, *Belgium* 8 B6 50 16N 4 55 E
Dinaric Alps, *Croatia* 12 C7 44 0N 16 30 E
Dingwall, *U.K.* 7 D4 57 36N 4 26W
Dir, *Pakistan* 23 B3 35 8N 71 59 E
Disteghil Sar, *Pakistan* 23 A5 36 20N 75 12 E
Diu, *India* 23 J3 20 45N 70 58 E
Diyarbakır, *Turkey* 15 G7 37 55N 40 18 E
Djakarta = Jakarta, *Indonesia* 22 D2 6 9S 106 49 E
Djerid, Chott, *Tunisia* 28 C8 33 42N 8 30 E
Djibouti ■, *Africa* 29 G15 12 0N 43 0 E
Dneprodzerzhinsk, *Ukraine* 15 E5 48 32N 34 37 E
Dnepropetrovsk, *Ukraine* 15 E5 48 30N 35 0 E
Dnieper →, *Ukraine* 15 E5 46 30N 32 18 E
Dniester →, *Europe* 15 E5 46 18N 30 17 E
Dobreta-Turnu-Severin, *Romania* 13 B10 44 39N 22 41 E
Dodecanese, *Greece* 13 F12 36 35N 27 0 E
Dodoma, *Tanzania* 32 F7 6 8S 35 45 E
Dogger Bank, *N. Sea* 4 E6 54 50N 2 0 E
Doha, *Qatar* 24 C4 25 15N 51 35 E
Dohazari, *Bangla.* 23 H14 22 10N 92 5 E
Dolbeau, *Canada* 43 A11 48 53N 72 18W
Dole, *France* 8 D6 47 7N 5 31 E
Dolomites, *Italy* 12 A4 46 30N 11 40 E
Dominica ■, *W. Indies* 44 M20 15 20N 61 20W
Dominican Rep. ■, *W. Indies* 45 D10 19 0N 70 30W
Don →, *Russia* 15 E6 47 4N 39 18 E
Don →, *U.K.* 7 D5 57 14N 2 5W
Doncaster, *U.K.* 7 F6 53 31N 1 9W
Dondra Head, *Sri Lanka* 25 E7 5 55N 80 40 E
Donetsk, *Ukraine* 15 E6 48 0N 37 45 E
Dongting, L., *China* 21 D6 29 18N 112 45 E
Donostia = San Sebastián, *Spain* 11 A5 43 17N 1 58W
Dorchester, *U.K.* 7 G5 50 42N 2 28W
Dordogne →, *France* 9 E3 45 2N 0 36W
Dordrecht, *Neths.* 8 B6 51 48N 4 39 E
Dordrecht, *S. Africa* 31 C4 31 20S 27 3 E
Doring →, *S. Africa* 31 C2 31 54S 18 39 E
Dortmund, *Germany* 10 C2 51 32N 7 28 E
Douai, *France* 8 B5 50 21N 3 4 E
Douala, *Cameroon* 30 D3 4 0N 9 45 E
Doubs →, *France* 8 D6 46 53N 5 1 E
Douglas, *S. Africa* 31 B3 29 4S 23 46 E
Douglas, *U.K.* 7 E4 54 9N 4 29W
Douro →, *Europe* 11 B1 41 8N 8 40W
Dover, *U.K.* 7 G7 51 7N 1 19 E
Dover, *Del., U.S.A.* 43 F10 39 10N 75 31W
Dover, *N.H., U.S.A.* 43 D12 43 12N 70 51W
Dover, Str. of, *Europe* 8 B4 51 0N 1 30 E
Dover-Foxcroft, *U.S.A.* 43 C13 45 14N 69 14W
Dovrefjell, *Norway* 6 F9 62 15N 9 33 E
Drac →, *France* 9 E6 45 12N 5 42 E
Draguignan, *France* 9 F7 43 32N 6 27 E
Drake Passage, *S. Ocean* 48 D23 58 0S 68 0W
Drakensberg, *S. Africa* 31 C4 31 0S 28 0 E
Drammen, *Norway* 6 G10 59 42N 10 12 E
Drava →, *Croatia* 13 B8 45 33N 18 55 E
Dresden, *Germany* 10 C5 51 2N 13 45 E
Dreux, *France* 8 C4 48 44N 1 23 E
Drina →, *Bos.-H., Yug.* 13 B8 44 53N 19 21 E
Drogheda, *Ireland* 7 F3 53 45N 6 20W
Dronne →, *France* 9 E3 45 2N 0 9W
Drumheller, *Canada* 38 C8 51 25N 112 40W
Drummond I., *U.S.A.* 42 B5 46 0N 83 40W
Drummondville, *Canada* 43 C11 45 55N 72 25W
Drygalski I., *Antarctica* 48 C17 66 0S 92 0 E
Du Bois, *U.S.A.* 42 E8 41 8N 78 46W
Dubai, *U.A.E.* 24 C4 25 18N 55 20 E
Dubbo, *Australia* 34 G8 32 11S 148 35 E
Dublin, *Ireland* 7 F3 53 20N 6 18W
Dubrovnik, *Croatia* 13 C8 42 39N 18 6 E
Dudinka, *Russia* 18 C10 69 30N 86 13 E
Duisburg, *Germany* 10 C2 51 27N 6 42 E
Duluth, *U.S.A.* 41 A8 46 48N 92 10W
Dumbarton, *U.K.* 7 E4 55 58N 4 35W
Dumfries, *U.K.* 7 E5 55 4N 3 37W
Dun Laoghaire, *Ireland* 7 F3 53 17N 6 9W
Dunbar, *U.K.* 7 E5 56 0N 2 32W
Dundalk, *Ireland* 7 E3 54 1N 6 25W
Dundee, *S. Africa* 31 B5 28 11S 30 15 E
Dundee, *U.K.* 7 D5 56 29N 3 0W
Dunedin, *N.Z.* 35 K13 45 50S 170 33 E
Dunfermline, *U.K.* 7 D5 56 5N 3 28W
Dunkerque, *France* 8 B5 51 2N 2 20 E
Dunkirk, *U.S.A.* 42 D8 42 30N 79 18W
Dunmore, *U.S.A.* 43 E10 41 27N 75 38W
Durango, *Mexico* 44 C4 24 3N 104 39W
Durban, *S. Africa* 31 B5 29 49S 31 1 E
Durg, *India* 23 J8 21 15N 81 22 E
Durgapur, *India* 23 H11 23 30N 87 20 E
Durham, *U.K.* 7 E6 54 47N 1 34W
Durham, *U.S.A.* 41 C11 36 0N 78 55W
Durrës, *Albania* 13 D8 41 19N 19 28 E
Dushanbe, *Tajikistan* 18 F8 38 33N 68 48 E
Düsseldorf, *Germany* 10 C2 51 15N 6 46 E
Duyun, *China* 20 D5 26 18N 107 29 E
Dvina, N. →, *Russia* 14 B7 64 32N 40 30 E
Dwarka, *India* 23 H2 22 18N 69 8 E
Dzerzhinsk, *Russia* 14 C7 56 14N 43 30 E
Dzhambul, *Kazakhstan* 18 E9 42 54N 71 22 E
Dzhugdzhur Ra., *Russia* 18 D15 57 30N 138 0 E
Dzungaria, *China* 20 B3 44 30N 86 0 E

E

Eagle L., *U.S.A.* 43 B13 46 23N 69 22W
East Beskids, *Europe* 10 D9 49 20N 22 0 E
East China Sea, *Asia* 21 C7 30 5N 126 0 E
East Indies, *Asia* 16 K15 0 0 120 0 E
East Lansing, *U.S.A.* 42 D5 42 44N 84 29W
East London, *S. Africa* 31 C4 33 0S 27 55 E
East Pt., *Canada* 43 B17 46 27N 61 58W
East Siberian Sea, *Russia* 18 B18 73 0N 160 0 E
Eastbourne, *U.K.* 7 G7 50 46N 0 18 E
Easter Dal →, *Sweden* 6 F10 61 30N 13 45 E
Easter Islands, *Pac. Oc.* 37 K17 27 0S 109 0W
Eastern Ghats, *India* 25 D6 14 0N 78 50 E
Easton, *Md., U.S.A.* 43 F9 38 47N 76 7W
Easton, *Pa., U.S.A.* 43 E10 40 41N 75 15W
Eastport, *U.S.A.* 43 C14 44 57N 67 0W
Eau Claire, *U.S.A.* 41 B8 44 46N 91 30W
Ebro →, *Spain* 11 B6 40 43N 0 54 E
Echo Bay, *Canada* 38 B8 66 5N 117 55W
Ecuador ■, *S. Amer.* 46 C2 2 0S 78 0W
Ede, *Nigeria* 30 C2 7 45N 4 29 E
Edendale, *S. Africa* 31 B5 29 39S 30 18 E
Edinburgh, *U.K.* 7 E5 55 57N 3 12W
Edmonton, *Canada* 38 C8 53 30N 113 30W
Edmundston, *Canada* 43 B13 47 23N 68 20W
Edward, L., *Africa* 32 E5 0 25S 29 40 E
Edward VII Land, *Antarctica* 48 C21 80 0S 150 0W
Effingham, *U.S.A.* 42 F3 39 8N 88 30W
Eganville, *Canada* 42 C9 45 32N 77 5W
Eger, *Hungary* 10 E9 47 53N 20 27 E
Egersund, *Norway* 6 G9 58 26N 6 1 E
Egypt ■, *Africa* 29 D13 28 0N 31 0 E
Eifel, *Germany* 10 C2 50 10N 6 45 E
Eindhoven, *Neths.* 8 B6 51 26N 5 28 E
El Aaiún, *W. Sahara* 28 D4 27 9N 13 12W
El Faiyum, *Egypt* 29 D13 29 19N 30 50 E
El Fasher, *Sudan* 29 G12 13 33N 25 26 E
El Iskandarîya = Alexandria, *Egypt* 29 C13 31 0N 30 0 E
El Mahalla el Kubra, *Egypt* 29 C13 31 0N 31 0 E
El Minya, *Egypt* 29 D13 28 7N 30 33 E
El Obeid, *Sudan* 29 G13 13 8N 30 10 E
El Paso, *U.S.A.* 40 D5 31 50N 106 30W
El Qâhira = Cairo, *Egypt* 29 C13 30 1N 31 14 E
El Salvador ■, *Cent. Amer.* 44 E7 13 50N 89 0W
Elba, *Italy* 12 C4 42 48N 10 15 E
Elbasan, *Albania* 13 D9 41 9N 20 9 E
Elbe →, *Europe* 10 B3 53 50N 9 0 E
Elbeuf, *France* 8 C4 49 17N 1 2 E
Elblag, *Poland* 10 A8 54 10N 19 25 E
Elbrus, *Asia* 15 F7 43 21N 42 30 E
Elburz Mts., *Iran* 24 B4 36 0N 52 0 E
Elche, *Spain* 11 C5 38 15N 0 42W
Eldoret, *Kenya* 32 D7 0 30N 35 17 E
Elephant I., *Antarctica* 48 C24 61 0S 55 0W
Elephants →, *Mozam.* 31 A5 24 10S 32 40 E
Eleuthera, *Bahamas* 45 C9 25 0N 76 20W

113
Kualakapuas
Malacca, Str. of

Kualakapuas, Indonesia 22 D3 2 55S 114 20 E
Kuching, Malaysia 22 C3 1 33N 110 25 E
Kudat, Malaysia 22 C3 6 55N 116 55 E
Kumanovo, Macedonia, Yug. 13 C9 42 9N 21 42 E
Kumasi, Ghana 30 C1 6 41N 1 38W
Kumayri, Armenia 15 F7 40 47N 43 50 E
Kumbakonam, India 25 D6 10 58N 79 25 E
Kunlun Shan, Asia 20 C3 36 0N 86 30 E
Kunming, China 20 D5 25 1N 102 41 E
Kuopio, Finland 6 F13 62 53N 27 35 E
Kupang, Indonesia 22 E4 10 19S 123 39 E
Kura →, Azerbaijan 15 G8 39 50N 49 20 E
Kurashiki, Japan 19 B3 34 40N 133 50 E
Kurdistan, Asia 24 B3 37 20N 43 30 E
Kure, Japan 19 B3 34 14N 132 32 E
Kurgan, Russia 18 D8 55 26N 65 18 E
Kuril Is., Russia 18 E17 45 0N 150 0 E
Kurnool, India 25 D6 15 45N 78 0 E
Kursk, Russia 14 D6 51 42N 36 11 E
Kuruman, S. Africa 31 B3 27 28S 23 28 E
Kuruman →, S. Africa 31 B3 26 56S 20 39 E
Kurume, Japan 19 C2 33 15N 130 30 E
Kushiro, Japan 19 F12 43 0N 144 25 E
Kushtia, Bangla. 23 H12 23 55N 89 5 E
Kütahya, Turkey 15 G5 39 30N 30 2 E
Kutaisi, Georgia 15 F7 42 19N 42 40 E
Kutch, Gulf of, India 23 H2 22 50N 69 15 E
Kutch, Rann of, India 23 G2 24 0N 70 0 E
Kuwait, Kuwait 24 C3 29 30N 48 0 E
Kuwait ■, Asia 24 C3 29 30N 47 30 E
Kuybyshev = Samara, Russia 14 D9 53 8N 50 6 E
KwaMashu, S. Africa 31 B5 29 45S 30 58 E
Kwangju, S. Korea 21 C7 35 9N 126 54 E
Kyōto, Japan 19 B4 35 0N 135 45 E
Kyūshū, Japan 19 C2 33 0N 131 0 E
Kyzyl Kum, Uzbekistan 18 E8 42 30N 65 0 E
Kzyl-Orda, Kazakhstan 18 E8 44 48N 65 28 E

L

La Chorrera, Panama 44 H14 8 50N 79 50W
La Ciotat, France 9 F6 43 10N 5 37 E
La Coruña, Spain 11 A1 43 20N 8 25W
La Flèche, France 8 D3 47 42N 0 4W
La Habana = Havana, Cuba 45 C8 23 8N 82 22W
La Mancha, Spain 11 C4 39 10N 2 54W
La Paz, Bolivia 46 D3 16 20S 68 10W
La Perouse Str., Asia 16 E18 45 40N 142 0 E
La Plata, Argentina 47 F4 35 0S 57 55W
La Porte, U.S.A. 42 E4 41 36N 86 43W
La Roche-sur-Yon, France 8 D3 46 40N 1 25W
La Sarre, Canada 42 A8 48 45N 79 15W
La Spezia, Italy 12 B3 44 8N 9 50 E
La Tour-du-Pin, France 9 E6 45 33N 5 27 E
La Tuque, Canada 43 B11 47 30N 72 50W
Labrador, Coast of, Canada 39 C13 53 20N 61 0W
Labuk B., Malaysia 22 C3 6 10N 117 50 E
Lac-Mégantic, Canada 43 C12 45 35N 70 53W
Laccadive Is. = Lakshadweep Is., Ind. Oc. 25 D6 10 0N 72 30 E
Lachine, Canada 43 C11 45 30N 73 40W
Laconia, U.S.A. 43 D12 43 32N 71 30W
Ladakh Ra., India 23 B6 34 0N 78 0 E
Ladoga, L., Russia 14 B5 61 15N 30 30 E
Ladybrand, S. Africa 31 B4 29 9S 27 29 E
Ladysmith, S. Africa 31 B4 28 32S 29 46 E
Lae, Papua N. G. 34 B8 6 40S 147 2 E
Lafayette, Ind., U.S.A. 42 E4 40 25N 86 54W
Lafayette, La., U.S.A. 41 D8 30 18N 92 0W
Lagos, Nigeria 30 C2 6 25N 3 27 E
Lagos, Portugal 11 D1 37 5N 8 41W
Lahn →, Germany 10 C2 50 17N 7 38 E
Lahore, Pakistan 23 D5 31 32N 74 22 E
Lahti, Finland 6 F13 60 58N 25 40 E
Laingsburg, S. Africa 31 C3 33 9S 20 52 E
Lake Charles, U.S.A. 41 D8 30 15N 93 10W
Lakewood, U.S.A. 42 E7 41 28N 81 50W
Lakshadweep Is., Ind. Oc. 25 D6 10 0N 72 30 E
Lalitapur, Nepal 23 F10 27 40N 85 20 E
Lamon Bay, Phil. 22 B4 14 30N 122 20 E
Lancaster, U.K. 7 E5 54 3N 2 48W
Lancaster, N.H., U.S.A. 43 C12 44 27N 71 33W
Lancaster, Pa., U.S.A. 42 E9 40 4N 76 19W
Lancaster Sd., Canada 39 A11 74 13N 84 0W
Landes, France 9 E3 44 0N 1 0W
Land's End, U.K. 7 G4 50 4N 5 43W
Langon, France 9 E3 44 33N 0 16W
Langres, France 8 D6 47 52N 5 20 E
Langres, Plateau de, France 8 D6 47 45N 5 3 E
Lannion, France 8 C2 48 46N 3 29W
L'Annonciation, Canada 43 B10 46 25N 74 55W
L'Anse, U.S.A. 42 B3 46 47N 88 28W
Lansing, U.S.A. 42 D5 42 47N 84 40W
Lanzhou, China 20 C5 36 1N 103 52 E
Laoag, Phil. 22 B4 18 7N 120 34 E
Laon, France 8 C5 49 33N 3 35 E
Laos ■, Asia 22 B2 17 45N 105 0 E
Lapeer, U.S.A. 42 D6 43 3N 83 20W
Lapland, Europe 6 E12 68 7N 24 0 E
Laptev Sea, Russia 18 B14 76 0N 125 0 E
Laredo, U.S.A. 40 E7 27 34N 99 29W
Largentière, France 9 E6 44 34N 4 18 E
Larisa, Greece 13 E10 39 49N 22 28 E
Larne, U.K. 7 E4 54 52N 5 50W
Larvik, Norway 6 G10 59 4N 10 4 E
Las Palmas, Canary Is. 28 D3 28 7N 15 26W
Las Vegas, U.S.A. 40 C3 36 10N 115 5W
Lashio, Burma 25 C8 22 56N 97 45 E
Latakia, Syria 24 B2 35 30N 35 45 E
Latina, Italy 12 D5 41 26N 12 53 E
Latvia ■, Europe 14 C3 56 50N 24 0 E
Launceston, Australia 34 J8 41 24S 147 8 E
Laurentian Plateau, Canada 39 C13 52 0N 70 0W
Lausanne, Switz. 8 D7 46 32N 6 38 E
Laut, Indonesia 22 C2 4 45N 108 0 E
Lauzon, Canada 43 B12 46 48N 71 10W
Laval, France 8 C3 48 4N 0 48W
Lawrence, U.S.A. 43 D12 42 40N 71 9W
Layla, Si. Arabia 24 C3 22 10N 46 40 E
Le Creusot, France 8 D6 46 48N 4 24 E
Le Havre, France 8 C4 49 30N 0 5 E
Le Mans, France 8 D4 48 0N 0 10 E
Le Puy, France 9 E5 45 3N 3 52 E
Leamington, Canada 42 D6 42 3N 82 36W
Lebanon, Ind., U.S.A. 42 E4 40 3N 86 28W
Lebanon, Ky., U.S.A. 42 G5 37 35N 85 15W
Lebanon, Pa., U.S.A. 42 E9 40 20N 76 28W
Lebanon ■, Asia 24 B2 34 0N 36 0 E
Lecce, Italy 13 D8 40 20N 18 10 E
Leduc, Canada 38 C8 53 15N 113 30W
Leeds, U.K. 7 F6 53 48N 1 34W
Leeuwarden, Neths. 8 A6 53 15N 5 48 E
Leeuwin, C., Australia 34 G2 34 20S 115 9 E
Leeward Is., Atl. Oc. 44 L18 16 30N 63 30W
Leghorn, Italy 12 C4 43 32N 10 18 E
Legnica, Poland 10 C7 51 12N 16 10 E
Leh, India 23 B6 34 9N 77 35 E
Lehututu, Botswana 31 A3 23 54S 21 55 E
Leicester, U.K. 7 F6 52 39N 1 9W
Leiden, Neths. 8 A6 52 9N 4 30 E
Leine →, Germany 10 B3 52 20N 9 50 E
Leipzig, Germany 10 C5 51 20N 12 23 E
Leith, U.K. 7 E5 55 59N 3 10W
Leitrim, Ireland 7 F2 54 0N 8 5W
Lena →, Russia 18 B14 72 52N 126 40 E
Leningrad = St. Petersburg, Russia 14 C5 59 55N 30 20 E
Leninsk-Kuznetskiy, Russia 18 D10 54 44N 86 10 E
Lens, France 8 B5 50 26N 2 50 E
Leominster, U.S.A. 43 D12 42 32N 71 45W
León, Mexico 44 C4 21 7N 101 30W
León, Guanajuato, Mexico 44 C4 21 7N 101 40W
León, Spain 11 A3 42 38N 5 34W
Lérida, Spain 11 B6 41 37N 0 39 E
Lerwick, U.K. 7 A6 60 10N 1 10W
Les Andelys, France 8 C4 49 15N 1 25 E
Les Sables-d'Olonne, France 9 D3 46 30N 1 45W
Leskovac, Serbia, Yug. 13 C9 43 0N 21 58 E
Lesotho ■, Africa 31 B4 29 40S 28 0 E
Lesparre-Médoc, France 9 E3 45 18N 0 57W
Lesvos, Greece 13 E12 39 10N 26 20 E
Leszno, Poland 10 C7 51 50N 16 30 E
Lethbridge, Canada 38 D8 49 45N 112 45W
Leti Is., Indonesia 22 D4 8 10S 128 0 E
Letiahau →, Botswana 31 A3 21 16S 24 0 E
Leuven, Belgium 8 B6 50 52N 4 42 E
Lévis, Canada 43 B12 46 48N 71 9W
Lewes, U.K. 7 G7 50 53N 0 2 E
Lewis, U.K. 7 C3 58 10N 6 40W
Lewiston, U.S.A. 43 C12 44 3N 70 10W
Lewistown, U.S.A. 42 E9 40 37N 77 33W
Lexington, U.S.A. 42 F5 38 6N 84 30W
Lexington Park, U.S.A. 42 F9 38 16N 76 27W
Leyte, Phil. 22 B4 11 0N 125 0 E
Lhasa, China 20 D4 29 25N 90 58 E
Liaoning □, China 21 B7 41 40N 122 30 E
Liaoyang, China 21 B7 41 15N 122 58 E
Liaoyüan, China 21 B7 42 58N 125 2 E
Liberec, Czech. 10 C6 50 47N 15 7 E
Liberia ■, W. Afr. 28 H5 6 30N 9 30W
Libourne, France 9 E3 44 55N 0 14W
Libreville, Gabon 32 D1 0 25N 9 26 E
Libya ■, N. Afr. 28 D10 27 0N 17 0 E
Lichinga, Mozam. 33 G7 13 13S 35 11 E
Lichtenburg, S. Africa 31 B4 26 8S 26 8 E
Liechtenstein ■, Europe 10 E3 47 8N 9 35 E
Liège, Belgium 8 B6 50 38N 5 35 E
Liepāja, Latvia 14 C3 56 30N 21 0 E
Ligurian Sea, Italy 12 C3 43 20N 9 0 E
Likasi, Zaïre 32 G5 10 55S 26 48 E
Lille, France 8 B5 50 38N 3 3 E
Lillehammer, Norway 6 F10 61 8N 10 30 E
Lilongwe, Malawi 33 G6 14 0S 33 48 E
Lim Fjord, Denmark 6 G9 56 55N 9 0 E
Lima, Peru 46 D2 12 0S 77 0W
Lima, U.S.A. 42 E5 40 42N 84 5W
Limerick, Ireland 7 F2 52 40N 8 38W
Límnos, Greece 13 E11 39 50N 25 5 E
Limoges, France 9 E4 45 50N 1 15 E
Limousin, France 9 E4 45 30N 1 30 E
Limoux, France 9 F5 43 4N 2 12 E
Limpopo →, Africa 33 K6 25 5S 33 30 E
Linares, Spain 11 C4 38 10N 3 40W
Lincoln, U.K. 7 F6 53 14N 0 32W
Lincoln, Maine, U.S.A. 43 C13 45 27N 68 29W
Lincoln, Nebr., U.S.A. 41 B7 40 50N 96 42W
Lindsay, Canada 42 C8 44 22N 78 43W
Lingga Arch., Indonesia 22 D2 0 10S 104 30 E
Linköping, Sweden 6 G11 58 28N 15 36 E
Linton, U.S.A. 42 F4 39 0N 87 10W
Linxia, China 20 C5 35 36N 103 10 E
Linz, Austria 10 D6 48 18N 14 18 E
Lions, G. of, France 9 F5 43 10N 4 0 E
Lipari Is., Italy 12 E6 38 30N 14 50 E
Lipetsk, Russia 14 D6 52 37N 39 35 E
Lippe →, Germany 10 C2 51 39N 6 38 E
Lisbon, Portugal 11 C1 38 42N 9 10W
Lisburn, U.K. 7 E3 54 30N 6 9W
Lisieux, France 8 C4 49 10N 0 12 E
Lismore, Australia 34 F9 28 44S 153 21 E
Listowel, Canada 42 D7 43 44N 80 58W
Lithuania ■, Europe 14 C3 55 30N 24 0 E
Little Current, Canada 42 C7 45 55N 82 0W
Little Karoo, S. Africa 31 C3 33 45S 21 0 E
Little Laut Is., Indonesia 22 D3 4 45S 115 40 E
Little Rock, U.S.A. 41 D8 34 41N 92 10W
Liuzhou, China 21 D5 24 22N 109 22 E
Liverpool, U.K. 7 F5 53 25N 3 0W
Livingstone, Zambia 33 H5 17 46S 25 52 E
Livonia, U.S.A. 42 D6 42 25N 83 23W
Livorno = Leghorn, Italy 12 C4 43 32N 10 18 E
Ljubljana, Slovenia 12 A6 46 4N 14 33 E
Ljusnan →, Sweden 6 F11 61 12N 17 8 E
Llandudno, U.K. 7 F5 53 19N 3 51W
Llanelli, U.K. 7 G4 51 41N 4 11W
Llanos, S. Amer. 46 B2 5 0N 71 35W
Lobatse, Botswana 31 B4 25 12S 25 40 E
Lobito, Angola 33 G2 12 18S 13 35 E
Loches, France 8 D4 47 7N 1 0 E
Lock Haven, U.S.A. 42 E9 41 7N 77 31W
Lodève, France 9 F5 43 44N 3 19 E
Łódź, Poland 10 C8 51 45N 19 27 E
Lofoten, Norway 6 E10 68 30N 15 0 E
Logan, Ohio, U.S.A. 42 F6 39 25N 82 22W
Logan, W. Va., U.S.A. 42 G7 37 51N 81 59W
Logan, Mt., Canada 38 B5 60 31N 140 22W
Logansport, U.S.A. 42 E4 40 45N 86 21W
Logroño, Spain 11 A4 42 28N 2 27W
Lohardaga, India 23 H10 23 27N 84 45 E
Loir →, France 8 D3 47 33N 0 32W
Loire →, France 8 D2 47 16N 2 10W
Lombardy □, Italy 12 B3 45 35N 9 45 E
Lomblen, Indonesia 22 D4 8 30S 123 32 E
Lombok, Indonesia 22 D3 8 45S 116 30 E
Lomé, Togo 30 C2 6 9N 1 20 E
Lomond, L., U.K. 7 D4 56 8N 4 38W
Łomza, Poland 10 B10 53 10N 22 2 E
London, Canada 42 D7 42 59N 81 15W
London, U.K. 7 G6 51 30N 0 5W
Londrina, Brazil 47 E4 23 18S 51 10W
Long Beach, U.S.A. 40 D3 33 46N 118 12W
Long Branch, U.S.A. 43 E11 40 19N 74 0W
Long I., Bahamas 45 C9 23 20N 75 10W
Long I., U.S.A. 43 E11 40 50N 73 20W
Long Xuyen, Vietnam 22 B2 10 19N 105 28 E
Longlac, Canada 42 A4 49 45N 86 25W
Lons-le-Saunier, France 8 D6 46 40N 5 31 E
Lop Nor, China 20 B4 40 20N 90 10 E
Lorain, U.S.A. 42 E6 41 28N 82 55W
Loralai, Pakistan 23 D2 30 20N 68 41 E
Lorca, Spain 11 D5 37 41N 1 42W
Lorient, France 8 D2 47 45N 3 23W
Lorn, Firth of, U.K. 7 D4 56 20N 5 40W
Lorraine, France 8 C6 48 53N 6 0 E
Los Angeles, Chile 47 F2 37 28S 72 23W
Los Angeles, U.S.A. 40 D3 34 0N 118 10W
Los Mochis, Mexico 44 B3 25 45N 108 57W
Lot →, France 9 E4 44 18N 0 20 E
Louis Trichardt, S. Africa 31 A4 23 1S 29 43 E
Louisa, U.S.A. 42 F6 38 5N 82 40W
Louiseville, Canada 43 B11 46 20N 72 56W
Louisiana □, U.S.A. 41 D8 30 50N 92 0W
Louisville, U.S.A. 42 F5 38 15N 85 45W
Lourdes, France 9 F3 43 6N 0 3W
Low Tatra, Slovakia 10 D8 48 55N 19 30 E
Lowell, U.S.A. 43 D12 42 38N 71 19W
Lower California, Mexico 44 B2 31 10N 115 12W
Lower Tunguska →, Russia 18 C10 65 48N 88 4 E
Lowestoft, U.K. 7 F7 52 29N 1 44 E
Lowville, U.S.A. 43 D10 43 48N 75 30W
Luanda, Angola 32 F2 8 50S 13 15 E
Luanshya, Zambia 33 G5 13 3S 28 28 E
Lubbock, U.S.A. 40 D6 33 40N 101 53W
Lübeck, Germany 10 B4 53 52N 10 41 E
Lublin, Poland 10 C10 51 12N 22 38 E
Lubumbashi, Zaïre 33 G5 11 40S 27 28 E
Lucknow, India 23 F8 26 50N 81 0 E
Lüda = Dalian, China 21 C7 38 50N 121 40 E
Lüderitz, Namibia 31 B2 26 41S 15 8 E
Ludhiana, India 23 D5 30 57N 75 56 E
Ludington, U.S.A. 42 D4 43 58N 86 27W
Ludwigshafen, Germany 10 D3 49 27N 8 27 E
Lugano, Switz. 10 F3 46 0N 8 57 E
Lugansk, Ukraine 15 E6 48 38N 39 15 E
Lugo, Spain 11 A2 43 2N 7 35W
Lule →, Sweden 6 E12 65 35N 22 10 E
Luleå, Sweden 6 E12 65 35N 22 10 E
Lüneburg Heath, Germany 10 B4 53 0N 10 0 E
Lunéville, France 8 C7 48 36N 6 30 E
Luni →, India 23 G3 24 41N 71 14 E
Luoyang, China 21 C6 34 40N 112 26 E
Luray, U.S.A. 42 F8 38 39N 78 26W
Lusaka, Zambia 33 H5 15 28S 28 16 E
Luton, U.K. 7 G6 51 53N 0 24W
Luxembourg, Lux. 8 C7 49 37N 6 9 E
Luxembourg ■, Europe 8 C7 49 45N 6 0 E
Luzern, Switz. 10 E3 47 3N 8 18 E
Luzhou, China 20 D5 28 52N 105 20 E
Luzon, Phil. 22 B4 16 0N 121 0 E
Lvov, Ukraine 15 E3 49 50N 24 0 E
Lyakhov Is., Russia 18 B16 73 40N 141 0 E
Lydda, Israel 29 C13 31 57N 34 54 E
Lydenburg, S. Africa 31 B5 25 10S 30 29 E
Lynchburg, U.S.A. 42 G8 37 23N 79 10W
Lynn Lake, Canada 38 C9 56 51N 101 3W
Lyonnais, France 9 E6 45 45N 4 15 E
Lyons, France 9 E6 45 46N 4 50 E

M

Ma'an, Jordan 24 B2 30 12N 35 44 E
Maastricht, Neths. 8 B6 50 50N 5 40 E
Macapá, Brazil 46 B4 0 5N 51 4W
Macau ■, China 21 D6 22 16N 113 35 E
Macclesfield, U.K. 7 F5 53 16N 2 9W
M'Clure Str., Canada 48 A11 75 0N 119 0W
Macdonnell Ras., Australia 34 E5 23 40S 133 0 E
Macedonia □, Greece 13 D10 40 39N 22 0 E
Macedonia ■, Macedonia, Yug. 13 D9 41 53N 21 40 E
Maceió, Brazil 46 C6 9 40S 35 41W
Macgillycuddy's Reeks, Ireland 7 F2 52 2N 9 45W
Mach, Pakistan 23 E1 29 50N 67 20 E
Machakos, Kenya 32 E7 1 30S 37 15 E
Machias, U.S.A. 43 C14 44 40N 67 28W
Machilipatnam, India 25 D7 16 12N 81 8 E
Mackay, Australia 34 E8 21 8S 149 11 E
Mackay, L., Australia 34 E4 22 30S 129 0 E
McKeesport, U.S.A. 42 E8 40 21N 79 50W
Mackenzie →, Canada 38 B6 69 10N 134 20W
Mackenzie Mts., Canada 38 B7 64 0N 130 0W
Mackinaw City, U.S.A. 42 C5 45 47N 84 44W
McKinley, Mt., U.S.A. 38 B4 63 2N 151 0W
Maclear, S. Africa 31 C4 31 2S 28 23 E
M'Clintock Chan., Canada 38 A9 72 0N 102 0W
McMurdo Sd., Antarctica 48 C19 77 0S 170 0 E
Mâcon, France 9 D6 46 19N 4 50 E
Macon, U.S.A. 41 D10 32 50N 83 37W
Macquarie Is., Pac. Oc. 36 N7 54 36S 158 55 E
Madadeni, S. Africa 31 B5 27 43S 30 3 E
Madagascar ■, Africa 33 J9 20 0S 47 0 E
Madaripur, Bangla. 23 H13 23 19N 90 15 E
Madeira, Atl. Oc. 28 C3 32 50N 17 0W
Madeira →, Brazil 46 C4 3 22S 58 45W
Madhya Pradesh □, India 23 H7 21 50N 78 0 E
Madinat al Shaab, Yemen 29 G16 12 50N 45 0 E
Madison, Ind., U.S.A. 42 F5 38 42N 85 20W
Madison, Wis., U.S.A. 41 B9 43 5N 89 25W
Madisonville, U.S.A. 42 G4 37 20N 87 30W
Madiun, Indonesia 22 D3 7 38S 111 32 E
Madras, India 25 D7 13 8N 80 19 E
Madrid, Spain 11 B4 40 25N 3 45W
Madurai, India 25 E6 9 55N 78 10 E
Mafeking, S. Africa 31 B4 25 50S 25 38 E
Mafeteng, Lesotho 31 B4 29 51S 27 15 E
Magadan, Russia 18 D17 59 38N 150 50 E
Magdalen Is., Canada 43 B17 47 30N 61 40W
Magdalena →, Colombia 46 A2 11 6N 74 51W
Magdeburg, Germany 10 B4 52 8N 11 36 E
Magelang, Indonesia 22 D3 7 29S 110 13 E
Magellan's Str., Chile 47 H2 52 30S 75 0W
Maggiore, L., Italy 12 A3 46 0N 8 35 E
Magnetic Pole (North), Canada 48 A4 77 58N 102 8W
Magnetic Pole (South), Antarctica 48 C18 64 8S 138 8 E
Magnitogorsk, Russia 14 D10 53 27N 59 4 E
Magog, Canada 43 C11 45 18N 72 9W
Mahakam →, Indonesia 22 D3 0 35S 117 17 E
Mahalapye, Botswana 31 A4 23 1S 26 51 E
Mahanadi →, India 23 J11 20 20N 86 25 E
Maharashtra □, India 23 J5 20 30N 75 30 E
Mahesana, India 23 H4 23 39N 72 26 E
Maidstone, U.K. 7 G7 51 16N 0 31 E
Maiduguri, Nigeria 30 B4 12 0N 13 20 E
Maijdi, Bangla. 23 H13 22 48N 91 10 E
Maikala Ra., India 23 J8 22 0N 81 0 E
Maimana, Afghan. 24 B5 35 53N 64 38 E
Main →, Germany 10 D3 50 0N 8 18 E
Maine, France 8 D3 47 55N 0 25W
Maine □, U.S.A. 43 C13 45 20N 69 0W
Mainz, Germany 10 D3 50 0N 8 17 E
Majorca = Mallorca, Spain 11 C7 39 30N 3 0 E
Makasar, Str. of, Indonesia 22 D3 1 0S 118 20 E
Makeyevka, Ukraine 15 E6 48 0N 38 0 E
Makgadikgadi Salt Pans, Botswana 31 A4 20 40S 25 45 E
Makhachkala, Russia 15 F8 43 0N 47 30 E
Makkah = Mecca, Si. Arabia 24 C2 21 30N 39 54 E
Makunda, Botswana 31 A3 22 30S 20 7 E
Malabar Coast, India 25 D6 11 0N 75 0 E
Malacca, Str. of, Indonesia 22 C2 3 0N 101 0 E

115
Naab Ostrava

N

Naab →, *Germany* **10 D5** 49 1N 12 2 E
Nābulus, *Jordan* **29 P21** 32 14N 35 15 E
Nadiad, *India* **23 H4** 22 41N 72 56 E
Nafud Desert, *Si. Arabia* **24 C3** 28 15N 41 0 E
Nagaland □, *India* **25 C8** 26 0N 94 30 E
Nagano, *Japan* **19 A6** 36 40N 138 10 E
Nagaoka, *Japan* **19 G11** 37 27N 138 51 E
Nagasaki, *Japan* **19 C1** 32 47N 129 50 E
Nagaur, *India* **23 F4** 27 15N 73 45 E
Nagercoil, *India* **25 E6** 8 12N 77 26 E
Nagoya, *Japan* **19 B5** 35 10N 136 50 E
Nagpur, *India* **23 J7** 21 8N 79 10 E
Nairn, *U.K.* **7 D5** 57 35N 3 54W
Nairobi, *Kenya* **32 E7** 1 17S 36 48 E
Najibabad, *India* **23 E7** 29 40N 78 20 E
Nakhichevan Republic □, *Azerbaijan* **15 G8** 39 14N 45 30 E
Nakhon Ratchasima, *Thailand* **22 B2** 14 59N 102 12 E
Nakhon Si Thammarat, *Thailand* **22 C2** 8 29N 100 0 E
Nakina, *Canada* **42 A4** 50 10N 86 40W
Nakuru, *Kenya* **32 E7** 0 15S 36 4 E
Nalchik, *Russia* **15 F7** 43 30N 43 33 E
Nam Co, *China* **20 C4** 30 30N 90 45 E
Namaland, *Namibia* **31 A2** 24 30S 17 0 E
Namaqualand, *S. Africa* **31 B2** 30 0S 17 25 E
Namib Desert, *Namibia* **31 A1** 22 30S 15 0 E
Namibe, *Angola* **33 H2** 15 7S 12 11 E
Namibia ■, *Africa* **31 A2** 22 0S 18 9 E
Namlea, *Indonesia* **22 D4** 3 18S 127 5 E
Nampula, *Mozam.* **33 H7** 15 6S 39 15 E
Namur, *Belgium* **8 B6** 50 27N 4 52 E
Nan Shan, *China* **20 C4** 38 30N 96 0 E
Nanaimo, *Canada* **38 D7** 49 10N 124 0W
Nanchang, *China* **21 D6** 28 42N 115 55 E
Nanchong, *China* **20 C5** 30 43N 106 2 E
Nancy, *France* **8 C7** 48 42N 6 12 E
Nanda Devi, *India* **23 D7** 30 23N 79 59 E
Nanded, *India* **25 D6** 19 10N 77 20 E
Nandurbar, *India* **23 J5** 21 20N 74 15 E
Nanga Parbat, *Pakistan* **23 B5** 35 10N 74 35 E
Nanking, *China* **21 C6** 32 2N 118 47 E
Nanning, *China* **20 D5** 22 48N 108 20 E
Nanp'ing, *China* **21 D6** 26 38N 118 10 E
Nantes, *France* **8 D3** 47 12N 1 33W
Nanticoke, *U.S.A.* **42 E9** 41 12N 76 1W
Nantong, *China* **21 C7** 32 1N 120 52 E
Nantua, *France* **9 D6** 46 10N 5 35 E
Napier, *N.Z.* **35 H14** 39 30S 176 56 E
Naples, *Italy* **12 D6** 40 50N 14 17 E
Nara, *Japan* **19 B4** 34 40N 135 49 E
Narayanganj, *Bangla.* **23 H13** 23 40N 90 33 E
Narbonne, *France* **9 F5** 43 11N 3 0 E
Narmada →, *India* **23 J4** 21 38N 72 36 E
Narvik, *Norway* **6 E11** 68 28N 17 26 E
Nashua, *U.S.A.* **43 D12** 42 50N 71 25W
Nashville, *U.S.A.* **41 C9** 36 12N 86 46W
Nasik, *India* **23 K4** 19 58N 73 50 E
Nasirabad, *India* **23 F5** 26 15N 74 45 E
Nassau, *Bahamas* **45 B9** 25 5N 77 20W
Nasser, L., *Egypt* **29 E13** 23 0N 32 30 E
Nata, *Botswana* **31 A4** 20 12S 26 12 E
Natal, *Brazil* **46 C6** 5 47S 35 13W
Natal □, *S. Africa* **31 B5** 28 30S 30 30 E
Nathdwara, *India* **23 G4** 24 55N 73 50 E
Natuna Is., *Indonesia* **22 C2** 4 0N 108 15 E
Nauru ■, *Pac. Oc.* **36 H8** 1 0S 166 0 E
Navarra □, *Spain* **11 A5** 42 40N 1 40W
Navsari, *India* **23 J4** 20 57N 72 59 E
Nawabshah, *Pakistan* **23 F2** 26 15N 68 25 E
Náxos, *Greece* **13 F11** 37 8N 25 25 E
Nazareth, *Israel* **29 N21** 32 42N 35 17 E
Ndjamena, *Chad* **28 G9** 12 10N 14 59 E
Ndola, *Zambia* **33 G5** 13 0S 28 34 E
Neagh, L., *U.K.* **7 E3** 54 35N 6 25W
Nebraska □, *U.S.A.* **40 B7** 41 30N 100 0W
Neckar →, *Germany* **10 D3** 49 31N 8 26 E
Neemuch, *India* **23 G5** 24 30N 74 56 E
Neenah, *U.S.A.* **42 C3** 44 10N 88 30W
Negaunee, *U.S.A.* **42 B4** 46 30N 87 36W
Negrais, C., *Burma* **25 D8** 16 0N 94 30 E
Negro →, *Argentina* **47 G3** 41 2S 62 47W
Negro →, *Brazil* **46 C4** 3 0S 60 0W
Negros, *Phil.* **22 C4** 9 30N 122 40 E
Neijiang, *China* **20 D5** 29 35N 104 55 E
Neiva, *Colombia* **46 B2** 2 56N 75 18W
Nejd, *Si. Arabia* **24 C3** 26 30N 42 0 E
Nellore, *India* **25 D6** 14 27N 79 59 E
Nelson, *N.Z.* **35 J13** 41 18S 173 16 E
Nelson →, *Canada* **38 C10** 54 33N 98 2W
Nelspruit, *S. Africa* **31 B5** 25 29S 30 59 E
Nemunas →, *Lithuania* **14 C3** 55 25N 21 10 E
Nepal ■, *Asia* **23 F10** 28 0N 84 30 E
Nérac, *France* **9 E4** 44 8N 0 21 E
Ness, L., *U.K.* **7 D4** 57 15N 4 30W
Netherlands ■, *Europe* **8 B6** 52 0N 5 30 E
Netherlands Antilles ■, *S. Amer.* **45 E11** 12 15N 69 0W
Neuchâtel, *Switz.* **10 E2** 47 0N 6 55 E
Neuchâtel, L., *Switz.* **10 E2** 46 53N 6 50 E
Neufchâteau, *France* **8 C6** 48 21N 5 40 E
Neuseidl, L., *Austria* **10 E7** 47 50N 16 47 E
Nevada □, *U.S.A.* **40 C3** 39 20N 117 0W
Nevada, Sierra, *Spain* **11 D4** 37 3N 3 15W
Nevada, Sierra, *U.S.A.* **40 C2** 39 0N 120 30W
Nevers, *France* **8 D5** 47 0N 3 9 E
New Albany, *U.S.A.* **42 F5** 38 20N 85 50W
New Bedford, *U.S.A.* **43 E12** 41 40N 70 52W
New Britain, *Papua N. G.* **34 B9** 5 50S 150 20 E
New Britain, *U.S.A.* **43 E11** 41 41N 72 47W
New Brunswick, *U.S.A.* **43 E10** 40 30N 74 28W
New Brunswick □, *Canada* **43 B14** 46 50N 66 30W
New Caledonia, *Pac. Oc.* **35 E12** 21 0S 165 0 E
New Castle, *Ind., U.S.A.* **42 F5** 39 55N 85 23W
New Castle, *Pa., U.S.A.* **42 E7** 41 0N 80 20W
New Glasgow, *Canada* **43 C16** 45 35N 62 36W
New Guinea, *Oceania* **36 H5** 4 0S 136 0 E
New Hampshire □, *U.S.A.* **43 D12** 43 40N 71 40W
New Haven, *U.S.A.* **43 E11** 41 20N 72 54W
New Jersey □, *U.S.A.* **43 E10** 40 30N 74 10W
New Lexington, *U.S.A.* **42 F6** 39 40N 82 15W
New Liskeard, *Canada* **42 B8** 47 31N 79 41W
New London, *U.S.A.* **43 E11** 41 23N 72 8W
New Mexico □, *U.S.A.* **40 D5** 34 30N 106 0W
New Orleans, *U.S.A.* **41 E9** 30 0N 90 5W
New Philadelphia, *U.S.A.* **42 E7** 40 29N 81 25W
New Plymouth, *N.Z.* **35 H13** 39 4S 174 5 E
New Siberian Is., *Russia* **18 B15** 75 10N 150 0 E
New South Wales □, *Australia* **34 G8** 33 0S 146 0 E
New York □, *U.S.A.* **43 D9** 42 40N 76 0W
New York City, *U.S.A.* **43 E11** 40 45N 74 0W
New Zealand ■, *Oceania* **35 J13** 40 0S 176 0 E
Newark, *Del., U.S.A.* **43 F10** 39 42N 75 45W
Newark, *N.J., U.S.A.* **43 E10** 40 41N 74 12W
Newark, *N.Y., U.S.A.* **42 D9** 43 2N 77 10W
Newark, *Ohio, U.S.A.* **42 E6** 40 5N 82 24W
Newaygo, *U.S.A.* **42 D5** 43 25N 85 48W
Newberry, *U.S.A.* **42 B5** 46 20N 85 32W
Newburgh, *U.S.A.* **43 E10** 41 30N 74 1W
Newburyport, *U.S.A.* **43 D12** 42 48N 70 50W
Newcastle, *Australia* **34 G9** 33 0S 151 46 E
Newcastle, *Canada* **43 B15** 47 1N 65 38W
Newcastle, *S. Africa* **31 B4** 27 45S 29 58 E
Newcastle-upon-Tyne, *U.K.* **7 E6** 54 59N 1 37W
Newfoundland □, *Canada* **39 C14** 53 0N 58 0W
Newman, *Australia* **34 E2** 23 18S 119 45 E
Newport, *Gwent, U.K.* **7 G5** 51 35N 3 0W
Newport, *I. of W., U.K.* **7 G6** 50 42N 1 18W
Newport, *Ky., U.S.A.* **42 F5** 39 5N 84 23W
Newport, *R.I., U.S.A.* **43 E12** 41 13N 71 19W
Newport, *Vt., U.S.A.* **43 C11** 44 57N 72 17W
Newport News, *U.S.A.* **41 C11** 37 2N 76 30W
Newry, *U.K.* **7 E3** 54 10N 6 20W
Nganglong Kangri, *China* **23 C8** 33 0N 81 0 E
Nha Trang, *Vietnam* **22 B2** 12 16N 109 10 E
Niagara, *U.S.A.* **42 C3** 45 45N 88 0W
Niagara Falls, *Canada* **42 D8** 43 7N 79 5W
Niagara Falls, *U.S.A.* **42 D8** 43 5N 79 0W
Niamey, *Niger* **30 B2** 13 27N 2 6 E
Nias, *Indonesia* **22 C1** 1 0N 97 30 E
Nicaragua ■, *Cent. Amer.* **44 E7** 11 40N 85 30W
Nicaragua, L. of, *Nic.* **44 E7** 12 0N 85 30W
Nice, *France* **9 F7** 43 42N 7 14 E
Nicholasville, *U.S.A.* **42 G5** 37 54N 84 31W
Nicobar Is., *Ind. Oc.* **25 E8** 9 0N 93 0 E
Nicosia, *Cyprus* **24 B2** 35 10N 33 25 E
Nicoya, Pen., *Costa Rica* **44 F7** 9 45N 85 40W
Niger ■, *W. Afr.* **28 F9** 17 30N 10 0 E
Niger →, *W. Afr.* **30 C3** 5 33N 6 33 E
Nigeria ■, *W. Afr.* **30 C3** 8 30N 8 0 E
Niigata, *Japan* **19 G11** 37 58N 139 0 E
Niihau, *U.S.A.* **40 H14** 21 55N 160 10W
Nijmegen, *Neths.* **8 B6** 51 50N 5 52 E
Nikolayev, *Ukraine* **15 E5** 46 58N 32 0 E
Nikolayevsk-na-Amur, *Russia* **18 D16** 53 8N 140 44 E
Nile →, *Africa* **29 C13** 30 10N 31 6 E
Nîmes, *France* **9 F6** 43 50N 4 23 E
Ningbo, *China* **21 D7** 29 51N 121 28 E
Ningxia Huizu Zizhiqu □, *China* **20 C5** 38 0N 106 0 E
Niort, *France* **9 D3** 46 19N 0 29W
Nipigon, *Canada* **42 A3** 49 0N 88 17W
Nipigon, L., *Canada* **42 A3** 49 50N 88 30W
Nipissing L., *Canada* **42 B8** 46 20N 80 0W
Niš, *Serbia, Yug.* **13 C9** 43 19N 21 58 E
Niterói, *Brazil* **47 E5** 22 52S 43 0W
Nitra, *Slovakia* **10 D8** 48 19N 18 4 E
Nitra →, *Slovakia* **10 E8** 47 46N 18 10 E
Niue, *Cook Is.* **35 D17** 19 2S 169 54W
Nivernais, *France* **8 D5** 47 15N 3 30 E
Nizamabad, *India* **25 D6** 18 45N 78 7 E
Nizhniy Novgorod, *Russia* **14 C7** 56 20N 44 0 E
Nizhniy Tagil, *Russia* **14 C10** 57 55N 59 57 E
Nkongsamba, *Cameroon* **30 D3** 4 55N 9 55 E
Nobeoka, *Japan* **19 C2** 32 36N 131 41 E
Noblesville, *U.S.A.* **42 E5** 40 1N 85 59W
Nogales, *Mexico* **44 A2** 31 20N 110 56W
Nogent-le-Rotrou, *France* **8 C4** 48 20N 0 50 E
Noirmoutier, I. de, *France* **8 D2** 46 58N 2 10W
Noranda, *Canada* **42 A8** 48 20N 79 0W
Norfolk, *U.S.A.* **41 C11** 36 40N 76 15W
Norfolk I., *Pac. Oc.* **35 F12** 28 58S 168 3 E
Norilsk, *Russia* **18 C10** 69 20N 88 6 E
Normandy, *France* **8 C4** 48 45N 0 10 E
Norristown, *U.S.A.* **43 E10** 40 9N 75 21W
Norrköping, *Sweden* **6 G11** 58 37N 16 11 E
Norrland, *Sweden* **6 F11** 62 15N 15 45 E
Norseman, *Australia* **34 G3** 32 8S 121 43 E
North Battleford, *Canada* **38 C9** 52 50N 108 17W
North Bay, *Canada* **42 B8** 46 20N 79 30W
North C., *Canada* **43 B16** 47 2N 60 20W
North Cape, *Norway* **6 D13** 71 10N 25 44 E
North Carolina □, *U.S.A.* **41 C11** 35 30N 80 0W
North Channel, *Canada* **42 B6** 46 0N 83 0W
North Channel, *U.K.* **7 E4** 55 0N 5 30W
North Dakota □, *U.S.A.* **40 A7** 47 30N 100 0W
North Downs, *U.K.* **7 G7** 51 17N 0 30 E
North European Plain, *Europe* **4 D11** 55 0N 25 0 E
North I., *N.Z.* **35 H14** 38 0S 175 0 E
North Ossetian Republic □, *Russia* **15 F7** 43 30N 44 30 E
North Pt., *Canada* **43 B15** 47 5N 64 0W
North Pole, *Arctic* **48 A1** 90 0N 0 0 E
North Rhine Westphalia □, *Germany* **10 C2** 51 45N 7 30 E
North Sea, *Europe* **4 D6** 56 0N 4 0 E
North Vernon, *U.S.A.* **42 F5** 39 0N 85 35W
North West Frontier □, *Pakistan* **23 C3** 34 0N 71 0 E
North West Highlands, *U.K.* **7 D4** 57 35N 5 2W
North West Territories □, *Canada* **38 B9** 67 0N 110 0W
North York Moors, *U.K.* **7 E6** 54 25N 0 50W
Northampton, *U.K.* **7 F6** 52 14N 0 54W
Northampton, *U.S.A.* **43 D11** 42 22N 72 31W
Northern Ireland □, *U.K.* **7 E3** 54 45N 7 0W
Northern Marianas □, *Pac. Oc.* **36 F6** 17 0N 145 0 E
Northern Territory □, *Australia* **34 E5** 20 0S 133 0 E
Northumberland Str., *Canada* **43 B16** 46 20N 64 0W
Norwalk, *U.S.A.* **42 E6** 41 13N 82 38W
Norway ■, *Europe* **6 F10** 63 0N 11 0 E
Norwegian Sea, *Atl. Oc.* **48 A7** 66 0N 1 0 E
Norwich, *U.K.* **7 F7** 52 38N 1 17 E
Norwich, *U.S.A.* **43 D10** 42 32N 75 30W
Nossob →, *S. Africa* **31 B3** 26 55S 20 45 E
Nottingham, *U.K.* **7 F6** 52 57N 1 10W
Nouâdhibou, *Mauritania* **28 E3** 20 54N 17 0W
Nouakchott, *Mauritania* **28 F3** 18 9N 15 58W
Nouméa, *N. Cal.* **35 E12** 22 17S 166 30 E
Noupoort, *S. Africa* **31 C3** 31 10S 24 57 E
Nova Scotia □, *Canada* **43 C16** 45 10N 63 0W
Novara, *Italy* **12 B3** 45 27N 8 36 E
Novaya Zemlya, *Russia* **18 B7** 75 0N 56 0 E
Novi Sad, *Serbia, Yug.* **13 B8** 45 18N 19 52 E
Novocherkassk, *Russia* **15 E7** 47 27N 40 15 E
Novokuznetsk, *Russia* **18 D10** 53 45N 87 10 E
Novomoskovsk, *Russia* **14 D6** 54 5N 38 15 E
Novorossiysk, *Russia* **15 F6** 44 43N 37 46 E
Novoshakhtinsk, *Russia* **15 E6** 47 46N 39 58 E
Novosibirsk, *Russia* **18 D10** 55 0N 83 5 E
Nowy Sącz, *Poland* **10 D9** 49 40N 20 41 E
Nubian Desert, *Sudan* **29 E13** 21 30N 33 30 E
Nuevo Laredo, *Mexico* **44 B5** 27 30N 99 30W
Nuku'alofa, *Tonga* **35 E16** 21 10S 174 0W
Nullarbor Plain, *Australia* **34 G4** 31 10S 129 0 E
Nuremburg, *Germany* **10 D4** 49 26N 11 5 E
Nuuk = Godthåb, *Greenland* **48 A9** 64 10N 51 35W
Nuweveldberge, *S. Africa* **31 C3** 32 10S 21 45 E
Nyasa, L., *Africa* **33 G6** 12 30S 34 30 E
Nyíregyháza, *Hungary* **10 E9** 47 58N 21 47 E
Nylstroom, *S. Africa* **31 A4** 24 42S 28 22 E
Nysa, *Poland* **10 C7** 50 30N 17 22 E
Nysa →, *Europe* **10 B6** 52 4N 14 46 E

O

Oahe L., *U.S.A.* **40 A6** 45 30N 100 25W
Oahu, *U.S.A.* **40 H16** 21 30N 158 0W
Oak Hill, *U.S.A.* **42 G7** 38 0N 81 7W
Oakland, *U.S.A.* **40 C2** 37 50N 122 18W
Oates Land, *Antarctica* **48 C19** 69 0S 160 0 E
Oaxaca, *Mexico* **44 D5** 17 2N 96 40W
Ob →, *Russia* **18 C8** 66 45N 69 30 E
Ob, G. of, *Russia* **18 C9** 69 0N 73 0 E
Oba, *Canada* **42 A5** 49 4N 84 7W
Oban, *U.K.* **7 D4** 56 25N 5 30W
Oberhausen, *Germany* **10 C2** 51 28N 6 50 E
Obi Is., *Indonesia* **22 D4** 1 23S 127 45 E
Ocean City, *U.S.A.* **43 F10** 39 18N 74 34W
Oconto, *U.S.A.* **42 C4** 44 52N 87 53W
October Revolution I., *Russia* **18 B11** 79 30N 97 0 E
Odendaalsrus, *S. Africa* **31 B4** 27 48S 26 45 E
Odense, *Denmark* **6 G10** 55 22N 10 23 E
Odessa, *Ukraine* **15 E5** 46 30N 30 45 E
Odessa, *U.S.A.* **40 D6** 31 51N 102 23W
Odra →, *Poland* **10 B6** 53 33N 14 38 E
Offa, *Nigeria* **30 C2** 8 13N 4 42 E
Ogbomosho, *Nigeria* **30 C2** 8 1N 4 11 E
Ogden, *U.S.A.* **40 B4** 41 13N 112 1W
Ogdensburg, *U.S.A.* **43 C10** 44 40N 75 27W
Ohio □, *U.S.A.* **42 E5** 40 20N 84 10W
Ohio →, *U.S.A.* **41 C9** 36 59N 89 8W
Ohre →, *Czech.* **10 C6** 50 30N 14 10 E
Oil City, *U.S.A.* **42 E8** 41 26N 79 40W
Oise →, *France* **8 C5** 49 0N 2 4 E
Ōita, *Japan* **19 C2** 33 14N 131 36 E
Ojos del Salado, Cerro, *Argentina* **47 E3** 27 0S 68 40W
Okahandja, *Namibia* **31 A2** 22 0S 16 59 E
Okaputa, *Namibia* **31 A2** 20 5S 17 0 E
Okara, *Pakistan* **23 D4** 30 50N 73 31 E
Okavango Swamps, *Botswana* **33 H4** 18 45S 22 45 E
Okayama, *Japan* **19 B3** 34 40N 133 54 E
Okazaki, *Japan* **19 B5** 34 57N 137 10 E
Okha, *Russia* **18 D16** 53 40N 143 0 E
Okhotsk, *Russia* **18 D16** 59 20N 143 10 E
Okhotsk, Sea of, *Asia* **18 D16** 55 0N 145 0 E
Oklahoma □, *U.S.A.* **40 C7** 35 20N 97 30W
Oklahoma City, *U.S.A.* **40 C7** 35 25N 97 30W
Okwa →, *Botswana* **31 A3** 22 30S 23 0 E
Öland, *Sweden* **6 G11** 56 45N 16 38 E
Old Town, *U.S.A.* **43 C13** 45 0N 68 41W
Oldenburg, *Germany* **10 B3** 53 10N 8 10 E
Oldham, *U.K.* **7 F5** 53 33N 2 8W
Olean, *U.S.A.* **42 D8** 42 8N 78 25W
Olekminsk, *Russia* **18 C14** 60 25N 120 30 E
Olenek →, *Russia* **18 B14** 73 0N 120 10 E
Oléron, I. d', *France* **9 E3** 45 55N 1 15W
Olney, *U.S.A.* **42 F3** 38 40N 88 5W
Olomouc, *Czech.* **10 D7** 49 38N 17 12 E
Oloron-Ste.-Marie, *France* **9 F3** 43 11N 0 38W
Olsztyn, *Poland* **10 B9** 53 48N 20 29 E
Olt →, *Romania* **13 C11** 43 43N 24 51 E
Olympia, *Greece* **13 F9** 37 39N 21 39 E
Olympus, Mt., *Greece* **13 D10** 40 6N 22 23 E
Omaha, *U.S.A.* **41 B7** 41 15N 95 55W
Oman ■, *Asia* **17 G9** 23 0N 58 0 E
Oman, G. of, *Asia* **24 C4** 24 30N 58 30 E
Omaruru, *Namibia* **31 A2** 21 26S 16 0 E
Ombai Str., *Indonesia* **22 D4** 8 30S 124 50 E
Omdurman, *Sudan* **29 F13** 15 40N 32 28 E
Ōmiya, *Japan* **19 B6** 35 54N 139 38 E
Omsk, *Russia* **18 D9** 55 0N 73 12 E
Ōmuta, *Japan* **19 C2** 33 5N 130 26 E
Ondo, *Nigeria* **30 C2** 7 4N 4 47 E
Onega →, *Russia* **4 C13** 63 58N 37 55 E
Onega, G. of, *Russia* **14 B6** 64 30N 37 0 E
Onega, L., *Russia* **14 B6** 62 0N 35 30 E
Oneida, *U.S.A.* **43 D10** 43 5N 75 40W
Oneida L., *U.S.A.* **42 D10** 43 12N 76 0W
Oneonta, *U.S.A.* **43 D10** 42 26N 75 5W
Onitsha, *Nigeria* **30 C3** 6 6N 6 42 E
Ontario □, *Canada* **42 A2** 48 0N 83 0W
Ontario, L., *N. Amer.* **42 D8** 43 40N 78 0W
Ontonagon, *U.S.A.* **42 B3** 46 52N 89 19W
Oostende = Ostend, *Belgium* **8 B5** 51 15N 2 54 E
Opava, *Czech.* **10 D7** 49 57N 17 58 E
Opole, *Poland* **10 C7** 50 42N 17 58 E
Oporto, *Portugal* **11 B1** 41 8N 8 40W
Oradea, *Romania* **10 E9** 47 2N 21 58 E
Orai, *India* **23 G7** 25 58N 79 30 E
Oran, *Algeria* **28 B6** 35 45N 0 39W
Orange, *Australia* **34 G8** 33 15S 149 7 E
Orange, *France* **9 E6** 44 8N 4 47 E
Orange, *U.S.A.* **42 F8** 38 17N 78 5W
Orange →, *S. Africa* **31 B2** 28 41S 16 28 E
Orange Free State □, *S. Africa* **31 B4** 28 30S 27 0 E
Orangeville, *Canada* **42 D7** 43 55N 80 5W
Oranjemund, *Namibia* **31 B2** 28 38S 16 29 E
Ordos, *China* **21 C5** 39 0N 109 0 E
Örebro, *Sweden* **6 G11** 59 20N 15 18 E
Oregon □, *U.S.A.* **40 B2** 44 0N 121 0W
Orekhovo-Zuyevo, *Russia* **14 C6** 55 50N 38 55 E
Orel, *Russia* **14 D6** 52 57N 36 3 E
Orenburg, *Russia* **14 D10** 51 45N 55 6 E
Orense, *Spain* **11 A2** 42 19N 7 55W
Orinoco →, *Venezuela* **46 B3** 9 15N 61 30W
Orissa □, *India* **23 J9** 20 0N 84 0 E
Oristano, *Italy* **12 E3** 39 54N 8 35 E
Orizaba, *Mexico* **44 D5** 18 51N 97 6W
Orkney Is., *U.K.* **7 C5** 59 0N 3 0W
Orlando, *U.S.A.* **41 E10** 28 30N 81 25W
Orléanais, *France* **8 D4** 48 0N 2 0 E
Orléans, *France* **8 C4** 47 54N 1 52 E
Orléans, I. d', *Canada* **43 B12** 46 54N 70 58W
Ormara, *Pakistan* **24 C5** 25 16N 64 33 E
Ormoc, *Phil.* **22 B4** 11 0N 124 37 E
Örnsköldsvik, *Sweden* **6 F11** 63 17N 18 40 E
Orsk, *Russia* **14 D10** 51 12N 58 34 E
Orumiyeh, *Iran* **24 B3** 37 50N 45 30 E
Oruro, *Bolivia* **46 D3** 18 0S 67 9W
Ōsaka, *Japan* **19 B4** 34 40N 135 30 E
Oshawa, *Canada* **42 D8** 43 50N 78 50W
Oshogbo, *Nigeria* **30 C2** 7 48N 4 37 E
Osijek, *Croatia* **13 B8** 45 34N 18 41 E
Osizweni, *S. Africa* **31 B5** 27 49S 30 7 E
Oskarshamn, *Sweden* **6 G11** 57 15N 16 27 E
Oslo, *Norway* **6 G10** 59 55N 10 45 E
Oslo Fjord, *Norway* **6 G10** 59 20N 10 35 E
Osnabrück, *Germany* **10 B3** 52 16N 8 2 E
Osorno, *Chile* **47 G2** 40 25S 73 0W
Ostend, *Belgium* **8 B5** 51 15N 2 54 E
Östersund, *Sweden* **6 F10** 63 10N 14 38 E
Ostrava, *Czech.* **10 D8** 49 51N 18 18 E

117
Rainier, Mt. — Sault Ste. Marie

Rainier, Mt., *U.S.A.* **40 A2** 46 50N 121 50W
Raipur, *India* **23 J8** 21 17N 81 45 E
Raj Nandgaon, *India* **23 J8** 21 5N 81 5 E
Rajahmundry, *India* **25 D7** 17 1N 81 48 E
Rajasthan □, *India* **23 F4** 26 45N 73 30 E
Rajasthan Canal, *India* **23 F3** 28 0N 72 0 E
Rajkot, *India* **23 H3** 22 15N 70 56 E
Rajshahi, *Bangla.* **23 G12** 24 22N 88 39 E
Rajshahi □, *Bangla.* **23 G12** 25 0N 89 0 E
Rakaposhi, *Pakistan* **23 A5** 36 10N 74 25 E
Rakops, *Botswana* **31 A3** 21 1S 24 28 E
Raleigh, *U.S.A.* **41 C11** 35 47N 78 39W
Ramgarh, *India* **23 H10** 23 40N 85 35 E
Ramotswa, *Botswana* **31 A4** 24 50S 25 52 E
Rampur, *India* **23 E7** 28 50N 79 5 E
Rancagua, *Chile* **47 F2** 34 10S 70 50W
Ranchi, *India* **23 H10** 23 19N 85 27 E
Randers, *Denmark* **6 G10** 56 29N 10 1 E
Rangoon, *Burma* **25 D8** 16 45N 96 20 E
Rangpur, *Bangla.* **23 G12** 25 42N 89 22 E
Rantoul, *U.S.A.* **42 E3** 40 18N 88 10W
Rasht, *Iran* **24 B3** 37 20N 49 40 E
Ratangarh, *India* **23 E5** 28 5N 74 35 E
Ratlam, *India* **23 H5** 23 20N 75 0 E
Raurkela, *India* **23 H10** 22 14N 84 50 E
Ravenna, *Italy* **12 B5** 44 28N 12 15 E
Ravi →, *Pakistan* **23 D3** 30 35N 71 49 E
Rawalpindi, *Pakistan* **23 C4** 33 38N 73 8 E
Raz, Pte. du, *France* **8 C1** 48 2N 4 47W
Ré, I. de, *France* **9 D3** 46 12N 1 30W
Reading, *U.K.* **7 G6** 51 27N 0 57W
Reading, *U.S.A.* **43 E10** 40 20N 75 53W
Recife, *Brazil* **46 C6** 8 0S 35 0W
Red →, *U.S.A.* **41 D8** 31 0N 91 40W
Red Deer, *Canada* **38 C8** 52 20N 113 50W
Red Sea, *Asia* **29 E14** 25 0N 36 0 E
Redon, *France* **8 D2** 47 40N 2 6W
Ree, L., *Ireland* **7 F3** 53 35N 8 0W
Regensburg, *Germany* **10 D5** 49 1N 12 7 E
Reggio di Calabria, *Italy* **12 E6** 38 7N 15 38 E
Reggio nell' Emilia, *Italy* **12 B4** 44 42N 10 38 E
Regina, *Canada* **38 C9** 50 27N 104 35W
Rehoboth, *Namibia* **31 A2** 23 15S 17 4 E
Reichenbach, *Germany* **10 C5** 50 36N 12 19 E
Reigate, *U.K.* **7 G6** 51 14N 0 11W
Reims, *France* **8 C6** 49 15N 4 1 E
Reindeer L., *Canada* **38 C9** 57 15N 102 15W
Reitz, *S. Africa* **31 B4** 27 48S 28 29 E
Remscheid, *Germany* **10 C2** 51 11N 7 12 E
Renfrew, *Canada* **42 C9** 45 30N 76 40W
Rennes, *France* **8 C3** 48 7N 1 41W
Reno, *U.S.A.* **40 C3** 39 30N 119 50W
Resistencia, *Argentina* **47 E4** 27 30S 59 0W
Rethel, *France* **8 C6** 49 30N 4 20 E
Réthímnon, *Greece* **13 G11** 35 18N 24 30 E
Réunion ■, *Ind. Oc.* **27 J9** 21 0S 56 0 E
Revilla Gigedo, Is., *Pac. Oc.* **37 F16** 18 40N 112 0W
Rewa, *India* **23 G8** 24 33N 81 25 E
Rewari, *India* **23 E6** 28 15N 76 40 E
Reykjavík, *Iceland* **6 B3** 64 10N 21 57W
Reynosa, *Mexico* **44 B5** 26 5N 98 18W
Rhine →, *Europe* **8 B7** 51 52N 6 2 E
Rhineland-Palatinate □, *Germany* **10 D2** 50 0N 7 0 E
Rhode Island □, *U.S.A.* **43 E12** 41 38N 71 37W
Rhodes = Ródhos, *Greece* **13 F13** 36 15N 28 10 E
Rhodope Mts., *Bulgaria* **13 D11** 41 40N 24 20 E
Rhön, *Germany* **10 C3** 50 24N 9 58 E
Rhône →, *France* **9 F6** 43 28N 4 42 E
Rhyl, *U.K.* **7 F5** 53 19N 3 29W
Riau Arch., *Indonesia* **22 C2** 0 30N 104 20 E
Ribeirão Prêto, *Brazil* **46 E5** 21 10S 47 50W
Richards Bay, *S. Africa* **31 B5** 28 48S 32 6 E
Richlands, *U.S.A.* **42 G7** 37 7N 81 49W
Richmond, *Ind., U.S.A.* **42 F5** 39 50N 84 50W
Richmond, *Ky., U.S.A.* **42 G5** 37 40N 84 20W
Richmond, *Va., U.S.A.* **42 G9** 37 33N 77 27W
Ridder, *Kazakhstan* **18 D10** 50 20N 83 30 E
Ridgway, *U.S.A.* **42 E8** 41 25N 78 43W
Riet →, *S. Africa* **31 B3** 29 0S 23 54 E
Riga, *Latvia* **14 C3** 56 53N 24 8 E
Riga, G. of, *Latvia* **14 C3** 57 40N 23 45 E
Rijeka, *Croatia* **12 B6** 45 20N 14 21 E
Rimini, *Italy* **12 B5** 44 3N 12 33 E
Rîmnicu Vîlcea, *Romania* **13 B11** 45 9N 24 21 E
Rimouski, *Canada* **43 A13** 48 27N 68 30W
Rio de Janeiro, *Brazil* **47 E5** 23 0S 43 12W
Río Gallegos, *Argentina* **47 H3** 51 35S 69 15W
Rio Grande →, *U.S.A.* **41 E7** 25 57N 97 9W
Ripon, *U.S.A.* **42 D3** 43 51N 88 50W
Riverhead, *U.S.A.* **43 E11** 40 53N 72 40W
Riversdale, *S. Africa* **31 C3** 34 7S 21 15 E
Riverside, *U.S.A.* **40 D3** 33 58N 117 22W
Rivière-du-Loup, *Canada* **43 B13** 47 50N 69 30W
Riyadh, *Si. Arabia* **24 C3** 24 41N 46 42 E
Roanne, *France* **9 D6** 46 3N 4 4 E
Roanoke, *U.S.A.* **42 G8** 37 19N 79 55W
Roberval, *Canada* **43 A11** 48 32N 72 15W
Robson, Mt., *Canada* **38 C8** 53 10N 119 10W
Rochechouart, *France* **9 E4** 45 50N 0 49 E
Rochefort, *France* **9 E3** 45 56N 0 57W
Rochester, *Ind., U.S.A.* **42 E4** 41 5N 86 15W
Rochester, *Minn., U.S.A.* **41 B8** 44 1N 92 28W
Rochester, *N.H., U.S.A.* **43 D12** 43 19N 70 57W
Rochester, *N.Y., U.S.A.* **42 D9** 43 10N 77 40W
Rockall, *Atl. Oc.* **4 D3** 57 37N 13 42W
Rockford, *U.S.A.* **41 B9** 42 20N 89 7W
Rockhampton, *Australia* **34 E9** 23 22S 150 32 E
Rockland, *U.S.A.* **43 C13** 44 6N 69 6W
Rocky Mts., *N. Amer.* **38 C7** 55 0N 121 0W
Rodez, *France* **9 E5** 44 21N 2 33 E
Ródhos, *Greece* **13 F13** 36 15N 28 10 E
Roermond, *Neths.* **8 B6** 51 12N 6 0 E
Roeselare, *Belgium* **8 B5** 50 57N 3 7 E
Rogers City, *U.S.A.* **42 C6** 45 25N 83 49W
Rohtak, *India* **23 E6** 28 55N 76 43 E
Roma, *Australia* **34 F8** 26 32S 148 49 E
Romania ■, *Europe* **13 B11** 46 0N 25 0 E
Romans-sur-Isère, *France* **9 E6** 45 3N 5 3 E
Rome, *Italy* **12 D5** 41 54N 12 30 E
Rome, *U.S.A.* **43 D10** 43 14N 75 29W
Romney, *U.S.A.* **42 F8** 39 21N 78 45W
Romorantin-Lanthenay, *France* **8 D4** 47 21N 1 45 E
Rondônia □, *Brazil* **46 D3** 11 0S 63 0W
Ronne Ice Shelf, *Antarctica* **48 C23** 78 0S 60 0W
Roodepoort, *S. Africa* **31 B4** 26 11S 27 54 E
Roosevelt I., *Antarctica* **48 C20** 79 30S 162 0W
Roquefort, *France* **9 E3** 44 2N 0 20W
Roraima □, *Brazil* **46 B3** 2 0N 61 30W
Rosario, *Argentina* **47 F3** 33 0S 60 40W
Roscommon, *U.S.A.* **42 C5** 44 27N 84 35W
Roseau, *Domin.* **44 M20** 15 20N 61 24W
Rosenheim, *Germany* **10 E5** 47 51N 12 9 E
Ross Ice Shelf, *Antarctica* **48 C20** 80 0S 180 0 E
Ross Sea, *Antarctica* **48 C19** 74 0S 178 0 E
Rossignol, L., *Canada* **43 C15** 44 12N 65 10W
Rosslare, *Ireland* **7 F3** 52 17N 6 23W
Rostock, *Germany* **10 A5** 54 4N 12 9 E
Rostov, *Russia* **15 E6** 47 15N 39 45 E
Rothaar Gebirge, *Germany* **10 C3** 51 0N 8 5 E
Rotherham, *U.K.* **7 F6** 53 26N 1 21W
Rothesay, *U.K.* **7 E4** 55 50N 5 3W
Rotorua, *N.Z.* **35 H14** 38 9S 176 16 E
Rotterdam, *Neths.* **8 B6** 51 55N 4 30 E
Roubaix, *France* **8 B5** 50 40N 3 10 E
Rouen, *France* **8 C4** 49 27N 1 4 E
Roussillon, *France* **9 F5** 42 30N 2 35 E
Rouxville, *S. Africa* **31 C4** 30 25S 26 50 E
Rouyn, *Canada* **42 A8** 48 20N 79 0W
Rovaniemi, *Finland* **6 E13** 66 29N 25 41 E
Royal Leamington Spa, *U.K.* **7 F6** 52 18N 1 32W
Royan, *France* **9 E3** 45 37N 1 2W
Rub' al Khali, *Si. Arabia* **24 D3** 18 0N 48 0 E
Rugby, *U.K.* **7 F6** 52 23N 1 16W
Rügen, *Germany* **10 A5** 54 22N 13 25 E
Ruhr →, *Germany* **10 C2** 51 25N 6 44 E
Rumania = Romania ■, *Europe* **13 B11** 46 0N 25 0 E
Rumford, *U.S.A.* **43 C12** 44 30N 70 30W
Rupat, *Indonesia* **22 C2** 1 45N 101 40 E
Ruse, *Bulgaria* **13 C11** 43 48N 25 59 E
Rushville, *U.S.A.* **42 F5** 39 38N 85 22W
Russia ■, *Eurasia* **18 C12** 62 0N 105 0 E
Rustenburg, *S. Africa* **31 B4** 25 41S 27 14 E
Ruteng, *Indonesia* **22 D4** 8 35S 120 30 E
Ruwenzori, *Africa* **32 D5** 0 30N 29 55 E
Rwanda ■, *Africa* **32 E5** 2 0S 30 0 E
Ryazan, *Russia* **14 D6** 54 40N 39 40 E
Rybinsk, *Russia* **14 C6** 58 5N 38 50 E
Rybinsk Res., *Russia* **14 C6** 58 30N 38 25 E
Ryūkyū Is., *Japan* **21 D7** 26 0N 126 0 E
Rzeszów, *Poland* **10 C9** 50 5N 21 58 E

S

Saale →, *Germany* **10 C4** 51 57N 11 56 E
Saar →, *Europe* **10 D2** 49 41N 6 32 E
Saarbrücken, *Germany* **10 D2** 49 15N 6 58 E
Saaremaa, *Estonia* **14 C3** 58 30N 22 30 E
Saba, *W. Indies* **44 K18** 17 42N 63 26W
Sabadell, *Spain* **11 B7** 41 28N 2 7 E
Sabah □, *Malaysia* **22 C3** 6 0N 117 0 E
Sabhah, *Libya* **28 D9** 27 9N 14 29 E
Sabie, *S. Africa* **31 B5** 25 10S 30 48 E
Sable, C., *Canada* **43 D15** 43 29N 65 38W
Saco, *U.S.A.* **43 D12** 43 30N 70 27W
Sacramento, *U.S.A.* **40 C2** 38 33N 121 30W
Safi, *Morocco* **28 C5** 32 18N 9 20W
Saginaw, *U.S.A.* **42 D6** 43 26N 83 55W
Saginaw B., *U.S.A.* **42 D6** 43 50N 83 40W
Saguenay →, *Canada* **43 A12** 48 22N 71 0W
Sahara, *Africa* **26 D4** 23 0N 5 0 E
Saharanpur, *India* **23 E6** 29 58N 77 33 E
Sahiwal, *Pakistan* **23 D4** 30 45N 73 8 E
Saidabad, *Iran* **24 C4** 29 30N 55 45 E
Saidpur, *Bangla.* **23 G12** 25 48N 89 0 E
St. Albans, *U.K.* **7 G6** 51 44N 0 19W
St. Albans, *Vt., U.S.A.* **43 C11** 44 49N 73 7W
St. Albans, *W. Va., U.S.A.* **42 F7** 38 21N 81 50W
St.-Amand-Mont-Rond, *France* **9 D5** 46 43N 2 30 E
St. Andrews, *U.K.* **7 D5** 56 20N 2 48W
St. Boniface, *Canada* **38 D10** 49 53N 97 5W
St.-Brieuc, *France* **8 C2** 48 30N 2 46W
St. Catharines, *Canada* **42 D8** 43 10N 79 15W
St. Christopher-Nevis ■, *W. Indies* **44 K19** 17 20N 62 40W
St. Clair, L., *Canada* **42 D6** 42 30N 82 45W
St.-Claude, *France* **9 D6** 46 22N 5 52 E
St.-Dié, *France* **8 C7** 48 17N 6 56 E
St.-Dizier, *France* **8 C6** 48 38N 4 56 E
St.-Étienne, *France* **9 E6** 45 27N 4 22 E
St-Félicien, *Canada* **43 A11** 48 40N 72 25W
St.-Flour, *France* **9 E5** 45 2N 3 6 E
St. Gallen, *Switz.* **10 E3** 47 26N 9 22 E
St.-Gaudens, *France* **9 F4** 43 6N 0 44 E
St-Georges, *Canada* **43 B12** 46 8N 70 40W
St. George's, *Grenada* **44 Q20** 12 5N 61 43W
St. George's Channel, *U.K.* **7 G4** 52 0N 6 0W
St.-Girons, *France* **9 F4** 42 59N 1 8 E
St. Gotthard P., *Switz.* **10 E3** 46 33N 8 33 E
St. Helena, *Atl. Oc.* **2 E9** 15 55S 5 44W
St. Helena B., *S. Africa* **33 L3** 32 40S 18 10 E
St. Helens, *U.K.* **7 F5** 53 28N 2 44W
St. Helier, *U.K.* **8 C2** 49 11N 2 6W
St-Hyacinthe, *Canada* **43 C11** 45 40N 72 58W
St. Ignace, *U.S.A.* **42 C5** 45 53N 84 43W
St-Jean, *Canada* **43 C11** 45 20N 73 20W
St-Jean, L., *Canada* **43 A11** 48 40N 72 0W
St.-Jean-d'Angély, *France* **9 E3** 45 57N 0 31W
St-Jérôme, *Canada* **43 C11** 45 47N 74 0W
St. John, *Canada* **43 C14** 45 20N 66 8W
St. John's, *Antigua* **44 K20** 17 6N 61 51W
St. John's, *Canada* **39 D14** 47 35N 52 40W
St. Johns, *U.S.A.* **42 D5** 43 0N 84 31W
St. Johnsbury, *U.S.A.* **43 C11** 44 25N 72 1W
St. Joseph, *Mich., U.S.A.* **42 D4** 42 5N 86 30W
St. Joseph, *Mo., U.S.A.* **41 C8** 39 46N 94 50W
St. Lawrence →, *Canada* **43 A13** 49 30N 66 0W
St. Lawrence, Gulf of, *Canada* **43 A16** 48 25N 62 0W
St.-Lô, *France* **8 C3** 49 7N 1 5W
St-Louis, *Senegal* **28 F3** 16 8N 16 27W
St. Louis, *U.S.A.* **41 C8** 38 40N 90 12W
St. Lucia ■, *W. Indies* **44 P21** 14 0N 60 50W
St. Lucia, L., *S. Africa* **31 B5** 28 5S 32 30 E
St.-Malo, *France* **8 C2** 48 39N 2 1W
St.-Malo, G. de, *France* **8 C2** 48 50N 2 30W
St-Martin, *W. Indies* **44 K19** 18 0N 63 0W
St. Marys, *U.S.A.* **42 E8** 41 27N 78 33W
St.-Nazaire, *France* **8 D2** 47 17N 2 12W
St. Niklass, *Belgium* **8 B6** 51 10N 4 9 E
St.-Omer, *France* **8 B5** 50 45N 2 15 E
St. Paul, *U.S.A.* **41 B8** 44 54N 93 5W
St. Peter Port, *Chan. Is.* **8 C2** 49 27N 2 31W
St. Petersburg, *Russia* **14 C5** 59 55N 30 20 E
St. Petersburg, *U.S.A.* **41 E10** 27 45N 82 40W
St.-Pierre et Miquelon □, *St- P. & M.* **39 D14** 46 55N 56 10W
St.-Quentin, *France* **8 C5** 49 50N 3 16 E
St.-Raphaël, *France* **9 F7** 43 25N 6 46 E
St. Stephen, *Canada* **43 C14** 45 16N 67 17W
St. Thomas, *Canada* **42 D7** 42 45N 81 10W
St.-Tropez, *France* **9 F7** 43 17N 6 38 E
St. Vincent and the Grenadines ■, *W. Indies* **44 Q20** 13 0N 61 10W
Ste-Marie de la Madeleine, *Canada* **43 B12** 46 26N 71 0W
Ste.-Menehould, *France* **8 C6** 49 5N 4 54 E
Saintes, *France* **9 E3** 45 45N 0 37W
Saintonge, *France* **9 E3** 45 40N 0 50W
Sak →, *S. Africa* **31 C3** 30 52S 20 25 E
Sakai, *Japan* **19 B4** 34 30N 135 30 E
Sakhalin, *Russia* **18 D16** 51 0N 143 0 E
Sala, *Sweden* **6 G11** 59 58N 16 35 E
Salado →, *Argentina* **47 F3** 31 40S 60 41W
Salamanca, *Spain* **11 B3** 40 58N 5 39W
Salamanca, *U.S.A.* **42 D8** 42 10N 78 42W
Salayar, *Indonesia* **22 D4** 6 7S 120 30 E
Saldanha, *S. Africa* **31 C2** 33 0S 17 58 E
Salekhard, *Russia* **18 C8** 66 30N 66 35 E
Salem, *India* **25 D6** 11 40N 78 11 E
Salem, *Ind., U.S.A.* **42 F4** 38 38N 86 6W
Salem, *Mass., U.S.A.* **43 D12** 42 29N 70 53W
Salem, *Ohio, U.S.A.* **42 E7** 40 52N 80 50W
Salem, *Va., U.S.A.* **42 G7** 37 19N 80 8W
Salerno, *Italy* **12 D6** 40 40N 14 44 E
Salford, *U.K.* **7 F5** 53 30N 2 17W
Salisbury, *U.K.* **7 G6** 51 4N 1 48W
Salisbury, *U.S.A.* **43 F10** 38 20N 75 38W
Salisbury Plain, *U.K.* **7 G6** 51 13N 1 50W
Salon-de-Provence, *France* **9 F6** 43 39N 5 6 E
Salonica = Thessaloníki, *Greece* **13 D10** 40 38N 22 58 E
Salt Lake City, *U.S.A.* **40 B4** 40 45N 111 58W
Salta, *Argentina* **47 E3** 24 57S 65 25W
Saltcoats, *U.K.* **7 E4** 55 38N 4 47W
Saltillo, *Mexico* **44 B4** 25 30N 100 57W
Saltillo, *Coahuila, Mexico* **44 B4** 25 25N 101 0W
Salto, *Uruguay* **47 F4** 31 27S 57 50W
Salvador, *Brazil* **46 D6** 13 0S 38 30W
Salween →, *Burma* **25 D8** 16 31N 97 37 E
Salyersville, *U.S.A.* **42 G6** 37 45N 83 4W
Salzburg, *Austria* **10 E5** 47 48N 13 2 E
Salzgitter, *Germany* **10 B4** 52 13N 10 22 E
Samar, *Phil.* **22 B4** 12 0N 125 0 E
Samara, *Russia* **14 D9** 53 8N 50 6 E
Samarkand, *Uzbekistan* **18 F8** 39 40N 66 55 E
Sambalpur, *India* **23 J10** 21 28N 84 4 E
Sambhal, *India* **23 E7** 28 35N 78 37 E
Sambhar, *India* **23 F5** 26 52N 75 6 E
Sámos, *Greece* **13 F12** 37 45N 26 50 E
Samsun, *Turkey* **15 F6** 41 15N 36 22 E
San →, *Poland* **10 C9** 50 45N 21 51 E
San Agustin, C., *Phil.* **22 C4** 6 20N 126 13 E
San Angelo, *U.S.A.* **40 D6** 31 30N 100 30W
San Antonio, *U.S.A.* **40 E7** 29 30N 98 30W
San Bernardino, *U.S.A.* **40 D3** 34 7N 117 18W
San Bernardino Str., *Phil.* **22 B4** 13 0N 125 0 E
San Diego, *U.S.A.* **40 D3** 32 43N 117 10W
San Francisco, *U.S.A.* **40 C2** 37 47N 122 30W
San Jorge, G., *Argentina* **47 G3** 46 0S 66 0W
San José, *Costa Rica* **45 F8** 9 55N 84 2W
San Jose, *U.S.A.* **40 C2** 37 20N 121 53W
San Juan, *Argentina* **47 F3** 31 30S 68 30W
San Juan, *Puerto Rico* **45 D11** 18 28N 66 8W
San Lucas, C., *Mexico* **44 C3** 22 50N 110 0W
San Luis Potosí, *Mexico* **44 C4** 22 9N 100 59W
San Marino ■, *Europe* **12 C5** 43 56N 12 25 E
San Miguel de Tucumán, *Argentina* **47 E3** 26 50S 65 20W
San Pedro Sula, *Honduras* **44 D7** 15 30N 88 0W
San Salvador, *El Salv.* **44 E7** 13 40N 89 10W
San Salvador de Jujuy, *Argentina* **47 E3** 24 10S 64 48W
San Sebastián, *Spain* **11 A5** 43 17N 1 58W
Sana', *Yemen* **24 D3** 15 27N 44 12 E
Sancy, Puy de, *France* **9 E5** 45 32N 2 50 E
Sand →, *S. Africa* **31 A5** 22 25S 30 5 E
Sandakan, *Malaysia* **22 C3** 5 53N 118 4 E
Sandusky, *U.S.A.* **42 E6** 41 25N 82 40W
Sangli, *India* **25 D6** 16 55N 74 33 E
Santa Ana, *U.S.A.* **40 D3** 33 48N 117 55W
Santa Clara, *Cuba* **45 C9** 22 20N 80 0W
Santa Cruz, *Bolivia* **46 D3** 17 43S 63 10W
Santa Cruz de Tenerife, *Canary Is.* **28 D3** 28 28N 16 15W
Santa Fe, *Argentina* **47 F3** 31 35S 60 41W
Santa Fe, *U.S.A.* **40 C5** 35 40N 106 0W
Santa Maria, *Brazil* **47 E4** 29 40S 53 48W
Santa Marta, *Colombia* **46 A2** 11 15N 74 13W
Santander, *Spain* **11 A4** 43 27N 3 51W
Santarém, *Brazil* **46 C4** 2 25S 54 42W
Santarém, *Portugal* **11 C1** 39 12N 8 42W
Santiago, *Chile* **47 F2** 33 24S 70 40W
Santiago de Compostela, *Spain* **11 A1** 42 52N 8 37W
Santiago de Cuba, *Cuba* **45 D9** 20 0N 75 49W
Santiago de los Cabelleros, *Dom. Rep.* **45 D10** 19 30N 70 40W
Santo André, *Brazil* **47 E5** 23 39S 46 29W
Santo Domingo, *Dom. Rep.* **45 D11** 18 30N 69 59W
Santos, *Brazil* **47 E5** 24 0S 46 20W
São Francisco →, *Brazil* **46 D6** 10 30S 36 24W
São José do Rio Prêto, *Brazil* **46 E5** 20 50S 49 20W
São Luís, *Brazil* **46 C5** 2 39S 44 15W
São Paulo, *Brazil* **47 E5** 23 32S 46 37W
São Roque, C. de, *Brazil* **46 C6** 5 30S 35 16W
São Tomé & Principe ■, *Africa* **28 J8** 0 12N 6 39 E
Saône →, *France* **9 E6** 45 44N 4 50 E
Sapporo, *Japan* **19 F12** 43 0N 141 21 E
Saragossa = Zaragoza, *Spain* **11 B5** 41 39N 0 53W
Sarajevo, *Bos.-H., Yug.* **13 C8** 43 52N 18 26 E
Saranac Lakes, *U.S.A.* **43 C10** 44 20N 74 10W
Sarangani B., *Phil.* **22 C4** 6 0N 125 13 E
Saransk, *Russia* **14 D8** 54 10N 45 10 E
Saratoga Springs, *U.S.A.* **43 D11** 43 5N 73 47W
Saratov, *Russia* **14 D8** 51 30N 46 2 E
Sarawak □, *Malaysia* **22 C3** 2 0N 113 0 E
Sarda →, *India* **23 F8** 27 21N 81 23 E
Sardinia, *Italy* **12 E3** 39 57N 9 0 E
Sargodha, *Pakistan* **23 C4** 32 10N 72 40 E
Sarh, *Chad* **28 H10** 9 5N 18 23 E
Sarlat-la-Canéda, *France* **9 E4** 44 54N 1 13 E
Sarnia, *Canada* **42 D6** 42 58N 82 23W
Sarrebourg, *France* **8 C7** 48 43N 7 3 E
Sarreguemines, *France* **8 C7** 49 5N 7 4 E
Sartène, *France* **9 G8** 41 38N 8 58 E
Sarthe →, *France* **8 D3** 47 33N 0 31W
Sasebo, *Japan* **19 C1** 33 10N 129 43 E
Saser, *India* **23 B6** 34 50N 77 50 E
Saskatchewan □, *Canada* **38 C9** 54 40N 106 0W
Saskatchewan →, *Canada* **38 C9** 53 37N 100 40W
Saskatoon, *Canada* **38 C9** 52 10N 106 38W
Sasolburg, *S. Africa* **31 B4** 26 46S 27 49 E
Sassari, *Italy* **12 D3** 40 44N 8 33 E
Sassnitz, *Germany* **10 A5** 54 29N 13 39 E
Satmala Hills, *India* **23 J5** 20 15N 74 40 E
Satna, *India* **23 G8** 24 35N 80 50 E
Satpura Ra., *India* **23 J6** 21 25N 76 10 E
Satu Mare, *Romania* **10 E10** 47 46N 22 55 E
Sauðarkrókur, *Iceland* **6 B4** 65 45N 19 40W
Saudi Arabia ■, *Asia* **24 C3** 26 0N 44 0 E
Sault Ste. Marie, *Canada* **42 B5** 46 30N 84 20W
Sault Ste. Marie, *U.S.A.* **42 B5** 46 27N 84 22W

119
Tabas Vanuatu

T

Tabas, *Iran* **24 B4** 33 35N 56 55 E
Tablas, *Phil.* **22 B4** 12 25N 122 2 E
Table Mt., *S. Africa* **31 C2** 34 0S 18 22 E
Tabora, *Tanzania* **32 F6** 5 2S 32 50 E
Tabriz, *Iran* **24 B3** 38 7N 46 20 E
Tacloban, *Phil.* **22 B4** 11 15N 124 58 E
Tacna, *Peru* **46 D2** 18 0S 70 20W
Tacoma, *U.S.A.* **40 A2** 47 15N 122 30W
Tacuarembó, *Uruguay* **47 F4** 31 45S 56 0W
Tadzhikistan = Tajikistan ■, *Asia* **18 F8** 38 30N 70 0 E
Taegu, *S. Korea* **21 C7** 35 50N 128 37 E
Taejon, *S. Korea* **21 C7** 36 20N 127 28 E
Taganrog, *Russia* **15 E6** 47 12N 38 50 E
Tagus →, *Europe* **11 C1** 38 40N 9 24W
Tahiti, *Pac. Oc.* **37 J13** 17 37S 149 27W
Taichung, *Taiwan* **21 D7** 24 12N 120 35 E
Taimyr Peninsula, *Russia* **18 B11** 75 0N 100 0 E
Tainan, *Taiwan* **21 D7** 23 17N 120 18 E
T'aipei, *Taiwan* **21 D7** 25 2N 121 30 E
Taiping, *Malaysia* **22 C2** 4 51N 100 44 E
Taiwan ■, *Asia* **21 D7** 23 30N 121 0 E
Taiyuan, *China* **21 C6** 37 52N 112 33 E
Ta'izz, *Yemen* **24 D3** 13 35N 44 2 E
Tajikistan ■, *Asia* **18 F8** 38 30N 70 0 E
Tak, *Thailand* **22 B1** 16 52N 99 8 E
Takamatsu, *Japan* **19 B4** 34 20N 134 5 E
Takaoka, *Japan* **19 A5** 36 47N 137 0 E
Takasaki, *Japan* **19 A6** 36 20N 139 0 E
Takla Makan, *China* **16 F12** 38 0N 83 0 E
Talaud Is., *Indonesia* **22 C4** 4 30N 127 10 E
Talca, *Chile* **47 F2** 35 28S 71 40W
Talcahuano, *Chile* **47 F2** 36 40S 73 10W
Taliabu, *Indonesia* **22 D4** 1 45S 124 55 E
Tallahassee, *U.S.A.* **41 D10** 30 25N 84 15W
Tallinn, *Estonia* **14 C3** 59 22N 24 48 E
Tamale, *Ghana* **30 C1** 9 22N 0 50W
Tambov, *Russia* **14 D7** 52 45N 41 28 E
Tamil Nadu □, *India* **25 D6** 11 0N 77 0 E
Tamo Abu Ra., *Malaysia* **22 C3** 3 10N 115 5 E
Tampa, *U.S.A.* **41 E10** 27 57N 82 38W
Tampere, *Finland* **6 F12** 61 30N 23 50 E
Tampico, *Mexico* **44 C5** 22 20N 97 50W
Tamworth, *Australia* **34 G9** 31 7S 150 58 E
Tana →, *Norway* **6 D13** 70 30N 28 23 E
Tana, L., *Ethiopia* **29 G14** 13 5N 37 30 E
Tanami Desert, *Australia* **34 D5** 18 50S 132 0 E
Tananarive = Antananarivo, *Madag.* **33 H9** 18 55S 47 31 E
Tando Adam, *Pakistan* **23 G2** 25 45N 68 40 E
Tanga, *Tanzania* **32 F7** 5 5S 39 2 E
Tanganyika, L., *Africa* **32 F6** 6 40S 30 0 E
Tangier, *Morocco* **28 B5** 35 50N 5 49W
Tangshan, *China* **21 C6** 39 38N 118 10 E
Tanimbar Is., *Indonesia* **22 D5** 7 30S 131 30 E
Tanjungbalai, *Indonesia* **22 C1** 2 55N 99 44 E
Tanzania ■, *Africa* **32 F6** 6 0S 34 0 E
Tapajós →, *Brazil* **46 C4** 2 24S 54 41W
Tapi →, *India* **23 J4** 21 8N 72 41 E
Tappahannock, *U.S.A.* **42 G9** 37 56N 76 50W
Tarābulus = Tripoli, *Lebanon* **24 B2** 34 31N 35 50 E
Tarābulus = Tripoli, *Libya* **28 C9** 32 49N 13 7 E
Tarakan, *Indonesia* **22 C3** 3 20N 117 35 E
Taranto, *Italy* **12 D7** 40 30N 17 11 E
Táranto, G. di, *Italy* **12 D7** 40 0N 17 15 E
Tarbagatai Ra., *Kazakhstan* **18 E10** 48 0N 83 0 E
Tarbes, *France* **9 F4** 43 15N 0 3 E
Tarim Basin, *China* **20 B3** 40 0N 84 0 E
Tarkastad, *S. Africa* **31 C4** 32 0S 26 16 E
Tarnów, *Poland* **10 C9** 50 3N 21 0 E
Tarragona, *Spain* **11 B6** 41 5N 1 17 E
Tarrasa, *Spain* **11 B7** 41 34N 2 1 E
Tashkent, *Uzbekistan* **18 E8** 41 20N 69 10 E
Tasman Sea, *Pac. Oc.* **36 L8** 36 0S 160 0 E
Tasmania □, *Australia* **34 J8** 42 0S 146 30 E
Tatar Republic □, *Russia* **14 C9** 55 30N 51 30 E
Tatarsk, *Russia* **18 D9** 55 14N 76 0 E
Tatta, *Pakistan* **23 G1** 24 42N 67 55 E
Tauern, *Austria* **10 E5** 47 15N 12 40 E
Taung, *S. Africa* **31 B3** 27 33S 24 47 E
Taunton, *U.K.* **7 G5** 51 1N 3 7W
Taunton, *U.S.A.* **43 E12** 41 54N 71 6W
Taunus, *Germany* **10 C3** 50 15N 8 20 E
Taurus Mts., *Turkey* **15 G5** 37 0N 32 30 E
Tawas City, *U.S.A.* **42 C6** 44 16N 83 31W
Tawau, *Malaysia* **22 C3** 4 20N 117 55 E
Tay →, *U.K.* **7 D5** 56 37N 3 38W
Tay, Firth of, *U.K.* **7 D5** 56 25N 3 8W
Tbilisi, *Georgia* **15 F7** 41 43N 44 50 E
Tchad, L. = Chad, L., *Chad* **28 G9** 13 30N 14 30 E
Tebingtinggi, *Indonesia* **22 C1** 3 20N 99 9 E
Tegal, *Indonesia* **22 D2** 6 52S 109 8 E
Tegucigalpa, *Honduras* **44 E7** 14 5N 87 14W
Tehran, *Iran* **24 B4** 35 44N 51 30 E
Tehuantepec, Gulf of, *Mexico* **44 D5** 15 50N 95 12W
Tehuantepec, Isthmus of, *Mexico* **44 D6** 17 0N 94 30W
Tel Aviv-Jaffa, *Israel* **29 P20** 32 4N 34 48 E
Telford, *U.K.* **7 F5** 52 42N 2 31W
Tell City, *U.S.A.* **42 G4** 37 55N 86 44W
Teluk Betung, *Indonesia* **22 C2** 4 13N 108 12 E
Tema, *Ghana* **30 C2** 5 41N 0 0 E
Temba, *S. Africa* **31 B4** 25 20S 28 17 E
Témiscaming, *Canada* **42 B8** 46 44N 79 5W
Tenerife, *Canary Is.* **28 D3** 28 15N 16 35W
Tennessee □, *U.S.A.* **41 C9** 36 0N 86 30W
Tennessee →, *U.S.A.* **41 C9** 37 4N 88 34W
Tepic, *Mexico* **44 C4** 21 30N 104 54W
Teramo, *Italy* **12 C5** 42 40N 13 40 E
Teresina, *Brazil* **46 C5** 5 9S 42 45W
Ternate, *Indonesia* **22 C4** 0 45N 127 25 E
Terni, *Italy* **12 C5** 42 34N 12 38 E
Terre Haute, *U.S.A.* **42 F4** 39 28N 87 24W
Teruel, *Spain* **11 B5** 40 22N 1 8W
Tetouan, *Morocco* **28 B5** 35 35N 5 21W
Tetovo, *Macedonia, Yug.* **13 C9** 42 1N 21 2 E
Teutoburger Wald, *Germany* **10 B3** 52 5N 8 20 E
Texas □, *U.S.A.* **40 D7** 31 40N 98 30W
Texel, *Neths.* **8 A6** 53 5N 4 50 E
Tezpur, *India* **23 F14** 26 40N 92 45 E
Thabana Ntlenyana, *Lesotho* **31 B4** 29 30S 29 16 E
Thabazimbi, *S. Africa* **31 A4** 24 40S 27 21 E
Thailand ■, *Asia* **22 B2** 16 0N 102 0 E
Thailand, G. of, *Asia* **22 B2** 11 30N 101 0 E
Thal, *Pakistan* **23 C3** 33 28N 70 33 E
Thal Desert, *Pakistan* **23 D3** 31 10N 71 30 E
Thames →, *Canada* **42 D6** 42 20N 82 25W
Thames →, *U.K.* **7 G7** 51 30N 0 35 E
Thane, *India* **23 K4** 19 12N 72 59 E
Thar Desert, *India* **23 E4** 28 0N 72 0 E
The Hague, *Neths.* **8 A6** 52 7N 4 17 E
The Pas, *Canada* **38 C9** 53 45N 101 15W
Thessalon, *Canada* **42 B6** 46 20N 83 30W
Thessaloníki, *Greece* **13 D10** 40 38N 22 58 E
Thessaloniki, Gulf of, *Greece* **13 D10** 40 15N 22 45 E
Thessaly □, *Greece* **13 E9** 38 25N 21 50 E
Thetford Mines, *Canada* **43 B12** 46 8N 71 18W
Thiers, *France* **9 E5** 45 52N 3 33 E
Thies, *Senegal* **28 G3** 14 50N 16 51W
Thimphu, *Bhutan* **23 F12** 27 31N 89 45 E
Thionville, *France* **8 C7** 49 20N 6 10 E
Thonon-les-Bains, *France* **9 D7** 46 22N 6 29 E
Thrace □, *Greece* **13 D11** 41 9N 25 30 E
Thule, *Greenland* **48 A10** 77 40N 69 0W
Thunder B., *U.S.A.* **42 C6** 45 0N 83 20W
Thunder Bay, *Canada* **42 A3** 48 20N 89 15W
Thuringian Forest, *Germany* **10 C4** 50 35N 11 0 E
Thurso, *U.K.* **7 C5** 58 34N 3 31W
Tianjin = Tientsin, *China* **21 C6** 39 8N 117 10 E
Tianshui, *China* **20 C5** 34 32N 105 40 E
Tiber →, *Italy* **12 D5** 41 44N 12 14 E
Tiberias, *Israel* **N21** 32 47N 35 32 E
Tibesti, *Chad* **28 E10** 21 0N 17 30 E
Tibet = Xizang □, *China* **20 C3** 32 0N 88 0 E
Ticino →, *Italy* **12 B3** 45 9N 9 14 E
Ticonderoga, *U.S.A.* **43 D11** 43 50N 73 28W
Tien Shan, *Asia* **16 E11** 42 0N 76 0 E
Tientsin, *China* **21 C6** 39 8N 117 10 E
Tierra del Fuego, I. Gr. de, *Argentina* **47 H3** 54 0S 69 0W
Tiffin, *U.S.A.* **42 E6** 41 8N 83 10W
Tignish, *Canada* **43 B15** 46 58N 64 2W
Tigris →, *Asia* **24 B3** 31 0N 47 25 E
Tijuana, *Mexico* **44 A1** 32 30N 117 10W
Tiksi, *Russia* **18 B14** 71 40N 128 45 E
Tilburg, *Neths.* **8 B6** 51 31N 5 6 E
Timaru, *N.Z.* **35 J13** 44 23S 171 14 E
Timbuktu = Tombouctou, *Mali* **30 A1** 16 50N 3 0W
Timişoara, *Romania* **13 B9** 45 43N 21 15 E
Timmins, *Canada* **42 A7** 48 28N 81 25W
Timor, *Indonesia* **22 D4** 9 0S 125 0 E
Tinaca Pt., *Phil.* **22 C4** 5 30N 125 25 E
Tipperary, *Ireland* **7 F2** 52 28N 8 10W
Tiranë, *Albania* **13 D8** 41 18N 19 49 E
Tîrgovişte, *Romania* **13 B11** 44 55N 25 27 E
Tîrgu-Jiu, *Romania* **13 B10** 45 5N 23 19 E
Tirich Mir, *Pakistan* **23 A3** 36 15N 71 55 E
Tiruchchirappalli, *India* **25 D6** 10 45N 78 45 E
Tirunelveli, *India* **25 E6** 8 45N 77 45 E
Tisa →, *Hungary* **10 E9** 46 8N 20 2 E
Tisza →, *Serbia, Yug.* **10 F9** 45 15N 20 17 E
Titicaca, L., *S. Amer.* **46 D3** 15 30S 69 30W
Titusville, *U.S.A.* **42 E8** 41 35N 79 39W
Tizi-Ouzou, *Algeria* **28 B7** 36 42N 4 3 E
Toamasina, *Madag.* **33 H9** 18 10S 49 25 E
Toba Kakar Hills, *Pakistan* **23 D2** 31 30N 69 0 E
Tobago, *W. Indies* **44 R21** 11 10N 60 30W
Tobermory, *Canada* **42 C7** 45 12N 81 40W
Tocantins →, *Brazil* **46 C5** 1 45S 49 10W
Togliatti, *Russia* **14 D8** 53 32N 49 24 E
Togo ■, *W. Afr.* **30 C2** 8 30N 1 35 E
Tokelau Is., *Pac. Oc.* **35 B16** 9 0S 171 45W
Tōkyō, *Japan* **19 B6** 35 45N 139 45 E
Tolbukhin, *Bulgaria* **13 C12** 43 37N 27 49 E
Toledo, *Spain* **11 C3** 39 50N 4 2W
Toledo, *U.S.A.* **42 E6** 41 37N 83 33W
Toliara, *Madag.* **33 J8** 23 21S 43 40 E
Toluca, *Mexico* **44 D5** 19 20N 99 40W
Tomaszów Mazowiecki, *Poland* **10 C8** 51 30N 19 57 E
Tombouctou, *Mali* **30 A1** 16 50N 3 0W
Tomini, G. of, *Indonesia* **22 D4** 0 10S 122 0 E
Tomsk, *Russia* **18 D10** 56 30N 85 5 E
Tonga ■, *Pac. Oc.* **35 D16** 19 50S 174 30W
Tonga Trench, *Pac. Oc.* **35 E16** 18 0S 173 0W
Tongaat, *S. Africa* **31 B5** 29 33S 31 9 E
Tongking, G. of, *Asia* **20 E5** 20 0N 108 0 E
Tonk, *India* **23 F5** 26 6N 75 54 E
Tonlé Sap, *Cambodia* **22 B2** 13 0N 104 0 E
Toowoomba, *Australia* **34 F9** 27 32S 151 56 E
Topeka, *U.S.A.* **41 C7** 39 3N 95 40W
Torino = Turin, *Italy* **12 B2** 45 4N 7 40 E
Torne →, *Sweden* **6 E12** 65 50N 24 12 E
Torne, L., *Sweden* **6 E11** 68 24N 19 15 E
Tornio, *Finland* **6 E12** 65 50N 24 12 E
Toronto, *Canada* **42 D8** 43 39N 79 20W
Torquay, *U.K.* **7 G5** 50 27N 3 31W
Torreón, *Mexico* **44 B4** 25 33N 103 26W
Tortosa, *Spain* **11 B6** 40 49N 0 31 E
Toruń, *Poland* **10 B8** 53 2N 18 39 E
Toteng, *Botswana* **31 A3** 20 22S 22 58 E
Toul, *France* **8 C6** 48 40N 5 53 E
Toulon, *France* **9 F6** 43 10N 5 55 E
Toulouse, *France* **9 F4** 43 37N 1 27 E
Touraine, *France* **8 D4** 47 20N 0 30 E
Tournai, *Belgium* **8 B5** 50 35N 3 25 E
Tournon, *France* **9 E6** 45 4N 4 50 E
Tours, *France* **8 D4** 47 22N 0 40 E
Touwsrivier, *S. Africa* **31 C3** 33 20S 20 2 E
Towanda, *U.S.A.* **42 E9** 41 46N 76 30W
Townsville, *Australia* **34 D8** 19 15S 146 45 E
Towson, *U.S.A.* **42 F9** 39 26N 76 34W
Toyama, *Japan* **19 A5** 36 40N 137 15 E
Toyohashi, *Japan* **19 B5** 34 45N 137 25 E
Trabzon, *Turkey* **15 F6** 41 0N 39 45 E
Trafalgar, C., *Spain* **11 D2** 36 10N 6 2W
Trail, *Canada* **38 D8** 49 5N 117 40W
Tralee, *Ireland* **7 F2** 52 16N 9 42W
Trang, *Thailand* **22 C1** 7 33N 99 38 E
Trangan, *Indonesia* **22 D5** 6 40S 134 20 E
Transkei □, *S. Africa* **31 C4** 32 15S 28 15 E
Transvaal □, *S. Africa* **31 A4** 25 0S 29 0 E
Transylvania, *Romania* **13 B11** 45 19N 25 0 E
Transylvanian Alps, *Romania* **4 F10** 45 30N 25 0 E
Trapani, *Italy* **12 E5** 38 1N 12 30 E
Traverse City, *U.S.A.* **42 C5** 44 45N 85 39W
Trent →, *U.K.* **7 F6** 53 33N 0 44W
Trentino-Alto Adige □, *Italy* **12 A4** 46 30N 11 0 E
Trento, *Italy* **12 A4** 46 5N 11 8 E
Trenton, *Canada* **42 C9** 44 10N 77 34W
Trenton, *U.S.A.* **43 E10** 40 15N 74 41W
Trier, *Germany* **10 D2** 49 45N 6 37 E
Trieste, *Italy* **12 B5** 45 39N 13 45 E
Trincomalee, *Sri Lanka* **25 E7** 8 38N 81 15 E
Trinidad & Tobago ■, *W. Indies* **44 S20** 10 30N 61 20W
Tripoli, *Lebanon* **24 B2** 34 31N 35 50 E
Tripoli, *Libya* **28 C9** 32 49N 13 7 E
Tripura □, *India* **23 H13** 24 0N 92 0 E
Tristan da Cunha, *Atl. Oc.* **2 F9** 37 6S 12 20W
Trivandrum, *India* **25 E6** 8 41N 77 0 E
Trnava, *Slovakia* **10 D7** 48 23N 17 35 E
Trois-Rivières, *Canada* **43 B11** 46 25N 72 34W
Trollhättan, *Sweden* **6 G10** 58 17N 12 20 E
Trondheim, *Norway* **6 F10** 63 36N 10 25 E
Trondheim Fjord, *Norway* **6 F10** 63 35N 10 30 E
Troy, *N.Y., U.S.A.* **43 D11** 42 45N 73 39W
Troy, *Ohio, U.S.A.* **42 E5** 40 3N 84 10W
Troyes, *France* **8 C6** 48 19N 4 3 E
Trujillo, *Peru* **46 C2** 8 6S 79 0W
Truk, *Pac. Oc.* **36 G7** 7 25N 151 46 E
Truro, *Canada* **43 C16** 45 21N 63 14W
Truro, *U.K.* **7 G4** 50 17N 5 2W
Tsau, *Botswana* **31 A3** 20 8S 22 22 E
Tselinograd, *Kazakhstan* **18 D9** 51 10N 71 30 E
Tshabong, *Botswana* **31 B3** 26 2S 22 29 E
Tshane, *Botswana* **31 A3** 24 5S 21 54 E
Tshwane, *Botswana* **31 A3** 22 24S 22 1 E
Tsimlyansk Res., *Russia* **15 E7** 48 0N 43 0 E
Tsu, *Japan* **19 B5** 34 45N 136 25 E
Tsumis, *Namibia* **31 A2** 23 39S 17 29 E
Tuamotu Arch., *Pac. Oc.* **37 J13** 17 0S 144 0W
Tubuai Is., *Pac. Oc.* **37 K12** 25 0S 150 0W
Tucson, *U.S.A.* **40 D4** 32 14N 110 59W
Tugela →, *S. Africa* **31 B5** 29 14S 31 30 E
Tula, *Russia* **14 D6** 54 13N 37 38 E
Tulcea, *Romania* **13 B13** 45 13N 28 46 E
Tulle, *France* **9 E4** 45 16N 1 46 E
Tulsa, *U.S.A.* **41 C7** 36 10N 96 0W
Tunis, *Tunisia* **28 B9** 36 50N 10 11 E
Tunisia ■, *Africa* **28 C8** 33 30N 9 10 E
Tunja, *Colombia* **46 B2** 5 33N 73 25W
Tura, *India* **23 G13** 25 30N 90 16 E
Turabah, *Si. Arabia* **24 C3** 28 20N 43 15 E
Turin, *Italy* **12 B2** 45 4N 7 40 E
Turkana, L., *Africa* **32 D7** 3 30N 36 5 E
Turkey ■, *Eurasia* **15 G6** 39 0N 36 0 E
Turkmenistan ■, *Asia* **18 F7** 39 0N 59 0 E
Turks Is., *W. Indies* **45 C10** 21 20N 71 20W
Turku, *Finland* **6 F12** 60 30N 22 19 E
Tuticorin, *India* **25 E6** 8 50N 78 12 E
Tuvalu ■, *Pac. Oc.* **35 B14** 8 0S 178 0 E
Tuxtla Gutiérrez, *Mexico* **44 D6** 16 50N 93 10W
Tuz Gölü, *Turkey* **15 G5** 38 45N 33 30 E
Tuzla, *Bos.-H., Yug.* **13 B8** 44 34N 18 41 E
Tver, *Russia* **14 C6** 56 55N 35 55 E
Two Rivers, *U.S.A.* **42 C4** 44 10N 87 31W
Tychy, *Poland* **10 C8** 50 9N 18 59 E
Tynemouth, *U.K.* **7 E6** 55 1N 1 27W
Tyre = Sūr, *Lebanon* **29 C14** 33 19N 35 16 E
Tyrol □, *Austria* **10 E4** 47 3N 10 43 E
Tyrrhenian Sea, *Europe* **12 E5** 40 0N 12 30 E
Tyumen, *Russia* **18 D8** 57 11N 65 29 E
Tzaneen, *S. Africa* **31 A5** 23 47S 30 9 E

U

Ubangi = Oubangi →, *Zaïre* **32 E3** 0 30S 17 50 E
Ube, *Japan* **19 C2** 33 56N 131 15 E
Uberaba, *Brazil* **46 D5** 19 50S 47 55W
Uberlândia, *Brazil* **46 D5** 19 0S 48 20W
Ucayali →, *Peru* **46 C2** 4 30S 73 30W
Udaipur, *India* **23 G4** 24 36N 73 44 E
Udaipur Garhi, *Nepal* **23 F11** 27 0N 86 35 E
Udine, *Italy* **12 A5** 46 5N 13 10 E
Udmurt Republic □, *Russia* **14 C9** 57 30N 52 30 E
Udon Thani, *Thailand* **22 B2** 17 29N 102 46 E
Ufa, *Russia* **14 D10** 54 45N 55 55 E
Uganda ■, *Africa* **32 D6** 2 0N 32 0 E
Uitenhage, *S. Africa* **31 C4** 33 40S 25 28 E
Ujjain, *India* **23 H5** 23 9N 75 43 E
Újpest, *Hungary* **10 E8** 47 32N 19 6 E
Ujung Pandang, *Indonesia* **22 D3** 5 10S 119 20 E
Ukraine ■, *Europe* **15 E5** 49 0N 32 0 E
Ulan Bator, *Mongolia* **20 B5** 47 55N 106 53 E
Ulan Ude, *Russia* **18 D12** 51 45N 107 40 E
Ulhasnagar, *India* **23 K4** 19 15N 73 10 E
Ullapool, *U.K.* **7 D4** 57 54N 5 10W
Ulm, *Germany* **10 D4** 48 23N 10 0 E
Ulyasutay, *Mongolia* **20 B4** 47 56N 97 28 E
Umbria □, *Italy* **12 C5** 42 53N 12 30 E
Ume →, *Sweden* **6 F12** 63 45N 20 20 E
Umeå, *Sweden* **6 F12** 63 45N 20 20 E
Umtata, *S. Africa* **31 C4** 31 36S 28 49 E
Umzimvubu, *S. Africa* **31 C4** 31 38S 29 33 E
Umzinto, *S. Africa* **31 C5** 30 15S 30 45 E
Ungava B., *Canada* **39 C13** 59 30N 67 30W
Ungava Pen., *Canada* **39 C12** 60 0N 74 0W
Uniontown, *U.S.A.* **42 F8** 39 54N 79 45W
United Arab Emirates ■, *Asia* **24 C4** 23 50N 54 0 E
United Kingdom ■, *Europe* **7 F5** 53 0N 2 0W
United States of America ■, *N. Amer.* **40 C7** 37 0N 96 0W
Upington, *S. Africa* **31 B3** 28 25S 21 15 E
Uppsala, *Sweden* **6 G11** 59 53N 17 38 E
Ural →, *Kazakhstan* **15 E9** 47 0N 51 48 E
Ural Mts., *Russia* **14 C10** 60 0N 59 0 E
Uralsk, *Kazakhstan* **14 D9** 51 20N 51 20 E
Uranium City, *Canada* **38 C9** 59 34N 108 37W
Urbana, *Ill., U.S.A.* **42 E3** 40 7N 88 12W
Urbana, *Ohio, U.S.A.* **42 E6** 40 9N 83 44W
Uruguay ■, *S. Amer.* **47 F4** 32 30S 56 30W
Uruguay →, *S. Amer.* **47 F4** 34 12S 58 18W
Ürümqi, *China* **20 B3** 43 45N 87 45 E
Usakos, *Namibia* **31 A2** 21 54S 15 31 E
Ushant, *France* **8 C1** 48 28N 5 6W
Üsküdar, *Turkey* **13 D13** 41 0N 29 5 E
Ussel, *France* **9 E5** 45 32N 2 18 E
Ust Urt Plateau, *Kazakhstan* **18 E7** 44 0N 55 0 E
Ústí nad Labem, *Czech.* **10 C6** 50 41N 14 3 E
Utah □, *U.S.A.* **40 C4** 39 30N 111 30W
Utica, *U.S.A.* **43 D10** 43 5N 75 18W
Utrecht, *Neths.* **8 A6** 52 5N 5 8 E
Utsunomiya, *Japan* **19 A6** 36 30N 139 50 E
Uttar Pradesh □, *India* **23 F8** 27 0N 80 0 E
Uttaradit, *Thailand* **22 B2** 17 36N 100 5 E
Uusikaupunki, *Finland* **6 F12** 60 47N 21 25 E
Uzbekistan ■, *Asia* **18 E8** 41 30N 65 0 E

V

Vaal →, *S. Africa* **31 B3** 29 4S 23 38 E
Vaal Dam, *S. Africa* **31 B4** 27 0S 28 14 E
Vaasa, *Finland* **6 F12** 63 6N 21 38 E
Vadodara, *India* **23 H4** 22 20N 73 10 E
Vadsø, *Norway* **6 D13** 70 3N 29 50 E
Váh →, *Slovakia* **10 E8** 47 43N 18 7 E
Val d'Or, *Canada* **42 A9** 48 7N 77 47W
Valdez, *U.S.A.* **38 B5** 61 14N 146 17W
Valdivia, *Chile* **47 F2** 39 50S 73 14W
Valence, *France* **9 E6** 44 57N 4 54 E
Valencia, *Spain* **11 C5** 39 27N 0 23W
Valencia, *Venezuela* **46 A3** 10 11N 68 0W
Valenciennes, *France* **8 B5** 50 20N 3 34 E
Valladolid, *Spain* **11 B3** 41 38N 4 43W
Valletta, *Malta* **12 G6** 35 54N 14 31 E
Valparaíso, *Chile* **47 F2** 33 2S 71 40W
Van, L., *Turkey* **15 G7** 38 30N 43 0 E
Van Buren, *U.S.A.* **43 B13** 47 10N 68 1W
Van Wert, *U.S.A.* **42 E5** 40 52N 84 31W
Vancouver, *Canada* **38 D7** 49 15N 123 10W
Vancouver I., *Canada* **38 D7** 49 50N 126 0W
Vanderbijlpark, *S. Africa* **31 B4** 26 42S 27 54 E
Vaner, L., *Sweden* **6 G10** 58 47N 13 30 E
Vännäs, *Sweden* **6 F11** 63 58N 19 48 E
Vannes, *France* **8 D2** 47 40N 2 47W
Vanrhynsdorp, *S. Africa* **31 C2** 31 36S 18 44 E
Vanua Levu, *Fiji* **35 D14** 16 33S 179 15 E
Vanuatu ■, *Pac. Oc.* **35 D12** 15 0S 168 0 E